OFFICIAL HISTORY OF THE INDIAN ARMED FORCES
IN THE SECOND WORLD WAR
1939-45

POST-WAR OCCUPATION FORCES:
Japan & South-East Asia

General Editor
BISHESHWAR PRASAD, D.LITT.

The Naval & Military Press Ltd

Published by

The Naval & Military Press Ltd
Unit 10 Ridgewood Industrial Park,
Uckfield, East Sussex,
TN22 5QE England

Tel: +44 (0) 1825 749494
Fax: +44 (0) 1825 765701

www.naval-military-press.com
www.nmarchive.com

In reprinting in facsimile from the original, any imperfections are inevitably reproduced and the quality may fall short of modern type and cartographic standards.

POST-WAR OCCUPATION FORCES:
JAPAN AND SOUTH-EAST ASIA

Rajendra Singh
Brigadier

Edited by
Bisheshwar Prasad, D.Litt.

TO ALL WHO SERVED

ADVISORY COMMITTEE

CHAIRMAN

Secretary, Ministry of Defence, India

MEMBERS

DR. TARA CHAND

DR. S. N. SEN

PROF. K. A. NILAKANTA SASTRI

PROF. MOHAMMAD HABIB

DR. R. C. MAJUMDAR

GENERAL K. S. THIMAYYA

LIEUT.-GENERAL SIR DUDLEY RUSSELL

LIEUT.-GENERAL S. P. P. THORAT

MILITARY ADVISER TO THE HIGH COMMISSIONER FOR PAKISTAN IN INDIA

SECRETARY

DR. BISHESHWAR PRASAD

CAMPAIGNS IN THE EASTERN THEATRE

Campaigns in South-East Asia 1941-42

Retreat from Burma 1941-42

Arakan Operations 1942-45

Reconquest of Burma 1942-45, Two Volumes

Post-War Occupation Forces: Japan and South-East Asia

PREFACE

I have great pleasure in presenting another volume of the Official History of the Indian Armed Forces in World War II, which has been prepared by the Combined Inter-Services Historical Section which was set up by the Government of India when that war ended and, after the Partition of India in 1947, was reconstituted as a joint venture of the two countries—India and Pakistan.

This Section planned the Official History of the Indian Armed Forces in the Second World War to appear in about twenty volumes, besides the seven volumes relating to the medical aspects of war. These twenty volumes were divided into three series, viz. campaigns in the eastern theatre, campaigns in the western theatre and general war administration and organisation.

Three volumes in the series relating to the campaigns in the eastern theatre have already been published. Unlike those volumes, the present one describes the responsibility shouldered by the Indian forces in the military administration of the territories occupied by the Allied Powers after the cessation of the war in Japan and South-east Asia. In Japan the Indian Contingent formed part of the British Commonwealth Occupation Force which was organised by the countries of the British Commonwealth to co-operate with the United States forces under the Supreme Commander Allied Powers, General MacArthur, while in South-east Asia the Indian forces worked under the control of Lord Mountbatten, the Supreme Allied Commander in this area. In both the zones the Indian Contingent had onerous duties to perform; and with the transfer of power in India in 1947 these troops were withdrawn.

This volume was written by one of the Editors in the Combined Inter-Services Historical Section, Lieut.-Colonel (now Brigadier) Rajendra Singh who had formed part of the Indian Contingent in Japan and thus had an intimate knowledge of the events narrated here. To him I acknowledge my indebtedness. The story is, however, based on the official records which were made freely available to the Combined Inter-Services Historical Section. For the statement of facts and the views expressed here I accept full responsibility.

The volume has been seen in the typescript by Shri H. M. Patel, I.C.S., then Secretary, Ministry of Defence, New Delhi; General S. M. Shrinagesh; Shri B. B. Ghosh, Joint Secretary, Ministry of Defence, New Delhi; Lieut.-General H. C. H. Robertson, CBE, DSO, Commander-in-Chief, Headquarters British Commonwealth Force, Japan; Major-General W. J. Cawthorn; Gavin Long Esq., General Editor, Australian Official History of War; Brigadier H. B. Latham, Cabinet Historical Section; and Major-General Orlando Ward, Chief Historical Division, Washington, to whom my thanks are due. I am indebted to General K. S. Thimayya, DSO, Dr. R. C. Majumdar, and Professor K. A. Nilakanta Sastri who read the volume as members of the Advisory Committee and offered their valuable comments. I am also grateful to Mr. P. N. Khera for seeing the book through the press, and Mr. T. D. Sharma for preparing the maps and charts.

In conclusion I acknowledge the encouragement and support which I have received from the Ministries of Defence, of India and Pakistan.

New Delhi,
October 1958.

BISHESHWAR PRASAD.

CONTENTS

		Page
Introduction		XIX

JAPAN

Chapter		
I.	Pre-surrender Period	1
II.	Supreme Command Allied Powers	7
III.	The Allied Control of Japan	25
IV.	The British Commonwealth Policy Regarding Occupation of Japan	30
V.	Joint Chiefs of Staff Australia	35
VI.	British Commonwealth Occupation Force	44
VII.	Concentration and Move of Brinjap to Japan	77
VIII.	British and Indian Troops in Japan	94
IX.	Responsibilities of Brindiv in Japan	107
X.	Navy, Air and Divisional Troops	124
XI.	Withdrawal of the Indian Contingent from Japan	156

SOUTH-EAST ASIA

XII.	The Overall Plan	169
XIII.	Recovery of Allied Prisoners of War and Internees	174
XIV.	Restoration of Law and Order in French Indo-China and Thailand after the Defeat of Japan	192
XV.	Restoration of Law and Order in the Netherlands East Indies	220
XVI.	The Disarming, Concentration and Repatriation of the Japanese Prisoners of War in South-East Asia	247
Appendices		259
Index		311

MAPS AND CHARTS

Facing Page

I.	Japan and Korea	1
II.	Zones of Occupation Japan and Korea	10
III.	Diagram showing relationship of JCOSA and Australian defence machinery for consideration of BCOF matters	36
IV.	Diagram showing channels of communication authorised for BCOF	55
V.	Diagram showing channels of communication authorised for officers nominated as representatives of National Contingent	95
VI.	Southern Japan dispositions of British Commonwealth Occupation Force as in June 1946	100
VII.	Southern Japan dispositions of British Commonwealth Occupation Force as on 1st March 1947	105
VIII.	Part map of Japan (Southern Honshu and Shikoku) showing roads with capacities BCOF area	109
IX.	South-East Asia	169
X.	French Indo-China	*Page* 198
XI.	Netherlands East Indies	*Facing Page* 221

ILLUSTRATIONS

	Facing Page
Major-General D. T. Cowan, Commander Brinjap	26
Indian Contingent arrives at Kure	27
March through Kure	27
RIAF in Japan	42
RIN in Kure	42
268 (Ind) Brigade and Battalion Commanders	43
4 Squadron RIAF	43
Major-General Cowan with 3 V.Cs. of Brinjap, Jemadar Gaje Ghale, Naik Agansing Rai and Namdeo Jadhao	66
268 Brigade Group Staff	67
Brigadier (later General) K. S. Thimayya, Commander 268 Indian Brigade	84
Brigadier (later General) S. M. Shrinagesh, Commander 268 Indian Brigade	85
Scenes of Earthquake, December 1946	128
Resettlement Training	129
Japan meets India	144
Indian Troops in Etajima	145
Admiral the Lord Louis Mountbatten, Supreme Allied Commander SEA, reading a message from His Majesty the King after the surrender of Japan	172
Lieut.-General Sir Philip Christison, Allied Force Commander in Netherlands East Indies	173
Lieut.-General E. C. Mansergh, Allied Force Commander in Netherlands East Indies	173
Lady Mountbatten, Chief Superintendent, Nursing Division, St. John Ambulance, talking to some ex-prisoners of war	186
Lady Mountbatten talking to a patient in a hospital in Saigon	187
Major-General G. C. Evans, Commander 7 Indian Division	202
Major-General O de T. Lovett, Commander 7 Indian Division	202
Major-General D. D. Gracey, Commander 20 Indian Division	203
Major-General D. C. Hawthorn, Commander 23 Indian Division	203
Major-General Cawthorn, representative of C-in-C India on Joint Chiefs of Staff, Australia	212
Major-General H. N. Chambers, Commander 26 Indian Division	212
Resettlement Training of Repatriates	213

ABBREVIATIONS

AA	..	Assistant Adjutant.
ACC	..	Allied Control Council.
ACNB	..	Australian Commonwealth Navy Board.
ACSEA	..	Allied Commander South-East Asia.
ADC	..	Aide-de-Camp.
AFHQ	..	Allied Forces Headquarters.
ALCNEI	..	Allied Land Command Netherlands East Indies.
ALFFIC	..	Allied Land Forces French Indo-China.
ALFNEI	..	Allied Land Forces Netherlands East-Indies.
ALFSEA	..	Allied Land Forces South-East Asia.
ALF Siam	..	Allied Land Forces Siam.
AMG	..	Allied Military Government.
AMGR	..	Allied Military Government Region.
AMGOT	..	Allied Military Government Occupied Territory
AMF	..	Australian Military Force.
APO	..	Army Post Office.
APWI	..	Allied Prisoners of War and Internees.
Aust	..	Australian.
BAFSV	..	British Armed Forces Special Vouchers.
BC	..	British Commonwealth.
BCAIR	..	Air Command of BCOF.
BCOF	..	British Commonwealth Occupation Force.
Bde Gp	..	Brigade Group.
BEO	..	Brigade Education Officer.
BOAC	..	British Overseas Airlines Corporation.
BORs	..	British Other Ranks.
BRICOSAT	..	British Commonwealth Sub-Area Tokyo.
Brindiv	..	British Indian Division.
Brinjap	..	British Indian Troops in Japan.
BT	..	British Troops.
CIEME	..	Commander, Indian Electrical and Mechanical Engineers.
CRE	..	Commander Royal Engineers.
DADPR	..	Deputy Assistant Director Public Relations.
DIC	..	Colonial Infantry Division.
Div Tps	..	Divisional Troops.

DMS	..	Director Medical Services.
DPR	..	Director Public Relations.
EME	..	Electrical and Mechanical Engineers.
ENSA	..	Entertainments National Service Association.
FANY	..	First Aid Nursing Yeomanry.
FEAC	..	Far Eastern Allied Commission.
F and F	..	Field and Fortress.
FCMA	..	Field Controller Military Accounts.
FF	..	Frontier Force.
FIC	..	French Indo-China.
GHQ	..	General Headquarters.
HK	..	Hikari Kikan (Japanese Intelligence Organisation).
HMIS	..	His Majesty's Indian Ship.
HMS	..	His Majesty's Ship.
HMT	..	His Majesty's Troopship.
HQ	..	Headquarters.
IA	..	Indian Artillery.
IAFS	..	Indian Air Formation Signals.
IAMC	..	Indian Army Medical Corps.
IE	..	Corps of Indian Engineers.
IEME	..	Corps of Indian Electrical and Mechanical Engineers.
IMB	..	Independent Mixed Brigade.
INA	..	Indian National Army.
Indn	..	Indian.
Inf.	..	Infantry.
ISLD	..	Indian Salvage and Local Disposal.
JCPS	..	Joint Chiefs Planning Staff.
JCOSA	..	Joint Chiefs of Staff Australia.
JIFs	..	Japanese Fifth Columnists (also for INA).
KNIP	..	Komite Nasional Indonesia Poesat.
KT	..	Kempei Tai (Japanese Intelligence Organisation).
Madras SM	..	Madras Sappers and Miners.

NEI	..	Netherlands East Indies.
NICA	..	Netherlands Indies Civil Affairs Organisation.
NZ	..	New Zealand.
NZMF	..	New Zealand Military Force.
ORs.	..	Other Ranks.
OSS	..	Office of Strategic Services.
P of W	..	Prisoners of War.
PACUSA	..	Pacific Air Command, United States Army.
PR	..	Public Relations.
PROs	..	Public Relations Officers.
QMG	..	Quartermaster General.
QVO	..	Queen Victoria's Own.
RA	..	Royal Artillery.
RAAF	..	Royal Australian Air Force.
RAF	..	Royal Air Force.
RAPWI	..	Repatriation (or Recovery) of Allied Prisoners of War and Internees.
RAN	..	Royal Australian Navy.
RASC	..	Royal Army Service Corps.
Regt.	..	Regiment.
REME	..	Royal Electrical and Mechanical Engineers.
RGR	..	Royal Gurkha Rifles.
RIA	..	Royal Indian Artillery.
RIAF	..	Royal Indian Air Force.
RIASC	..	Royal Indian Army Service Corps.
RIC	..	Colonial Infantry Regiment.
RIE	..	Royal Indian Engineers.
RN	..	Royal Navy.
RNZAF	..	Royal New Zealand Air Force.
SACSEA	..	Supreme Allied Commander South-East Asia.
SAS	..	Special Army Service.
SCAP	..	Supreme Command Allied Powers.
SEAC	..	South-East Asia Command.
SO	..	Staff Officer.
SSAFA	..	Sailors, Soldiers and Airmen Families Association.
SSAHA	..	Sailors, Soldiers and Airmen Home Association.
Sqn.	..	Squadron.
SWB	..	South Wales Borderers.
SWPA	..	South-West Pacific Area.

TKR	..	People's Protection Army (Tentara Keamanon Rakyat later changed to TKI.)
UK	..	United Kingdom.
UKINDEL	..	United Kingdom/Indian Element.
USSR	..	Union of Socialist Soviet Republics.
VC	..	Victoria Cross.
VCOs	..	Viceroy's Commissioned Officers.
VIPs	..	Very Important Persons.
VJ	..	Victory over Japan.
WAS	..	Women's Auxiliary Service.
WAS(B)	..	Women's Auxiliary Service (British).
WIS	..	Weekly Intelligence Summary.
WVC(I)	..	Women's Voluntary Corps (India).
WVC(UK)	..	Women's Voluntary Corps (United Kingdom).

INTRODUCTION

Japan entered the war with the stunning blow of Pearl Harbour. Similarly, the United States closed the scene by atomic explosions of Hiroshima and Nagasaki. But neither the opening of the armageddon nor its conclusion was as sudden as it appears to be. The beginning of Japanese aggression in China and the interest evinced by the United States in limiting the sphere of Japanese economic expansionism had made inevitable a conflict between the two great naval Pacific Powers. The war in Europe and the easy victories of Nazi Germany in its earlier phases brought the clash nearer, for the militarists of Japan could have no better opportunity of ensuring their naval security in the Pacific and bringing under their control the economic resources of the Southwest Pacific than when the United States and Great Britain were involved in a war in Europe and their more numerous and stronger fleets were dispersed over the distant seas. British diplomatic activity had been directed in Tokyo from the very commencement of the war, if not before that, towards keeping the kingdom of the Mikados away from the global conflict; and appreciations did not fail to take cognizance of the hostile attitude of the eastern imperialist. But actual hostilities took long to begin. The occupation of Indo-China by the Japanese forces in collusion with the Vichy Government of France evoked countervailing measures by the United States and her Allies. These reacted further on the bellicosity of the Japanese militarists, and, when diplomacy failed to close the widening gap, Japanese navy enacted the Pearl Harbour to cripple the United States Navy and thereby gained a respite for her plans of closing the Pacific from the south-west. Her immediate successes were spectacular and for the moment she had swept the Pacific waves of Anglo-American ships of war, had annexed its land fringes on the southern and western sides and brought within her grips the vast economic resources and the fields of oil and mineral supplies of Burma, Malaya and the Netherlands East Indies.

This concurrence of Japanese victories with the successes of her Axis partners in Europe created a complex problem for the Allies whose war potential, though mighty, could not cope with the situation. But soon the war machinery in the United States and the British Empire was geared to the needs, and their giant productive capacity was harnessed to turn out a stream of men and armaments, battle-ships and planes, to stem back the tide of Axis aggression. By the end of 1943 the ultimate defeat of Japan had become a certainty, though it took more than twelve months to drive her armed forces back from the vast periphery which encroached on the preserves of western imperialisms. The two-pronged attack, landward from India, and seaward in the Pacific islands by the United States navy, was slowly but steadily battering its way to the core of the Japanese Empire. The frustration of Japanese invasion of Imphal in the spring of 1944 by the Indian forces and the capture of Okinawa and Iwo Jima by the American marines, paved the way for the ultimate surrender of Emperor Hirohito and his cabinet.

Japan's economy was not up to the strain of a long and exhausting war. The mainland did neither produce enough food for the growing population nor had a sufficiency in mineral resources to feed the war industries. Oil and steel were both in short supply. As long therefore as Manchuria and the vast region of ' Eastern Asia Co-prosperity Sphere ' could be maintained in direct contact with the homeland and their products exploited, the Japanese offensive could proceed unabated. But the moment the United States had pierced the line of island defence in the Pacific, the communications with Indo-China, Malaya and Netherlands were intercepted and the Japanese mainland faced a continuous barrage of air bombing. Industry was crippled, food resources were depleted and the timber and paper cities of Japan were burnt to ashes. Her " productive machinery was approaching paralysis as a result of a shortage or complete lack of almost everything. Air raids and blockade had compressed steel fingers around the economic throat of the nation ".[1] The production of planes had fallen from the peak figure of 2,857 during the month of June 1944 to only about 1,000 in July 1945. Her naval fleet had been practically wiped out in the battles of the Philippine Sea and Leyte Gulf and by air attacks in the Inland Sea. The food situation was growing critical and malnutrition was sapping the " nation's war potential " and affecting human efficiency. Black-marketing was prevalent and embraced not only the supply of food but of clothing, shoes and other necessaries of life. Allied air attacks had disrupted the country's transport system. Shortage of fuel was causing a feeling of dismay at the prospect of a cold winter. To add to the grimness of this story may be calculated the loss in personnel and property by the ever-recurring air raids which had destroyed or badly damaged about 100 cities and had accounted at a minimum

---

[1] Masuo Kato: *The Lost War*, p. 13.

for a loss of 280,000 men in killed and 4,20,000 in injured. No less than 95,00,000 persons had been rendered homeless losing practically all they possessed. The consciousness of inevitable defeat was there but the spirit of the people had been kept up by the propaganda that they would go down fighting a glorious war to the last man. Preparations were on foot in 1945 for the defence of the homeland and farmers were busy on the vulnerable coast-line putting up walls and preparing an " iron ring ".

This propaganda front, however, was hollow from within. The Suzuki Cabinet from the day of its installation in office had been looking for a way out of the war. Their determination was reinforced by the Russian notification in April 1945 to terminate the neutrality agreement which had " lost its significance ". The German defeat in Europe made Japan apprehensive of Soviet entry into the war in the east. And, in the words of Kato, " Japan's number-one diplomatic job from that moment on was to find some new basis for an understanding with Russia that would prevent her from joining the Allies in the Pacific war ".[2] Not only were talks begun with Russia for a new agreement, but even the proposal was made for the Soviet to " act as a mediator in bringing the war with the Allies to a close ". Even a peace feeler was transmitted to America by the Japanese representative in Switzerland. Soon after, the Potsdam Declaration of the three supreme Allied heads issued on 26 July 1945 paved the way for the acceptance of defeat and the surrender of Japan. The Declaration was considered but not rejected, though a section in the Government desired to interpose certain conditions affecting the occupation and trial of war criminals. But the suspense did not last long when the United States used the atom bomb to break it and Russia chose to declare war against Japan on August 8, to shatter the will of the people. The war party had not lost its enthusiasm completely and in the army there was still a group which was prepared even for a *coup de main* to prevent the pacifist Suzuki from accepting the demand for surrender. But all opposition was drowned by the Emperor's determination to end the war when he spoke to his people on the radio for the first time on 15 August. Japan had lost the war and was prepared for peace, but a negotiated peace with all its preliminaries of truce and armistice did not square with the objcets of the United States, and the new weapon of destruction was employed, not to secure the end of war but the unconditional surrender of the Japanese people and the occupation of their land by the Allied forces. The purpose was not peace alone, but the

[2] *Ibid* p. 231.

moulding of Japanese will and psychology for all times and training that people in the ways of democracy. Surrender was thus to be followed by a period of occupation and military government by the Allies.

After the first World War also certain territories of the defeated Powers had been occupied by the British, French or American forces and a form of military administration had been established. But early in World War II except for the opening of the School of Military Government by the United States in Charlottesville, Virginia, in May 1942, for the training of officers for civil affairs and liaison, no preparations appear to have been made by any of the Allied Powers for the disposal of Axis possessions during the " post-hostilities period ". Nor had any concrete peace aims been declared beyond the general principles contained in the Atlantic Charter. However, in January 1943 after his meeting at Casablanca with Prime Minister Churchill, President Roosevelt " announced unconditional surrender as the only terms on which the United States would deal with the Axis Powers ".[3] This principle was applied first in the case of Italy which surrendered on 3 September 1943. The document signed by General Eisenhower, which offered military armistice, specified the right of the Commander-in-Chief of the Allied Forces firstly to " establish Allied Military Government over such parts of Italian territory as he may deem necessary in the military interests of the Allied Nations ", and secondly " to impose measures of disarmament, demobilization and demilitarization ". By another document signed on 29 September 1943 the conditions of such military control were fully defined. But apart from defascization which involved the surrender of Mussolini and his Fascist collaborators, Italy did not experience the full weight of military occupation. It was so because of the formation of Government by Badoglio and the administration of Italy as a co-operator in the war against Germany. Owing to the existence of an established government there and its recognition by the Allied Powers, military government was enforced only in such areas as were required for the purpose of prosecuting war against Germany. Nevertheless, the Moscow Declarations of 1 November 1943 enunciated the object of Allied policy towards Italy, which it was announced, " must be based upon the fundamental principle that Fascism and all its evil influences and emanations shall be utterly destroyed and that the Italian people shall be given every opportunity to establish governmental and other institutions based upon democratic principles ".

[3] Hajo Holborn: *American Military Government*, p. 16.

An Advisory Council of the representatives of the Governments of the United Kingdom, Russia, United States, French Committee of National Liberation and Greece and Yugoslavia was also set up to deal with all day to day questions, other than military operations, and co-ordinate Allied policy in regard to Italy. Italian example could not, however, be effective in the case of other Axis partners who were dealt with not as co-operators but as enemies whose unconditional surrender and complete transformation from totalitarianism was desired. But the object of occupation remained the same everywhere, and the measures outlined at Moscow were followed in their essentials in Japan or Germany.

Germany's turn came next. As early as 1 November 1944, Moscow Declarations took cognizance of German atrocities and threatened punishment of war criminals. But it was at the Crimea Conference in February 1945, that the post-hostilities policy towards Germany was determined. On her unconditional surrender and cessation of armed resistance, Germany was to be occupied by the forces of the three Powers and France, each occupying a separate zone. Co-ordination was to be secured by a central control commission consisting of the Supreme Commanders of the three Powers with its headquarters in Berlin. The purpose of such military occupation was " to destroy German militarism and Nazism and to ensure that Germany will never again be able to disturb the peace of the world ". To secure this object it was declared: " We are determined to disarm and disband all German armed forces; break up for all time the German General Staff that has repeatedly contrived the resurgence of German militarism; remove or destroy all German military equipment; eliminate or control all German industry that could be used for military production; bring all war criminals to just and swift punishment and exact reparation in kind for the destruction wrought by the Germans; wipe out the Nazi Party, Nazi laws, organizations and institutions, remove all Nazi and militarist influences from public office and from the cultural and economic life of the German people; and take in harmony such other measures in Germany as may be necessary to the future peace and safety of the world. It is not our purpose to destroy the people of Germany, but only when Nazism and militarism have been extirpated will there be hope for a decent life for Germans, and a place for them in the comity of nations ".[4] The occupation thus would not be for any momentary object such as exacting an armistice but was for a permanent purpose of ensuring peace in the world for all times by preventing " Germany

---

[4] *Ibid*, Appendix VI, pp 154-5.

from ever again becoming a threat to the peace of the world ".[5] It was also made clear that Germany would be occupied " as a defeated enemy nation " and not " for the purpose of liberation ". An essential aspect of the occupation was to effect " the decentrallization of the political and administrative structure and the development of local responsibility ".[6]

Before we proceed to the analysis of the principles and measures for the occupation of Japan, it may be useful to examine the method of Allied military government in Germany. With the surrender on 8 May, Germany had no central government or authority " capable of accepting responsibility for the maintenance of order, the administration of the country and compliance with the requirements of the victorious Powers ".[7] Hence the Allied Supreme Commands assumed " supreme authority " which encompassed every aspect of civil or military government. Holborn has rightly interpreted the declaration to imply determining the law for the Germans without recognizing any internal political authority.[8] The authority thus assumed was a " common responsibility " to be exercised in concert by the four Powers. The Allied Control Council was established as an instrument to achieve this object. Demilitarization of the country and exaction of the reparations were its main functions. But in the matter of occupation the principle of separatism or individuality had full sway. The country was divided into four zones, each under the military occupation of one of these four Powers. Though initially zones were created merely for convenience of Allied administration yet gradually these introduced virtually a " political partition of Germany ", and the Control Council lapsed into a mere formal gathering of the representatives of the Powers to determine general policies which did not always govern practice. No central government was created in Germany and the lack of cohesion among the occupying Powers led to the development of diverse policies and methods for the " democratisation of Germany ". Economic and other controls enunciated at the Potsdam Conference could not be given effect to uniformly, and the political system which had evolved as a result of occupation had contributed to decentralization and dualism. Occupation has also led to friction between the western and eastern occupation authorities and has been one of the most potent post-war international irritants.

[5] Directive to C-in-C United States Forces, Holborn, p. 159.
[6] *Ibid* p. 158.
[7] Holborn, Appendix X, The Declaration of Berlin 5 June 1945, p 173.
[8] Holborn, p. 33.

Principles on which occupation was to be carried out were defined by the three national leaders, Churchill, Stalin, and Truman, at the Potsdam Conference in August 1945. These provided for the complete elimination of all weapons of war and the means of their production, the abolition of the National Socialist Party and a "complete purge" of all its members, convincing the German people of their total defeat and guilt for war, and finally for measures to train the Germans in the "democratic and peaceful ways of life". These objects were sought to be achieved by the repeal of all Nazi legislation discriminating between races and people, by the trial and punishment of all war criminals, by inculcating democratic ideas and establishing an impartial judiciary and creating local government institutions. The Allied Control Council was definitely desired to take effective measures for the gradual democratisation of Germany for which local self-government and other democratic techniques were to be employed. Re-establishment of the elective principle, initially in the sphere of local government, and the restoration of freedom of speech and vote were to be used as methods for this consummation. The whole idea was to build up the edifice of democratic government from the bottom and in the absence of a central indigenous authority, the training in self-government of the German people was to begin in the sphere of local government only.

The Allied Control Council also created a number of administrative departments, manned by Germans, to assist it in general supervision. These related to finance, transport, communications, foreign trade and industry and provided a substitute for a central administration. The Council was also entrusted with certain economic responsibilities, which related to the reconstruction of German economic life on an agricultural basis. All industry connected with war was forbidden, and all "unneeded productive capacity", measured in terms of the lower standard of living of the German people, was to be removed and utilised for the payment of reparations. The denudation of German industrial potential and the agrarianisation of her whole economy were believed to be the best correctives against future militarism of the people. However, there was no intention to efface German nationality or to condemn the people to political helotage, for, at Potsdam, solicitude was expressed for treating them "fairly and without discrimination" and for handing over the entire administrative machinery to them gradually. Rapidly changing conditions made complete adherence to those policies and programmes impracticable; nevertheless, these provided a model for occupation policy in Japan.

Before Japan had surrendered, as has been mentioned earlier, the heads of the three Allied states, the United States, Great Britain and the Republic of China, had outlined at Potsdam on 26 July 1945 the terms on which Japan could expect the cessation of war. These called for the complete elimination, for all times, of " the authority and influence of those who have deceived and misled the people of Japan into embarking on world conquest ". This was believed to be essential for establishing in the world " a new order of peace, security and justice " which would be incompatible with " irresponsible militarism ". No mention was made in it of the Emperor specifically, but his advisers and all leaders of the army, navy and war governments were to be ousted from all positions of power and influence. Next was announced the desire to occupy " points in Japanese territory " until such time as the new order was established and convincing proof was available that the " war-making power " of Japan had been destroyed. These were the " basic objectives " of occupation. The Potsdam Declaration also limited Japanese territory to the four islands of the mainland. No other limitations were imposed. It was further declared that the Japanese forces after being disarmed would be returned to their homes and opportunity would be afforded to them " to lead peaceful and productive lives ". Beyond the punishment of war criminals, there was no retribution or intention to enslave the Japanese people or to destroy their nationality. The Japanese Government was exhorted to " remove all obstacles to the revival and strengthening of democratic tendencies among the Japanese people " and to establish " freedom of speech, of religion, and of thought, as well as respect for the fundamental human rights ". Only such industries as had war significance and would enable Japan to rearm were to be forbidden, but other industries " as will sustain her economy and permit the exaction of just reparations in kind " were to be maintained and access to raw materials was to be permitted. The duration of the occupation was also defined in a clause which laid down that " the occupying forces of the Allied shall be withdrawn from Japan as soon as these objectives have been accomplished and there has been established in accordance with the freely expressed will of the Japansese people a peacefully inclined and responsible government ". This Declaration, mild yet firm, was accepted by the Japanese Government and the instrument of surrender was signed on 2 September 1945.

The United States having the sole control of war in the Pacific, Japan, unlike Germany, was initially occupied by the United States forces only and was saved from partition which is incidental to zonal occupation by diverse Powers. The United

States Government was also keen to retain unity of control in Japan and not share power or responsibility with other members of the United Nations. Thus, while the form of United Nations authority was kept up by instituting advisory organisations, supreme control vested in the United States Government and was exercised without restraint or interference by its representative, General MacArthur, who was designated the Supreme Commander for the Allied Powers. That Government had also defined its occupation policy in a Directive issued by the President to the Supreme Commander Allied Powers on 6 September 1945, when the instrument of surrender was signed. Though the occupation was considered to have the " character of an operation on behalf of the principal Allied Powers acting in the interests of the United Nations at war with Japan " and the forces of those powers were invited to participate in the occupation, all such forces were to be under the command of the " Supreme Commander designated by the United States ". It was also clearly mentioned that while every effort would be made to formulate policies by common consultation and " the constitution of appropriate advisory bodies ", in the event of difference of opinion, " the policies of the United States will govern ". These limitations on Allied control were imposed to achieve a unity of command and to prevent the repetition of divided authority as in Germany and Austria.

In the Directive of 6 September 1945, the United States had defined ultimate objectives of occupation, the mode and extent of Allied authority and the political and economic programme of occupation. This Directive together with the principles enunciated at Potsdam became the basis of Allied occupation policy in Japan. The ultimate United States objectives were laid down as:

" a. To insure that Japan will not again become a menace to the United States or to the peace and security of the world.

" b. To bring about the eventual establishment of a peaceful and responsible government which will respect the rights of other states and will support the objectives of the United States as reflected in the ideals and principles of the Charter of the United Nations. The United States desires that this government should conform as closely as may be to the principles of democratic self-government but it is not the responsibility of the Allied Powers to impose upon Japan any form of government not supported by the freely expressed will of the people ".

The above objectives were to be achieved by limiting the sovereignty of Japan to the main islands, completely disarming and demilitarising the country, encouraging the Japanese people "to develop a desire for individual liberties and respect for fundamental human rights", particularly freedom of speech, thought and religion, and affording them an opportunity to develop their economy for the peaceful needs of the community. Disarmament and demilitarisation were the primary tasks of military occupation and were to be carried out promptly and with determination. Japan was not allowed to have any army, navy, air force, secret police organisation or civil aviation. All ground, naval and air forces were to be disbanded and the General Headquarters and the General Staff were to be dissolved. All naval and military material as well as installations were to be handed over to the Supreme Commander. High officials of the General Headquarters and General Staff, high naval and military officials, and leaders of ultra-nationalist and militarist organisations were to be taken into custody and all such institutions were to be dissolved and prohibited. Constructively, freedom of worship and formation of political parties were to be encouraged. The Japanese people were also to be afforded an opprotunity "to become familiar with the history, institutions, culture and the accomplishments of the United States and other democracies". For this purpose association of Japanese people with the personnel of the occupation forces was to be provided. Judicial, legal and police systems were also to be reformed and all discriminatory laws were to be abrogated. In the economic field, the whole industrial basis of "Japanese military strength" was to "be destroyed and not permitted to revive". But organisations of labour, industry or agriculture with a democratic basis were to be encouraged. All economic activity with a bias towards "the peaceful disposition of the Japanese people" was to be supported and reconstructed. Japan was also expected to provide goods and services for the needs of the occupying forces but to the extent that her people would not be exposed to starvation, disease or acute physical distress. The Japanese authorities were themselves made responsible for establishing and administering controls over their economic activities. In the Directive provision was made for reparations, monetary and banking policies, and international trade etc. Control was to be maintained over exports and imports, and their administration was to be subject to the approval and supervision of the Supreme Commander.

An important departure from German occupation was in respect of the continuance of the Japanese central authority.

The Supreme Commander was required to " exercise his authority through Japanese governmental machinery and agencies, including the Emperor, to the extent that this satisfactorily furthers United States objectives ". Hence the Japanese Government was permitted under the instructions of the Supreme Commander " to exercise the normal powers of government in matters of domestic administration ". In other words, " the authority of the Emperor and the Japanese Government " was subject to control by the Supreme Commander who alone possessed " all powers necessary to effectuate the surrender terms and to carry out the policies established for the conduct of the occupation and the control of Japan ". The policy was to use the existing form of government in Japan, though not to support it. Consequently, the continuity of government could be possible there and no lacunae did arise as in Germany. This made easy the administration of military occupation and secured the United States objectives more expeditiously.

It has been mentioned earlier that the military occupation of Japan had the character of an Allied operation and that the armed forces of the other Allied states were also invited to join in its enforcement. Of course co-operation was to be in a subordinate capacity for all control and command vested in the American Supreme Commander who would execute the directives issued to him by the American Joint Chiefs of Staff. However, advisory bodies were to be formed for establishing policies. The American Government was keen to have such co-operation and established a Far Eastern Advisory Commission with the function of making " recommendations to the participating governments " on some matters without having any controlling powers. According to Holborn, " the Far Eastern Advisory Commission, as proposed on August 21, 1945, was a rather weak instrument for reaching such political agreements, the more so since its establishment would not provide any clear system of regular information to its members by the United States Government. The proposed Far Eastern Advisory Commission would have contributed merely a forum for the exchange of views ".[9] This system had the merit of preserving " unity of command over the actual operations of American military government in Japan ". And the American view was that nothing should be done which would in any manner weaken the authority of General MacArthur who had been accepted by the other Allied Powers as Supreme Commander. Any tampering of his actions by an Allied Control Council or any hindrance to the United

[9] Holborn, p. 95.

States Government in giving him " adequate policy guidance ", would, according to Holborn, have opened the gates " to the same elements of political disunity and ensuing stagnation that had marred the occupations of Germany and Austria ".[10] The United States did not desire any serious limitation in her powers to control the military occupation of Japan, for in the Pacific and in so important a base as Japan, the United States did not want any powerful partners. Hence, the machinery for Allied participation had to be weak, ineffective and limited in the extent and scope of its controlling authority. But such a machinery could not be acceptable to the other Allied Powers. The Far Eastern Advisory Commission could not suit their conception of inter-Allied co-operation. Britain and China had misgivings about it, and Soviet Russia declined to join it in September 1945. Invitations were then issued to Australia, Canada, France, India, the Netherlands, New Zealand and the Philippines to join. The first meeting of the enlarged Far Eastern Advisory Commission was held in Washington on 30 October 1945, and the members were taken to Japan in December to review the conditions there. But even before they had reached Japan, the Moscow Conference had decided on replacing the Commission by the Far Eastern Commission.

The new Far Eastern Commission was a " body of higher political standing than its predecessor ".[11] It was to be composed of one representative each of the participating governments, viz. the Union of Socialist Soviet Republics, the United Kingdom, the United States, China, France, the Netherlands, Canada, Australia, New Zealand, India and the Philippines. Its functions were defined to be:

1. " To formulate the policies, principles, and standards in conformity with which the fulfilment by Japan of its obligations under the Terms of Surrender may be accomplished.

2. " To review, on the request of any member, any directive issued to the Supreme Commander for the Allied Powers or any action taken by the Supreme Commander involving policy decisions within the jurisdiction of the Commission ".

The Commission had no power to make " recommendations with regard to the conduct of military operations " or territorial adjustments and was bound to " respect existing control machinery in Japan ". The policy decisions of the Commission were to be

[10] *Ibid* p. 95.
[11] *Ibid* p. 96.

interpreted by the United States Government in the form of directives issued to the Supreme Commander who was bound to implement them. But such directives could be reviewed by the Commission. Thus theoretically the Commission was vested with the "ultimate power for the determination of general policy", but in actual practice the policies adopted by the Commission were formulated into directives for the Supreme Commander Allied Power (SCAP) by the State, War and Navy Department Co-ordinating Committee of the United States Government which also served the Joint Chiefs of Staff in formulating their policies into directives for the Supreme Commander. The result was that while the Allied Powers had " a part in mapping out plans for occupied Japan, the fact that they were channeled through wholly American agencies subjected the outcome to dominant American ideas ".[12]

The Supreme Commander was initially without any check on his authority, but the Moscow Conference instituted an Allied Council for Japan in Tokyo under the Chairmanship of the Supreme Commander or his Deputy " for the purpose of consulting with and advising the Supreme Commander in regard to the implementation of the Terms of Surrender, the occupation and control of Japan, and of directives supplementary thereto; and for the purpose of exercising the control authority herein granted ". The Council was to be composed of the Supreme Commander who was its Chairman and the United States member, a member each for USSR and China, and one member representing jointly the United Kingdom, Australia, New Zealand and India. This Council was to meet once every two weeks. All orders for the implementation of the Terms of Surrender were issued by the Supreme Commander, who was the 'sole executive authority', but he was required to " consult and advise with the Council in advance of the issuance of orders on matters of substance, the exigencies of the situation permitting ". But in respect of fundamental changes in the structure of Japanese constitution or change in the Japanese government as a whole, any disagreement with the members of the Council would involve suspension of orders and reference to the Far Eastern Commission. But this did not affect changes of individual Ministers or filling of vacancies in the Cabinet there. However, General MacArthur is reported to have " strictly construed this grant of power to the Allied Council and refused to be controlled by it ".[13]

[12] Floyd A. Cave: *Origins and Consequences of World War II*, p. 565.
[13] *Ibid.*

Within this framework of Allied supervision and American execution of occupation policies, the British Commonwealth Occupation Force was invited to participate in the military occupation of Japan. Among the four Powers constituting the Allied Council, the USSR and China had no share in the actual occupation and their forces did not come into Japan. Initially, the United States had the control of the whole mainland of Japan and with her forces initiated the new regime of military government. But soon after the British Commenwealth agreed to participate by sending the Occupation Force, which had to work under the supreme command of General MacArthur and had limited functions and restricted authority within the areas allotted to it. The British Commonwealth Occupation Force had no responsibility for policy formulation but had merely to execute the directives issued to it by the Supreme Commander for Allied Powers. The chain of command was linked to the United States chain of command though in its internal affairs of administration and discipline, each one of the component elements was autonomous. Their subordination to Supreme Commander for Allied Powers extended to the enforcement of occupation policies and execution of SCAP directives or in matters which brought the Force into contact with the Japanese people or their Government.

The British Commonwealth Occupation Force was itself an integrated force composed of the elements of the Armed Forces of Australia, India, New Zealand and the United Kingdom. Apparently the intention was to demonstrate the solidarity of the British Commonwealth, on which basis Great Britian sought the co-operation of other members of the Commonwealth in participating in the occupation of Japan. Australia also was eager to supervise the changeover of Japan from totalitarianism to democracy in view of her vital Pacific interests. India was not a free agent then and responded to the call of the United Kingdom. Thus a force was raised and sent to Japan early in 1946 under the command of an Australian Commander-in-Chief and to this force was allotted a part of the Japanse territory for military occupation and government under the control, supervision and authority of the Supreme Commander for the Allied Powers in Japan. A joint organisation known as Joint Chiefs of Staff Australia (JCOSA) was set up in Australia for the discussion and determination of common matters and that represented the defence authorities of the various component states. But the JCOSA had to function in most cases through the Australian Defence Department, which caused friction and occasional protests by the representatives of the other Commonwealth countries. In Japan, however, the integration of forces had a smooth working and the BCOF could function effectively within its limited sphere.

The main function of the occupation forces was to destroy Japan's capacity to make war and for that purpose a dual programme of disarmament and democratisation had been outlined. Rapid progress had been made in realising the first objective, which was facilitated and greatly expedited by the continuance of the Japanese Government and the prestige which attached to the Emperor. "Under orders of the Supreme Commander, the Japanese Government dissolved the Imperial General Headquarters and disarmed and demobilized the armed forces located in Japan". Armies outside Japan were disarmed by the local Allied commanders and sent back to Japan. The demobilized soldiers soon settled into peaceful avocations. The war material was also quickly destroyed, for the Japanse made no effort to hide it. Thus the task of demilitarising Japan was completed within a few months and when the British Commonwealth Occupation Force and particularly the Indian Contingent assumed their duties, little was left to be done to accomplish this objective.

The process of democratisation however was a long one though in this field also success was both rapid and appreciable. The task of eliminating persons guilty of war crimes was not difficult. The Government organised a purge and carried out orders of SCAP most zealously. All persons suspected of pro-Fascist leanings were removed from office, all anti-democratic organisations were abolished and the secret police was demobilised. But the positive advance towards a democratic psychology and constitutional and social set-up was necessarily a long process. But even in this direction some progress had been made early. Immediately after occupation, the Supreme Commander issued a directive ordering the release of all political prisoners and the removal of limitations on political and civil liberties. All aid was stopped to the cult of Shintoism. Freedom of association was allowed and political parties and labour unions were encouraged to reorganise. A new constitution was also drafted and on the Diet approving it, was brought into effect on 3 May 1947. Elections were held and the new democratic government modelled on European parliamentary and American systems began functioning. All this came about by the efforts of the Japanse people and their Government, who rendered co-operation in altering the outlook of the country. The occupation forces had also contributed towards such consummation by their example. But burden was not heavy and mostly their job was limited to rendering aid in times of natural calamities or in relieving economic distress resulting from the breakdown of the machinery of production.

The Indian Contingent of the British Commonwealth Occupation Force, was sent to Japan early in 1946 and was withdrawn consequent on the change of Government in India in 1947. Originally it had the character of a British officered force with a secondary role. But when in 1946 there was popularisation of the Government of India and with the withdrawal of the British Contingent, the Indian force had its own officers; and General H. C. H. Robertson, the Commander-in-Chief of British Commonwealth Occupation Force, gave it the recognition of an autonomous unit with an independent charge. The occupational task of the force did not involve any warlike operations. Mostly it was engaged on internal security duties, had to deal with the smugglers, black-marketeers and other anti-social elements. It played its part in relieving distress arising from natural calamities. Yet it would not be incorrect to add that having no control over policy decisions, and having no major responsibilities, it acted merely as a component unit of a large British Commonwealth force which had been sent to Japan largely for reasons of prestige. The narrative in the following pages, therefore, is only a record of the organisation of the force, its move to Japan, the functions it performed and the manner in which it disposed itself in a foreign land under Allied military occupation. The machinery of inter-governmental relationship, the links between SCAP, JCOSA and the component contingents and the mutual contact between the national contingents and the BCOF command have been discussed to focus attention on the main aspects of an inter-state organisation for military co-operation.

Bisheshwar Prasad

ERRATA

In Plate II, facing page 27, *for* " Indian Contingent arrives at Kure " *read* " Brindiv arrives at Kure."

In Plate V, facing page 66, *add* " In the centre is Field Marshal Auchinleck."

In Appendix 'J', facing page 310, *for* " PART 'A'—USSR Arms Basis " *read* " PART 'A' User Arms Basis."

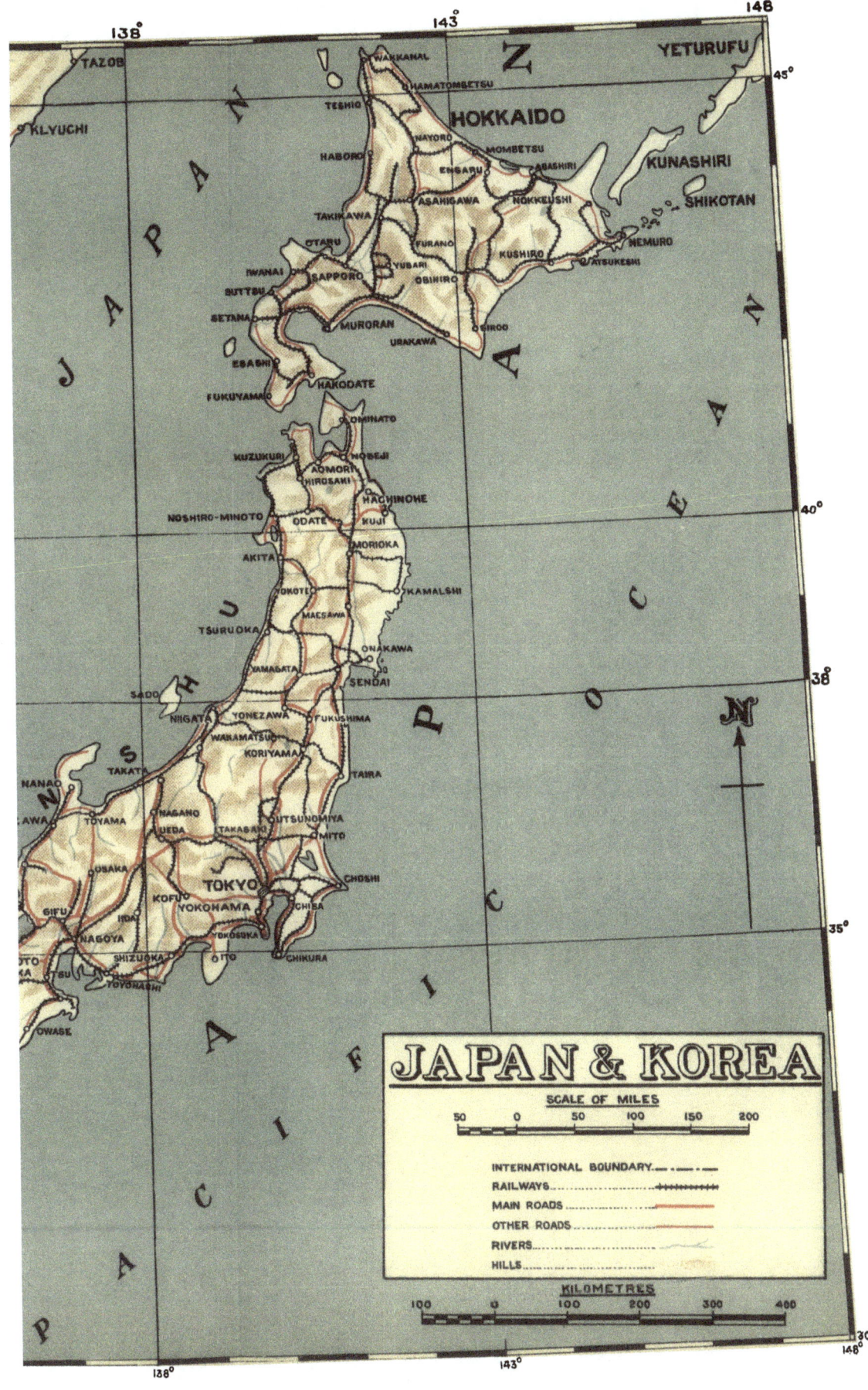

CHAPTER I

Pre-Surrender Period

WAR WITH JAPAN

On 7 December 1941, the Imperial Japanese Headquarters in Tokyo announced that Japan had entered into a state of war with Great Britain and the United States of America. Many hours before this announcement, and while peace parleys were still going on in Washington between the American and Japanese representatives, Japanese carrier-borne planes had made heavy attacks on Pearl Harbour, the main American base in the Pacific Ocean. The war in the Pacific had already started when the Government of India declared war on Japan on 8 December 1941.

The same day Japanese forces landed in Thailand (Siam) and north-east Malaya. The battle-trained Japanese crack troops who had prepared long for this war, with the elements of initiative and surprise in their favour, began to spread like wild-fire into French Indo-China, Siam and Malaya, while with their naval superiority, the other prong struck the oil-bearing Dutch islands of Sumatra and Java and started heading towards New Guinea. The two prongs were directed against India and Australia, the two main bases from where offensive action to stem and turn this tide could be mounted against Japan.

Many set-backs were in store for the Allies. On 25 December 1941, the British outpost of Hong Kong, where Indian troops along with British and Canadian units had fought gallantly against immensely superior Japanese forces, surrendered. The menace to Singapore began to grow. Strong dissatisfaction with the conduct of the Malayan Campaign, where considerable Australian forces were fighting alongside Indian and British troops, began to be voiced in the Australian press. On 3 January 1942, to meet this persistent demand and to organise the whole area stretching from Malaya, through Dutch East Indies, to New Guinea and Australia, into a combat zone, General Sir A. P. Wavell was appointed Supreme Commander in the South-West Pacific area, while General Chiang Kai-shek became the Commander of the Allied forces in the Indo-China and Thailand region.

Meanwhile twenty-six Allied nations including India expressed their determination to prosecute a relentless war against Japan by signing the Atlantic Charter on 1 January 1942 and made a joint declaration that:

"(a) Each Government pledges itself to employ its full resources, military or economic, against the Tripartite Pact and its adherents, with which such a Government is at war.

(b) Each Government pledges itself to co-operate with the governments signatory hereto, and not to make a separate armistice or peace with the enemies".

The war in the Pacific moved with great rapidity involving serious threats to Malaya, Borneo, Dutch East Indies and the Philippines. January 1942 saw the siege of Singapore, the main bastion of Allied defence in the South-West Pacific.

The Japanese had acquired air and naval supremacy in the South-West Pacific and thus menaced the security of vast territories held by many nations, British, Dutch, French, Portuguese, Australian and American. To co-ordinate properly the war effort of those regions and direct the operations from a centrally located headquarters was impracticable for General Wavell. Hence an organisation known as the Combined Chiefs of Staff Committee was formed in Washington for the purpose of ensuring effective unified command in the South-West Pacific and co-ordinating war effort in all the theatres. Thus alone could the Australian demand for a voice in the control of war be met, which had been voiced at the time.

The Combined Chiefs of Staff Committee was set up in Washington and was to consist of the representatives of the British Chiefs of Staff and the United States Chiefs of Staff. This body had to co-ordinate and correlate the policy in all the theatres of war where British and/or United States forces were operating. In case of a difference of opinion between the service representatives the dispute had to be referred to the heads of the two states, Mr. Roosevelt and Mr. Churchill.

The United States Chiefs of Staff was made responsible for the eastern approaches to Australia and New Zealand, which was designated "ANZAC Area". The northern area which centred around Singapore was made a British responsibility under the designation of "ABDA Area". The China theatre under Marshall Chiang Kai-shek, though not directly controlled by the Combined Chiefs of Staff, was closely linked to it by high-powered services liaison staffs at Chungking, Washington and London.

The war in the South-West Pacific took an adverse turn for the Allies. Following on the surrender of Singapore on 15 February 1942, the Japanese landed in Java and Sumatra, thus cutting off the link between India and Australia, and invaded Burma, involving a threat to the defences of India. The fall of Rangoon and the easy entry of the Japanese navy into the Indian Ocean made them masters of south-east Asia. Moreover, India was threatened on her eastern frontier. If the surging tide of Japanese advance was to be checked, India and Australia, the two bases, must be defended at all cost and their industrial resources developed to gain material superiority over the Japanese. For this purpose it was necessary to bring about closer co-operation between the Governments and their fighting services.

Sir Stafford Cripps, the Chancellor of Exchequer, Government of the United Kingdom, arrived in India in March 1942 to endeavour to settle the political issue in India and obtain maximum Indian effort for war against Japan. General Douglas MacArthur, "the hero of Bataan", arrived in Australia by air on 17 March 1942, to become the Supreme Commander of all the United Nations forces in the South-West Pacific region, at the request of the Australian Government. The Australian Prime Minister, Mr. John Curtin, announced on 12 March 1942 that the conduct of operations in the ANZAC Area would be vested in the Supreme Commander, South-West Pacific Area (SWPA). Australia had imposed two major conditions for this organisation, viz.:—
  (a) that the machinery set up should not be complicated,
  (b) that at the final stage of any decision Australia should have a direct and equal voice.

The Australian Chiefs of Staff were directly linked to South-West Pacific Area and Australia had an accredited representative with General MacArthur to influence policy at all stages. A close link-up was created between the Australian and South-West Pacific Area Service Headquarters.

To obtain a voice for the component units at the governmental level in influencing policy regarding the South-West Pacific, a Pacific War Council was established whose first meeting was held in Washington on 1 April 1942. India was a member of this Council and was greatly interested in its deliberations. The importance of Australia and India in the war was emphasised by Mr. Curtin who said: "Australia and India must be held as the pillars of the Allied position in Asia and the Pacific for the final defeat of Japan".[1]

The war was coming nearer to these two pillars. In the north General Alexander's forces, after a fighting retreat in Burma against overwhelming odds, had reached "the eastern gates of India". But this supreme effort of the out-numbered, worn-out

[1] John Curtin's speech in Canberra.

Indian and British troops had given India time, five precious months, to prepare her defences.

Further advance of the two Japanese prongs was held up—that towards India in the jungle-clad, mosquito-infested hills of eastern India; that towards Australia in the knife-edged mountain peaks of the Owen-Stanley Range in New Guinea. In both bases vast forces and resources were being assembled and organised, not only to check the Japanese advance, but to put it back into reverse gear.

REORGANISATION OF ABDA AREA

On 19 June 1943, General Sir Claude Auchinleck took over as Commander-in-Chief, India, from Lord Wavell, who became Viceroy of India. On his appointment Lord Wavell said: " India is a vital supply base for the United Nations in the east, and the more fully and rapidly India can develop and extend the war effort she is already making, the sooner will this shadow of war pass from her, and the earlier can she achieve her aim of full self-government ".[2]

To conduct operations against Japan a separate South-East Asia Command (SEAC) was also set up. Admiral Lord Louis Mountbatten was appointed the Supreme Commander of this area which consisted of the former territories of ABDA Area less India, which came under the Commander-in-Chief, India. South-East Asia Command came directly under the British Chiefs of Staff and was organised on the same basis as the Allied Forces Headquarters (AFHQ) for General Eisenhower's campaign in North Africa. All the Allied forces in this theatre were placed under Lord Louis Mountbatten's command. The policy in the two Pacific theatres, South-East Asia Command and South-West Pacific Area, was co-ordinated through the Combined Chiefs of Staff in Washington. With the creation of these two new commands and the appointment of a distinguished sailor and soldier respectively at the head of each, the war in the Pacific took a definite turn for the better.

PROSECUTION OF WAR IN THE EAST

General MacArthur's Headquarters announced that combined and co-ordinated operations had begun in New Guinea, while South-East Asia Command forces had declared a halt to the

---

[2] Lord Wavell's speech to the Pilgrim's Society in London.

westward threat of the Japanese in Imphal-Kohima area. For the next two years, a relentless war was carried on in Burma and the islands of South-West Pacific in which America, United Kingdom, Australia, India and New Zealand paid tremendous price for victory. The story of the campaigns in Burma, Gaudalcanal, Chindwin, Mandalay, Arakan and Leyte has been written in other histories.

Throughout 1944-45, the Indian Navy, Army and Air Force played a major part in holding the invading hordes against severe odds, and ultimately turned the tables on the Japanese in early 1945. After many gallant deeds which added fresh laurels to their martial glory, the Indian forces swept the Japanese off their feet and drove them down the Irrawaddy and Chindwin rivers to Rangoon with the speed of those mighty torrents.

The war in Europe came to an end at 0245 hours on 7 May 1945 with the unconditional surrender of Germany to the Allies. Italy had fallen before and there remained only one and the last partner of the Tripartite Pact—Japan. It was obvious that the mighty effort of all the Allies would be turned against their remaining foe.

Despite the Allied warning and the Potsdam Declaration, Japan showed no sign of giving up the fight. Still the Japanese fought on, attacking time and again with blind persistence and destroying everything in their path or getting destroyed themselves. While the Allied land forces were destroying the Japanese Imperial Army in their "fox holes", the American Super-Fortresses were raining havoc on the Japanese mainland by persistent and heavy bombing. All important towns were razed to the ground, one after the other, by high explosive and incendiary bombs. The Fourteenth Army, three-fourths of which were Indian troops, had chased the Japanese from one end of Burma to the other.

The Atom Bomb

The American forces captured Okinawa and were preparing to assault the Japanese mainland. It was anticipated that the Japanese would put up a stout resistance in defence of their homeland and that the Allies would have to pay a heavy price for conquering every inch of the Japanese mainland. But, late in the evening of 6 August 1945, President Truman announced: "Sixteen hours ago, an American aeroplane dropped an atomic bomb on Hiroshima. The use of an atomic bomb for the first time in the history of warfare was a consequence of epoch-making discovery".

Hiroshima, the target, was a great port and army base with a population of about 340,000. It covered an area of 7·5 square miles, 4·1 square miles of which was completely obliterated with heavy additional damage outside the area. More than 70,000 people were killed. A wave of consternation submerged the Government and people of Japan.

The second atomic bomb was dropped at noon of 9 August 1945 on the great port of Nagasaki, a city of 250,000 people. One-third of Nagasaki was wiped out. The fear of the annihilation of Japan gripped the Government who now saw the writing on the wall.

THE JAPANESE SURRENDER

On 8 August 1945, the Soviet Foreign Minister, Mr. Molotov, handed a note to the Japanese Ambassador that Russia would be at war with Japan as from 9 August 1945. Within thirty-six hours of Russia's entry into the Far Eastern war, and after the complete destruction of Hiroshima and Nagasaki by atomic bombs, the Japanese offered to surrender according to the terms of the Potsdam Declaration. On 14 August 1945, the Japanese Cabinet accepted the Allied terms and the war against Japan came to an end. General MacArthur was appointed the Supreme Commander Allied Powers (SCAP) to accept the Japanese surrender.

CHAPTER II

Supreme Command Allied Powers

THE ARTICLE OF SURRENDER

On 2 September 1945, on board the U.S.S. *Missouri*, in Tokyo Bay, the Japanese envoys signed the unconditional surrender. The terms of the surrender were as follows:—

" (i) We, acting by command of and on behalf of the Emperor, the Japanese Government, and the Japanese Imperial General Headquarters, hereby accept the provisions in the declaration issued by the Heads of the Governments of the United States, China and Great Britain on 26 July at Potsdam, and subsequently adhered to by the Soviet Union.

(ii) We hereby proclaim the unconditional surrender to the Allied Powers of Japanese Imperial General Headquarters and of all Japanese armed forces and all armed forces under Japanese control wherever situated.

(iii) We hereby command all Japanese forces wherever situated, and Japanese people, to cease hostilities forthwith, to preserve and save from damage all ships, aircraft, and military and civil property, and to comply with all requirements which may be imposed by the Allied Supreme Commander or by agencies of the Japanese Government at his direction.

(iv) We hereby command Japanese Imperial General Headquarters to issue at once orders to commanders of all Japanese Forces and all forces under Japanese control wherever situated to surrender unconditionally themselves and all forces under their control.

(v) We hereby command all civil, military and naval officials to obey and enforce all proclamations, orders and directives deemed by the Allied Supreme Commander to be proper to effectuate this surrender and issued by him or under his authority, and direct all such officials to remain at their posts and continue to perform their non-combatant duties unless specifically relieved by him or under his authority.

(vi) We hereby undertake for the Japanese Government and their successors to carry out the provisions of the Potsdam Declaration in good faith and to issue whatever command

and take whatever action may be required by the Allied Supreme Commander or by any other designated representative of the Allied Powers for the purpose of giving effect to the Declaration.

(vii) We hereby command the Japanese Imperial Government and Japanese Imperial General Headquarters at once to liberate all Allied prisoners of war and civilian internees now under Japanese control, and provide for their protection, care, maintenance and immediate transportation to places as directed.

(viii) The authority of the Emperor and the Japanese Government to rule the state shall be subject to the Allied Supreme Command, who will take such steps as he deems proper to effectuate these terms of surrender ".

On behalf of the Allies the following affixed their signatures to it: General MacArthur (as Supreme Commander), Fleet-Admiral Chester Nimitz (for the United States), General Hsu Yung-Chang (for China), Admiral Sir Bruce Fraser (for Great Britain), Lieutenant-General Kuzma Nikoyayevitch Dervyanko (for the Soviet Union), General Sir Thomas Blamey (for Australia), Colonel L. Moore Cosgrave (for Canada), General Phillip Leclerc (for France), Admiral Conrad Helfrich (for Netherlands) and Air Vice-Marshal Isitt (for New Zealand). There was no Indian delegate present at the ceremony.

The Imperial Script

At 1030 hours on that date, World War II came to an end and Emperor Hirohito issued an Imperial Script calling on all Japanese forces to lay down their arms forthwith and " faithfully to carry out all provisions of the instrument of surrender ". The surrender and subsequent occupation were made easy by this proclamation, which the Japanese considered it their sacred duty to obey. There were no incidents with the Japanese military or civil population.

Japanese Surrender in South-East Asia Command

While the main surrender took place on board the U.S.S. *Missouri*, other Japanese formations surrendered in various theatres. In Singapore, the Supreme Allied Commander, Admiral Lord Louis Mountbatten, accepted the surrender on 12 September 1945, of all Japanese forces in South-East Asia. Count Terauchi, the Japanese overall commander in South-East Asia, could not attend as he was suffering from a paralytic stroke but sent his sword to be surrendered by General Itagaki, Commander of the Imperial

Japanese Seventh Army Area, who signed the surrender on his behalf. Representatives of the Armed Forces of Great Britain, United States, India, Australia, China, France and Holland were present, Brigadier (now General) K. S. Thimayya, D.S.O., affixed his signature on behalf of India.

Thus ended the Japanese threat, which in 1942 had reached the gates of India. To stem and turn back this tide thousands of Indians had laid down their lives and India had to make heavy sacrifices of material and money for the common cause. In the words of President Truman, " It was a long road to Tokyo and a bloody one, " and India having paid dearly in blood and sweat became a partner in the occupation of Japan.

American Troops Land in Japan

It was agreed with the Japanese surrender envoys, who had arrived in Manila on 19 August 1945 that the American occupation troops would begin to land on the Japanese soil on 28 August. On that date a few thousand American troops went ashore and occupied strategic places on the four Japanese Islands of Honshu, Shikoku, Kyushu and Hokkaido. On the same day General MacArthur issued a directive:

(a) authorising his Army Commanders to requisition anything they needed in Japan; and
(b) calling for the immediate demobilization and disarmament of the Japanese forces.

On 8 September 1945, General MacArthur at the head of his troops made his formal entry in Tokyo. In a statement from Supreme Command Allied Powers Headquarters it was announced, " that Japan would be occupied by 500,000 American troops, that every opportunity would be given to the Japanese to carry out their instructions without compulsion, that the civilian population would be allowed freedom from all unwarranted interference with their personal liberty and that the Japanese economy would be controlled to the extent necessary to achieve the United Nations objectives ".

As a United Nations Organisation had already come into being it was expected that Japan would be occupied by an Allied Force, composed of contingents of various countries. But General MacArthur, perhaps being influenced by the none too pleasant experience of the joint control of Germany, placed the military control of Japan solely under the United States Eighth Army Commander, General Eichelberger.

While Americans were landing in Japan, the Soviet troops of the 2nd Far Eastern Front occupied the whole of Japanese

Sakhalin Peninsula, the northern half of which already belonged to Russia. In Korea and Manchuria there was a race to occupy the largest area of foreign territory formerly held by Japan. In Korea, however, the line of division between the Russian and American troops was agreed to as the 38th parallel.[1]

JAPAN'S MAIN TERRITORY

Japan's main territory consists of four main islands: Hokkaido in the north, separated from Sakhalin by a 40-mile narrow channel; the biggest of the four islands, Honshu; the island of Shikoku; and the southern-most island of Kyushu. A backbone of volcanic mountains runs through the four islands, with the sacred mountain Fuji in Honshu dominating them all. The hills are steep and wooded and in some places snow-covered. At most places they end up precipitously at the seashore. Thus most of Japan is mountainous with narrow coastal plains skirting the hills, and fast flowing streams and steep ravines intersecting them. There are four large level areas in Japan, Tokyo, Nagoya, Sendai and Osaka, all in Honshu, where live most of Japan's teeming millions with their factories and dwellings.

The communications of Japan consisted of railways, roads and a highly developed ferry system which connected the four islands. Its wireless, telephone and other communication systems were all placed under the complete supervision and control of the Supreme Commander Allied Powers. With her exits completely sealed off by the Allied naval forces, her system of inland communications under Allied control, and the seizure of her mercantile marine, Japan was completely isolated from the outside world.

THE OBJECTS OF OCCUPATION

Japan was an occupied territory and the objects and aims of occupation were laid down in a Directive issued by President Truman to General MacArthur. It laid down:
   (a) that the authority of the Japanese Emperor and Government would remain subordinate to General MacArthur;
   (b) that the control of Japan would be exercised through the Japanese Government as long as it remained satisfactory;
   (c) that the Potsdam Declaration would be the basis of the United States policy for treatment of Japan.

---

[1] The division of boundaries in Japan and Korea is shown on chart opposite.

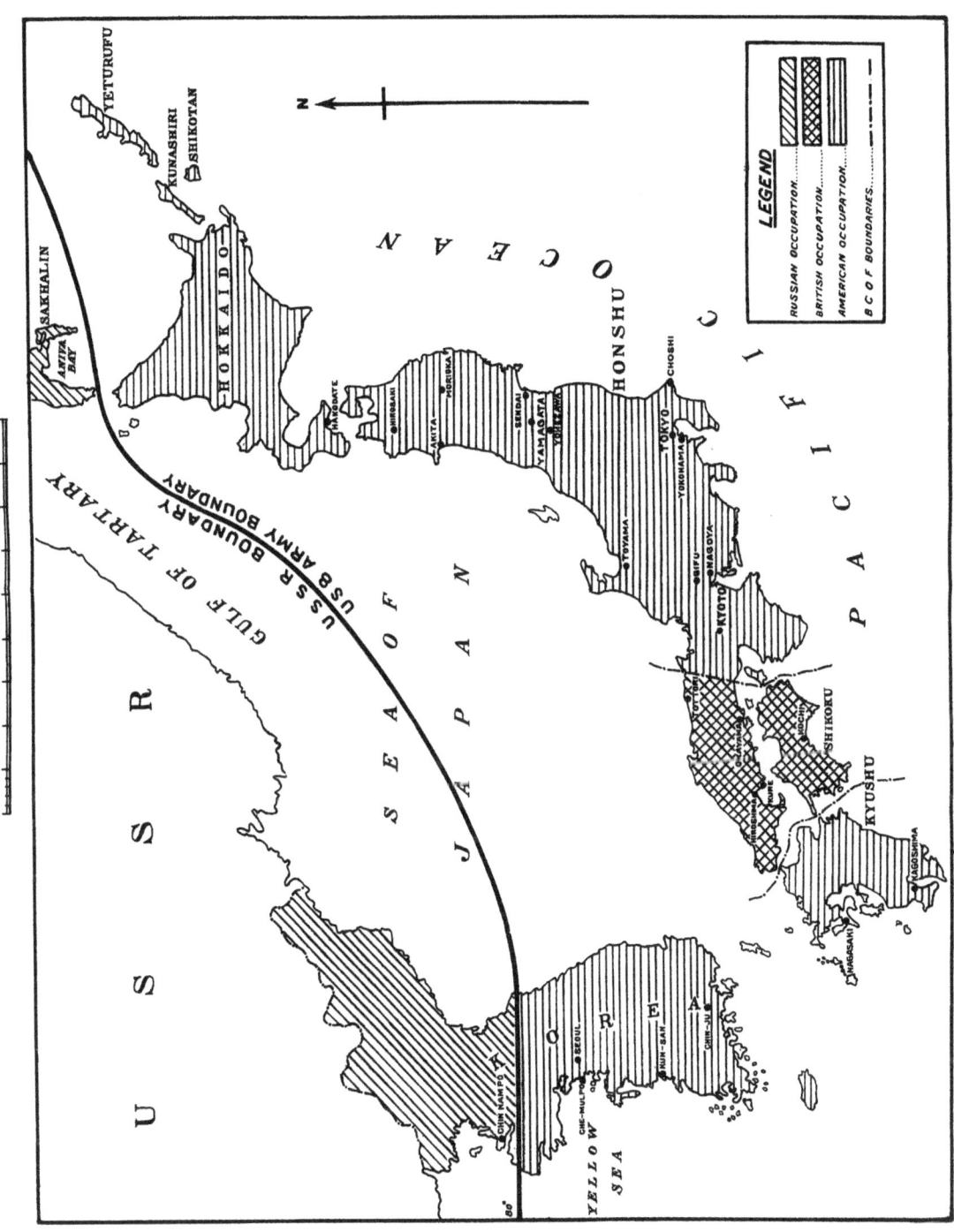

In conformity with these principles General MacArthur issued many directives to the Japanese Imperial Government and created a complex machinery to conduct his policies, as far as possible, through the Imperial Japanese Government, and failing that, directly through the occupation channels illustrated on the chart opposite.

SUPREME COMMAND ALLIED POWERS MACHINERY

Unlike Germany, where normal Government had ceased to exist, in Japan the Government of the Emperor was maintained in power and governed the country, though Supreme Commander Allied Powers' Headquarters supervised the governmental acts and controlled various aspects of administration by directives issued to the Japanese Government. This continuance of the emblem of the Emperor, without effective political power but invested with all the forms of a constitutional machinery, made the task of military occupation easy. All directives to the Japanese people were issued through the Emperor's Government and were obeyed by them owing to their instinctive obedience to the Emperor. That insured people's co-operation rather than their resistance. At the same time it facilitated the conduct of business for General MacArthur, the overall political and military authority, who had to deal only with two channels, for political matters with the Japanese Government and for military control through the United States Eighth Army.

Supreme Commander Allied Powers was invested with the powers to supervise and direct the Japanese Government. All legislation by the Diet required his approval to be effective. Supreme Commander Allied Powers could also secure necessary legislation through the Diet which could be dissolved by him and fresh elections ordered. The Supreme Commander Allied Powers also controlled the formation of ministries and allocation of portfolios. It was also found necessary to retain the administrative machinery of the old Japanese regime, purged of the " suspects " or " war criminals ". But in fact the real controlling authority in their respective regions was retained by the operational commanders, the Commander United States Eighth Army, Commander-in-Chief British Commonwealth Occupation Force, and the commanders of the United States Corps and Divisions who were responsible for policing the Japanese people to see that the operation directives were not violated by them. In addition, throughout the Japanese islands, personnel of the Allied Military Government were stationed at important centres to help the local prefectural authorities with advice and to guide them in democratic methods. One of the main functions of this Allied Military Government came to be to supervise the issue and distribution of the food and medical supplies which were made available by the United States Government throughout the whole of Japan.

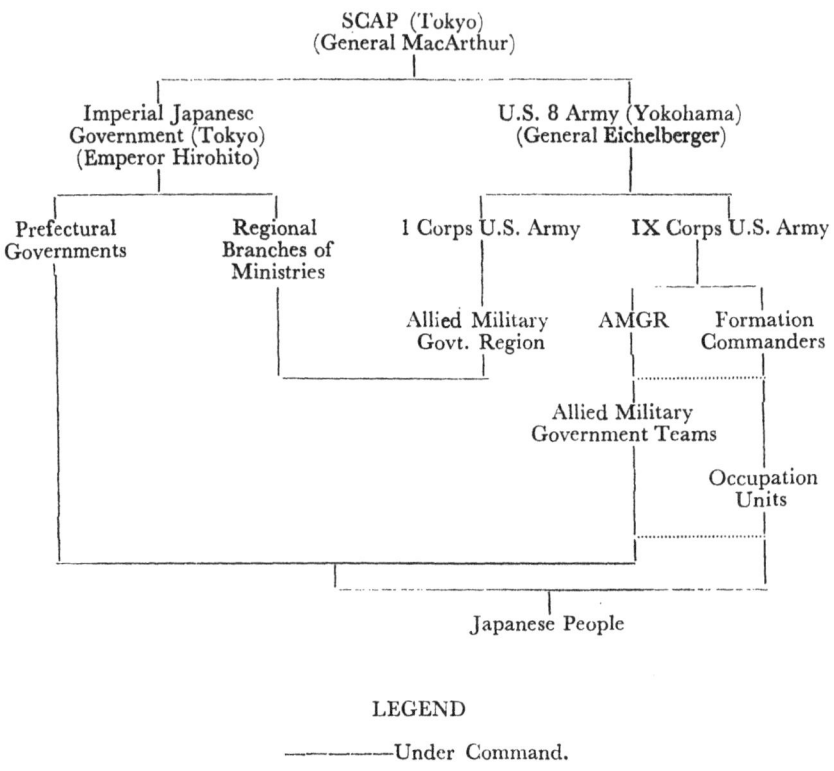

LEGEND

————————Under Command.

..........................Contact.

The Allied Military Government was organised into regions and operated through teams, which were largely manned by American personnel. But in the British Commonwealth Occupation Force area, commonwealth co-operation was not unwelcome and the British Commonwealth Occupation Force supplied a number of teams in its regions, whose work evoked admiration from the American authorities. It was, however, not possible for the British Commonwealth to render effective co-operation in the Allied Military Government owing to the inability to share in the costly liability involved in providing food and medical supplies for a population of between eleven and fourteen million Japanese people who inhabited the area controlled by the British Commonwealth

Occupation Force. Nevertheless, through its personnel in the Allied Military Government teams, British Commonwealth Occupation Force could have all the contact it needed with the Japanese people without any cost to itself or to the participating Governments. The Allied Military Government teams in their prefectures maintained an intimate control over the people and effectively participated in all forms of Japanese social, political and economic activity. These teams were not directly under the authority of the United States Eighth Army, but were dependent on it for the supply of food, stores etc. and for telegraphic and postal communications. It may also be emphasised that these teams did not in any manner override the controlling authority of the Commander-in-Chief British Commonwealth Occupation Force in his area of responsibility.

The Military Objects of Occupation

President Truman's Directive of 6 September 1945, laid down the objectives of occupation as:

    (i) the complete disarmament and demilitarisation of Japan;
    (ii) the eradication of military education;
    (iii) the dissolution of the large industrial and banking concerns;
    (iv) the encouragement of democratic organisation;
    (v) freedom of worship (military organisation not to be allowed to hide behind the cloak of religion—Shintoism);
    (vi) the ensuring of payment of reparations (provided this did not interfere with the country's peace-time economy); and
    (vii) enabling the Japanese to conduct their economic life within stated safeguards and under the approval of the Supreme Commander.

The attainment of the above objects required the destruction of Japanese militarism in all its stages; the location and subsequent destruction of all military stores and equipment, the liquidation of all Japanese war organisations; the demobilisation of all armed forces; and the suppression of all subversive activities in any form. To carry out these tasks the American forces were initially located at all important centres. At the same time the Japanese military authorities being well aware of their altered position carried out the Supreme Commander Allied Powers directives with great promptitude and exactitude. By 30 September 1945, only 28 days after the surrender, 81 per cent of the Japanese troops in Japan had been demobilised and it was estimated that full demobilisation would be completed by 15 October 1945.

The biggest problem was, however, the repatriation of the Japanese forces in the far-flung theaters of war. Arrangements were therefore made for their quick repatriation and demobilisation. Similarly the huge stocks of military stores had to be traced, catalogued and destroyed. The Japanese military authorities being well aware of the impossibility of armed resistance gave themselves up. The Japanese war machinery was thus liquidated overnight and all military officers who were not wanted for war-crimes retired to their country homes to till their scanty farms. The Japanese masses, accustomed to strict discipline and proverbial obedience of orders, also adopted a non-militant attitude. Japan changed overnight.

The military object having been attained in such a short time and without any resistance whatsoever, General MacArthur declared on 26 September 1945, "that within six months 200,000 troops would be sufficient for the occupation of Japan and Korea"—a reduction of 300,000 troops.

Henceforth the political object, the democratisation of Japan, became more important and, in consonance with world opinion and public pressure from America, Supreme Commander Allied Powers machinery was put in top-gear to achieve this end.

ALLIED TROOPS FOR JAPAN

Meanwhile some of the Allied Powers were also showing keenness to participate in the occupation in accordance with President Truman's Directive, which had laid down that "the occupation shall have the character of an operation on behalf of the principal Allied Powers, that the participation of the forces of other nations that had taken a leading part in the defeat of Japan would be welcomed and expected", and thereby to change the United States control into Allied control.

Such a demand was made particularly by Australia, presumably on behalf of the British Commonwealth, and by virtue of her being a principal Pacific Power which had borne a major share of the struggle against Japan, as measured by the casualties suffered (some 50,000) and the cost incurred [£(Australia) 2,111,000,000].[2] On 17 August 1945, Mr. Chifley, the Australian Prime Minister, informed the United Kingdom Government of

---

[2] Killed in action against the Japanese.   10627
Died of wounds in action.   1196
Died of wounds on sickness while P of W.   5597
Died of injuries or sickness in operational areas.   1470
Wounded in action.   14081
Prisoners of War repatriated.   14519.

the wish of Australia " to furnish a composite force to participate in the occupation of Japan under an Australian Commander subject only to General MacArthur's consent ". Thereupon it was ultimately decided to send a Commonwealth Force consisting of British, Australian, Indian and New Zealand troops to Japan under an Australian Commander, and under the overall control of a Joint Chiefs of Staff in Australia composed of the representatives of the participating states.

Negotiations to this effect were opened with the United States State Department in Washington by Dr. Evatt, Australian Minister of External Affairs, and in Tokyo with General MacArthur by Lieutenant-General Northcott of the Australian Army, on behalf of the Commonwealth.

NEGOTIATIONS WITH SUPREME COMMANDER ALLIED POWERS

Their concurrence took long to come. Negotiations dragged on for many months. The chief point at issue was whether the British Commonwealth forces should have an independent zone for their occupation.[3] The State Department was not prepared to accept this, because of its opposition to the allocation of national zones in Japan similar to those in Germany.[4] It was felt that this would create a bad precedent which could be taken advantage of by Russia and China also. Hence in the principles adopted for the participation of the British Commonwealth forces in the occupation of Japan, it was specifically laid down that the army portion of British Commonwealth Occupation Force would be placed under the command of the United States Eighth Army while the Air Force and the Navy could work under the United States Air Force and United States Navy respectively.

MacArthur—Northcott Agreement

The proposals of the United States Government as to the general principles and the tentative arrangements made in Tokyo, following discussions between General MacArthur and Lieutenant-General Northcott, were embodied in a 'Memorandum for Record' (also known as ' MacArthur—Northcott Agreement ') which were accepted by the British Commonwealth Governments concerned in the following form:—

" The British Commonwealth Governments welcome the agreement reached between General MacArthur and Lieutenant-General Northcott as a logical outcome of the general principles

[3] Document dated 20 December 1945.
[4] Britel/36 of 26 December 1945 to Troopers and Armindia.

set out by United States Government and propose that this agreement be accepted and placed on record as the agreed basis on which the British Commonwealth Force will proceed to, and participate in the occupation of, Japan, subject to further consideration of such matters as detailed financial arrangements, supply of stores, internal organisation of British Commonwealth Occupation Force ".

The main points of MacArthur-Northcott agreement were:[5]

(a) The British Commonwealth Occupation Force will constitute a component of occupation forces in Japan under the supreme command of the Supreme Commander for the Allied Powers. It will be charged with the normal military duties of a force of its size and composition, including military control of Hiroshima Prefecture etc. These areas do not constitute a National Zone. Relationship of British Commonwealth Occupation Force with the Japanese and routine security functions will be prescribed by the Commanding General, United States Eighth Army.

(b) Supreme Commander Allied Powers will assign ground forces of British Commonwealth Occupation Force to the operational control of the Commanding General, United States Eighth Army and the Air component of British Commonwealth Occupation Force to United States Fifth Air Force. General Officer Commanding, British Commonwealth Occupation Force will be responsible for the maintenance and administration of British Commonwealth Occupation Force as a whole.

(c) General Officer Commanding, British Commonwealth Occupation Force will have the right of direct access to the Supreme Commander for the Allied Powers on matters of major policy affecting the operational capabilities of the Force.

(d) For matters of Governmental concern affecting the policy and operations of British Commonwealth Occupation Force, the channel of communication lies from the Australian Government as representative of the British Commonwealth of Nations through the United States Government and Joint Chiefs of Staff to Supreme Commander Allied Powers.

[5] Memorandum for Record, General Headquarters, Supreme Allied Commander for the Allied Powers, dated 18 Dec. 45, in Appx. "A".

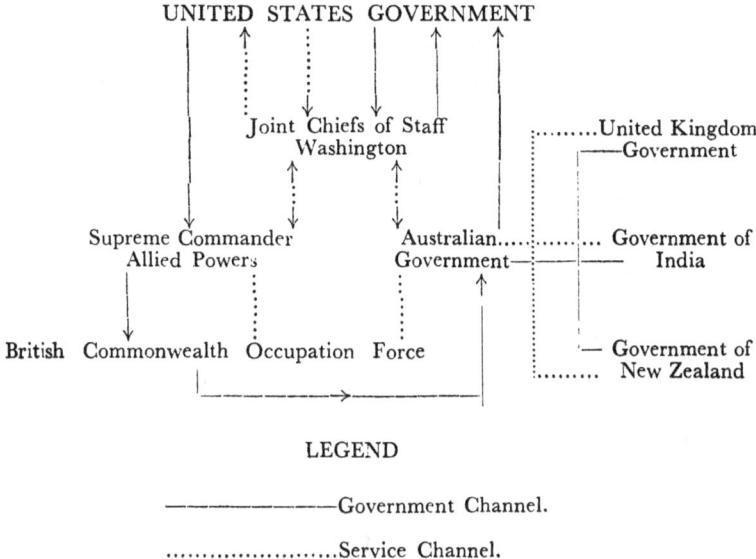

LEGEND

———————Government Channel.

..................Service Channel.

(e) British Commonwealth Occupation Force may be withdrawn wholly or in part upon agreement between the Governments of United States and Australia or upon six months notice by either party.

(f) Reductions will be made in British Commonwealth Occupation Force from time to time in conformity with progressive reductions in the United States Occupation Forces in Japan.

(g) The Australian Service Mission in Tokyo will be disbanded and its functions taken over by an Advance Echelon, Headquarters British Commonwealth Occupation Force.

(h) Improvements made to Japanese facilities with United States materials will be accepted by British Commonwealth Occupation Force on dollar reimbursement basis, when such facilities are needed and desired by the British Commonwealth Force.

This agreement defined the functions of the British Commonwealth Occupation Force and determined its relationship with Supreme Commander Allied Powers and the United States Eighth Army. The force was placed under the supreme command of Supreme Commander Allied Powers, but its relationship with the Japanese and the routine security functions concomitant on the military control of the Hiroshima Prefecture allotted to it, were to be determined by the Commander of the United States Eighth

Army. It was made perfectly clear that the areas under direct occupation of the British Commonwealth Occupation Force would " not constitute a National Zone ". This specifically differentiated the role of the component units in Japan from that of AMGOT in Italy and Germany and ensured centralised control under the Supreme Commander Allied Powers. The anxiety for unity of control is clearly emphasised in clause (b) which provided for operational control of the ground and air forces respectively by the commanding generals of the United States Eighth Army and Fifth Air Force. But such control did not comprehend the " maintenance and administration of the British Commonwealth Occupation Force for which its independence was clearly expressed". The British Commonwealth Occupation Force had to make its own provisioning, and any materials obtained from the United States had to be paid for in dollars unless required for operational purposes. Clause (h) further laid down that all Japanese facilities improved by the United States forces with their materials, when utilised by the British Commonwealth Occupation Force would have to be paid for in dollars. This condition might have affected the choice of Hiroshima Prefecture as the area of occupation of the British Commonwealth Occupation Force owing to the limited nature of such improvements there; for elsewhere the Americans had, owing to their prior occupation, made considerable improvements in the matter of accommodation etc.

The other clauses of this agreement prescribed the channels of communication between the Supreme Commander Allied Powers and British Commonwealth Occupation Force both for operational and political purposes; while in the first case the General Officer Commanding British Commonwealth Occupation Force had the right of direct access to the Supreme Commander Allied Powers, in the latter category the approach was through the Australian Government, United States Government and the Joint Chiefs of Staff. There was provision for the withdrawal of the British Commonwealth Occupation Force also, which was either by agreement with the United States Government or upon six months' notice.

SELECTION OF AN AREA FOR BRITISH COMMONWEALTH OCCUPATION FORCE

In selecting the area for BCOF the following basic factors had to be taken into consideration:
(a) the area must have prestige value;

(b) it must have an important port of entry under the exclusive control of British Commonwealth Occupation Force;
(c) it must have facilities for recreation;
(d) it must have sufficient accommodation for Headquarters and troops;
(e) it must be proportionate in relation to the Force and its possible operational role;
(f) it must be available immediately;
(g) it should, as far as possible, be climatically suitable.

There were four important areas in Japan, important from the point of social, industrial and political development. All of them were located in the main Japanese island of Honshu. They were:

(a) *Tokyo Area*—This was the capital area, the seat of Imperial Japanese Government and of Supreme Commander Allied Powers. The port of Yokohama, only 8 miles away, was occupied by the United States Eighth Army Headquarters. This area of major importance and great prestige value for the Japanese was not offered to British Commonwealth Occupation Force as it was fully occupied by very large United States forces, and British Commonwealth Occupation Force would not have been fitted in as an independent entity with all the facilities mentioned above.

(b) *Nagoya Area*—This was an industrially developed area south of Tokyo, and was earmarked for the Chinese, who never came. This area was not offered to British Commonwealth Occupation Force because Supreme Commander Allied Powers might have desired to locate the Chinese forces between two American formations in the north and south.[6]

(c) *Kobe-Osaka Area*—This was the second largest and highly developed area with the former Japanese capital of Kyoto located in its centre. In pre-war days this area was of great commercial value and the harbour of Kobe handled the largest amount of shipping in Japan. Kobe had thus great prestige value particularly because Japanese sacred cities and the centres of civilisation of Kyoto and Nara were located there. It was also highly industrialised and socially developed and had an important port. It had modern beautiful hotels, all important places of sight-seeing and the best opera, Takarazuka. It had at the same time sufficient

[6] PACCOS 38 dated 11 September 1946.

accommodation both for the Headquarters and the troops. But as Kobe was designated " the first major port " of the American forces in Japan through which far more supplies passed than through any other port, and which was also the base for their forces in Korea, it was unlikely that this area could be offered to British Commonwealth Occupation Force. Therefore the Supreme Commander Allied Powers declared that it could not be made immediately available to British Commonwealth Occupation Force. It was stated that the port had to be cleared of mines and United States stores had to be shifted to other areas,[7] which required at least a period of eight months to execute. This naturally could not suit the British Commonwealth Occupation Force which had already been marking time for a long period and was getting restive to take up its role. Moreover, the occupation of the area would have involved payment in dollars of a colossal amount, the cost for developments made by the United States forces. The density of its population which was considered to be a potential danger owing to its highly industrialised character inclining towards communism, was also a factor against the selection of Kobe-Osaka area as General Northcott's forces were not adequate to control this area[8] in the event of any trouble.

(d) *Hiroshima—Kure Area*—It bordered the narrow Japanese inland sea with Honshu on the north and Shikoku to the south. It had an important port of Kure, the great Japanese naval dockyards. With the atom bombing of Hiroshima this area had become notorious though it had no great prestige value in the eyes of the Japanese. It was industrially and socially backward; and as a large number of military installations were located there it had been badly bombed. Except for the sacred Miyajima (Paradise Island) it offered no recreational facilities. Accommodation was limited except at Etajima which was the former Japanese naval academy and only a few minutes sea journey from Kure harbour. This area was immediately available for British Commonwealth Occupation Force and could be easily taken over as it was sparsely occupied by United States forces.

Out of the two areas available, Kobe-Osaka area was not offered by Supreme Commander Allied Powers, but even if it had

---

[7] PACCOS No. 11 dated 20 March 1946.
[8] Ibid.

been offered it is problematical if General Northcott would have selected it for the reasons mentioned above, viz. the time-lag, cost involved in taking over American facilities and the inadequacy of British Commonwealth Occupation Force to control it in the event of trouble. As it turned out later, however, the time lag was of no importance, for British Commonwealth Occupation Force could not arrive before February 1946; and the cost consideration could have been obviated by taking over alternative accommodation and developing it from Japanese resources. Finally, there was luckily no trouble in the area. But these could not have been visualised in advance and that too only four months after the surrender. General Northcott who did not have a previous opportunity to reconnoitre thoroughly any of these areas[9] accepted the only alternative—Hiroshima, which he considered as " satisfactory from climatic and other aspects of British Commonwealth Occupation Force. This area may be extended if necessary ".[10] Nevertheless, some dissatisfaction was felt owing to the limited nature of amenities and facilities for recreation and shopping. Climatic and expansion aspects could not override this consideration for it was believed that climatic disparity could not be great between it and the area on the south coast of Honshu and that the direction of expansion had not been indicated.

No provision was made initially for stationing British Commonwealth Occupation Force troops in Tokyo and the Cabinet Office in London cabled to Joint Chiefs of Staff Australia on 21 December 1945, that " the MacArthur-Northcott agreement does not even mention a Detachment of the Force being stationed in Tokyo Prefecture, which we consider desirable ".[11]

The Supreme Commander Allied Powers readily agreed to the location, in rotation, of one battalion in Tokyo to carry out guard duties under the control of United States 2nd Cavalry Division stationed there. Later a British Commonwealth Sub-area (BRICOSAT) was formed in Tokyo which played an important part in raising Commonwealth prestige and in the maintenance of British Commonwealth civil agencies in Tokyo.

FINAL ACCEPTANCE OF BRITISH COMMONWEALTH OCCUPATION FORCE

After his agreement with General MacArthur, Lt.-General Northcott returned to Australia to report to the Joint Chiefs of

[9] BRITEL Signal No. 62 dated 8 January 1946.
[10] BRITEL/36 of 26 December 1945 to Troopers and Armindia.
[11] Signal dated 21 December 1945 from Cabinet Offices to Joint Chiefs of Staff Australia.

Staff in Australia. On 24 December 1945, he gave a resume of his discussions with General MacArthur. The main points stressed were:—[12]

(a) whole-hearted welcome and co-operation of MacArthur and his staff;

(b) affirmation by MacArthur that British Commonwealth Occupation Force was urgently needed and that, far from opposing it, he had always pressed for its early arrival.

Even after the agreement and final acceptance of all terms laid down by the Supreme Commander Allied Powers, the formal agreement from the United States Government was not immediately forthcoming. The New Zealand Government was getting tired of this delay and the Prime Minister of New Zealand cabled to Mr. Chifley, Prime Minister of Australia:

"We have considered the terms of agreement between General MacArthur and Northcott and are quite prepared to participate on that basis. We would be less than frank, however, if we did not say that in view of the time which has elapsed since the first tentative announcement was made regarding the provision of this Force and the way in which negotiations have dragged, that enthusiasm for it had flagged very considerably in New Zealand. There is a general feeling that this Force is not needed and it appears questionable whether, in the circumstances, it is likely to yield any increase in British Commonwealth prestige. We are, however, willing to go on ".

The Australian Government, as representing the British Commonwealth Governments concerned, pressed for the United States Government's agreement so that a movement programme could be drawn up and submitted to General MacArthur for approval. The time schedule of arrival of British Commonwealth Occupation Force depended on the capacity of Kure harbour, the only port in the area. The detailed reconnaissance of this area was to be carried out by the Advance Echelon of General Northcott's Headquarters in Tokyo and a Port Party to be despatched from the East Indies Fleet. No person could be moved to Japan without Supreme Commander Allied Powers clearance, and Supreme Commander Allied Powers was not willing to give this clearance till United States Government approval was received to the entry of British Commonwealth Occupation Force in Japan.[13] This greatly handicapped the Advance Headquarters in carrying out the detailed reconnaissance and making out plans of allocation.

[12] BRITEL/36 dated 26 December 1945.
[13] Signal dated 15 December 1945 from Tokyo to Australia.

On 31 January 1946, the United States Government gave their final approval and a combined communique was issued from all Allied capitals. The following communique was issued by General MacArthur:[14]

"The present Occupation Forces in Japan extend the heartiest possible welcome to the British Commonwealth Forces who are about to share with them the arduous and difficult duties which are involved. Their presence will materially broaden the base along international lines of a burden which up to this time has of necessity been carried to a large extent unilaterally by the United States Forces and cannot fail to be beneficial in effect. It will enable a diminution in our own strength and will thereby bring welcome relief to many individuals. The Australian contingent served under my personal command with brilliant honour during the long and arduous campaigns on the road back and I take a special personal pride in again being associated with it. The reception of the entire force will be of the warmest".

In addition, the United States Government State Department issued the following communique:[15]

"When the exact composition and time of arrival of the British Commonwealth Force are known to General MacArthur he will determine the number and schedule of withdrawal of American troops from his command.

The participation of British Commonwealth Forces in the occupation of Japan is in line with the policy made public by the President on 22 September which stated that the participation of the Forces of other Nations that have taken a leading part in the war against Japan will be welcome and expected.

In accordance with this declaration invitations were extended also to the Governments of China and Union of Soviet Socialist Republics to send troops to participate in the occupation. The Chinese Government has informed this Government that while it is willing to provide a contingent of troops it is not in a position to do so at the present time. The Union of Soviet Socialist Republics has not accepted the invitation to participate".

Thus ended the period of protracted negotiations. It appears that the United Kingdom was initially not keen to participate in the occupation of Japan but was persuaded to do so by the persistence of Australia. The attitude of the New Zealand Government

---

[14] Signal 1 dated 30 January 1946, from Washington to Australia.
[15] Signal 2 dated 30 January 1946 from the Australian Legation Washington to Australia.

was lukewarm; they were merely going as part of a common show and to further Commonwealth co-operation. The Government of India, it is stated, on being asked by His Majesty's Government in the United Kingdom to provide a British–Indian Division at His Majesty's Government's expense, decided to participate on their own account in the occupation and meet the charges for the Indian element.[16]

On arrival in Japan British Commonwealth Occupation Force became an instrument in the Allied control of Japan.

[16] General Cawthorn's note:
"India was asked initially to provide a British-Indian Division on behalf of His Majesty's Government in UK who would meet all charges. The Government of India on their own initiative decided that in preference to this they would participate in the occupation and provide and pay for part of the forces."

CHAPTER III

The Allied Control of Japan

JAPAN AS AN AMERICAN BASE

The political and military objectives for the occupation of Japan were clearly laid down in President Truman's Directive to General MacArthur of 6 September 1945. The main purpose of occupation was to so completely demilitarise Japan as to make her powerless for aggression both politically and economically. However, the uneventful occupation and co-operation given to the Supreme Commander Allied Powers by the Japanese Government and people and the changing world situation soon after the end of war, operated to soften the rigours of occupation policy. It is not unnatural to suppose, at the same time, that American policy in this respect might have been affected by the growing tension between the Union of Soviet Socialist Republics and United States of America in the matter of Germany and Korea. Japan's strategic position in the Far East and the anti-communist tendencies of her people could be reckoned upon as assets in any future Russo-American conflict in the Pacific. Moreover, Japan could not be left wholly unprotected at the mercy of her powerful neighbours. These factors may have influenced the Supreme Commander Allied Powers in following a policy which *prima facie* might not have squared with the declared object of occupation. Its directions and actions might have been directed by these considerations particularly in so far as they were guided towards making Japan economically self-sufficient and politically democratic.

Japan's anti-communism and her potentialities led America to develop such political and economic institutions there as might contribute to ensure Japanese loyalty to the cause of democracy. This was facilitated by the co-operation extended by the Japanese who saw in the American control of all their activities, economic and political, an opportunity of re-establishing Japan and of emerging as a great power. To achieve this object, then a mere dream, the Japanese gave all-out help to the Supreme Commander Allied Powers authorities, geared up their production with American assistance and indocrinated the Japanese masses with anti-communism.

This spirit of total support to America convinced the Supreme Commander Allied Powers of the good intentions of the Japanese Government and its people. General MacArthur must also have begun to feel that it might after all not be necessary to occupy Japan for such a long period as had been planned before and declared, " the occupation will last for five years and if necessary for a longer period ".

The chief object of such occupation, then, was to maintain administrative and political stability which was achieved by vesting more power to the Japanese authorities and retaining the emblem of the Emperor. It was also essential to produce an anti-communist psychology by popularising democratic institutions. It is not unlikely that the idea of making Japan a defensive base against communism might have been entertained by some American authorities which could be easily effected by keeping United States land, naval and air forces there and maintaining them by developing the industries of Japan. The eventual stoppage by the Supreme Commander Allied Powers of the removal of Japanese capital industries and their rehabilitation by the Economic Section of the Supreme Command Allied Powers lent support to this view.

It was, however, unlikely that these objectives could be pursued unilaterally by United States of America without opposition from some of the Allied Powers. Hence the appearance of Allied control was maintained for which an Allied Control Council had been established.

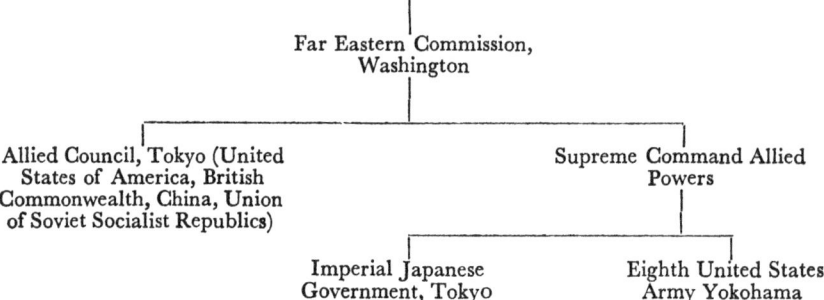

ALLIED CONTROL COUNCIL (ACC)

The Allied Control Council in Tokyo was intended to be an advisory body for Supreme Commander Allied Powers, and the United States Department of State made it quite clear that " United States of America will not allow any interference with the control of Japan by the Army of General MacArthur ".[1]

[1] Signal dated 27 August 1946.

Major-General D. T. Cowan, Commander Brinjap.

PLATE II

Indian Contingent arrives at Kure

March through Kure

The Allied Control Council had one representative each from United States of America, British Commonwealth, Union of Soviet Socialist Republics and China, with an American as its President. This body was an agent of the Far Eastern Commission in Washington and was vested with no executive powers to influence or direct policy. It could only discuss and raise issues with the Far Eastern Commission and advise Supreme Commander Allied Powers who was free to accept or reject the advice without giving reasons.

THE ALLIED GOVERNMENTS

The British Commonwealth seat on the Allied Control Council was filled by an Australian, Mr. MacMahon Ball. Dr. L. C. Jain, an Indian economist, was appointed Economic Adviser to the Commonwealth Representative.

The differences of opinion amongst the Allies regarding Japan were voiced in this Council and General Derevyanko, the Russian representative, was the most vehement exponent of views in opposition to those of the United States of America. The Russian attitude to Supreme Commander Allied Powers policy was diametrically opposed to the Americans. The main Russian criticism of Supreme Commander Allied Powers policy centred on the American attitude towards the Japanese Government. These criticisms were naturally resented by the American representatives who were fully convinced of the genuineness of Japanese co-operation. Mr. Acheson said, " that the Japanese authorities never seemed to get credit in the Council for the good work they did. If the Council was to have influence with the Japanese it should be just and fair minded ".

In order to gain Japanese confidence it was essential for America to support the Japanese Government. On 18 October 1946, Mr. Acheson remarked " That the time had come when Japanese aims had become virtually identical with Allied aims."[2] This remark was strongly criticised by Russia who saw in it the growing menace of Japan, and by Mr. MacMahon Ball, who said, " I would like to say that I would not, without the most careful further consideration, be able to identify myself with you in the expression of cordiality and confidence towards the present Japanese Government."[3] Australia was against the resurgence of Japan as a power in the Pacific. But General MacArthur was of the opinion that the Japanese had shed their Imperial coat and that the April 1946 elections were very fair and devoid of any corruption and

[2] Signal dated 28 October 1946.
[3] *Ibid.*

pressure from the Allied Occupation Forces and showed the democratic conversion of Japan.

LIAISON MISSIONS IN JAPAN

In order to obtain more influence with Supreme Commander Allied Powers, the United Kingdom strengthened its Liaison Mission and appointed Mr. Gascoigne, with the rank of an Ambassador. General Gairdner also remained as the Personal Representative of the Prime Minister of the United Kingdom.

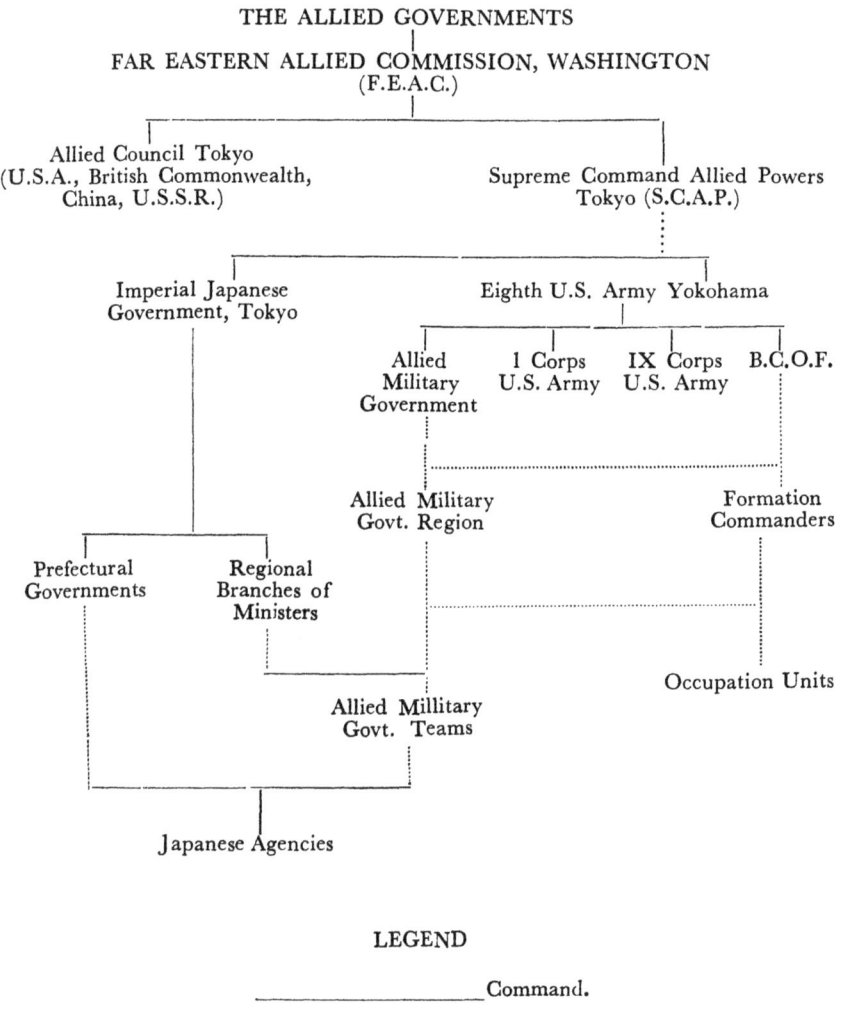

With the formation of an Interim Government in India in September 1946, Dr. L. C. Jain was promoted as the Head of the Indian Liaison Mission in Tokyo. He still retained his post as the Economic Adviser and in this dual role he was both equal and subordinate to Mr. MacMahon Ball at one and the same time. In any case the Indian Liaison Mission did not have much influence with Supreme Commander Allied Powers and it could not further India's interest without proper reorganisation.[4]

Despite these various agencies Supreme Commander Allied Powers remained the sole arbiter of Japanese destiny. Although British Commonwealth Governments had sent their troops to Japan they could not either effectively interfere or influence Supreme Commander Allied Powers policy. In order to ensure continuity of occupation and military government, the Supreme Commander Allied Powers had laid down the condition of six months' notice before any Allied Government could withdraw its contingent from Japan and then only with the Supreme Commander's concurrence, and military government was made a sole American responsibility. In February 1947 the United Kingdom withdrew its main force and only left a token force in Japan to satisfy the Australian susceptibilities. India on attaining her independence also withdrew her forces while New Zealand first reduced its contingent and later withdrew it completely. Only Australian forces stayed on though their numbers were considerably reduced.

To evaluate the achievements of the British Commonwealth Occupation Force in relation to the Supreme Commander Allied Powers, we will have to examine the objects of British Commonwealth policy in Japan for which that Force was sent there.

[4] Signal No. 1826 dated 14 August 1946. File No. 6325/1-11/SD5.

CHAPTER IV

The British Commonwealth Policy Regarding Occupation of Japan

In order to assess the objects for which the British Commonwealth of Nations took part in the occupation of Japan, it may be necessary here to examine the economic, political and military advantages which were supposed to accrue from the despatch of British Commonwealth Occupation Force to Japan and which might have influenced the decision.

Strategic Considerations[1]

The Pacific had, after World War II, loomed large in the diplomatic arena as a region of immense strategic potentialities. Japan as its centre naturally attracted close attention of the Powers wanting to play a role in the Far East. The British Commonwealth could not therefore neglect the developments there. For Australia and New Zealand particularly, and Canada, India and the United Kingdom generally, the future of Japan and the situation in the Pacific were of intimate concern. The events of World War II were still fresh in memory and Australia could not afford to take any risks with her own security. That may account for her keenness to locate forces in Japan which now became an outpost of her defence. She may also have been influenced by the growing menace of the spreading communism in China and South-East Asia, which she viewed as a potential danger to her security, her position as a world power and her whole tradition of friendly relations with the United States. Australia's keenness for an effective position in the Pacific and the sense of obligation for the assistance derived from the United States may also have prompted her to take an active share in the occupation of Japan. The interests of the other members of the Commonwealth did not materially differ from those of Australia. It was therefore considered necessary to have the Commonwealth forces in Japan so as to be able to influence the future course of treaty and to control her economic resources and war potential.

Political Considerations[2]

In addition to these strategic considerations there were important political considerations also which prompted

[1] Memorandum on the usefulness of British Commonwealth Occupation Force by Australian Defence Committee (Extended) and Joint Chiefs of Staff Australia.
[2] Australian Defence Committee (Extended) and Joint Chiefs of Staff Australia Memorandum on the advantages of BCOF.

participation in the occupation of Japan. It was believed that British Commonwealth Occupation Force in Japan would

 (a) increase British prestige in the eyes of the Japanese people as among the victors of the last war, also as a power to be reckoned with in future;

 (b) raise in the eyes of the Allies and other countries, specially those interested in the Pacific, the prestige of the British Commonwealth of Nations and its potentialities as a world power;

 (c) demonstrate to the world that Australia had attained political maturity and was prepared to play her part in the councils of the world;

 (d) ensure for Australia the position of a principal in the peace settlement;

 (e) strengthen the position of the Commonwealth representatives on the Far Eastern Commission and on the Allied Control Council for Japan.

The main political factor was that of prestige. It was felt that the presence of British Commonwealth Occupation Force in Japan would increase British Commonwealth prestige in the eyes of the Japanese people and would impress on their mind the fact that they were defeated not by the United States alone but by a combination of the British and American forces. The presence of Indian troops did largely contribute to raise the prestige of India which was naturally enhanced after the declaration of Independence and the establishment of the National Government at home. An element in prestige is the behaviour of diplomatic representatives. In the beginning, though the Indian diplomatic representative could not make much impression owing to lack of contacts, poor accommodation and lack of transport, particularly as compared with the resources of other missions, yet ultimately Dr. L. C. Jain and Shri B. Rama Rao did not fail to lay the foundation of India's prestige in Japan.

Economic Considerations

One of the objects of occupation would be the economic exploitation of Japan. Though not mentioned in the directive to the Commander-in-Chief British Commonwealth Occupation Force yet it may have been one of the primary reasons which induced the British Commonwealth to participate in the occupation. These economic motives, while not being direct, included the development of contacts with the influential sections of the Japanese people, securing of suitable ports of entry for commerce, sharing in the shipping tonnage of Japanese overseas trade, which was to be carried in Allied shipping owing to the ban on Japanese mercantile marine, and developing future trade with the British Commonwealth.

India had no conception of these economic advantages and having neither the means nor the freedom to exploit them, her contingent was unable to enhance India's economic interests in Japan. The same was not the case with the other participating members of the Commonwealth who had their own shipping and had surpluses of food and raw material to carry on a favourable barter trade with Japan.

Military Objects

The military objects assigned to British Commonwealth Occupation Force were more or less the same as outlined by the President of the United States for Supreme Commander Allied Powers. They were:

(a) to assist in demilitarisation and disposal of Japanese war installations and armaments,
(b) to safeguard the Allied installations and equipment,
(c) to give military protection to British Commonwealth civil missions engaged in selecting goods and equipment for reparations,
(d) to maintain internal security in Japan, and
(e) to provide military backing to the United States military government in British Commonwealth Occupation Force area.

The necessity to employ troops to give protection to the Allied nationals, agencies or installations fortunately never arose except in very minor cases. At the same time, the Japanese maintained perfect internal peace. Tabulation of military stores and their destruction became a matter of routine which was carried out without any interference or hindrance. Thus, in the event, it never became necessary for British Commonwealth Occupation Force to carry out practically most of the military tasks, which it was originally expected it might be called upon to perform.

Commonwealth Co-operation Considerations [3]

An important consideration which governed the mounting of British Commonwealth Occupation Force was to develop a system of Commonwealth co-operation, need for which was felt during World War II. British Commonwealth Occupation Force was as such an experiment to determine the basis of integration of British Commonwealth forces. It was intended to:

---

[3] Australian Defence Committee (Extended) and Joint Chiefs of Staff Australia Memorandum on Lessons of British Commonwealth Occupation Force.

(a) foster maximum integration of services and personnel,
(b) foster integration between personnel and the services of the various contingents,
(c) provide data for the administration of a similar combined force overseas in war, and
(d) provide data for the control machinery of a similar combined force.

But unfortunately these results could not be achieved, for, firstly, the principle of such integration had not been defined initially, and secondly lack of mutuality and national differences did not afford sufficient scope for its experimentation. Integration was started sometime in the middle of 1946 but by the end of the year the British Brigade was under orders of withdrawal causing a major reorganisation in the British/Indian element, and before this could be stabilised, the Indian Contingent was itself withdrawn. Even in this limited time British Commonwealth Occupation Force was able to indicate the lines on which an experiment could be conducted in the future. It indicated the trends on which the future Commonwealth defence policy might be developed.

When British Commonwealth Occupation Force was mounted it was decided to apportion the responsibility for its control to a body known as the Joint Chiefs of Staff Australia (JCOSA) and the Australian Government machinery was made the agent to execute its policy.

The experience of British Commonwealth Occupation Force in Japan and its controlling agency in Australia, must provide useful lessons for the control and administration of such a force, on behalf of the countries contributing it, irrespective of its location and role. The points of general application to be examined are:—[4]

(a) *The Controlling Body:* the machinery necessary to control such a combined force, the inter-Governmental difficulties, relationship of this body to the respective national Governments and their agents, and the staff and organisation for such a body.

(b) *The Combined Force:* the principles governing the composition, organisation and administration of such a force, inter-Dominion and inter-service integration, outline plan, defence arrangements and control.

(c) *The Executive Agency:* to determine the division of responsibility between the controlling body and executive agency, channels of communication between various governments taking part in the combined force. To

[4] Australian Defence Committee (Extended) and Joint Chiefs of Staff Australia Memorandum on Lessons of British Commonwealth Occupation Force.

determine the basis and staff for liaison between the controlling body and agents.

The controlling body and British Commonwealth Occupation Force were a combined organisation while the executive organisation was solely Australian. To view the achievements of Joint Chiefs of Staff Australia and British Commonwealth Occupation Force in their correct perspective it is essential to remember the various handicaps under which these organisations had to work. Joint Chiefs of Staff Australia was never treated as a pet child and British Commonwealth Occupation Force had no powers to formulate policy. The Supreme Commander Allied Powers alone had the complete control of the Allied Military Government.

CHAPTER V

Joint Chiefs of Staff Australia

The setting up of Joint Chiefs of Staff Australia and the formation of British Commonwealth Occupation Force was an experiment in British Commonwealth co-operation. The Governments of four countries—the United Kingdom, Australia, India and New Zealand—and the national service headquarters in each country were equally concerned in framing the policy for British Commonwealth Occupation Force and sharing the responsibility for providing man-power and meeting the cost of the force.

Joint Chiefs of Staff Australia was set up in Australia on behalf of the British Commonwealth Governments concerned, and was vested with the right to control and administer the British Commonwealth Occupation Force, subject to:—[1]

(a) the supreme control of the British Commonwealth Governments concerned;
(b) the responsibility of the British Commonwealth Governments concerned for the interior economy and administration of their own contingents;
(c) the conformity with the procedure laid down by the British Commonwealth Governments concerned for the authorisation of commitments relating to the maintenance of their own contingents, or accepted in respect of British Commonwealth Occupation Force as a whole;
(d) the reservations regarding operational control; and
(e) the reservations regarding financial control.

Joint Chiefs of Staff Australia consisted of the Australian Chiefs of Staff and representatives of the Chiefs of Staff in the United Kingdom and New Zealand and of the Commander-in-Chief of the three Indian Services. It was supposed to foster within its own organisation and within British Commonwealth Occupation Force the policy of maximum integration on an inter-service and inter-Dominion basis.

The directive issued to Joint Chiefs of Staff Australia on behalf of, and with the approval of, His Majesty's Governments concerned laid down that Joint Chiefs of Staff Australia had to look to the Australian Government's machinery for:—

(a) obtaining inter-governmental guidance on matters of political significance;

---

[1] Australian Minister of Defence Memorandum of 1946.

(b) executive action to implement Joint Chiefs of Staff Australia policy and decisions; and

(c) administrative machinery required for Joint Chiefs of Staff Australia and British Commonwealth Occupation Force matters.[2]

Joint Chiefs of Staff Australia was made responsible for drawing up plans for the participation of British Commonwealth Occupation Force in the occupation of Japan and to ensure that Commander-in-Chief, British Commonwealth Occupation Force, was provided with all facilities to enable him

(a) to represent worthily the British Commonwealth in the occupation of Japan;

(b) to maintain and to enhance British Commonwealth prestige and influence in the eyes of the Japanese and of our Allies; and

(c) to illustrate to, and to impress upon, the Japanese people as far as may be possible the democratic way and purpose in life.

As the executive responsibility to implement Joint Chiefs of Staff Australia policy was vested in Australian Service machinery, it was agreed that overseas members (representatives of countries other than Australia) of Joint Chiefs of Staff Australia would sit as members of the Australian Defence Committee (Extended) when matters concerning overseas contingents of British Commonwealth Occupation Force or concerning the force as a whole were under consideration. The relationship between Joint Chiefs of Staff Australia, British Commonwealth Occupation Force and Australian Defence Ministry, is shown in the diagram opposite.

For all matters upon which Joint Chiefs of Staff Australia was not authorised to pronounce without consultation on a governmental level, it had to refer to the national governments concerned. Matters having political significance were to be submitted through the Secretary, Australian Department of Defence, to the Australian Minister of Defence and of service significance to the respective Chiefs of Staff.

The complicated machinery which was created to integrate national interests of the countries taking part in British Commonwealth Occupation Force would not work smoothly. There was constant friction between the Australian Defence Department and the overseas members of Joint Chiefs of Staff Australia.

The overseas members of Joint Chiefs of Staff Australia represented their respective Chiefs of Staff or Commander-in-Chief, India, and their task was:

[2] Joint Chiefs of Staff Australia No. 276, minute No. 255/1946.

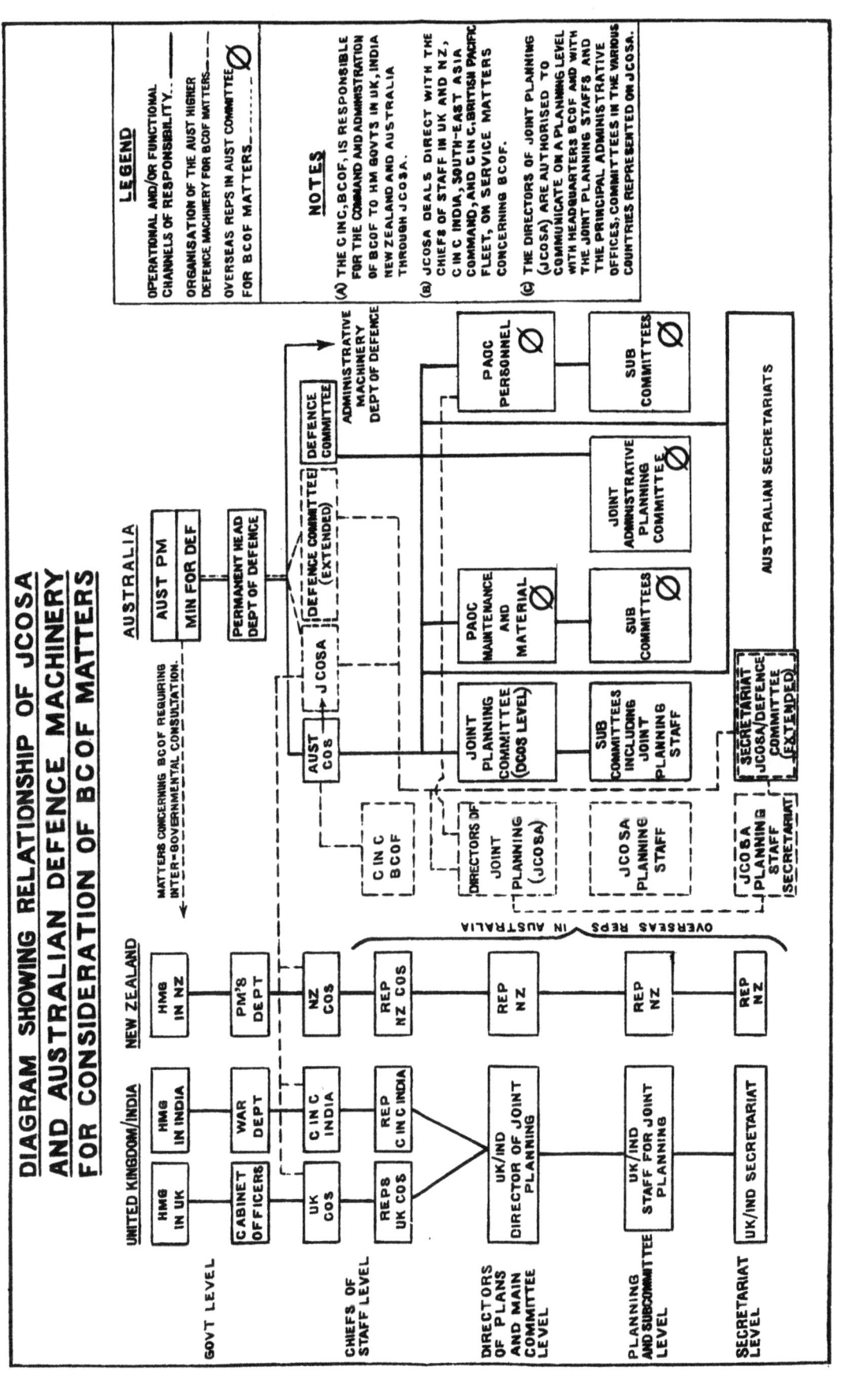

(a) to represent the views of their respective Chiefs of Staff or Commander-in-Chief in India with special reference to the control and administration of British Commonwealth Occupation Force;

(b) to maintain touch with the various branches of the Australian service departments, and provide overseas representatives in those departments so as to assist in dealing with British Commonwealth Occupation Force matters; and

(c) to ensure that representatives were provided to sit on the various committees that met under the direction of the Australian Defence Committee or Joint Chiefs of Staff Australia whenever these committees were dealing with British Commonwealth Occupation Force matters of common interest.

The position of Joint Chiefs of Staff Australia *vis-a-vis* Australian service machinery is illustrated below:

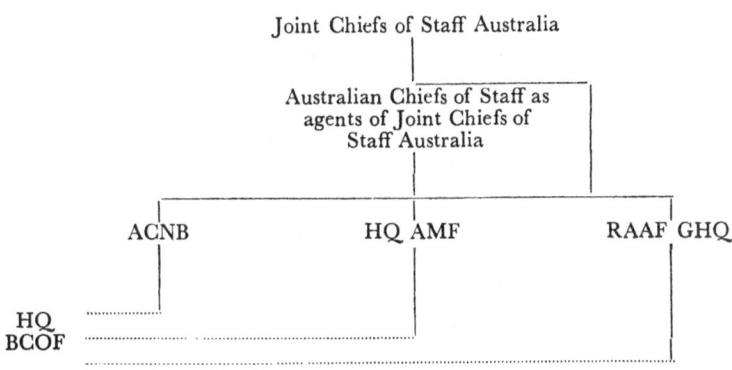

LEGEND

————— Joint policy of control and joint policy of administration.

·············· Executive Instructions based on this policy issued by the Service Headquarters.

Thus all policy decisions of Joint Chiefs of Staff Australia were passed to the Australian Chief of Staff, who as agents of Joint Chiefs of Staff Australia then issued appropriate instructions to the Australian Commonwealth Navy Board, Headquarters Australian Military Forces or Royal Australian Air Force Headquarters, as the case might be. These Headquarters were then responsible for issuing executive instructions implementing Joint Chiefs of Staff Australia policy. It was a circuitous channel and was often liable to considerable delays and misunderstandings.

The Chairman of Joint Chiefs of Staff Australia, (Chief of Staff, Australian Army) clearly defined the functions of its members *vis-a-vis* the Australian Service Headquarters. He wrote in his memorandum of 24 July 1946, " It has become apparent that friction has arisen between various authorities concerned with British Commonwealth Occupation Force in carrying out their respective functions. This friction is entirely due to a lack of clearness in the definition of where the duties of one authority begin and of the other end....... It has therefore become necessary to clarify the relationship of the overseas members of Joint Chiefs of Staff Australia and their staff to the Australian Service Headquarters ".[3] According to him the functions of the overseas members were:

(i) to assist in the framing of joint policy for Joint Chiefs of Staff Australia and maintaining touch with the branches of Australian Headquarters;
(ii) to assist Australian Headquarters in planning by providing a portion of the Joint Chiefs of Staff Australia Planning Staff and its secretariat;
(iii) to provide advice to the Australian Headquarters when requested by that Headquarters to do so; and
(iv) to keep their own authorities adequately informed.

He made it absolutely clear, " that overseas members of Joint Chiefs of Staff Australia had no responsibility for the detailed work connected with the issue of the executive instructions required to implement Joint Chiefs of Staff Australia policy and the members of Joint Chiefs of Staff Australia Planning Staff only have access to the branch of the Australian Headquarters concerned, and then only for planning purposes and *NOT* to query how the branch is carrying out its duties in connection with the implementation of Joint Chiefs of Staff Australia policy ".

He further wrote:

" Australian Service Headquarters are embarrassed by frequent enquiries and suggestions received concerning ways and means of implementing Joint Chiefs of Staff Australia policy ....members of Joint Chiefs of Staff Australia and their staff who devote the greatest part of their time solely to Joint Chiefs of Staff Australia and British Commonwealth Occupation Force will think of various ways of framing executive instructions............ However, the Australian Staffs are more fully acquainted with all the factors involved. In any case, in Australia the responsibility for the execution of Joint Chiefs of Staff Australia policy has

---

[3] Memorandum of Chairman Joint Chiefs of Staff Australia dated 24 July 1946.

been placed upon the Australian Service Headquarters who can carry out this task. Having been given a job to do they should be left alone to do the job ".[4]

Moreover, he made comprehensive recommendations to determine the relationship between Joint Chiefs of Staff Australia and Australian Chiefs of Staff in order to remove occasions of conflict. These were that

" (a) the Australian Chiefs of Staff arrange to have made to Joint Chiefs of Staff Australia such general statements as the Australian Chief of Staff considers necessary to the execution of this responsibility for British Commonwealth Occupation Force;

(b) Joint Chiefs of Staff Australia invite the Australian Chief of Naval, General and Air Force Staff to provide replies to such questions as Joint Chiefs of Staff Australia considers necessary;

(c) in regard to matters which are, or are likely to be, the subject of Planning Staff action, the overseas members make their enquiries from Australian Headquarters through the Australian members of Joint Chiefs of Staff Australia;

(d) where possible, all overseas offices be integrated with each branch of Australian Headquarters;

(e) information from a Branch may be provided only with the authority of a Senior Australian Staff Officer of that branch;

(f) copies of correspondence concerning executive action by Australian Headquarters on Joint Chiefs of Staff Australia policy should *NOT* be passed to Overseas members. Only when necessary for planning, they will be provided to the Planning Staff by Australian Service Headquarters ".

Strong exception to these proposals was taken by the overseas members, and one of them wrote:[5]

" The overseas representatives, as part of Joint Chiefs of Staff Australia are charged with the administration and control of British Commonwealth Occupation Force. In the present circumstances they can only discharge their responsibility by keeping a close eye on the agent and the result of his labours. If the agent was perfect, many questions could be left entirely to him after policy had been decided. But he is not perfect and that is one reason why, in my opinion, we cannot accept the proposal that

[4] Memorandum of Chairman Joint Chiefs of Staff Australia, 24 July 1946.
[5] Note of 2 August 1946.

the overseas representatives should sit in a darkened room and view British Commonwealth Occupation Force by such shafts of light as the Service Headquarters may choose to turn on from time to time. The other reason is that we cannot exercise control, or shape a policy, unless we are fully informed about what is happening, not only in Australia in meeting the instructions given by Joint Chiefs of Staff Australia, but also in British Commonwealth Occupation Force as the result of the execution or attempted execution of Joint Chiefs of Staff Australia policy.

We cannot blindly accept an agent's views on these subjects—and thus make the agent judge, jury and advocate of his own case—as we are virtually asked to do ".

This statement was representative of the views of the overseas members who greatly resented any assumption of overriding authority by the Australian Defence Department. Their apprehension was that Australia was appropriating the position of a " dominant partner, who would hear the views of the interested parties but who might, in his capacity as the executive agent for the Region, ignore them when it came to saying what was to be done ". Their feeling was that " equal responsibility for the framing of policy was denied " to them. They suspected Australia of a desire for unilateral control which they regarded as destructive of the very basis of Joint Chiefs of Staff Australia which was organised on a combined basis. There was protest against Australian action in taking up certain matters at Governmental level without going through Joint Chiefs of Staff Australia. On 3 May 1946, India's representative on it protested that " the Australian Government had shown lack of courtesy to him by short circuiting Joint Chiefs of Staff Australia, by referring to India the matter regarding supply of meat on hoof, without referring the matter to him first ".[6] They did not fully agree with the enunciation of the functions of the overseas members of Joint Chiefs of Staff Australia by the Chairman, and considered that his interpretation would reduce that authority into a mere advisory body, which has to beg for information from Australian service machinery both in respect of the framing of policy and its implementation. It would appear that overseas members desired to have close and intimate association with the Australian service agencies and some sort of a supervisory authority in matters pertaining to British Commonwealth Occupation Force. That this role was incompatible with the independence of a self-governing nation did not occur to them. Australian defence services however could not tolerate interference with their freedom

---

[6] Agenda 95/1946. Supplement No. 1 of discussion on 31 May 1946.

of action and viewed with disfavour all attempts by the overseas members to encroach on their discretion. The whole episode was an unfortunate one and was born of misunderstandings arising from the undefined nature of the respective roles of the two authorities, Joint Chiefs of Staff Australia and the Australian Defence Department; ultimately this omission was rectified by the issue of detailed instructions for the guidance both of the overseas members and the Australian services concerned. This was formally issued as a directive by the Australian Government on behalf of the Commonwealth Governments in December 1946. But in the interval the indefiniteness of the position had led to misunderstandings and frictions which adversely affected the work of Joint Chiefs of Staff Australia. It is no wonder that this experience influenced the Prime Minister of Australia to make the statement on 1 December 1946 " that he did not consider Joint Chiefs of Staff Australia to be a suitable model on which to base future Imperial defence developments ".[7] Nevertheless Joint Chiefs of Staff Australia continued to fulfill its responsibilities and brought out many lessons which are contained in its Plan issued on 15 May 1946.

On Joint Chiefs of Staff Australia, India was represented by an Indian element under Major-General Cawthorn, who was designated as the representative of the Commander-in-Chief of India. This section joined the United Kingdom element to form a combined organisation briefly known as UKINDEL (United Kingdom/Indian/Element). Its functions were to look after the interests of the United Kingdom and India and to this extent it succeeded admirably. It assisted to a large extent in the work of planning and organisation by Joint Chiefs of Staff Australia for British Commonwealth Occupation Force.

With the withdrawal of the British Brigade from Japan in January 1947 and Indian troops in October 1947 the Joint Chiefs of Staff Australia organisation was dissolved and the Australian Defence Department took over the responsibility of British Commonwealth Occupation Force, which had by now become almost an Australian /New Zealand Group.

In order to sum up the functions and achievements of Joint Chiefs of Staff Australia it is desirable to point out the lessons learnt during its tenure, September 1945 to December 1947. These lessons are in respect of the controlling body (Joint Chiefs of Staff Australia) and the executive agents (Australian Defence Machinery) and their relationship:[8]

[7] Indel/71 dated 17-6-1947.
[8] *Ibid.*

The Controlling Body
- (a) Need to issue in advance an agreed inter-governmental definition of the aims and objects of the force and of broad principles on which it is organised, controlled and administered.
- (b) Need for a controlling body to be nominated and administratively established before detailed planning for the raising and despatch of the force is started.
- (c) Need for an agreed directive to all the members at the outset, even though this has to be modified in the light of actual working.
- (d) Need for a considerable degree of decentralisation of power to the controlling body by the National Service Headquarters whom the members individually represent, particularly in such matters as alterations to War Establishments and integration of services, within the manpower ceilings laid down by the respective Governments.
- (e) Need for early decision by the Governments concerned on the manpower ceilings for their contribution to the force.
- (f) Need for early decision on broad outline of financial arrangements likely to affect organisation and administration both within and without the force.
- (g) Need for early preparation of an outline plan of organisation for command and administration of the force and its despatch to concentration areas.
- (h) Need for the staff of the controlling body to be properly organised at the outset to allow of Naval, General, and Air Staff aspects to be given early and adequate weight so that administrative planning can be based on well thought out, clearly defined and co-ordinated " general staff " policy.
- (i) Need for a Public Relations Organisation, together with amenities and other matters which must essentially be co-ordinated on a force as opposed to a component basis, to be considered from the outset.

The Executive Agents
- (a) Need for early definition of responsibility and allocation of subjects.
- (b) Need for clearly defined machinery and procedure from the outset to facilitate adequate consultation with overseas representatives and to ensure that they are kept adequately informed.

PLATE III

RIAF in Japan

RIN in Kure

PLATE IV

268 (Ind) Brigade and Battalion Commanders

4 Squadron RIAF

(c) Need for early decision as to the extent to which existing staffs of the national headquarters made executively responsible for the force should be augmented to cope with the extra work, so as to avoid necessity for setting up special machinery.

CHAPTER VI

British Commonwealth Occupation Force

THE COMMUNIQUE

On 2 February 1946, after agreement with the Governments concerned, the following communique was issued simultaneously in the United Kingdom, Australia, New Zealand and India:—

" 1. As a result of discussion between the members of the British Commonwealth, and reference on their behalf to the Government of United States by the Australian Government, it has been agreed that a Joint British Commonwealth Force should participate in the occupation of Japan. Arrangements are now well advanced for the Force to proceed on the following basis:

2. The Force is drawn from the United Kingdom, Australia, New Zealand and India. The Commander-in-Chief of the Force is Lieutenant-General J. Northcott, C. B., M.V.O., of the Australian Military Forces. His Headquarters is fully integrated with representatives drawn from each Service and from each Commonwealth country contributing to the force. Air Commodore F. M. Bladin, C.B.E., of the Royal Australian Air Force has been appointed Chief of Staff to Lieutenant-General Northcott.

3. The Force comprises:—
   (a) Force and Base troops drawn from each of the contributing countries.
   (b) A land component organised as a Corps of one British-Indian Division and two independent brigade groups, one each from Australia and New Zealand.
   (c) An air component comprising Squadrons drawn from the Royal Air Force, the Royal Australian Air Force, the Royal New Zealand Air Force and the Royal Indian Air Force.

4. Units of the British Pacific Fleet are also stationed in Japanese waters.

5. The British-Indian Division is commanded by Major-General D. T. Cowan, C.B.E., D.S.O., M.C., Indian Army, and includes 5 Brigade of the 2nd Division and 268 Indian Infantry Brigade.
The Australian Infantry Brigade Group includes 34 Australian Infantry Brigade commanded by Brigadier

Nimmo. The Commander of the New Zealand Brigade, which is coming from Italy, is Brigadier K. L. Stewart, C.B.E., D.S.O.

6. The British Commonwealth Force (BCOF) will form part of the occupation forces in Japan under the supreme command of General Douglas MacArthur, Supreme Commander for the Allied Powers (SCAP). He has assigned the land component to the general operational control of the Commanding General, 8th United States Army, who is in military control of the whole area of Japan. The air component has been assigned to the general operational control of the Commanding General, Pacific Air Command, United States Army (PACUSA). Lieutenant-General Northcott, as Commander-in-Chief, British Commonwealth Occupation Force, is entirely responsible for the maintenance and administration of the British Commonwealth Force as a whole. He has direct access to General MacArthur on matters of major policy affecting the operational capabilities of the Force. On policy and administrative matters affecting the Force, the Commander-in-Chief is responsible to the British Commonwealth Governments concerned through a British Commonwealth organisation set up in Melbourne and known as the "Joint Chiefs of Staff in Australia".

7. Their instructions to the Commander-in-Chief, British Commonwealth Occupation Force, will be issued by the Australian Chiefs of Staff. The Joint Chiefs of Staff in Australia (JCOSA) comprise the Australian Chiefs of Staff and representatives of the Chiefs of Staff in the United Kingdom and New Zealand, and of the Commander-in-Chief in India. This organisation is fully associated with the Australian joint service machinery. The Commander-in-Chief, British Commonwealth Occupation Force, has the right of direct communication with the Joint Chiefs of Staff in Australia on administrative matters affecting the Force. On matters of Governmental concern affecting the policy and operations of British Commonwealth Occupation Force he will communicate through Joint Chiefs of Staff in Australia to the Australian Government who act as the representative of the other Commonwealth Governments concerned.

8. The area allotted to British Commonwealth Occupation Force is the Hiroshima Prefecture, including the

cities of Kure and Fukuyama. British Commonwealth Occupation Force will be responsible for the demilitarisation and disposal of Japanese installations and armaments and for exercising military control of the area but not for its military government which remains the responsibility of the United States agencies. The British Commonwealth Occupation Force area will not constitute a national zone. The British Commonwealth Occupation Force may be called upon to conduct military operations outside its normally allocated area. When air support for the land component of British Commonwealth Occupation Force is required, this will primarily be provided by the British Commonwealth Occupation Force air component. Kure will be the base port for the British Commonwealth Occupation Force who will be responsible for the working of the entire port, the Kure naval yard remaining under United States naval control.

9. Provision is being made for the British Commonwealth Occupation Force to be represented in Tokyo Prefecture by a detachment which will probably be of battalion strength. This detachment will be drawn in turn from each national component in the Force.

10. The British Commonwealth Force may be withdrawn wholly or in part by agreement between the United States Government and the Commonwealth Governments concerned, or upon six months' notice by either party. It has also been agreed that progressive reductions in the strength of the Force will be made from time to time in conformity with progressive reductions which may be made in the strength of the United States Occupation Forces in Japan.

11. The Australian Services Mission hitherto located in Tokyo has been transformed into an advanced echelon of Headquarters British Commonwealth Occupation Force with the addition of officers from other Commonwealth components. For the present it remains in the Tokyo area to facilitate liaison with General MacArthur's Headquarters.

12. Details of the move to Japan of the various components of British Commonwealth Occupation Force cannot yet be announced but detailed planning is now in progress on the following basis:—
   (a) Naval Port Parties for the working of Kure port to arrive in the first week of February.

(b) Leading elements of the Australian component to arrive in the third week of February.
(c) Leading elements of the British-Indian Division to arrive about 1st March.
(d) Leading elements of the New Zealand Brigade, which is moving from Italy, to arrive about 23rd March.

13. The organisation of British Commonwealth Occupation Force and the arrangements for its control through Joint Chiefs of Staff in Australia which are outlined above constitute a further development in the closer integration of British Commonwealth co-operation. They ensure that each of the Governments concerned has a full and effective voice in this joint undertaking ".

The course of events leading to the publication of the above communique has already been traced in earlier chapters and it is not necessary to reiterate the causes of delay which occurred. Authority having been obtained from the United States it was now expected that there would be no further delay in the move of the force, which had been marking time for a considerable period. This, of course, depended on the formulation of policy and plans by Joint Chiefs of Staff in Australia and the issue of orders for the mounting of the force, which in its turn depended on the following factors:

(a) reception facilities in the area allotted,
(b) information about capacity of Kure Port to handle British Commonwealth Occupation Force shipping,
(c) the availability of shipping to carry troops from various theatres, and
(d) the availability of troops for the move.

INFORMATION ABOUT HIROSHIMA AREA

The initial reconnaissance of the Hiroshima area, allotted to British Commonwealth Occupation Force, provided the following information:[1]

" About one-third of the area is broken land, the uplands with heights ranging from 800 to 2,000 feet have thin, sandy rocky soil with thin forest cover, while the lowlands consist of coastal strips with narrow valleys. Within the few miles of the coast-line, the altitude sometimes exceeds 2,000 feet, although the average altitude along the south coast is usually

---

[1] Joint Chiefs of Staff in Australia Plan 141/13A G(ops).

less than 1,500 feet. Movement across country is difficult due to steep gradients, swift unbridged streams, the narrow valleys, and the density of the jungles with which the entire mountainous section is covered. The area is hot, humid, with rainy summers and relatively mild winters with the mean temperature in coldest month above freezing point. Despite the southernly location snowfalls are frequent, but they only last for a short time. The prefecture is located in the typhoon area and the south-eastern portion is subject to the greatest damage. Sufficient accommodation for personnel, equipment, ammunition and supplies is available in the prefecture to meet British Commonwealth Occupation Force's requirements. Cool rooms, freezing rooms, ice-making plant and ice-storage rooms are available. Roads are adequate, but their condition is only fair.

There is no shortage of manual labour in the area though skilled labour is in short supply. No difficulty is anticipated in obtaining sufficient labour for unloading ships and other work concerned with setting up of British Commonwealth Occupation Force ".

On the above information, it was planned that the whole of British Commonwealth Occupation Force could be dispersed in Hiroshima Prefecture with sufficient amount of covered space for men and material. But contrary to expectations the inadequacy of accommodation and facilities for 37,000 troops was revealed soon after the arrival of the first contingent. This necessitated taking over a few more prefectures. The Australians being first to arrive, occupied Hiroshima Prefecture; here, however, accommodation did not seem to correspond with their wishes. The *Sun* (Melbourne) in its issue of 28 March 1946, reported: " Nobody here (Tokyo) denies that the Australians in 34 Brigade at Kaitaichi are at present in the worst barracks area for occupation troops in the whole of British Commonwealth Zone. The British and New Zealand forces now arriving in Japan more than a month behind the Australians are being favoured with better billets and more pleasant surroundings ".

This was associated with the nationality of the Commander-in-Chief of the Force and was thus commented upon by the *Sun*: "It was explained to-day that the Australians were penalised because the Commander-in-Chief of the British Forces, General Northcott, is an Australian, and it may have been misunderstood if the Diggers (Australians) had been given the pick of the places ".[2]

---

[2] The *Sun*, Melbourne, 28 March 1946.

The facts, however, were that after the arrival of the Australian Brigade it was felt necessary to occupy additional prefectures of Yamaguchi, Shimane, Tottori and the island of Shikoku. It was decided to allot the last three to the British-Indian Division which was the largest formation, and the prefecture of Yamaguchi to the New Zealanders who were coming last. It was not deemed necessary to move the Australians from Hiroshima Prefecture to the new areas because accommodation in all areas was more or less of the same type, which on the whole was not of high quality until new barracks were constructed.

CAPACITY OF SEA AND AIR PORTS OF ENTRY

" Kure which was selected as the port of entry for the force was the site of the largest naval base in Japan and is located in a small valley bounded on three sides by high hills and, on the fourth, by the harbour. To the west and south, the harbour is protected by two groups of rugged, granite islands. The port had ample anchorage, but only a limited number of berths, three alongside berths being available for Liberty-type cargo ships and two additional anchor berths being available for discharge of mechanical transport and stores. Sufficient Japanese tugs and lighters were available to discharge simultaneously two ships from the anchorage. Mobile and floating cranes were available. The tide range was eleven feet ".[3]

The air-port of entry was Iwakuni in the Yamaguchi Prefecture. This air-field, during the war, was a fairly large Japanese naval and army training and operational air-field. It was the nearest air-field from Hong Kong which could accept heavy planes. It had one concrete strip (4-inch depth) 3,900 feet long. Taxi tracks and dispersal areas were inadequate. An aeroplane slipway was available nearby. There were good hangars and domestic accommodation was available, although it needed considerable rehabilitation. The air-field was also served by a railway siding.[4]

Kure Port and Iwakuni air-port had sufficient capacity to handle all British Commonwealth Occupation Force's sea and air traffic. The difficulty anticipated was in reception and dispersal, and maintenance of troops because no initial stocks were available to tide over the transit period and accommodation could not be improved until the troops were actually in occupation.

[3] Joint Chiefs of Staff in Australia Plan 141/13 AG (Ops).
[4] *Ibid.*

THE AVAILABILITY OF SHIPPING

The shipping programme had to be chalked out after consultation with the various authorities responsible as shipping was in short supply, and was heavily booked. But when the final sanction of United States of America for the mounting of British Commonwealth Occupation Force was not available, Joint Chiefs of Staff in Australia was naturally worried. On 18 January 1946, the Australian Government informed their legation in Washington that " embarrassment was arising from the delay of the reply from the United States Government because shipping had already been ordered by the several contingents of British Commonwealth Occupation Force and some loading instructions had been issued": But still from the United States confirmation was not forthcoming. The Australian Government further pressed for the grant of clearance for the Naval Port Party so as to avoid inconvenience on the date of arrival of the rest of the force. After great pressure from General Northcott's Headquarters in Tokyo, Supreme Commander for the Allied Powers clearance for the Naval Port Party was granted on 21 January 1946, with the proviso that it would arrive on or after 1 February 1946, and without prejudice to the United States final agreement regarding the basis of participation. The Naval Port Party had, therefore, a very limited time to carry out reconnaissance and prepare detailed shipping time-table before the arrival of the force which was scheduled to begin by the middle of that month.

The responsibility of mounting the force was:
(a) United Kingdom/Indian Army component—General Headquarters India in consultation with Headquarters Allied Land Forces South-East Asia.
(b) Royal Air Force/Royal Indian Air Force component—
    (i) Units in Malaya—Headquarters Air Command South-East Asia.
    (ii) Units in India—Headquarters British Air Force South-East Asia.
(c) Australian Military Force component—AHQ Melbourne in conjunction with HQ Morotai Force.
(d) Royal Australian Air Force component—AHQ Melbourne in conjunction with HQ Morotai Force.
(e) New Zealand Army component—HQ Central Mediterranean Force.

(f) Royal New Zealand Force component—Air Department, Wellington.

(g) Naval Port Party—C-in-C East Indies.

THE AVAILABILITY OF TROOPS

The British-Indian troops had been marking time at Nasik in India, the Australians at Morotai in South-West Pacific and the New Zealand Brigade in Italy since 15 August 1945. It was only on 9 January 1946 that the Joint Chiefs of Staff in Washington signalled their approval for a Naval Port Party to arrive in Kure for the purpose of making arrangements in advance for British Commonwealth Force. General Northcott, who was on a visit to India, was so informed. On 12 February 1946 Supreme Commander for the Allied Powers issued Operation Instruction No. 3, giving a practical shape to the MacArthur-Northcott Agreement.[5] On receipt of these instructions Joint Chiefs of Staff in Australia issued a directive to C-in-C, British Commonwealth Occupation Force, for the mounting of the force.

DIRECTIVE TO COMMANDER-IN-CHIEF BRITISH COMMONWEALTH OCCUPATION FORCE[6]

The Directive to the Commander-in-Chief, *inter alia* laid down the following responsibilities;

" (a) to represent the Armed Forces of the British Commonwealth Governments in the Allied occupation of Japan, and to ensure that that role was carried out in such a way as worthily to represent the British Commonwealth Governments concerned and so as to enhance British Commonwealth prestige and influence in the eyes of the Japanese and our Allies and of the World. The force has to exemplify and impress upon the Japanese people the British Commonwealth way and purpose in life.

(b) to follow the principle of maximum integration of services and personnel of national components in British Commonwealth Occupation Force Headquarters and in the Force and Base organisations ".

The process by which British prestige had to be impressed on the Japanese and the Allies has already been discussed and the

---

[5] Occupation Instruction No. 3 dated 12 February 1946, at Appendix 'B'
[6] Directive to Commander-in-Chief, British Commonwealth Occupation Force No. JCPS 45/19 dated 18 February 1946 at Appendix 'C'

part played by Indian troops to raise the prestige of India will be explained in greater detail in the following chapters. In brief, the Force played a very great part in bringing home to the Japanese the power, prestige and position of the British Commonwealth of Nations in world politics.

The other objective, that of integration, was difficult to achieve; firstly, because no basis was laid down in advance on which such integration was to be carried out and, secondly, there were many differences which could not be removed by the touch of the magic wand, but could only be smoothed by experience and time. Integration is only possible if the fundamental principle of equality in all aspects is firmly adhered to. But this could not be applied to British Commonwealth Occupation Force to a very great degree, because there were not only differences of pay, service, and allowances but also of religion, culture and tradition, which could not be easily reconciled by executive action.

Integration was to be applied mainly in Headquarters British Commonwealth Occupation Force, Britcom Base and in administrative units under these formations. In Headquarters British Commonwealth Occupation Force the senior staff positions were reserved for the officers of the Australian Military Forces (AMF). This was done because they were conversant with the Australian service machinery at home, which was the source of supply for British Commonwealth Occupation Force. In the earlier stages the various vacancies below them were not allotted on a nationality basis but had to be filled up haphazardly. The ideal might have been to have well balanced teams, consisting of officers of different nationalities, but this was made more difficult by the fact that, where the vacancy was allotted by nationality, it was not filled by that nation due either to lack of qualified persons or shortage of manpower. India perhaps, due to her own fault, was the greatest sufferer in this respect. While it provided the greatest number of integrated units and a force as large as Australia's, its representation in British Commonwealth Occupation Force was negligible. Till December 1946, there were hardly six Indian officers in junior appointments in a Headquarters consisting of more than two hundred officers. It can mainly be explained by the fact that British officers were borne on Indian Army strength, and Indian officers were required in India for nationalisation of the forces then taking place. When the replacement of a proportion of British officers by Indians in the Integrated Headquarters was urged on General Headquarters India by Joint Chiefs of Staff in Australia, it was pointed out: " It is essential in the interests of the Indian Contingent of British Commonwealth Occupation Force that there should be adequate Indian Army representation in integrated Headquarters and integrated units. British officers are still an integral part of the Indian Army and if they are excluded from the manpower ceiling of Indian component, it is inevitable that Indian Army representation in integrated Headquarters will suffer, firstly, because responsibility for allocating British officers of Indian Army to appointments in British Commonwealth Occupation Force will really rest with the War Office who will consciously or unconsciously tend to give preference to British Service officers, secondly, because the bulk of the senior staff and integrated command appointments outside Brindiv are held by Dominion officers who equally consciously or unconsciously prefer to have British rather than Indian officers appointed to more senior posts under them as they are used to dealing with the former and latter are strange to them ".[7] Could this attitude be conducive to integration? It is only fair to add however that Commander-in-Chief India expressed his inability to find more Indian officers for British Commonwealth Occupation Force in response to these urgings.

Integration in Britcom Base on the other hand was achieved to a greater degree and produced some good results. But all formations were always trying to have more British personnel in place of Indian. A particular case was the demand by British Commonwealth Occupation Force for additional United Kingdom Provost units. There was already a preponderance of British Provost sections over the Indians, though the Indians were far greater in number. "The preponderance of British Military Police indicated that Indian Military Police could not be used independently and that British Military Police were required to deal with both Indian and British troops.[8]

Nevertheless, there were not many occasions for friction. Deputy Chief of the General Staff, India, who visited Japan in 1947 remarked: "The Force comes from the three different Services of four separate countries, which made friction unavoidable, especially in the early days. The miracle is that there has been so little ".[9]

To obviate misunderstandings, India proposed the integration of Indian administrative units for functional control only and opposed carrying this policy of integration below sub-units; " Indian Other Ranks in an integrated unit should be so organised that they work under their own officers and non-commissioned officers as complete sub-units ", and would remain under command

[7] Indel/200 of 2 December 1946,
[8] Indel/45/11/1 notes of visit of Chief of General Staff (India) to Delhi 4-7 October 1946,
[9] No, 2504/B/DCGS (B) Tour notes of DCGS (B) India 5 February to 1 March 1947.

of the Commander, Brindiv, for domestic, administrative and welfare purposes.[10]

The Commander-in-Chief in India stressed very strongly, "the necessity for avoiding 'incidents' arising out of disregard for the religious and class susceptibilities of Indian personnel. He was anxious that any impression of discrimination in the treatment of, or outlook towards, Indian personnel, should be avoided and that it should be apparent that Indian formations and units were treated on the same basis as those of other components".[11]

With the political changes in India, the policy of integration in British Commonwealth Occupation Force received a further set-back. All the Indian units and services were to be nationalised, which should not have affected integration in British Commonwealth Occupation Force if the Indian element had been an independent entity like other components from the very start.[12] Now the mixed British/Indian Units had to be broken up so that Indian units could become independent of British control. This "created a paradox for British Commonwealth Occupation Force, for while advocating integration in general on one hand, on the other it was destroying what had already been built up. It is suggested that British and Indian mixed units in British Commonwealth Occupation Force be allowed to remain as before and that the Indian component be nationalised like contingents of other nations."[13] The suggestion was accepted with the proviso that Indian personnel would serve under their own and not under British Warrant Officers and Non-Commissioned Officers.

It may be to a certain extent due to the fact that India's acquiescence in integration was only given in part or that integration in British Commonwealth Occupation Force was not fully achieved. A further reason undoubtedly was that different national elements did not really have time to know each other sufficiently to form a "palatable" mixture at an early enough stage.

As has already been pointed out, given more time and means, and good faith and understanding on all sides from the outset, integration should have succeeded admirably as was proved in many units where integration was applied. It would be wrong to say that it succeeded in every case because there were a few mixed units which were unhappy, the causes being mostly national jealousies and lack of human understanding. It was once again

---

[10] Britel 540 of 7 March 1946.
[11] Notes on General Cawthorn's visit to India dated 4 February 1946.
[12] Notes on the Liaison visit of Colonel Roberts, DD of O (India) to Japan.
[13] Personal signal from General Cawthorn to PAO (I).

DIAGRAM SHOWING CHANNELS OF COMMUNICATION AUTHORISED FOR BCOF

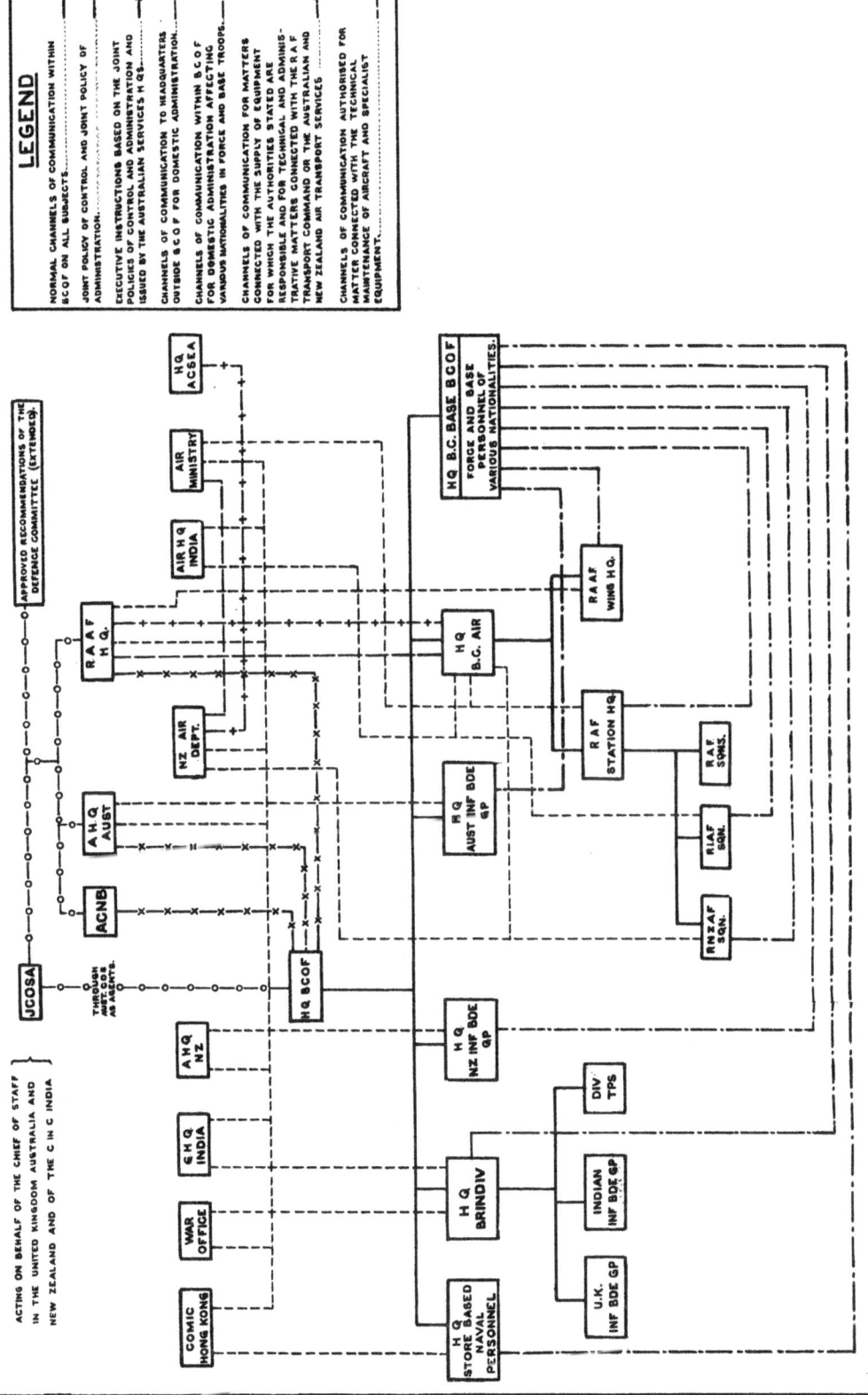

proved that to understand and work together it is necessary to lay down rules of precedence and command, and define responsibilities and channels of communication from the very beginning. Where this was omitted or not insisted upon by higher formations, the different elements instead of coalescing began to disintegrate.

THE CHANNELS OF COMMUNICATION

In order to carry out his various responsibilities the Commander-in-Chief, British Commonwealth Occupation Force, had to deal with many authorities on different levels. The channels through which British Commonwealth Occupation Force communications had to pass are illustrated on the chart opposite. These were[14]:—

(a) *On matters requiring ministerial or Governmental advice but not of a command or administrative nature:*
Commander-in-Chief British Commonwealth Occupation Force ... Secretary of Defence Department, Australia.

(b) *On matters of joint policy:*
Commander-in-Chief British Commonwealth Occupation Force ... Australian Chiefs of Staff to JCOSA.

(c) *On matters of command and administrative responsibility:*
Commander-in-Chief, British Commonwealth Occupation Force ... Joint Chiefs of Staff Australia—Governments concerned.

(d) *For all executive action by Australian Service machinery:*
Commander-in-Chief British Commonwealth Occupation Force ... Australian Services—Chiefs of Staff Australia

(e) *On all matters of domestic administration from the aspect of the personnel of any particular national contingent:*
Headquarters British Commonwealth Occupation Force ... ... National Service Headquarters.

[14] Joint Chiefs of Staff in Australia Plan 114/13 AG(Ops),

The above summary covers the arrangements in respect of both land and air forces.

The channels of command and for orders from British Commonwealth Occupation Force to various components were according to the established rules of procedure but the nominated national representative had the right of direct communication with his national Service Headquarters on any matters of national importance but had to submit two copies of such communication to Headquarters British Commonwealth Occupation Force. It was very rarely that this prerogative was used and never in fact had it to be invoked to protect any contingent or component against a policy or decision of Headquarters British Commonwealth Occupation Force.

The organisation of British Commonwealth Occupation Force was:

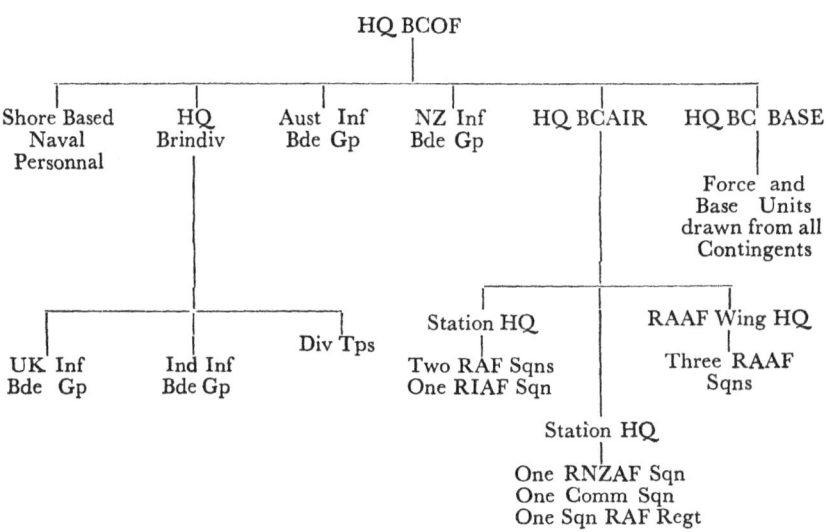

It was presumed that all contingents of British Commonwealth Occupation Force would be self-contained and would also provide, separately, additional troops for Headquarters British Commonwealth Occupation Force and Base Installations, but the orders of battle for the various national contingents neither specified the numbers to be detailed nor gave the breakdown of units earmarked for Integrated Headquarters. In consequence the transfer of units by Headquarters British Commonwealth Occupation Force, from national contingents to Integrated Formations, created a good deal of misunderstanding.

COMPARATIVE STRENGTHS BY SERVICES AND NATIONALITIES[15]

The comparative strength for various nationalities was initially:

Country	Total	Percentage
Great Britain	9,954	28·1
India	9,611	27·1
Australia	11,466	32·3
New Zealand	4,425	12·5
Total British Commonwealth Occupation Force	35,456	100

The breakdown of strengths between integrated units and national contingents was approximately as shown on the next page.

BRITISH COMMONWEALTH OCCUPATION FORCE ORDER OF BATTLE

From the outset it was clear that Australia and New Zealand could not provide their share of Base and technical troops, hence larger demands were placed on India and the percentage of Indian troops increased with each shipment.[16] India accepted this additional commitment under the belief that this would provide an opportunity to gain experience. For financial and administrative reasons it was essential that Indian units be kept on the Brindiv Order of Battle. British Commonwealth Occupation Force allotted certain Indian units to the Force and Base Order of Battle, and in case of Base placed such units under the command of the Base Commander in accordance with "normal procedure". Commander-in-Chief British Commonwealth Occupation Force stated that "experience has shown that any departure from the established principles of command, general and local administration, leads only to difficulties and inefficiency. Such command has been limited to the extent that domestic personnel administration and welfare of the troops remains the responsibility of the nominated national representative".[17]

[15] INDEL L/7.
[16] UK/INDEL 115/2 dated 28 February 1946.
[17] Headquarters, British Commonwealth Occupation Force GSOS 0·421 SD dated 19 October 1946.

Breakdown Strength—BCOF

DETAIL	Naval Component			Army Component							Air Component						All Components Total
	RN	RAN	Total	UK & Indian Armies			AMF	NZMF	Total		RAF/RIAF			RAAF	RN-ZAF	Total	
				UK	India	Total					RAF	RIAF	Total				
(a)	(b)	(c)	(d)	(e)	(f)	(g)	(h)	(i)	(j)		(k)	(l)	(m)	(n)	(o)	(p)	(q)
Force troops (including HQ British Commonwealth Occupation Force, BCAIR Headquarters and integrated Headquarters and Units)	...	1	1	634	2735	3369	4703	283	8355		188	7	195	113	27	335	8691
Percentage	...	100	100	...	...	40·3	56·3	3·4	100		...	...	58·2	33·7	3·1	100	...
Formations (i.e. Division, Brigades, Wings, etc. and their Headquarters)	350	...	350	5774	6295	12069	4551	3838	20458		3008	574	3582	2078	277	5937	26745
Percentage	100	...	100	...	...	58·9	22·3	18·8	100		...	...	60·3	35·0	4·7	100	...
Total Force	350	1	351	6408	9030	15438	9254	4121	28813		3196	581	3777	2191	304	6272	35436
Percentage	99·7	0·3	100	...	...	53·6	32·0	14·4	100		...	...	60·2	34·9	4·9	100	...

This transfer was in respect of the United Kingdom and Indian elements only as New Zealand was unable to provide any Force or Base troops. After discussion with Joint Chiefs of Staff in Australia and in order to avoid confusion Indian units were retained on the Brindiv Order of Battle, while on the British Commonwealth Occupation Force Order of Battle, for domestic use only, they were shown with the formation under which they were serving. It was also agreed that, whenever the nominated representative or component commander wished to take action in respect of any aspect of domestic administration and welfare of units not under his direct command, he would initiate such action through the commander under whom the unit was then actually serving.[18]

The following Indian administrative units were transferred to the general administration of British Commonwealth Occupation Force to fuse with the administrative services of British Commonwealth Occupation Force, so as to effect greatest economy in operations:[19]

Serial	Designation
626	489 Indian Supply Platoon.
627	591 Indian Supply Platoon.
628	8 Indian Field Bakery Section.
629	69 Indian Field Bakery Section (BT).
630	67 Indian Field Butchery Section (BT).
631	38 Indian Rear Holding Supply Depot.
632	59 Indian Supply Company Headquarters.
633	756 Indian Supply Section.
634	858 Indian Petroleum Platoon.
634a	861 Indian Petroleum Platoon.
634b	92 Indian Field Bakery Section.
635	92 Indian General Hospital (Combined) (250 Bed).
636	80 British General Hospital (200 Bed).
638	51 Indian Sub Depot Medical Stores.
640	25 Indian Field Laboratory.
644	25 Indian Ophthalmic Unit.
645	5 Sub Spec Centre.
648	Detachment 221 Advance Ordnance Depot.
649	One Ammunition Platoon (ex 64 Ordnance Field Depot.)
650	Half 223 Vehicle Park.

[18] Indel/7A/1 dated 18 November 1946.
[19] General Headquarters (India) No. 7240/01/A/SD 5 dated 25 January 1946.

Serial	Designation
673	Detachment ISLD.
676	1548 Indian Pioneer Company.
696	Detachment Graves Registration and Enquiry Unit.
717	Press Detachment.
719A	9 Recovery of Allied Prisoners of war and Civilian Internees Searcher Team.
665	Headquarters Movement and Transportation.

ADMINISTRATION OF BRITISH COMMONWEALTH OCCUPATION FORCE

The administration and maintenance of British Commonwealth Occupation Force was difficult because all supplies, stores, vehicles and equipment were imported. The Force came from three different services of four separate countries. The various administrative problems of particular interest to the Indian Contingent will be dealt with in the following chapters, but those problems were faced and solved very bravely and expeditiously and "great credit is due to the Commanders, their staffs and the Units for what they have achieved in so short a time ".[20]

Maintenance of discipline and morale was the most important administrative problem. The discipline of British Commonwealth Occupation Force troops, on the whole, remained very good. It is not necessary to compare one contingent with the other but the discipline of the Indian Contingent was of a high order of which they could be well proud.

FRATERNISATION

The most controversial subject in British Commonwealth Occupation Force was fraternisation on which policy was clearly laid down in a Personal Instruction issued by Lieut.-General J. Northcott, Commander-in-Chief, British Commonwealth Occupation Force, with the approval of Joint Chiefs of Staff in Australia and after reference to the Commonwealth Governments. This stated:

> " 1. Fraternisation is one of the most difficult problems with which we shall be faced. I consider that it is quite impracticable to issue stringent orders defining what is to be done in an infinite variety of possible contingencies. My policy regarding fraternisation can best be stated

[20] General Scott's Tour Notes No. 2504/B/DCGS(B) dated 8 March 1947.

in the following terms. Every member of British Commonwealth Occupation Force must bear in mind that he is present in Japan in a dual capacity. He is not only a sailor, a soldier or an airman. He is also a representative of the British Commonwealth of Nations and all that it stands for in the world.

In dealing with the Japanese he is dealing with a conquered enemy who has by making war against us, carried deep suffering and loss in many thousands of homes throughout the British Empire. Your relation with this defeated enemy must be guided largely by your own individual good judgement and your sense of discipline. You must be formal and correct, you must not enter their homes or take part in their family life. Your unofficial dealings with the Japanese must be kept to the minimum. You must obey strictly all instructions regarding establishment or areas which are placed out of bounds to personnel forming part of the British Commonwealth Occupation Force. Above all you must remember that dual capacity in which you came to Japan and, beyond that the fact that the eyes of the Japanese *and* our Allies and indeed of the world will be watching you. Much depends on your conduct and on your bearing. Be sure that they remain normal and that they are in keeping with the dignity and courtesy which are part of our common heritage and tradition.

2. No games will be scheduled between any organisation of British Commonwealth Occupation Force and any teams composed altogether or in part of Japanese nationals.
3. No military personnel will engage in any athletic contests with Japanese nationals.
4. Japanese should be encouraged to conduct their own athletic and recreational programmes.
5. It is the policy of the Occupation Force to make provision for all its requirements of food and not to acquire any food whatsoever from local sources. Local procurement of food depletes the food resources available to the inhabitants of Japan. Members of British Commonwealth Occupation Force will not purchase or otherwise obtain, receive, possess or consume any foodstuffs of any description from local sources ".[21]

---

[21] Joint Chiefs of Staff in Australia Plan Minute No. 102.

These comprehensive instructions issued with the approval of the participating Governments were intended to limit contacts between the Japanese and the members of the component units of British Commonwealth Occupation Force. It was not possible to rigidly define the conditions of such contact, but the general principle that the members of the Occupation Force should not commit acts which could react on the prestige or honour of the participating nations was fully emphasised. The troops were admonished to keep their conduct and bearing normal and act with dignity and courtesy in their dealings with the Japanese people. It was at the same time essential to impose restrictions on the procurement of food stuffs from the local sources so as not to interfere with the local economy which was then in the grips of a crisis. On the other hand, black-marketing was rife in the country and many Japanese were prepared to utilise prospects of fraternisation with the troops for obtaining supplies of food, clothing, cigarettes, soap etc. from the occupation forces. It is unfortunate that many members of these forces could be made unwitting agents of uncrupulous black-marketeers. This situation had led therefore to occasional rigorous application of these instructions regarding fraternisation which might have been resented by some members of the occupation forces. But such limitations on the conduct of the individuals were essential, though these should not have been allowed to deteriorate into racial or national arrogance. It was also essential to limit fraternisation between the Japanese women and the members of the Occupation Force, owing to its social reactions in the parent countries. One means by which such liaison could be minimised was to permit the move of service families to Japan, which was done by British Commonwealth Occupation Force. At the same time better recreational and amenity services for the troops were organised.

DEPENDENT FAMILIES IN BRITISH COMMONWEALTH OCCUPATION FORCE

In October 1946 it was decided to allow service families in Japan depending on the availability of accommodation. The first families to arrive in British Commonwealth Occupation Force were of Brindiv, who had been able to procure and develop the facilities a little earlier than other formations. In Headquarters British Commonwealth Occupation Force, Britcom Base and the Australian Brigade areas, construction of new accommodation was taken in hand. New Zealand did not permit the move of families to Japan. As the British Brigade was withdrawn in early

1947 and there were rumours of the withdrawal of the Indian Contingent, the move of Brindiv families was stopped in May 1947.

The maintenance of families in Japan was not an easy task, it involved procurement and distribution of supplies, household necessities and other arrangements concerned with families.

AMENITIES AND WELFARE

For the troops in general the arrangements for amenities and welfare were organised on a centralised basis.

Headquarters British Commonwealth Occupation Force was to co-ordinate and control all amenity units, canteens and clubs to provide the maximum benefit to the general welfare of the whole Force. The Australian Army Canteen Service, through Commander-in-Chief, British Commonwealth Occupation Force, was made responsible for the supply of canteen stores for British Commonwealth Occupation Force and for establishing and directing British Commonwealth Occupation Force Canteen Service, which was to operate in Japan throughout British Commonwealth Occupation Force as a financially independent organisation.

The Canteen Service provided clubs for officers and men, ran various gift shops and gift trains and was responsible for welfare in general. The shops were well stocked with Australian materials and the Japanese souvenirs were sold at reasonable prices. The opening of these shops was an important occasion at all centres.

The amenities services ran a circuit of cinemas where Indian pictures were screened for the benefit of Indian troops. Occasional concert parties from Australia, United Kingdom and India toured the various formations.

Many hotels in different sight-seeing places were taken over from the Japanese, rehabilitated and organised as Leave Centres. The most popular were those in Kobe and Tokyo area. For the Indian Contingent, British Commonwealth Occupation Force organised a separate hotel at Uijji, about ten miles from Kobe. This became very popular. Indians were also allowed to visit Tokyo on leave during the tour of duty of Indian battalion there.

Trips to various beauty-spots and inland cruises were also organised by the Amenities Service. In the latter half of 1947 the welfare and amenities were of a very high standard and compared well with those of the Americans. The only drawback was the scarcity of imported goods, which were in abundance in American Post Exchanges but could not be bought by British

Commonwealth Occupation Force personnel due to currency restrictions.

MAINTENANCE OF BRITISH COMMONWEALTH OCCUPATION FORCE[22]

The maintenance of British Commonwealth Occupation Force was to be carried out from Australian or New Zealand sources through Australian channels so as to ensure economy of personnel and shipping and to produce the most effective method of administration. The above policy was implemented in three phases:
- (a) Phase I—The "Initial Phase", during which each component was maintained from the supplies and stores which accompanied it to Japan.
- (b) Phase II—The "Interim Phase", during which Australia had to assume added responsibilities for other contingents, beginning on 1 August 1946 and continuing until 31 December 1946.
- (c) Phase III—The "Long-term Phase", beginning on 1 January 1947 which was based on the full implementation of maintenance policy by Australia.

Army Headquarters Melbourne was made responsible for providing all services, supplies and stores for the maintenance of the whole Force. It had also to supply all medical and dental stores and had also to arrange to ship fresh supplies for all components of the Force.

SUPPLIES

The most difficult problem was the supply of fresh vegetables, which were neither available nor could be produced in Japan. These supplies had to come from Australia and the course from the market to the consumer was set with many difficulties;[23] such as:
- (a) the quantity and quality of vegetables available at Sydney at the time of loading,
- (b) transportation from market to army stores at White Bay,
- (c) refrigeration temperatures on reefers,
- (d) reefer storage facilities at Kure,
- (e) internal distribution to scattered units of British Commonwealth Occupation Force,
- (f) preservation in outstations.

[22] Joint Chiefs of Staff in Australia Plan, paras 129-140.
[23] Australian Military Forces QL/2308 dated 1 October 1946.

It will be pertinent to mention here that there is summer in Australia when it is winter in Japan and vice versa; hence the vegetables which could be made available during summer in Japan were those which grew in winter in Australia. The problem of transport was further complicated by the fact that all shipping from Australia had to cross the equator and pass for some days through very hot areas. That made shipment of vegetables in deck cargo impossible, and required refrigeration facilities which were not easily available. Nevertheless, these difficulties were overcome by persistent effort and, by December 1946, the following scales of fresh supplies were available to all British Commonwealth Occupation Force troops:—

Meat	6 days weekly
Butter	6 days weekly
Eggs	3 days weekly
Fresh Fruit	4 days weekly
Potatoes	5 days weekly
Onions	5 days weekly
Other vegetables (including swedes, cabbages, cauliflowers, carrots, pumpkin, beetroot etc.)	5 days weekly

ORDNANCE

The supply of ordnance stores until 1 January 1947, was arranged by providing automatic maintenance packs for each component from its own sources. After 31 December 1946, Army Headquarters Melbourne had to arrange for the supply of all ordnance stores required by all component units.

The British Commonwealth Occupation Force Ordnance Service was responsible for providing common user items of ammunition. The plan was:
  (a) units to hold one first-line refill,
  (b) formation to hold one first-line refill,
  (c) the Base Ammunition Depot to hold 30 days supply of ammunition at contact rate.

All units had to maintain field system of accounting for ordnance stores and all ordnance establishments were to use the AMF accounting system.

ACCOMMODATION, ENGINEER WORKS AND STORES

An initial supply of engineer works stores, furniture and essential accommodation stores was to accompany all components.

But after 31 December 1946 Army Headquarters Melbourne was made responsible for the supply of all such stores, required by British Commonwealth Occupation Force. As regards accommodation, Supreme Commander Allied Powers had issued general instructions relating both to the rehabilitation of existing buildings and the construction of new ones. A lavish scale of furniture was also sanctioned for the messes. But gradually, in view of its effect on Japanese economy, the provisions regarding requisition and procurement of houses, facilities and stores had to be tightened up by Supreme Commander for the Allied Powers. Yet British Commonwealth Occupation Force had full power and authority to handle all its own affairs. It was responsible for procuring construction material and furniture from the Japanese sources, which it provided to its component units on a generous scale. The scale of accommodation and furnishing provided by British Commonwealth Occupation Force compared well with the American standards.

MOVEMENT AND TRANSPORTATION

Army Headquarters Melbourne, in close consultation with Headquarters British Commonwealth Occupation Force, was responsible for the general control of merchant shipping into Kure. All arrangements for movement by rail and by sea from and within Japan were made by British Commonwealth Occupation Force Movement Control Group, an integrated body. All air movement was made by the Air Booking Centre, Iwakuni, subject to the priorities allotted by Air Priorities Board, Headquarters British Commonwealth Occupation Force. Scheduled air transport services to Japan for British Commonwealth Occupation Force were provided by Royal Air Force from Hong Kong. Non-schedule services within Japan were carried out by the BCAIR Communication Squadron.

The Transportation Service, under Headquarters British Commonwealth Occupation Force, was responsible for the operation and maintenance of the port of Kure. As local skilled labour was available for port maintenance, only supervision was required.

Railways in Japan were operated and maintained by the Japanese Government Railways under the United States supervision. In British Commonwealth Occupation Force area Movement Control Organisation of British Commonwealth Occupation Force was responsible for all moves of men, stores and vehicles by rail.

PLATE V

Major-General Cowan with 3 V.Cs. of Brinjap, Jemadar Gaje Ghale, Naik Agansing Rai and Namdeo Jadhao

PLATE VI

268 Brigade Group Staff

POSTAL ARRANGEMENTS[24]

Postal Set-up: Army Postal Units were provided by all contingents and components for service with their units and for maintaining communication with the home countries. Indian Army Postal Units were responsible for serving Indian and British army units and for providing postal services for Royal Air Force/Royal Indian Air Force units.

An integrated Base Post Office was established at Kure. A detachment of Brindiv Postal Unit formed the Indian Section of the integrated Base Post Office. Forward Post Offices were established at all stations.

Mail Routes in British Commonwealth Occupation Force: The layout of the Force over an extensive area required long lines of communication. There was a network of railway lines in the area, but even so some places on the north coast of Honshu and the south coast of Shikoku were more than 24 hours journey from the Base. The Postal Services were further handicapped by the lack of alternative roads and the ban on travel by civilian trains. The main routes were as follows:—

(i) *Tokyo—Iwakuni Main Line:* Two express Allied trains were run on this line, and postal couriers were permitted the use of separate accommodation in the mail van in one of the trains called, "Allied Limited". Couriers were provided by the Australian Advance Post Office.

(ii) *Okayama—Shikoku:* Daily courier services was run by train from Okayama to Uno connecting with railway ferry between Uno and Takamatsu across the Inland Sea. The couriers were provided by Royal Indian Army Services Corps units. From Takamatsu railhead the Brigade arranged to collect and distribute the mail bags to Tokushima, Takuma, Matsuyama, Gomen and Kochi. All these places were connected by fast railway service to Takamatsu.

(iii) *Okayama—Matsue:* There was a daily service which was run from Okayama to the north coast by couriers provided by 268 Indian Infantry Brigade. From Matsue the mail bags were conveyed to the Field Post Offices at Hamada and Tottori by unit representatives.

(iv) *Okayama—Kure:* In addition to the despatches made on the "Allied Limited" military special, secondary despatches were made daily by Japanese civilian trains

---

[24] Report by Major D.S. Virk DDPS (Brindiv).

to connect with outgoing and incoming air mails. This was the only route on which couriers were provided by the Indian Advance Post Office.

(v) *Kure—Iwakuni*: After trying the rail and road services for a few months a special launch was procured to bring in air mails direct from Iwakuni to Kure, saving many hours in transit and assuring mail connections from Kure onwards.

Postal facilities: The following postal facilities were available at the Indian Forward Post Office:

(i) Sale of postal stamps and stationery (Indian postage stamps).
(ii) Delivery and acceptance for despatch of first class and second class mails including parcels through the post orderlies.
(iii) Registration of letters and parcels.
(iv) Issue of Indian Money Orders.
(v) Sale and encashment of British Postal Orders.
(vi) Acceptance of Indian Saving Bank Deposits.
(vii) Facilities for the receipt and despatch of private telegrams.

Air Mail: Initially, air mail was routed from India via. Australia, but the United Kingdom insisted on sending their despatches via. Hong Kong because an air-link had been established between Hong Kong and Japan from the beginning of April 1946. The same route was adopted by India. The receipts and despatches on this route were extremely irregular and transit time varied from 10 days to 20 days. High level representations were made but there was no improvement till BOAC commercial service was established towards the end of 1946 and even then receipts from the United Kingdom were only once a week while those from India were as irregular as before. The root cause of the trouble was the adverse flying weather on the Calcutta—Rangoon—Saigon—Hong Kong route. Royal Air Force machines had frequent breakdowns and responsibility for the carriage of mail was shared by at least three separate squadrons.

Telegrams: In August 1946 a limited direct cable service was introduced between Osaka and London and this was later expanded to normal cable service. The financial aspect of the new service was very favourable because telegrams could be sent at almost one-third of the normal world rate.

Money Orders and Postal Orders

Restrictions were placed from the beginning on the booking of Money Orders and sale of British Postal Orders. No Money

Order could be booked or Postal Order purchased unless the Commanding Officer of the unit certified that the money was drawn by the purchaser from his entitlement. Maximum monthly limits of remittances were also fixed for all ranks.

Postal Concessions: The normal war-time concessions of postage and customs duty were sanctioned. As silk was sold at all gift shops the Government of India was requested to increase the annual limit of duty-free silk from 4 yards to 6 yards and this was approved. Free airmail postage was replaced by concessional rate of postage in May 1947 as for members of the other forces overseas.

Lessons: The experience of postal services in British Commonwealth Occupation Force brought out the following lessons:

(a) an unambiguous, catching and indicative address should be adopted and promulgated well in advance,
(b) the civil post offices in India should be given adequate instructions for the routing of the mail of the Force to the proper offices of exchange,
(c) adequate postal units should be allotted to the Force from the very beginning,
(d) the postal units should not be dependent on India for day to day supply of postage stamps etc. and for rendering of accounts,
(e) firm air and surface routes should be selected for despatch of mails before the Force leaves India, and regularity and speed should be the objective,
(f) postal representatives should be detailed at all important points where mails have to be transferred *en route* from one air service/ship to another,
(g) postage stamps should be overprinted 'APO' to eliminate hoarding for use and sale,
(h) the controlling postal officers should be permitted to fix the postage and telegram rates to suit local conditions,
(i) the controlling postal officers should have direct liaison with the other postal administrations represented on the spot.

CURRENCY ARRANGEMENTS IN BRITISH COMMONWEALTH OCCUPATION FORCE

In the beginning the Japanese Yen was made legal tender in British Commonwealth Occupation Force, whose Yen requirements were met by Supreme Commander for the Allied Powers from Japanese sources. It is not known on what basis this money was obtained and how it was to be adjusted but it became apparent very soon that more and more Japanese Yen were being deposited with Paymaster British Commonwealth Occupation Force than were actually issued to the troops. This was bound to happen when there was nothing to distinguish between Yen obtained from legal sources such as pay and allowances and those obtained from illegal sources, such as black-market and sale of War Department property.[25]

In order to stop conversion of illegal Yen into world currencies, restrictions were imposed and conversion was allowed only for one half of the amount issued during the previous month. The withdrawals through Paymaster were very insignificant and this check forced the black-marketeers to buy postage stamps so that at one time no postage stamps were available in British Commonwealth Occupation Force post offices. This rash was stopped by rationing stamps and, as soon as arrangements could be made, by overprinting them for sale to British Commonwealth Occupation Force personnel in Japan.

It was anticipated that the high percentage of Yen obtained by illegal sources, and converted by British Commonwealth Occupation Force agencies in Japan into world currencies by Chief Paymaster British Commonwealth Occupation Force would be lost to the pool account of the Force. It was threfore decided to introduce cash vouchers for all transactions in British Commonwealth Occupation Force agencies.[26]

Satisfactory vouchers could not be produced locally in Japan and it was not possible to use vouchers used by American troops because that would have meant reimbursement to the United States Treasury of an equivalent amount of dollars. Hence these vouchers had to be obtained from outside, and as Australia could not produce them within six months it was agreed to introduce the British Armed Forces Special Vouchers (BAFSV) which were being used by British Occupation Force in Germany.[27]

British Commonwealth Occupation Force required British Armed Forces Special Vouchers to the value of 880,625 pounds sterling and the United Kingdom Government wanted the Australian Treasury to reimburse the face value of the cash vouchers in full. To this the Australian Government rightly demurred and wrote that the Australian Government as agent for the British Occupation Commonwealth Force had assumed primary responsibility for supply and maintenance which required great financial

---

[25] Brindel 1412 of 23 December 1946.
[26] *Ibid.*
[27] Defence Melbourne Joint Chiefs of Staff in Australia 305 dated 20 December 1946.

accommodation and should not be called upon to reimburse the full value of vouchers to the extent of 900,000 pounds sterling.

Ultimately in view of the mounting loss to all countries due to illegal Yen transactions it was agreed that:

(a) Australia would treat British Armed Forces Special Vouchers received from His Majesty's Government as public moneys which would be subject to conditions prescribed under Australian Audit Act and Treasury Regulations.

(b) On termination of use, Vouchers would be returned to His Majesty's Government and any losses charged to Pool Account and reimbursed to His Majesty's Government.

(c) Vouchers would retain their British Sterling rating, and articles and services for which they are used would be priced accordingly.[28]

From 6 May 1947, British Armed Forces Vouchers denominated in sterling became the only legal tender within British Commonwealth Occupation Force for all British Commonwealth Occupation Force service personnel, non-British Commonwealth Occupation Force service personnel and British Commonwealth Occupation Force accredited civilians, for the issue of pay and allowances and for payment of:

(i) purchases in all Force establishments including post offices, canteens, gift shops, officers' shops, institutes, hotels, clubs, cafeterias, messes etc;

(ii) mess bills;

(iii) services, stores and supplies provided on pre-payment or repayment.

British Armed Forces Vouchers could be exchanged for Japanese Yen currency through Paymasters, Field Cashiers, and Account Officers at the rate of 200 yen to £1 sterling, but Yen currency could not in any circumstances be reconverted to British Armed Forces Vouchers.

FINANCIAL ARRANGEMENTS OF BRITISH COMMONWEALTH OCCUPATION FORCE

The final financial arrangements for British Commonwealth Occupation Force were not approved till December 1947, by which

---

[28] Joint Chiefs Staff in Australia 305 of December 1946.

time the British, Indian and New Zealand contingents had completely or partly left Japan for their home countries. The finalisation of financial arrangements between four Governments for apportioning costs of British Commonwealth Occupation Force was however bound to take time as lengthy inter-Governmental negotiations were involved. In the interim, Australia made all the joint payments and each country kept an account of its own payments. The main problem was the basis on which charges had to be apportioned between the various countries.

General Cawthorn on his return from India in February 1946 informed Joint Chiefs of Staff in Australia that India had agreed to meet the cost of the Indian component on the following basis:[29]

(a) Pay of all personnel to be borne by the Indian Government.

(b) All other charges to be debited to the Japanese Government.

(c) One-fourth of the overall cost of British Commonwealth Occupation Force to be charged to India, as the strength of the Indian component was approximately in that ratio.

(d) No dollar payments to be made to the United States authorities for any material or services provided by or through United States authorities, which the latter obtained from Japanese sources, e.g., Japanese Yen obtained from Supreme Commander Allied Powers for use in British Commonwealth Occupation Force.

These financial intricacies had not been thought out before and Joint Chiefs of Staff in Australia Planning Staff expressed their inability to advise, "being unaware, of the political and politico-legal aspects of cost of British Commonwealth Occupation Force being borne by the Japanese.[30]"

The United Kingdom Government desired to recover from the Japanese Government the cost of stores and supplies for the maintenance of the Force as a first charge against the proceeds from Japanese exports. It also intended that stores obtained locally should be paid for, either by the Japanese or by the payment of Yen received from the Japanese free of charge.

There were many other difficulties in levying this charge on the Japanese Government and this could only be settled on an

---

[29] General Cawthorn's notes on his visit to India in Jan '46.
[30] JCPS 45/17 of 14 February 1946.

inter-Governmental level. It also depended on the policy of Supreme Commander for the Allied Powers and the capacity of Japan to pay. It was intertwined with the complex problem of "Reparations", which was never thrashed out. As this affair could only be settled after a Japanese Peace Treaty had been signed, it was essential to make some financial arrangements between the four countries taking part in British Commonwealth Occupation Force.

The arrangements for computing, and the policy for allocating overall cost of British Commonwealth Occupation Force among the various countries concerned was based on a "per capita" basis:

- (a) each country to be responsible for meeting all charges for pay of the personnel of its components,
- (b) one of the Governments concerned (Australia) to assume primary responsibility for financing and computing all other expenditure incurred for British Commonwealth Occupation Force,
- (c) all participating countries to reimburse the Pool Account according to the ratio fixed for them,
- (d) any recoveries from the Japanese to be allocated between the four Governments proportionately to the strength of their component with the Force,
- (e) the cost of all stores and supplies sent to Japan for the maintenance of British Commonwealth Occupation Force, and the cost of transport thereof, to be borne by the Pool Account,
- (f) the cost of any major requirement of a unit to be borne direct by the Government concerned.[31]

India's share in the Pool Account[32] was provisionally and initially fixed at 32 per cent but this did not take into consideration the following facts:

- (i) India provided the largest amount of initial equipment and stores, which were taken over by British Commonwealth Occupation Force.
- (ii) India provided more ancillary personnel to make up for deficiencies in other national components. (United Kingdom paid for the troops provided by India to make up United Kingdom's deficiencies).
- (iii) India provided direct certain items peculiar to Indian troops.

[31] JCPS 46B/22 dated 1 August 1947.
[32] DCGS/G/100. Remarks by General Cawthorn.

In view of the above India's proportionate share was reduced to 27·4 per cent.[33]

The long term maintenance for British Commonwealth Occupation Force was based on the following:[34]

(i) Base Depots to be integrated.

(ii) No actual costing of the maintenance of each component to be carried out in Japan.

(iii) The financial adjustment regarding the cost of maintenance of British Commonwealth Occupation Force between various Governments to be on a proportionate basis (the integrated nature of the force made actual costing out of question).

(iv) Australia to be responsible for the maintenance of British Commonwealth Occupation Force of all stores and supplies.

(v) All demands from British Commonwealth Occupation Force to be placed on Australia.

(vi) Demands to be forwarded by Headquarters, British Commonwealth Occupation Force as one co-ordinated demand for the whole of the Force and not separately for each contingent.

(vii) Australia to meet, as far as possible, demands from her own sources and the balance of demands to be laid off on other countries according to pre-arranged schedules.

(viii) All stores to be demanded on a co-ordinated basis for the whole of British Commonwealth Occupation Force and no separate account to be kept for different contingents.

In the beginning it may not have been possible to appreciate what might be the outcome of these arrangements at the final disbandment of the Force. If no credit was to be given for the "initial issues" the country which had contributed most to the integrated installations was bound to lose. Each country was responsible for the initial cost of the units it supplied and those should therefore have been returned in the same state as they were mounted irrespective of the source of supply of the replacements[35]. The position, however, remained indeterminate and was fruitful of controversy.

These disputes could have been avoided if the financial implications had been thrashed out earlier and Financial Advisers from each participating country were appointed with Joint Chiefs

---

[33] Britel No. 88 dated 25 January 1946.
[34] DCGS/G/100. Note by General Cawthorn.
[35] Indel/183 dated 22 October 1947.

of Staff in Australia and British Commonwealth Occupation Force. India had a Financial Adviser with British Commonwealth Occupation Force for a period of a few months but on the insistence of India[36] this post was declared redundant and Mr. Zahir Ahmad was returned to India.

THE LESSONS FROM BRITISH COMMONWEALTH OCCUPATION FORCE

The mounting, build-up, administration and maintenance of British Commonwealth Occupation Force was an important experiment which brought out many useful lessons and revealed the need for:—

(a) early receipt by the Commander-in-Chief of Outline Plan of force to cover broad principles of organisation and administration, including degree of inter-service and international integration, financial arrangements and control,

(b) early receipt of directives by the Commander-in-Chief and the component commanders,

(c) assembly of headquarters staff in time to permit of detailed planning before despatch of the force/ components,

(d) decentralisation of powers to the Commander-in-Chief to adjust establishment etc. within the force to meet local conditions subject to an agreed degree of control by the controlling body,

(e) standardisation of relations between the Commander-in-Chief and all components and contingents to enable the Commander-in-Chief to exercise effective control on a uniform basis throughout the force,

(f) early provision of entertainment allowances on a force basis,

(g) revision of nomenclature of staffs and appointments to meet the case of a force integrated from both the service and international aspects,

(h) avoidance of undue adherence to the national nomenclature etc., in respect of administration so as to foster the idea of a British Commonwealth Force and prevent from the outset any feeling that one component predominates or that others are dependent on its " bounty ". This particularly applies to supply, ordnance and canteen units,

[36] DCGS/G/100.

(i) adherence to the Chief of Staff organisation and avoidance of duality of responsibility between the Principle Administrative Officer and the Chief of Staff,

(j) headquarters of the force to be organised and to function as an inter-service headquarters and not primarily as an Army Headquarters.

CHAPTER VII

Concentration and move of Brinjap to Japan

Chief of Staff Telegram Cossea 314 of August 13, 1945 gave the following estimate of the occupational forces for Japan to be provided by India Command:—
- (a) One Indian Brigade Group.
- (b) One British Brigade Group.
- (c) Divisional Troops.

It was decided that this force should be known as Brinjap and the following principles were laid down for the selection of the units[1]:—
- (a) as many classes and arms as possible to be represented,
- (b) units with maximum war experience (for political and sentimental reasons contingent to be drawn from regiments known to have done especially well against the Japanese in Burma)[2],
- (c) subject to the above, units to be readily available in India,
- (d) limitation of movement, so as to avoid uneconomical use of the limited shipping resources,
- (e) no interference with the forces in Zipper, which had already been mounted,
- (f) before dispatch, the force to be brought on standard establishment and equipped to a high standard,
- (g) proper organisation of administrative units, as administrative problems for this force in Japan were expected to be considerable,
- (h) concentration of the force in one place in India prior to its mounting.

This force was to be formed from the selected units of 36th (Indian) Infantry Division and 2nd (British) Infantry Division. The British Brigade from 2nd (British) Infantry Division was to consist of English, Welsh and Scottish battalions. It was further decided to form a Headquarters similar to a normal Division Headquarters but containing certain additional personnel, usually found at a Corps Headquarters, such as Education, Welfare etc. These additional troops were provided to make Brinjap a completely independent and self sufficient unit.

[1] File No. 7240/01/SD5.
[2] Telegram 73913/SD5 dated 17 August '45.

It was also agreed to provide an initial maintenance lift for all stores and supplies for 90 days with the exception of cigarettes and tobacco and tinned and dehydrated equivalent of fresh meat, fruits and vegetables, and tinned butter, which were to be for 45 days only.[3]

The second maintenance lift was to include Royal Air Force stores, all petrol, oil, lubricants and mechanical transport spirit for 90 days as for the first lift, and ammunition at contact rates for 15 days. For reasons of prestige, and the fact that this force had to serve in the closest contact with Americans, it was decided that the unit messes should be equipped to a high scale with crockery and other peace-time ancillaries, for which loans were provided on the following basis[4] :—

(a) *Officers' Messes* Scale per officer

Headquarters Force, Force Signals and all units raised especially for this force ... ... Rs. 300/-
All other units including British units, and regular and non-regular units ... ... Rs. 200/-

(b) *Sergeants' Messes*

Headquarters Force, Force Signals and all units raised especially for this force ... ... Rs. 150/-
All other British regular and non-regular units Rs. 150/-

A special clothing scale for officers was sanctioned and the following items on loan were issued to all the officers proceeding to Japan:

	No.
Battle dress serge	2
Caps G.S. serge	1
Greatcoat dismounted	1
Shirts Angola drab with collars ...	2
Camp Comforter	1
Gloves knitted	1
Jerkin leather	1
Blankets	3

Major-General D. T. Cowan, C.B., C.B.E., D.S.O., M.C., well known in military circles as "Punch" Cowan, was selected to command this force.[5] General Cowan had commanded the

[3] Britel 141 of 14 February '46, Britel 517 of 6 Feb.
[4] File No. 7240/01/SD5.
[5] Signal No. 73913/SD5 dated 17 August 45 from Auchinleck to Slim.

17th Indian Division which captured Meiktila, a major victory, and changed the tide of events in the Burma campaign. This division had fought against the Japanese longer than any formation—from February 1942 until June 1945. In that period the division had won seven Victoria Crosses and more than 600 other decorations. The achievements of this division were a fair sample of the whole range of Indian effort on land in the war against Japan.

Major-General Cowan who commanded this famous formation was the right person to command Brinjap and to show to the Japanese people the victors of war and builders of peace. He said on assuming command:—

> " I am proud to be leading to Japan, men and women of British and Indian armies who through so many years of endurance and hard fighting have so well earned the right to be there after the common victory.
>
> These men and their predecessors, whose effort and achievement they represent saved India and reconquered Burma. Many of them were on the edge of still greater enterprise when the enemy capitulated.
>
> I hope our time of duty in Japan will help to consolidate and enlarge the fellowship and unity of effort which were forged with our friends and allies in War ".

The personnel of Division Headquarters began to assemble in Delhi from 10 September 1945, and moved to Nasik after a fortnight to join the force which they had to command.

Brinjap, as this force was then called, had begun to assemble in August 1945, but the Headquarters was not in position till the end of September. The concentration of the force which, in normal course, should be organised by its own Headquarters was carried out haphazardly without any proper planning before the Headquarters was ever formed. This handicap was also evident in a marked degree in the mounting of British Commonwealth Occupation Force. The Joint Chiefs of Staff Australia Plan, which was to be the working plan for this force, was not, as has been mentioned before, in print till after six months of the concentration of the force in Japan. However, Headquarters Brinjap by dint of labour soon organised the force into a well equipped and trained force before it left India for duty overseas.

SELECTION OF UNITS

The selection of units was an important task because all units had done very well. After careful consideration, the following units were selected:—

(a) *Indian Brigade*

Headquarters 268 Indian Infantry Brigade which had fought in Burma during 1944-45 was selected as the Brigade Headquarters to command the three battalions, which had been specially selected to represent the Indian Army. These were:—

  (i) 5th Battalion 1st Punjab Regiment from 26th Indian Division. This unit had fought in Arakan and taken part in the capture of Rangoon.

  (ii) 1st Battalion, the Mahratta Light Infantry, which, although it had not taken part in the Burma Campaign, had been in the Western Desert and Italy, where it had won two Victoria Crosses.

  (iii) 2nd Battalion, 5th Royal Gurkhas which had fought throughout the greater part of the Burma campaign and which headed the list of honours and awards for the infantry in the Indian Army, the famous " Triple VC " Battalion.

(b) *British Brigade (5 Infantry Brigade)*
    2nd Battalion Dorsetshire Regiment
    1st Battalion the Queen's Own Cameron Highlanders
    2nd Battalion the Royal Welch Fusiliers.

The 7th Light Cavalry was selected to represent the Indian Armoured Corps, for its excellent work during the Burma campaign, where it had won more awards than any other Indian cavalry regiment. For its role in Japan it was changed to an armoured car regiment and issued with Daimler armoured cars.

The artillery was represented by 30 Field Battery, RA, from 2nd Infantry Division, with whom it had served in France and Burma. 16 Indian Field Battery, IA, which had served in Burma was to represent the Indian Artillery, which was granted the title of Royal in December 1945.

The Engineer Units were 5 Field Company and 21 Field Park Company. 429 Field Company (Queen Victoria's Own Sappers and Miners) represented the famous Corps of Sappers and Miners.

CONCENTRATION AT NASIK

These famous units of the Indian Army began to assemble at Mashrul Camp near Nasik from the middle of July 1945. They came from far off corners of the world, the Punjabis from Burma, the Mahrattas from Italy, and the Engineers from Jamshedpur. The deserted camp once again came back to life. Its distance from any large town and lack of facilities made it difficult for the troops to find sufficient amenities and relaxation, which were so necessary for a force of this kind. The reason for the selection of this site might have been its vicinity to the port of embarkation. But this absence of amenities fully prepared the troops for lack of them in Japan where initially no ready made facilities could be available.

268 Indian Infantry Brigade: 268 Brigade as an independent brigade had done excellent work in the Burma Campaign. It had to represent in Japan the might and valour of the Indian Army. India had made a very great contribution in stopping and later defeating the Fascist aggression on all fronts. She had raised the greatest volunteer fighting force of all time—more than 2,000,000 men. More than two-thirds of the Allied Land Forces in South-East Asia were Indian Army men and among them were the original battalions of 268 Indian Infantry Brigade. It was now to be commanded by Brigadier (later General) K. S. Thimayya D.S.O., who had won great honour and renown in the fighting against Japan. Brigadier Thimayya was most suited by his personality, charm of manners and unassailable reputation, to impress on the Japanese the calibre of Indian commanders. He had been present at the ceremony of Japanese surrender in Singapore and had signed on behalf of India.

The staff was a mixed one which was selected from many Indian units but had few Indians in it. For an Indian brigade, commanded by an Indian, it was expected that the majority of the staff must be Indian, as this would have impressed the Japanese a great deal more and saved the constant American comment " peculiar Indian contingent commanded by British officers ".[6]

Indian Camp at Mashrul: The Brigade staff soon after arrival at Nasik got down to the task of organisation, reception and accommodation of Indian units coming to join them in the Mashrul Camp.

The camp was a beehive of activity, everyone preparing furiously for the impending move to Japan. They did not know that they would have to wait many long months before they could actually move to the country of " cherry blossoms " about which they had heard so much from officers who came to lecture about Japan. In the tented camps the various units vied with each other in the reputation they had gained in the last war. The Punjabis were proud because the Commander-in-Chief of India was their Colonel-in-Chief and considered themselves as his " blue-eyed boys ". In 1941 this unit was in garrison duty at Mandalay and

---

[6] Interview by Lt-Col. J. G. Singh, ADC to General Robertson.

had withdrawn to India with General Alexander's Army. It had very nearly completed a circle via. Arakan, Ramree and Rangoon.

The Mahrattas with their gaudy red-green hackles, talked proudly of their achievements in the Western Desert and Italy. They did not like the huts and tents of Mashrul after the villas of Italy. The Italian Campaign had made them tough. They had taken part in smashing the Gustav and the Hitler lines and had seen action in South Florence. They had advanced to Pisa and helped to cross the Senio and Santerno rivers. They had won many decorations including two VCs. Having taken part in the defeat of one enemy they were now going to occupy the land of the other, defeated by their brothers-in-arms.

The Gurkhas from Nepal had already won great renown for valour by winning three VCs in the grim battles of Kohima. Two VCs were won at Mortar Bluff in the Imphal area, on successive days in June 1944. In five months of bloody fighting this unit had 820 battle casualties. They had also the proud privilege of having been commanded by General "Punch" Cowan, who was now their Force Commander.

There were many other Indian units about whom we will hear a great deal later. There was the 7th Light Cavalry which was an Indian unit, though being Divisional Troops, was not with 268 Indian Infantry Brigade.

429 Indian Field Company IE arrived at Mashrul Camp from Tatanagar on 16 September 1945 and got down to making roads and culverts in the Camp. It was happy to be back again within the fold of 268 Brigade, having fought along with it in Burma.

Force 152

Force 152, which was being raised at Mashrul Camp was christened British and Indian Troops Japan (Brinjap) with effect from 1 November 1945 when General Cowan, the General Officer Commanding, inspected all the troops on the inauguration day. It was the intention of the Commander-in-Chief, India, that this force proceeding to Japan should be well equipped, clothed and provided with all articles of amenities, welfare and training. The long stay at Nasik was therefore devoted to fitting all personnel properly with summer and winter clothings. The veterans were put through many ceremonials and trained to carry out Internal Security tasks.

The fame of Brinjap had spread far and wide in India and many officers came to inspect this force. On 27 November 1945 the force marched past Lieut.-General R. M. Lockhart C.B., C.I.E., M.C., General Officer Commanding, Southern Command.

7th Light Cavalry took part partly in armoured cars and partly in soft vehicles. In the evening the massed pipes and bugles of the force played Retreat at 57 Indian General Hospital (C). Bands of 5/1 Punjab Regiment, 2/5 RGR (FF) and 2 Camerons took part. The General Officer Commanding-in-Chief congratulating the forces said: " I congratulate all ranks on their soldierly bearing, turn-out and steadiness on parade. I consider that the standard reached in a ceremonial parade in so short a period of training, reflects great credit on all concerned. I appreciate that the standard reached so far is the result of the hard work, which has been so enthusiastically put in by all ranks of the Force. The Retreat sounded by the massed Bands was most impressive. The obviously happy Force spirit made the visit most enjoyable one. Best of luck in Japan ".

The date of departure from India was still not certain. Negotiations were going on in Washington and Tokyo. The earlier indications were that the force would be embarking before the end of the year, but as no definite decision was forthcoming the move was postponed for early next year. This period of enforced delay was utilised in arranging inter-unit and inter-brigade exercises, sports tournaments and recreation camps near Lake Beale. Welfare parties were also organised to visit Bombay and to go out shooting in the neighbouring jungle. During December 1945, 7th Light Cavalry was busy equipping itself with Dodges, and British units were making arrangements for the celebration of Christmas and New Year's Day in Nasik. Most of the units were able to send leave parties to Bombay and had holidays for X' mas and New Year's Day.

Commander-in-Chief's Visit

For the first fortnight of the new year, 1946, all units of the force were busily preparing for the Commander-in-Chief's visit. General Sir Claude Auchinleck inspected 268 Indian Infantry Brigade on parade, with 7th Light Cavalry, 16 Indian Field Battery RIA, 429 Indian Field Company (QVO) Madras S & M, Indian Light Field Ambulance, IAMC, and 111 Indian Infantry Workshop Company (IEME). After inspection he presented 48 medals and orders to officers and men of the brigade, and presented a Union Jack to the Brigade Commander. Addressing the parade he said:—

" I am very glad that you are going to Japan to represent the Indian Army there.

The Indian Army did much to bring about the defeat of the Japanese and all the world knows how well it fought in Assam and Burma.

The Indian Army also helped greatly in the defeat of Germany by its bravery and skill in the hard fighting in Africa, Germany and Syria.

Amongst you, are units and officers and men who have fought in all these countries and have made the name of the Indian Army famous.

All parts of the Indian Army are represented here to-day—Cavalry, Artillery, Engineers, Signals, Infantry, IAMC, IEME and all had their share in securing Victory.

In Japan you will meet soldiers not only from Britain, but also from Australia and New Zealand and other countries.

I know that you will show them by your conduct, bearing and efficiency that the Indian Army is second to none in peace as well as in war. The honour of the Army is in your hands.

Your Commander is the first Indian Officer to command a brigade in war and I have much pleasure in presenting this flag to him and I know that you will guard it well.

I wish you good luck and a safe and pleasant journey.

I wish I were going with you ".

The Brigade then marched past to the tune of the pipes and drums of the 5th Battalion 1st Punjab Regiment and 2nd Battalion 5th Royal Gurkha Rifles (Frontier Force).

The Commander-in-Chief met the three heroes of the force, the three VCs: Jemadar Gaje Ghale of 2/5 Gurkhas, Sepoy Nam Deo Jadhao of 1/5 Mahratta LI, and Naik Agansing Rai 2/5 Gurkhas, who were going to Japan to show to the Japanese the type of brave sons of India who had gained the highest awards fighting against them.

Another Postponement

The departure of the force was again postponed, and the camp rumours were that it would be moving out in March. This was confirmed when leave details were sent out and leave was to close on 15 March. These postponements were having an adverse effect on the morale of the troops and General Cawthorn apprised the Joint Chiefs of Staff Australia of the position. " The advantages of an early arrival are considerable. Political and public enthusiasm are already waning and further delays may cause complete disinterest. This tendency was reflected as far back as 19 November 1945 when British troops of Brindiv began cancelling deferments of release. The divisional commander considered an early firm date of sailing, and implicit adherence

Brigadier (later General) K. S. Thimayya, Commander 268 Indian Brigade

Plate VIII

Brigadier (later General) S. M. Shrinagesh, Commander 268 Indian Brigade

to it, very important to maintaining morale. It must be remembered that all British troops hate India,[7] and they are located very close to the Transit Depot at Deolali where they see large numbers of men leaving for United Kingdom on release and repatriation.

"A factor exists which cannot yet be quoted officially but which may cause difficulties if further delays occur, i.e., internal disorders in India may arise in March. These would probably be directed against the railways and ports".[8]

Against this desire to secure the early arrival of Brinjap in Japan was the fact that no Indian Advance Party had gone there and it was not definite that adequate advance base facilities were available at Kure port for a sound peace-time scale of administration.

It was suggested by the United Kingdom/India Element of Joint Chiefs of Staff Australia that, " this administration could best be secured by the setting up of a self-contained Brit/Ind/Anzac/Advance Base prior to the introduction of the main body of Brinjap ".[9] The latter was self-contained as far as the divisional rear boundary, and could be sailed as such without any delay. Some of the units required in rear of this boundary, however, were still to be raised, as also personnel, whose details were unknown, belonging to various integrated headquarters in the Base.

General Cowan, Commander Brinjap, signalled: "If it was desired to sail Brinjap without Brinjap element in Base a very firm undertaking would be required that satisfactory alternative administrative arrangements were guaranteed. This was not possible to assess until the British Commonwealth Occupation Force administrative reconnaissance report was received. It was recognised that the period of maximum stress in the Base will be during the arrival period, when short cuts and expedients are unsound. Reliance upon such means, or upon United States aid, would subject United Kingdom/India force to the risk of:—

    (a) failure to provide the high peace-time standard which United Kingdom/Indian troops have been led to expect and to which they are entitled,

    (b) in the worst but foreseeable cases, possible complete administrative breakdown particularly in the more complex problem of Indian troops maintenance ".[10]

This sound advice was not heeded and the move of Brinjap Advance Party was further dealyed. The matter was again raised with Joint Chiefs of Staff Australia but decision was postponed

---

[7] DCGS/G/100 dated 8-4-49. General Cawthorn explains that 'British troops hated service in India and *not* India itself'.
[8] JCO PS/48/A/3 dated 4 January 46.
[9] JCPS 48/A/43 dated 4 January 46.
[10] *Ibid.*

till after the return of General Northcott, Commander-in-Chief, British Commonwealth Occupation Force, who had come to India to inspect Brinjap, accompanied by Major-General W. J. Cawthorn, C.B., C.I.E., C.B.E., India's representative on Joint Chiefs of Staff Australia.

On 18 January 1946, Lieut.-General J. Northcott, C.B., M.V.O., Commander-in-Chief, British Commonwealth Occupation Force visited the force. He inspected 268 Brigade Group, took the salute at a march past and conferred with selected officers and VCOs. He said: " Our job in Japan is to play our part in winning the peace which is just as important as the task we had in winning the war. We are not going there as Indians, Britons, Australians and New Zealanders in separate units, but for the first time we form a completely integrated British Commonwealth Force. The success of our job will depend a great deal on the behaviour, discipline, military efficiency of every individual in the force as part of the Commonwealth team.

"Very soon the Australians from Australia, the New Zealanders from Italy, yourselves from India, and air force squadrons from many parts of the world will begin moving to Japan to carry out the important task in front of us. We have to take over the occupation of a large area in southern Japan called the Hiroshima Prefecture. It is an area stiff with armaments, coastal defences, ammunition works, naval workshops and so on. The whole area is to be demilitarised and we have to do it. We have to supervise the Japanese who will do the labour and to see they do not put any thing over us. It is a man-size job and it will take us some time to complete it. Another most important task which is the object of this force is to occupy this country and to show the Japanese what it means to enjoy the personal freedom we know but of which they have not the slightest understanding.

" For the first time in their lives they have been freed from the tyranny of their own authorities, the police and gestapo organisations, and the only reason they are now free from this fear is because of the presence of Allied occupation forces. As representatives of the British Empire your behaviour, discipline, military efficiency and the whole manner in which you comport yourselves both on parade and off duty will be a great example to this cowed and defeated nation ".

The General was entertained by officers of the force, and the Kumaon Brass Band in full ceremonial dress made its first official appearance. This band thereafter was always in great demand at all social functions.

On his visit to General Headquarters (India), New Delhi, General Northcott asked for an Indian Officer to be appointed as his ADC to keep him acquainted about Indian Army matters and customs.

THE MOVE

When planning the move it was appreciated that it would be essential to have sufficient elements of administrative units functioning on the ground when the main party arrived, as this was not a purely tactical move. It was considered necessary to send an Advance Party to Japan as early as possible. This question was referred to Joint Chiefs of Staff Australia. On 28 December 1945, Joint Chiefs of Staff Australia signalled " that the subject of Brinjap Staff Advance Party was discussed with General Northcott and A. V. M. Boucher and conclusion was reached that except for those RAF officers no party should be sent forward but held in India when a final stage is reached in discussions now taking place in Washington ".

General Northcott assured General Headquarters India that the Advance Party would be called forward in ample time and proceed direct to Japan. In the meantime the Australian Liaison Mission which had been in Japan for some weeks, and had become the advanced element of British Commonwealth Occupation Force Headquarters was to carry out reconnaissances of the area allotted to British Commonwealth Occupation Force and communicate to Brinjap their future locations.

The appreciation of the time factor for mounting Indian contingent was submitted to Supreme Allied Commander South-East Asia, who was responsible for the provision of shipping for this move, on 30 November 1945. This clearly stated that 4 personnel ships, 11 fitted M. T. ships and 4 store ships were required. Taking D-Day as the day of sailing ex-Bombay, where the contingent was concentrated, the time-table was:—

Day	Event
D-30	Orders to mount contingent received.
D-26	Shipping selected.
D-8	Shipping arrives Bombay.
D-7	Loading commences Bombay.
D-Day	Contingent sails.

A clear 30 days warning was required to mount the contingent from the date the order ' to go ' was received by Armindia.

The planned build-up of United Kingdom/Indian Contingent in Japan was as follows:—

Serial No.	Formation, Units	Number of Personnel	ETA Kure
1	Naval Port Party	400	1–11 Feb 1946
2	Air Advance Party	20	6–12 Feb 1946
3	Advance Sea Party Brindiv—RAF/RIAF	2,055	1 Mar 1946
4	First Echelon Brindiv—RAF/RIAF	2,048	16–23 Mar 1946
5	RAF/RIAF (Malaya)	1,025	16 Mar 1946
6	RAF/RIAF (Air Parties)	400	21 Mar 1946
7	RAF/RIAF (Carrier Party) Second Echelon	126	15-18 Apr 1946
8	Brindiv—RAF/RIAF	8,909	15 Apr to 3 May 1946
9	RAF/RIAF (Burma, Malaya)	1,380	15 Apr 1946

Schedule of Movement
Air Advance Party: A party of 10 officers and 7 BORs, selected representatives of staff and services, left India by air on 16 February 1946 and arrived at Kure on 19 February 1946.

Sea Advance Party
When planning this move, it was appreciated that it would be essential to have a sufficient element of administrative units functioning on the ground to receive and maintain the main body of the division on arrival. Hence an advance party of 1600 personnel was despatched from India on 8 February 1946 and arrived in Kure on 1 March 1946. To make this party self-contained in itself it was allotted a lift of 100 vehicles and 850 tons of balanced stores.

Main Body
The main body was divided into two echelons, roughly corresponding to the two infantry brigades each, plus a proportion of divisional troops.
    (a) *First Sea Echelon:* Division Headquarters
                            Divisional Troops (less 7 Cavalry),

169 General Transport Company,
5 Infantry Brigade.
Shipping allocated: HT *Dunera*
HT *Orduna*
HT *Arundel Castle,*

(b) *Period 17 March—5 April 1946*
First Flight: Balance Divisional Troops and Advance Party 268 Indian Infantry Brigade.
Shipping allocated: HT *Rajula.*
Second Flight: 268 Indian Infantry Brigade.
Shipping allocated: HT *Orduna.*

Final embarkation of 6,761 personnel of first sea echelon was completed on 17 March 1946 and final debarkation in Kure by 5 April 1946. 112 personnel of the second echelon were embarked by 29 April 1946 and arrived in Kure on 19 May 1946 completing the move of the whole division.

Vehicles/Stores/G1098—1st Sea Echelon

8 Mechanical Transport/Stores Vessels were allotted to lift the vehicles of this echelon together with Unit G1098 and half of the first 90 days maintenance stores tonnage.

Total vehicles shipped	824
Total stores shipped	12,248 tons
Total G1098 shipped	1,288 tons

2nd Vehicle/Store Sea Echelon

7 Mechanical Transport/Stores vessels were allotted to this echelon to lift the balance of vehicles and balance of Unit G1098 and first lift of 90 days maintenance stores.

Total vehicles shipped	859
Total stores shipped	6,895 tons
Total G1098 shipped	218 tons

Personnel on Mechanical Transport/Stores Vessels

All vessels with the exception of five were fitted to carry personnel. This helped out the personnel lift considerably as a total of 1417 personnel were carried over the two echelons.

First 90 Days Maintenance Tonnage

Shipment of this tonnage balanced over the first and second echelons was completed on 21 April 1946.

MOVE FROM NASIK TO BOMBAY

The move by rail from Nasik to Bombay once again demonstrated that units as a whole did not appreciate the necessity for Unit Standing Orders to cover moves by rail, road and sea. The fact that the successful move of a unit depended entirely on the preparedness of the unit to move was brought home to most of the units.

Nasik being only 100 miles from Bombay, and connected by main road, proved to be an excellent concentration area. No duplication of lines of communication resulted in continual hold-ups in the passing of order and in case of necessity War Transport link could be used for effective link-up.

Movement of troops overseas calls for accurate and complete documentation and where the implications were not appreciated in advance, considerable difficulty was felt in embarkation. In this connection it was found imperative not only to insist on correct documentation but orders were issued for officers of units to accompany their men on board and into troops' decks. This also helped in the correct stowing of kit and economy in space.

Travel in troops transport is never luxurious and there were general complaints about the cramped space. But as the troops were keen to get to Japan and as light entertainment was available on board the ships the complaints gradually disappeared, troops making the best of the available facilities.

The setting up of Divisional Control Headquarters at the port of embarkation was considered essential. Though this duplicated the control with the Movement Control authorities, yet it proved very effective in the accurate allocation of personnel to the ships and in the continuity in calling forward troops from the concentration area in Nasik to the port of embarkation at Bombay.

The vehicles and personnel had to be split up in many groups, but as the vehicles and stores had preceded the personnel ships it was expected that the units on arrival in Japan would be self-sufficient and mobile.

On the departure of Brinjap from Bombay the following message was received from General Officer Commander-in-Chief Southern Command, India:—

"All in Southcom join me in wishing you and those under your command the very best of Good Luck and success on the great and important task that lies before you. We shall watch your activities with pride and confidence".

ARRIVAL IN SINGAPORE

The ships carrying Brinjap arrived in Singapore on 16 March 1946, and in the early morning of 17 March the main party of Brinjap paraded through the streets of Singapore. Admiral Lord Louis Mountbatten, Supreme Allied Commander, South-East Asia, took the salute as a column of representatives of Brinjap troops marched past the historical municipal building where Lord Louis Mountbatten had accepted the Japanese surrender of Singapore on 19 Spetember 1945. Lord Mountbatten inspected the contingents of Queen Alexandra's Imperial Military Nursing Service, Field Army Nursing Yeomanry, Women's Auxiliary Service (B), Women Volunteer Services (United Kingdom), Young Women's Christian Association, Entertainments National Service Association, formed up on the steps of the municipal building.

H.M.T. *Dunera* carrying Headquarters 268 Indian Infantry Brigade and 5/1 Punjab arrived at Singapore on 7 April 1946. All ranks were greatly disappointed at not being allowed ashore although the ship remained in stream for more than two days.

ARRIVAL IN HONG KONG

Major-General Frank Festing, C.B.E., D.S.O., General Officer Commanding Allied Land Forces Hong Kong, came on board the ship *Dunera* to welcome Brinjap on 22 March, 1946. On 23 March, the crowded streets at Kowloon, on the mainland across Hong Kong, welcomed the first contingent of Brinjap troops going to Japan. Major-General Festing took the salute as the representatives of all the units marched past the building of the Peninsula Hotel.

DEBARKATION IN KURE

The port of debarkation was Kure, the old Japanese Naval Dockyard, one of the biggest in the world, now a mass of twisted steel. Three alongside berths were available for the discharge of vehicles and stores, while personnel could be disembarked alongside pontoons or in the stream on to Landing Ship Tanks depending on the size of the vessel.

Personnel: Disembarkation of personnel was effected smoothly throughout, and rapid clearance to unit areas was facilitated through the excellent arrangements made by the advance parties to receive and accommodate units.

Vechicles: Majority of vehicles on arrival were runners and facilitated easy discharge. There had been extensive pilferage en route from the vehicles in ships which were not fitted to carry escorts. Strict precautions and quick clearance were required to prevent pilfering in Kure.

Stores: Discharge of stores was at first handicapped because the Port Organisation was not efficiently geared up to handle the tonnage. This was soon remedied by the assistance of Brinjap troops.

It was found that the port working facilities, including Movement and Transportation and Base Units, should be well established and geared up to receive a force of any considerable size before such a force is mounted for ultimate disembarkation at the port.

The following units co-operated in the disembarkation of the Division, which was effected during the period 1 March to 19 May 1946.

    British Combined Movement Control Group.
    241 Indian Docks Operating Company.
    Australian Docks Operating Unit.
    One British Combined Base General Transport Company.

The above units had only arrived in Kure in the last week of February, and their settling-in period coincided with the arrival of the New Zealand and Australian contingents. None-the-less, their rapid discharge of stores and vehicles and embarkation of personnel was a creditable performance in view of the limited port facilities and unpreparedness of the port to receive so large a force, whilst catering also for the Australian and New Zealand contingents.

The first Indian element arrived in Kure on 28 March while the main body in H. T. *Dunera* arrived on 18 May 1946. At the docks, 5/1 Punjab escort to Colours was inspected by Commander-in-Chief, British Commonwealth Occupation Force, Lieut.-General J. B. Northcott, C.B., M.V.O. The troops then disembarked and marched past Generals Northcott and Cowan on their way to the railway station.

The Indian troops for the first time had a good look at the Japanese mainland which they were going to occupy and saw the havoc that had been caused by American bombings. Everywhere large Japanese warships were lying aground in various positions of abandonment while all naval structures on the island along the narrow Japanese Inland Sea were no more than a mass of twisted steel. Brigadier Thimayya had a good look at this desolate scene and as he stepped ashore said: " We are sorry to have left India at this stage of political changes but there is a job to be done here and the Indian Army has definitely earned a share in the honour of the occupation of Japan. We are looking forward to happy associations with Empire and other Allied troops ".

MOVE OF NO. 4 SQUADRON RIAF

On 2 April 1946, after six months of standing by, nineteen Spitfire Mk. XIV aircraft were airborne from Yallahanka for Cochin, where they were embarked on an aircraft carrier which took the air party of No. 4 Squadron to Japan for occupation duties.

After landing at Cochin the engines were inhibited to prevent corrosive action at sea, and then wheeled down to the quay. By the morning of the 7th all aircraft were loaded and lashed on the carrier deck. The carrier steamed out of the harbour at 1400 hours on 8 April 1946, and after a voyage of 15 days anchored at Iwakuni, on the 23rd in the morning. According to the original plan the aircraft were supposed to be flown off the carrier and landed at the airfield, but due to bad weather and some technical complications no aircraft was allowed to take off from the carrier. This caused great disappointment to the pilots who had received concentrated training on deck take-offs. By the 24th all the aircraft were off-loaded and transported to the wharf by means of barges, from where they were pushed down to the airfield.

The squadron was originally based at British Commonwealth Air Station, Iwakuni, for one week, from where it was moved to British Commonwealth Air Station Miho and formed a group with two other Royal Air Force Spitfire Squadrons."

[11] Report by Squadron Leader Barker RIAF.

CHAPTER VIII

British and Indian Troops in Japan

THE CHANGE OF DESIGNATION

Brinjap arrived in Japan as a self-contained formation fully organised to carry out any role allotted to it in an independent capacity. However, as a part of the British Commonwealth Occupation Force, an integrated force, under the command of General Northcott, it had no independent role allotted to it. Soon, on the recommendation of Joint Chiefs of Staff Australia, the designation of United Kingdom/Indian Contingent, Brinjap, was changed to Brindiv. In its new role Brindiv was placed under the direct overall command of the Commander-in-Chief British Commonwealth Occupation Force. The national contingents were autonomous in their domestic affairs and responsible for their own Governments, though for international contingent purposes and overall supervisory control they were under the command of the Commander-in-Chief, British Commonwealth Occupation Force. There was some misunderstanding initially about this change in designation, but in the end it was admitted by all, even General Cowan, that Joint Chiefs of Staff, Australia policy was sound and in the best interests of the Indian Contingent.[1]

DIRECTIONS TO CONTINGENT COMMANDERS

It was necessary to define the relationship between National Contingent/British Commonwealth Occupation Force/National Headquarters, hence a directive was issued to General Cowan as Commander of the British/Indian National Contingent which *inter alia* laid down that:[2]

"(a) National Contingent Commander was responsible to Commander-in-Chief, British Commonwealth Occupation Force, for the command, employment, administration and training of the Indian element of the British-Indian Division and such formations and units as might be allotted to it from time to time.

(b) National Contingent Commander was made responsible to the Commander-in-Chief, British Commonwealth Occupation Force, and to General Headquarters, India,

---

[1] DCGS/G/100. General Robertson had been responsible for this organisation.
[2] Directive to the Nominated Representative of India contingent Indel/50/4 of 15 Oct., 46 at Appendix. "D"

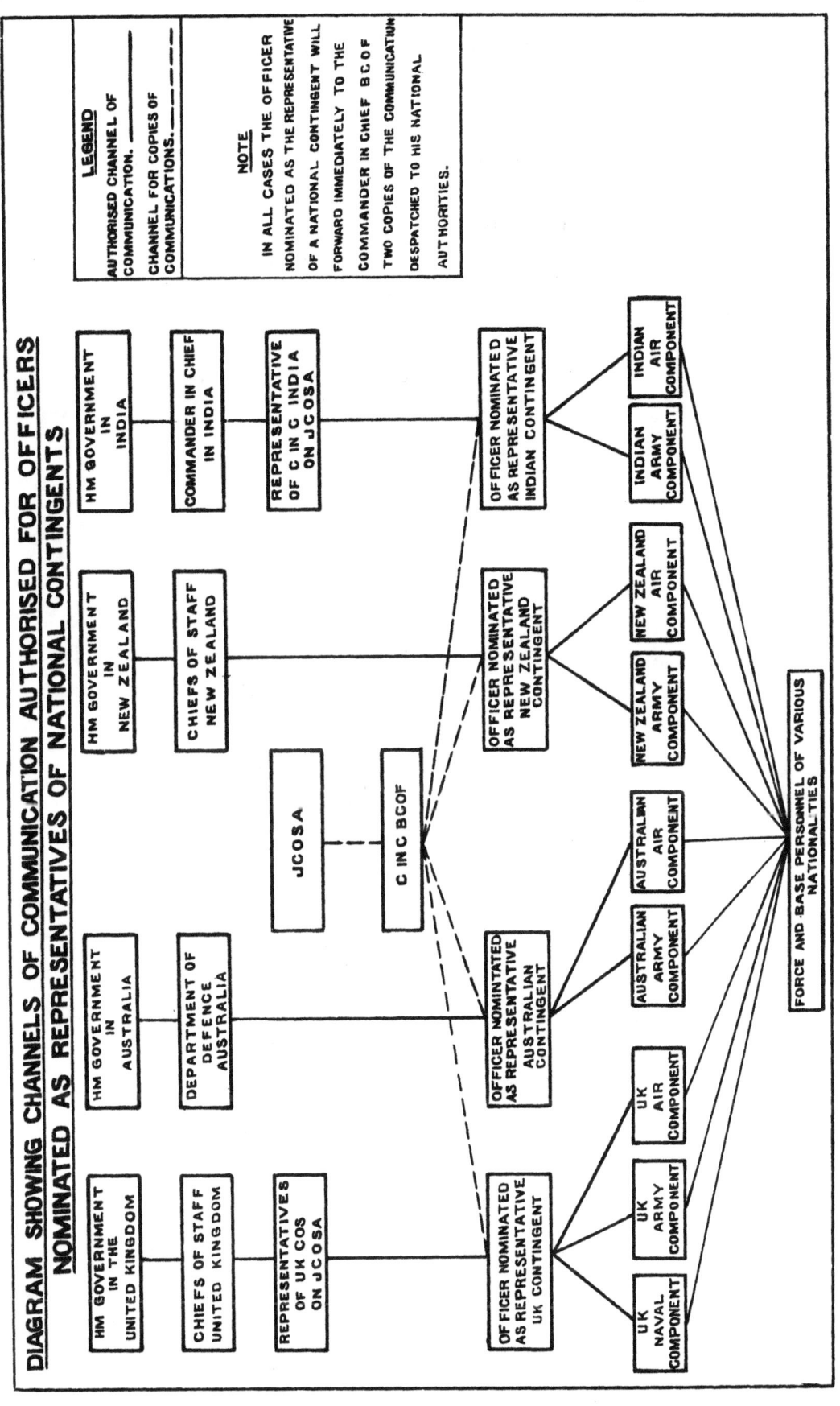

for matters of domestic administration including disciplinary action in respect of all the personnel of the Indian Army wherever serving in British Commonwealth Occupation Force and to ensure that the arrangements for their welfare were satisfactory.

(c) National Contingent Commander was to communicate direct with General Headquarters, India, but to provide the Commander-in-Chief, British Commonwealth Occupation Force, with two copies of any such communications ".

The channels of communication authorised for Contingent Commanders and nominated representatives are given in the diagram opposite.

Domestic Subjects: The following subjects were classified under " routine domestic personnel administration " and were the responsibility of the National Contingent Commander:

(i) Reinforcements, replacements.
(ii) Re-engagements in Japan.
(iii) Leave, including compassionate leave outside Japan.
(iv) Discharges, including discharges for compassionate reasons.
(v) Return to countries of origin of undesirable, unsuitable, and medically unfit personnel.
(vi) Conditions of Service (except policy concerning service in Japan).
(vii) Education, repatriation, rehabilitation and post-war reconstruction.
(viii) Promotion, reduction etc.
(ix) Honours and awards of medals and stars other than for service in Japan.
(x) Promotion and posting of officers up to the rank of Colonel.
(xi) Confidential and special reports on officers below the rank of Lieut.-Colonel.
(xii) Officers' records.
(xiii) Records, including the reporting of casualties.
(xiv) National elections and referendums.
(xv) Philanthropic bodies.
(xvi) National patriotic funds.

NOMINATED REPRESENTATIVE

Major General D. T. Cowan, C.B., C.B.E., D.S.O., M.C. was appointed the Commander of the Army Component of the Indian

Contingent and also its nominated representative. Squadron Leader J. G. Chandra was the Commander of the Air Force component of the Indian Contingent of British Commonwealth Occupation Force. As the national representative General Cowan was made responsible for:[3]

(a) all personnel of all services in the Indian Contingent and for bringing to the notice of the Government of India any matter which affected either the general well-being of the personnel in the contingent or the interests of the Government;

(b) ensuring in conjunction with Commander-in-Chief, British Commonwealth Occupation Force that Indian personnel were not employed on any task or in such manner as to conflict with religion or caste susceptibilities.

TASKS FOR THE INDIAN CONTINGENT

The National Contingent Commander was to ensure that those under his command, at all times:—

" (a) represent India worthily in the occupation of Japan,

(b) maintain and enhance British Commonwealth prestige and influence in the eyes of the Japanese and/or our Allies; and

(c) illustrate to, and impress on, the Japanese people as far as may be possible, the democratic way and purpose in life"[4].

In the fulfilment of these objects, General Cowan had a very difficult task. Any degree of propaganda and advertisement could not change the political position of India *vis-a-vis* the United Kingdom. India was not politically independent and the fact that Indian troops had defeated the Japanese in the far flung battlefields was a matter of the past. The actual position at the moment was depicted by Indian troops mostly commanded by British officers. In the beginning the Indian contingent could not adequately demonstrate to the Japanese people, who, not very long ago, were one of the big powers of the world, the democratic way and purpose of life, which their countrymen themselves were fighting for. It could only show, what it was, a sound, efficient and disciplined military force. The turn-out, efficiency, sense of duty and discipline of the Indian troops was the one redeeming feature of the whole situation. By their treatment of the Japanese, their all-round behaviour and conduct, the Indian troops created a good impression among the Allies and the Japanese.

[3] Indel/50/5 of 15 October, 46 at Appendix " E."
[4] *Ibid.*

After the dissolution of Brindiv and the formation of an Indian Brigade Group, with complete nationalisation of the officer cadre and the attainment of independence on 15 August 1947, the position of Indians in the eyes of the Allies and the Japanese was greatly enhanced. On the foundation of sincere freindship which was bulit up gradually, rose the edifice of Indian prestige, sound and shining.

THE MEANS TO INCREASE INDIAN PRESTIGE

The tasks laid down above for the Indian Contingent were to be achieved by:—
" (i) efficiency and smartness of turn-out and the standard of equipment and drill of troops;
(ii) preservation of the dignity of all ranks on or off duty;
(iii) the influence and conduct of British system of obtaining and administering justice; and
(iv) the contact of service personnel with the Japanese to influence their opinion in favour of India ".

The efficiency and smartness of the Indian troops was second to none in Japan and contributed equally with others to the reputation of British Commonwealth Occupation Force. On the many occasions of the change of guard at the Imperial Plaza, Tokyo, their turn-out and drill movements exacted admiration from numerous Allied and Japanese spectators. The preservation of dignity of all ranks on or off duty was not only a matter for the individual but mostly depended on the attitude of the senior members of the Force.

Indians were appointed by General Robertson to the Provost Courts and conducted their business with decorum and disposed of cases on merits, and no national prejudice or war venom was ever allowed to affect the course of justice. Generally the behaviour of the Indian troops towards the Japanese also showed no feelings of revenge and few cases of misbehaviour were reported. There were, however, not many occasions for contact with the people of Japan. Yet, despite these handicaps, many Indians came in contact with the Japanese and thoroughly impressed on them the Indian way of life, their austere simplicity and genuine sincerity. On the other hand, the Japanese also made a lasting impression on the Indian mind by their customs and mode of life, which in many instances were admired by the Indian soldiers. Their high standard of education and wide literacy existing even in the remotest villages, the number of schools and the large attendance there did not fail to affect the soldier, who could contrast the conditions in his homeland. They also marked the advance in technical sciences and cognate fields. Another aspect of Japanese life which appealed to the Indian soldiers was the discipline of the masses there and many felt that for progress in their own country inculcation of discipline was essential.

The Indian troops who used to do the journeys by rail or road were impressed by the fact that no space was wasted in Japan. A law forbids the peasant to cultivate more than one-third space on any hillside. The virgin forest at the top and in the re-entrants stops erosion which is bound to occur where gradients are so steep and rainfall so heavy. The cultivated space is terraced in small fields according to the contours. This zig-zag pattern is a pleasing sight in the Japanese landscape, for it is covered with various plantations of different hues. All the space, along the roads, along the railway lines, almost anywhere where there is soil, is laboriously and tenderly cultivated. Not only do the Japanese cultivate every inch of their land but they also excel in the number of crops and the quantity of yield from that limited space. The rotation of crops is achieved by careful timing and planning, while the quantity is increased by improving the quality, in which the Agriculture Department of the Imperial Japanese Government played an important part.

Many Indians were quick to learn the Japanese language and were thus enabled to get a better insight into the Japanese mind and manners. Some of them were invited to Japanese homes and were struck by their artistic simplicity. In brief, the Indians by their contact with the Japanese learnt a great deal which was for their good and of their country, while they in turn by their bearing may have left a lasting impression on the Japanese mind.

LOCATION OF BRINDIV

Brindiv, of which only 5 British Brigade had arrived, was allotted the Hiro and Fukuyama areas at the eastern end of Hiroshima and Shimane Prefectures:—

Hiro Area: Divisional Headquarters
                     Divisional Troops
                     Headquarters 5 Brigade
                     1st Battalion Queen's Own Cameron Highlanders.
Northern Area: 2 Dorset.
(Shimane-Ken)
Shikoku Island: 2 RWF
Kure Area: Base Troops.

System of Maintenance: The system of maintenance was normal and presented no difficulties. The supplies and stores were drawn from the various depots in Kure and then distributed in the normal way througout the division. But difficulty was encountered in the despatch of fresh supplies to outlying units, as refrigerator vans and plants were not available in the beginning.

Accommodation at Hiro: Accommodation in Japan was classified according to its use during the war. The Target Property, which was used by the Japanese armed forces, automatically belonged to the occupation authorities who had complete rights of alteration, removal and destruction, as they thought fit. The Imperial Japanese Government property was reserved for the use of the Japanese Government and it was difficult to acquire this property for the use of occupation forces. Such property included schools, hospitals and other official and non-official institutions. The third category was known as "Procured Proprety" which was Japanese civilian accommodation procured for the use of occupation troops. To obtain this the requisitioning authority had to go through strict procurement channels.

The accommodation in the Hiro area was seized Japanese property, old naval barracks and armament factories, which was hardly in a condition to be considered hospitable, particularly as it lacked lights, doors or windows. For the most part, officers and members of the Women's Services were housed in houses procured from the Japanese. These were flimsy structures, the walls consisting of sliding paper screens were adequate for the summer but not for the rigorous Japanese winter. Other ranks were accommodated in practically every case in ex-Japanese military barracks, which were mostly double-storied wooden structures.

It was not considered advisable to use stoves and heaters in these barracks due to the frequent risk of fire for which strict fire orders were issued to all units. Arrangements were therefore made to instal steam-heating. To assist in the reconstruction of this accommodation and make it comfortable for the troops, all the engineer resources were employed on this task, assisted by Japanese labour. Extensive reconnaissance of the area was carried out to find engineer stores. The Japanese labour in the beginning proved very unsatisfactory. They were slow in the uptake and grumbled at long hours of work.

But it was hoped that with the move of the formation to the new area of responsibility the accommodation situation would be eased.

MOVE OF BRINDIV TO OKAYAMA

In May, 1946, it was decided to allocate the prefectures of Okayama, Tottori and Shimane and the whole of Shikoku Island to Brindiv. This move was made difficult and had to be taken piecemeal as it depended on the move-out of the United States 24th Division which was in occupation of this area.

The move of 5 Infantry Brigade to occupy the whole of Shikoku Island presented several problems. First, it entailed sea transportation from Uno to Takamatsu and then dispersal of units to their destinations inland. The maintenance and administration of 5 British Brigade had, therefore, to be more or less independent.

Shimane and Tottori Prefectures were allotted to 268 Indian Infantry Brigade which began to arrive in Japan from 18 May 1946 onward. They were lucky not to have made two shifts but moved straight to their permanent locations. Brigade Headquarters was located at Matsue, a pleasant spot on the western coast of Japan, while the two battalions were located, 5/1 Punjab at Tottori and 1/5 Mahrattas at Hamada, on the same coast. 2/5 Gurkhas went to Okayama as Divisional reserve.

TAKING OVER OF THE NEW AREA

The Okayama area was taken over formally by Brindiv from United States 24th Division by 1715 hours on 11 June 1946. Major-General James Lester, Commander of the United States Division, visited 7th Light Cavalry on 29 May 1946, and attended a regimental durbar. On his departure, a guard of honour was provided by 429 Field Company. The parade was a great success and was followed by a volley-ball match with the United States Anti-Tank Company which was won by the Indians after an exciting game.

To avoid the dismantling of accommodation as had happened in Hiro area, the accommodation was taken over by Brindiv troops before the withdrawal of the Americans.

By 30 June 1946, most of the units of Brindiv were settled in their permanent locations.

OKAYAMA PREFECTURE

Okayama Prefecture forms a rough square between Hiroshima Prefecture to the west, Tottori Prefecture to the north, Hyogo Prefecture to the east, and the Inland Sea to the south. Distances between north-south and east-west boundaries average some 55

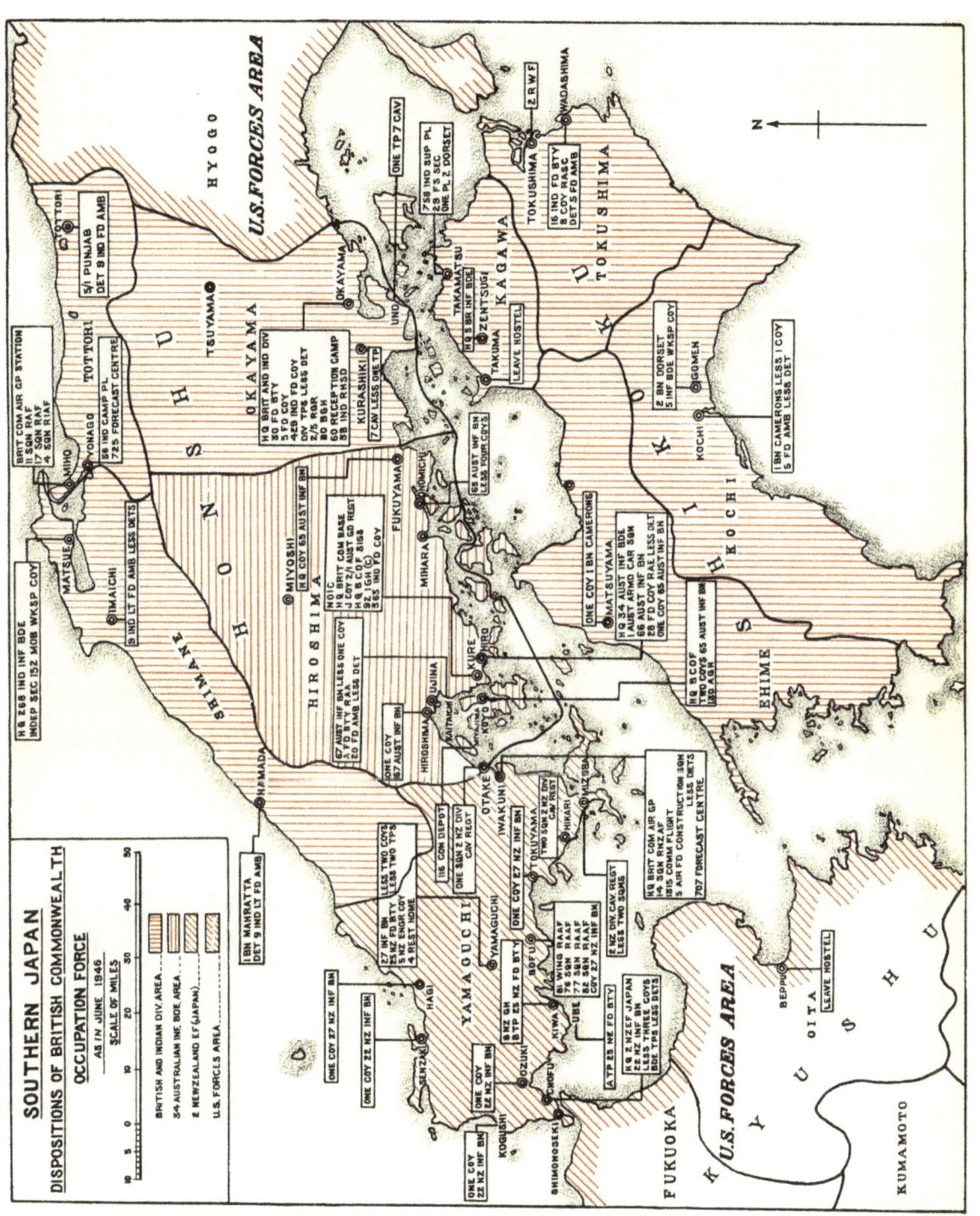

miles. The main lines of communication were from east to west and consisted of the Sanyo Railway system and the Sanyo-Do Highway, both of which extended from Tokyo to Shimonoseki. Two railway lines crossed the prefecture from Okayama to Tottori and Yonago (in the north) and there were several "feeder" lines. Road movement from south to north was limited by difficult natural conditions—narrow, winding tracks, occasional steep inclines and the inevitable paddy fields.

Before the war, Okayama City was the permanent headquarters of a Japanese brigade and a Japanese regiment of the 10th (Himeji) Division. With the movement of this division to China the base at Himeji became the headquarters of a Depot Division and the facilities at Okayama were converted to suit a Regimental Replacement Unit, responsible for raising Japanese "new type" regiments (roughly equivalent to British brigades). A similar organisation for raising engineer units was located at Okayama. Among regiments and engineer units raised there during the war were units of the 54th Division which fought in Burma (154 Infantry Regiment and 54 Engineering Regiment). Other formations raised there fought in Luzon, the Solomons and New Guinea, and in North China, the remainder serving only in Japan. The army barracks were situated on the north-west outskirts of the town. An Ordnance Depot was in the north-eastern sector, in Sanganya area.

This accommodation was taken over by Brindiv for headquarters and divisional troops.

MAINTENANCE

Advance Base Depots were organised in Okayama which were replenished from the Base Depots in Kure—Hiro area. The maintenance channels from Headquarters Brindiv to 5 Brigade were by rail and road to Uno from where the supplies were carried by rail and passenger ferry to Takamatsu on the Shikoku Island, where detachments of maintenance and administrative units were located. From there the forward supplies were by rail. The supply system for 268 Brigade was from Okayama to Yonago and then to the two battalions at Tottori and Hamada direct. Yonago also supplied 4 Royal Indian Air Force Squadron at Miho.

SOME EVENTS

Soon after the arrival of the units in their locations they had to start performing many duties. The first ceremonial in which the Indian troops took part was the celebration of the Empire Day in Tokyo on 22 May 1946. General Northcott, C.B., M.V.O., Commander-in-Chief British Commonwealth Occupation Force, took the salute.

On 16 June 1946, Brigadier Thimayya, D.S.O., commanding 268 Brigade left for Tottori to meet the Commander-in-Chief on his last visit to the Indian Contingent as he was soon returning to Australia to take up his new appointment as Governor of New South Wales. After inspecting 5/1 Punjab at Tottori the General went to Matsue, inspected a Guard of Honour at the railway station and met American and Japanese officials of the prefecture. He stayed on for the night and dined in the Officers' Mess. The Kumaon Band played during the dinner. After completion of his tour he sent the following message:

" Before leaving Japan I wish to thank the Headquarters Staff, Commanders and Staffs and the units of British Commonwealth Occupation Force, for the splendid work that has been done by them during the difficult period of concentrating our force from so many widely scattered parts of the Empire and settling into the occupation areas. The first phase of our task has been successfully accomplished but much remains to be done and I am confident that the same co-operation and loyal support that I have experienced will be afforded to the new Commander-in-Chief, Lieut-General Robertson. The British Commonwealth Occupation Force is a great experiment in the integration of Empire forces and Empire co-operation.

Success is of the greatest importance to the future security of the British Commonwealth of Nations and I hope that every man, whatever his rank or job may be, will wholeheartedly contribute towards its success by his conduct, devotion to duty and by playing the game as a member of this great Empire team. Our association with the United States Forces in the Pacific has been a very happy one. Their co-operation and desire to assist us in the common task of the occupation of Japan has been greatly appreciated by us all and the friendships which have been made will endure long after we have finished our work together. I cannot let this opportunity pass without thanking the British Commonwealth Base troops for the excellent work carried out under most arduous and difficult conditions. In conclusion I wish you all good luck and success to British Commonwealth Occupation Force. Keep the Flag flying ".

During the months of July, August and September 1946 there were many changes in the disposition of troops. 1548 Indian Pioneer Company which was employed at Kure docks for menial work was repatriated back to India because it was considered invidious to have Indian troops doing the same menial work alongside the Japanese. The Indians had resented doing so and their employment was also considered an un-economical commitment.

Brigadier K. S. Thimayya, D.S.O., who had returned from Manilla on 17 July 1946 after attending the Philippines Independence celebrations, received orders of another posting in India in December 1946. On his departure he sent the following message to all ranks:

"I have commanded 268 Indian Infantry Brigade for over a year and have now to leave you for another appointment in India. It has been a great honour to me, and I have taken great pride in having under command those Battalions who have distinguished and gallant records in World War II. During our raising in Nasik and subsequently since our arrival in Japan all of you have had a difficult time settling in and now you face a severe winter. In all this time your drill, discipline and your duties of occupation have been of a very high order and you have set and maintained a standard which is difficult to beat. You have won the respect and admiration of the Japanese people and you have therefore kept high the reputation of the Indian Army. I wish to thank you all for the loyalty and co-operation you have shown me and specially my staff who have worked unceasingly on your behalf".

On 21 December 1946, there was a very severe earthquake. At 0411 hours, without warning, the buildings began to rattle like a toy in the hands of a mischievous child. The wooden floors began to move away from under the feet. Chunks of cement began to fall from the walls and all electric fittings began to strike against each other in mad fury. Orders were given to evacuate all buildings. In pitch darkness, all electric power being switched off at the source, everyone rushed towards the doors and windows. At times it appeared as if the sea was rushing in to engulf the whole area and, at others, as if the buildings were going to have a headlong collision with the adjacent hills. Thousands of homeless people were trekking towards higher ground to find refuge, which they knew would not be available. Food, clothes and shelter was the problem, to solve which British Commonwealth Occupation Force rose to the occasion. Supplies of all kinds, thousands of blankets, warm garments, and tons of foodstuffs were rushed to Shikoku by air.

British and Indian troops who garrisoned this island gave away their rations to feed the hungry. They provided them shelter in their own billets, gave them warm clothes to wear. The doctors worked day and night to inoculate the masses against the spread of cholera and other infectious diseases. The gratitude of the Japanese masses at this prompt help given without any obligation, was to be seen to be believed.

On 19 January 1947 sudden orders were received for the withdrawal of 5 (British) Infantry Brigade from Japan to Malaya. This put further pressure on the Indian troops, who had to move to Shikoku Island to guard the installations being left behind by the British. The withdrawal of 5 Infantry Brigade was completed during February and only small detachments of Indian troops and AMG were left behind. Subsequently, however, it was decided to post 34 Australian Infantry Brigade in Shikoku and Indian detachments were withdrawn as soon as stores were removed and installations closed.

With the withdrawal of 5 British Brigade the reorganisation of the forces in British Commonwealth Occupation Force was essential. 34 Australian Infantry Brigade which was located at Hiro became responsible for the Shikoku Island. As this force was short of men it was decided not to locate any major units there, but to supervise by frequent patrolling. At Headquarters British Commonwealth Occupation Force, the formation of a Headquarters Land Forces was favoured by Joint Chiefs of Staff, Australia, but strongly opposed by Commander-in-Chief, British Commonwealth Occupation Force, who believed that it would fail to relieve Headquarters British Commonwealth Occupation Force of its administrative work but would rather duplicate it. The withdrawal of 5 Brigade had also the effect of disbanding the Brindiv. But the Indian Contingent was still there and it was almost one-third of the total Commonwealth Occupation Force in Japan. A plan of reorganisation was suggested by which the Indian force would have effective representation at Headquarters British Commonwealth Occupation Force. It was proposed that—

(a) the Units of Brindiv remaining in Japan should form 268 Indian Infantry Brigade Group, and its Commander, who, General Robertson insisted, should be an Indian, should be the " national representative ";

(b) the appointment of AA and QMG at Headquarters Britcom Base, Kure, should be held by an officer of the Indian Army.

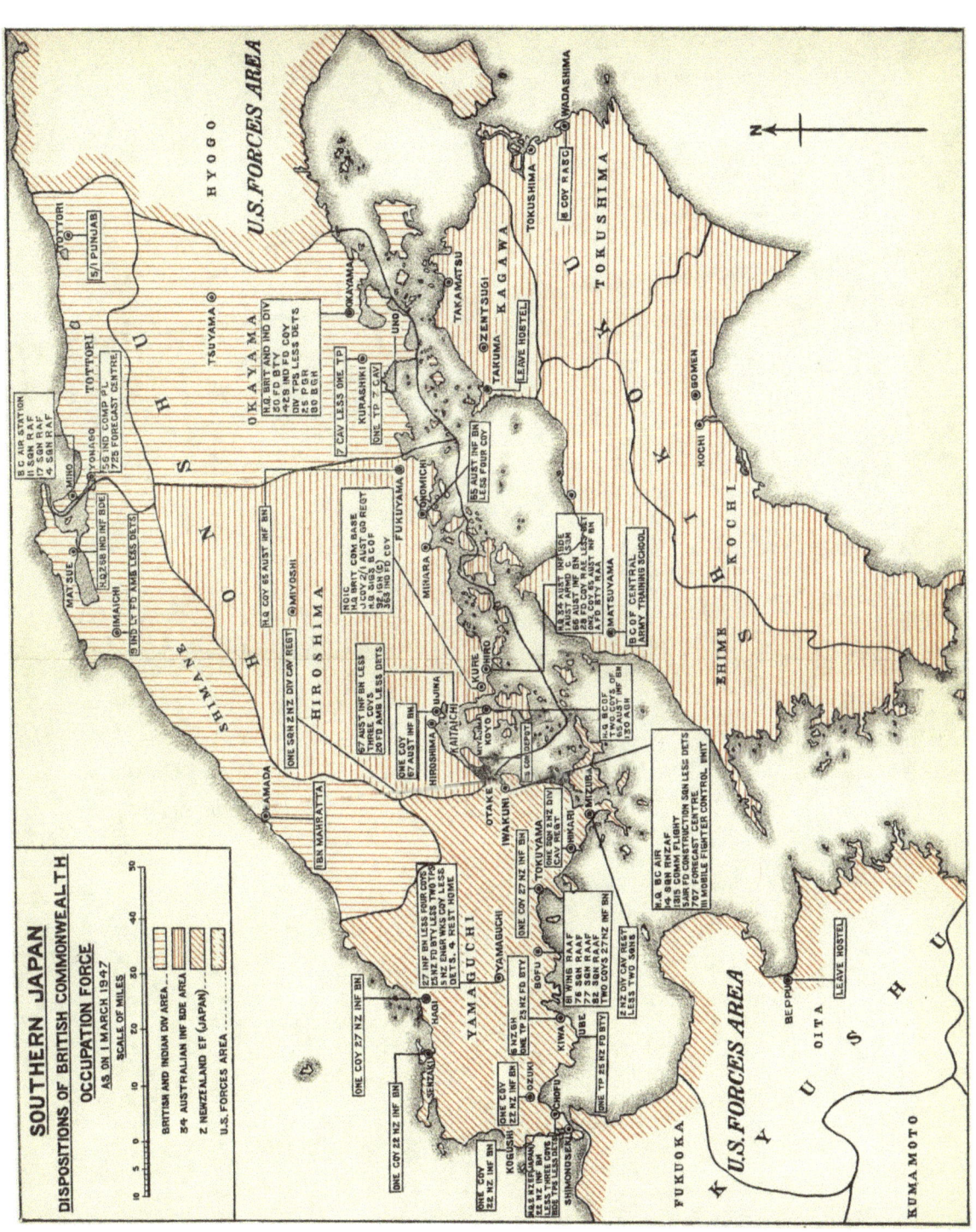

The proposal to appoint a Principal Administrative Officer at Headquarters British Commonwealth Occupation Force and to upgrade it to Major-General was turned down by General Robertson.

Brigadier S. M. Shrinagesh (later General) who had taken over command of 268 Brigade in January 1947, was selected to command the 268 Brigade Group to be formed by the amalgamation of certain divisional units with the existing units of 268 Brigade. On 12 March 1947, he took over command from Major-General Cowan, who sent the following message to all ranks:

" On my departure from Japan I wish all members of Brindiv past and present ' *Au Revoir* ' and the very best of good luck.

I can express my feelings on departure by saying to you all, men and women of Brindiv, how deeply I have appreciated your very loyal support, co-operation and hard work throughout our time together. As a result of the team work of the Brindiv family your reputation stands high amongst the occupational forces in Japan. I leave you under the command of my friend Brigadier S. M. Shrinagesh, your new Commander, secure in the knowledge, that you will support him as well as you have backed me throughout my period of command. Thank you ".

The following signal was sent to Major-General D. T. Cowan on board the ship H. T. *Ranchi* from Brigadier Shrinagesh:

" On behalf of the officers, VCOs and ORs of 268 Indian Infantry Brigade I would like to express our deep regret on the breaking up of a famous division whose name will always remain in history. I would like also to convey to you and your staff our deep sense of appreciation and gratitude for all that you have done for us. No troops have been better cared for or in better mettle than those of Brindiv under command, this speaks volumes for the work you and your staff have done in overcoming the difficulties that beset British Commonwealth Occupation Force when the force first moved in. To you personally we offer our warm appreciation of your brilliant leadership and submit that we have been proud to serve under you. On behalf of all members of Brindiv remaining behind in Japan we wish you *bon voyage*, a happy reunion with your family and a good, well-earned leave ".

On 19 March 1947, 268 Brigade Headquarters moved from Matsue to take over Brindiv responsibility in Okayama while 9th Light Field Ambulance from Imaichi moved in its place.

With the withdrawal of Headquarters 268 Brigade from the north coast more districts (*Guns*) were allotted to units in that area.

From 1 May 1947, Brindiv was dissolved and 268 Brigade Group came into being. An Order of Battle as on 30 June 1947, is in Appendix 'F'. As the war establishment of this Group was not published till about the middle of September 1947, many officers and ranks had to be held on the old divisional establishment which created a lot of misunderstanding and heart-burning among the officers.

Along with the complete control of the three prefectures passing over to the Indian formation, the units themselves were being completely nationalised, and every officer helped to make this first Indian formation overseas a great success.

With the achievement of Independence in August 1947, it was decided to withdraw the Indian Contingent from Japan. The Shimane Prefecture was taken over by BCAIR and Okayama Prefecture passed to the 34 Australian Infantry Brigade. By 25 October 1947, the whole of the Indian Contingent was withdrawn from Japan.

CHAPTER IX

Responsibilities of Brindiv in Japan

Each formation was allotted an area in which it was responsible for operational duties, internal security, occupational duties, and general duties. The original area allotted to Brindiv was approximately the eastern half of Hiroshima and Shimane Prefectures but with effect from 1 June 1946 the Prefectures of Shimane, Tottori, Okayama and the island of Shikoku, an area of approximately 14,000 square miles and containing at least 6 million inhabitants, were placed under Brindiv.

This area was subdivided as follows:—

    5 (Br.) Infantry Brigade—Shikoku island

    268 (Ind.) Infantry Brigade (Less one battalion)—Shimane, Tottori.

    Divisional troops (plus one battalion)—Okayama.

The layout within the prefectures was throughout based on battalion garrisons with an occasional company detachment in order to cover satisfactorily the large area.

By the end of June 1946, the divisional troops, which had been so far located in the Hiro area, completed their move to Okayama while the British Brigade had already occupied Shikoku island. The Indian Brigade on arrival in Japan moved direct to its new locations.[1]

The proper control of this large area depended on good means of communication and availability of transport.

COMMUNICATIONS IN BRINDIV AREA

Except for rail, other communication facilities in Japan were poor. Moreover 5 (Br.) Brigade in Shikoku was completely isolated from the Brindiv units located on Honshu island by the Inland Sea. The development of the communication system was *Priority One* on United States Eighth Army list of developments.

Road Communications:[2] Due to scarcity of space and lack of level areas, the roads in Japan are very narrow and run along steep embankments and through numerous tunnels. During the summer months it was possible to use 15 cwts trucks and Jeeps on the roads between large towns, but large convoys with heavier loads were out

---

[1] For dispositions as in June 1946 see map opposite p. 100.
[2] For road communications in British Commonwealth Occupation Force Area see map opposite page 109.

of the question owing to the sandy nature of the top surface, which disintegrated very quickly, and the weak wooden tressle bridges. During the winter months only Jeeps could be used on those roads which had not been blocked by land-slides or snow.

United States Eighth Army started an ambitious road repair plan throughout Japan together with re-classification and road marking schemes. But as blast and road-making materials were scarce progress was very slow and effort was mainly concentrated on highways which interconnected important centres. Reconnaissance of all roads in Brindiv area was carried out. These were properly marked and all bridges indicated with their load carrying capacity. Roads were the second best means of communication.

Railway Communications: As road communication in Japan was relatively poor it was necessary to rely largely on the railway for the movement of troops and supplies, especially in the winter months. The Japanese railways were fortunately excellent and it was very easy to move troops, vehicles and stores by this means as all important towns were interlinked by a well controlled railway system.

The railway system in Japan was controlled by United States Eighth Army, Railway Division, which had its control offices at all important centres. In the British Commonwealth Occupation Force area, Headquarters British Commonwealth Occupation Force Movement Control Organisation handled all movements of whatever force by rail within its area. All operating staff was Japanese, and the trains were run by the Japanese Government Railways. Movement of personnel was made possible by:

(a) Running special trains for Allied personnel only. No Japanese were permitted to board these trains. In the beginning all travel on such trains was free for all Allied personnel, but from March 1947 all railway movement was on payment. Travelling Cash Vouchers could be purchased by the Allied personnel with occupation currency.

(b) *Reserved Accommodation*: In other areas where Allied traffic was not so great, railway accommodation was reserved in certain trains.

(c) *Requisitioned Accommodation*: As and when necessary railway accommodation could be requisitioned from the Japanese Government Railways through United States Eighth Army.

Sea Communications: As Japan is a land of scattered islands with a vast coast-line it had a highly developed coastal mercantile marine. This was taken over by the occupation authorities.

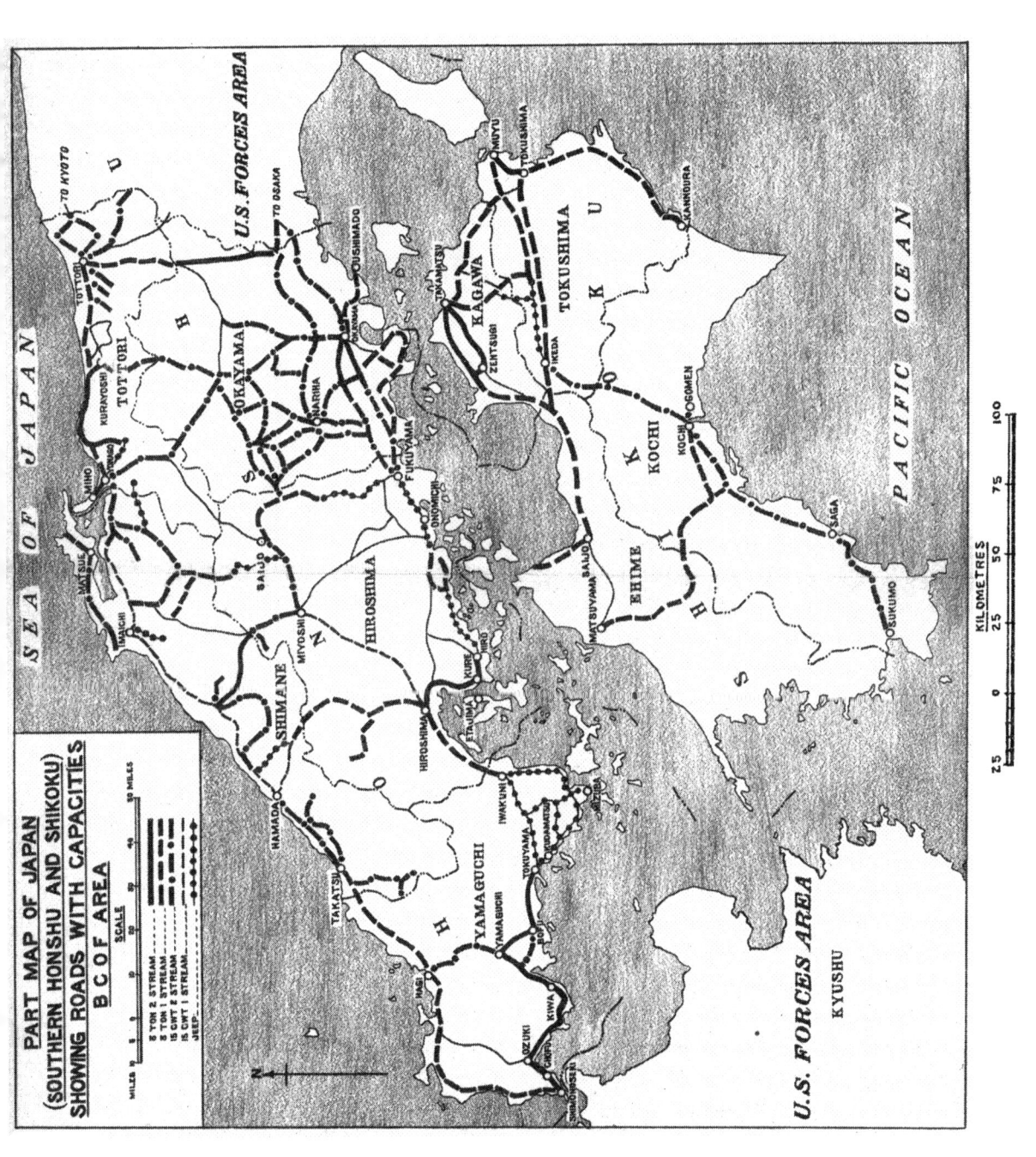

In Brindiv area the sea communications were important because all supplies and maintenance had to go from Honshu to Shikoku by sea. Bulk supplies were delivered direct from Kure, while the daily maintenance was through Uno ferry terminus to Takamatsu. The sea journey from Uno or Kure took approximately six hours in passenger ferries but in fast motor-boats it could be done in three hours.

Air Communications: There were a certain number of airfields for both Dakotas and light aircraft at Okayama, Tokushima, Goman, Kochi and Miho which were maintained in good condition.

TRANSPORT

Road Transport: Before the Indian Contingent left India it was given the wrong information that roads in Japan were of good quality. Brindiv was accordingly equipped with heavier type vehicles, which in Japan could be used only in important towns but could not be moved across country. The only vehicle found suitable in the narrow, winding roads of Japan was the Jeep and, even where heavier vehicles could ply, they had to be four-wheel drive due to the poor surface of the roads. As Jeeps in India were in short supply the operational efficiency of the force suffered a great deal.

Rail Transport: On the other hand, the rail transportation system was very efficient and plenty of stock was available. It was undoubtedly a very sensible move to avoid the bombing of Japanese railway communications during the war, as without these it would have been impossible to carry out any large move. Rail accommodation was good and steam heated during winter months and the trains were always punctual. The Japanese railway staff was most efficient.

Sea Transport: Movement by sea was limited due to the scarcity of landing craft. This deficiency was made good by procuring Japanese craft and rehabilitating them for the use of occupation troops. About 80 craft were requisitioned by Brindiv to be used for maintenance, patrolling and recreation. The crew were always Japanese, supervised by a Transportation Non-Commissioned Officer.

Air Transport: Due to the lack of aircraft and persistent bad weather no great use was made of this type of transportation but in an emergency the Air Force Transportation Squadron could be called in to assist.

OPERATIONAL DUTIES

For operational duties Brindiv was under command of British Commonwealth Occupation Force, which in turn was controlled by United States Eighth Army.

In view of their rapid demobilisation and the destruction of military stores and equipment it was considered doubtful if the Japanese could resort to large-scale armed revolution. But this contingency could not be completely ignored. All units had to prepare "Keep" schemes and had to practise them regularly. Throughout Brindiv's stay in Japan there was never any danger of an uprising. But there was a greater danger, that of ever recurring natural disasters in Japan. The British Commonwealth Occupation Force area was particularly subject to severe typhoons. It is however believed that adequate measures were available to meet the problems arising out of the natural calamities. Each area had a Disaster Plan[3] which was to be put into operation the moment the warning order was received from the Japanese Warning System. On the warning being issued everyone had to take precautions, but in over-crowded, over-populated Japan it was difficult to get away. No place was safe. The Japanese police and civil authorities always co-operated with the occupation forces in carrying out practices and putting the plans into action.

On 29 July 1946 a typhoon warning was received from the Japanese meteorological centre, and troops, Japanese police and civilians were alerted. Strong gales at 50 miles per hour started in the evening and by midnight a violent typhoon was raging. No one had a wink of sleep in pitch darkness, all electric power having been cut off. All the low lying areas were flooded and the howling wind kept blowing the whole night. Luckily the morning was quiet and damage was negligible.

A more severe typhoon struck the southern coast of Japan, particularly Tokyo area, on 17 September 1947, when the fierce "Kathleen", code-name for the typhoon, hit Atami and Kawana areas. The incessant rain for many days flooded the rivers, which broke their embankments and washed away thousands of houses and miles of precious paddy.

Despite all this loss of life and property and complete paralysis of communications, there was never any breach of peace and troops had never to be called out to quell disturbances. This speaks very highly for Japanese self-control and discipline.

---

[3] Disaster Plan 268 Brigade Group in Appendix 'G',

INTERNAL SECURITY

Maintenance of internal security was by far the greatest problem in Japan. The internal conditions in the country were not stable, and could not be, after a major defeat which had followed great destruction of life and property, and most important of all, economic dislocation. The problem of internal security was varied and required constant vigilance and immediate action to nip trouble in the bud.

Security in the area of Brindiv responsibility was achieved by:—

(a) *Having a network of intelligence centres:* These centres were manned by Combined Inter-Services Detailed Interrogation Centre personnel who were assisted in this task by American Counter Intelligence Corps and Japanese police.

(b) *Garrisoning important centres:* Garrisons were located at all important communication centres and at the seats of Japanese civil government.

(c) *Patrolling:* All outlying areas were constantly patrolled in Jeeps and on foot.

(d) *Flag marches:* Units carried out flag marches in their respective areas at reasonable intervals. These marches restored confidence in the local population, who had anticipated a hostile attitude on the part of the occupation troops.

(e) *Checks and searches:* Regular checks and searches were carried out by units and formations.

Each garrison had a security scheme, which was based on the overall divisional security scheme. The infantry battalion in Okayama was the divisional reserve and each garrison had a " mobile reserve " ready to move out by rail, road or air to the assistance of the neighbouring garrison or garrisons.

As armoured cars could only operate in the Okayama area and certain parts of Shikoku island, 7th Light Cavalry was based outside Okayama with a squadron on the island of Shikoku.

The problem of the Koreans: The Koreans in Japan were the cause of some trouble. Many of them indulged in criminal activities and often duped the Japanese. In the beginning they claimed privileges as " Allied Nationals ", who could not be apprehended by Japanese police under Japanese law, but later, with the clarification of their position, they were brought to book. But the Japanese police did not dare to take action against them without the support of the occupation forces. Many Koreans had to be kept under surveillance and constant patrolling and checks had to be carried out to break their combines and prevent them from criminal action. They were also guilty of inducing illegal Korean immigration into Japan. Supreme Commander Allied Powers had decided to repatriate every Korean who did not want to be a Japanese citizen back to Korea and declared all unauthorised Korean immigration illegal. It was therefore necessary for the occupation troops to blockade all ports of entry and apprehend the blockade runners.

Illegal Korean immigration: The Koreans mostly came from the southern part of Korea, which was in the occupational zone of United States Eighth Army, but it was not possible for American forces located there alone to frustrate every attempt at blockade-running as the coast-line was very long and the resources very limited. The Korean technique was to make all arrangements secretly in some remote village in Korea from where the junk usually left in darkness. If detected, all occupants will give out that they were fishermen going out to sea for a night catch. If they were lucky to get through the intercepting naval patrols, they landed on the Japanese coast in darkness. Shimonoseki in Japan was the nearest place from Korea and the trip in the junk took about six hours if the sea was calm. Therefore the whole operation was completed under the cover of darkness and detection was made more difficult as no night air reconnaissance was possible.

The blockade-running used to start generally after the monsoons; it began in August and lasted till October, when the seas again became too rough for junks to hazard the journey. The immigrants generally landed in the Prefecture of Yamaguchi, New Zealand area of responsibility, and from there infiltrated into other areas overland. The reasons for running the blockade were:
    (i) better food conditions in Japan,
    (ii) black-market activities under the impression that they would not be apprehended, and
    (iii) escaping the economic mess in Korea.

Prices paid for the trip were fantastic and, in most cases, all family possessions were sold to pay for the passage. The escapes after landing in Japan were well organised and the general impression was that these were supported by the Communists.

In order to stop this illegal traffic it was necessary:
    (i) To carry out patrolling of the China Sea, between Korea and Japan. This was done by units of the Pacific Fleet, which had ships from the American, British and Indian navies.
    (ii) To carry out air reconnaissance patrols. This was carried out by air forces based on Miho. 4 Squadron

Royal Indian Air Force which was stationed there did this task admirably.

(iii) To carry out coastal patrols. This was done by infantry units located in Shimane and Tottori Prefectures in patrol boats, which were procured from the Japanese.

(iv) To institute a good warning system. As soon as information was received about a suspected boat it was passed to the Japanese police, and the nearest occupation forces. This system was poor in the beginning but when the Japanese police were placed on the occupation forces warning system the results were good.

(v) To use search patrols. Once the Koreans were landed it was necessary to search and apprehend them. This was done by the Japanese police assisted by troops.

(vi) To use interception patrols. In order to discourage blockade running it was necessary to intercept and seize the junks. This was done during the day time on the return journey to Korea by air and sea patrols.

(vii) To repatriate apprehended Koreans. All illegal immigrants had to be transported to Senzaki in Yamaguchi Prefecture, where a repatriation camp was built for them.

With the introduction of a quick warning system, with patrols constantly on the alert and with the full co-operation of the local Japanese population all blockade-runners, who landed in Brindiv area, were easily caught.

Patrolling: Prevention is better than cure and it was necessary to patrol constantly the area of responsibility for any sign of unrest or illegal activities. Such patrolling was generally carried out by parties in jeeps or on foot. The main tasks were to check the towns and villages for Korean immigrants, black-market activities and civilian unrest. They had also to reconnoitre and report on the condition of communicatons. The Japanese police always assisted in these checks and accompanied all patrols. They were of great help in detecting many cases of illegal sale of War Department property. The co-operation shown by the Japanese officials and police throughout the period of occupation was highly satisfactory. They made genuine efforts to carry out all orders and instructions by Brindiv. The Japanese police was both capable and efficient considering the relatively small size of the force and the lack of transport, which made them comparatively immobile.

Due to this constant vigilance the situation throughout the area remained generally quiet and there was never an indication that the Japanese civilian population would cease to co-operate with the occupation forces. There were hardly half a dozen cases of insubordination and insolence and the culprits were generally the Koreans.

OCCUPATIONAL DUTIES

The occupation duties related to Supreme Commander Allied Powers directives regarding the occupation and to insuring that they were being carried out by the Japanese. The occupation troops had to protect Allied life and property, which meant provision of guards and patrolling. The most important duty was detection of crime.

Detection of Crime: Counter Intelligence Corps and Combined Intelligence Service Detailed Interrogation Centre were mainly responsible for this task but the occupation troops helped to keep a check of the vast area.

The incidence of crime in Japan was relatively small and generally involved theft of property, mainly foodstuffs and clothes. Japanese police was generally able to trace every culprit and once apprehended, the Japanese generally confessed the crime and disclosed all connecting links.

The cases were tried by Provost Courts composed of Allied officers, and the accused had to serve sentences in Japanese prisons, where the prisoners had to provide their own food. As these thefts were mainly to obtain food, imprisonment was a very severe punishment. 256 such cases were tried by Provost Courts in Brindiv area.

With the spread of poverty and increasing scarcity of food and clothing crime increased among Koreans, who instigated Japanese juveniles to carry out their nefarious designs.

Disposal of Japanese war equipment: The location and disposal of Japanese war material was an important function of the Intelligence Staff. As these dumps were scattered over a large area, a comprehensive Intelligence Directive was issued to all units so that all ranks could assist in the detection of war material and the tabulation of information.

The Disposal of Enemy Equipment Section was responsible for the co-ordination of all activities connected with the disposal of Japanese equipment. Large quantities of arms and ammunition were traced and destroyed. These included such items as 3,000 twelve-inch naval shells and air-bombs and mines, which were disposed of by dumping in the sea. Extensive patrolling had to be carried out to check new undisclosed " targets ".[4] Though a thorough search of the area was carried out, no clandestine dumps were revealed.

Supervision of repatriated Japanese soldiers: Another important function of the Brindiv was to supervise the repatriation of a large number of Japanese soldiers who were repatriated through Hiroshima, where a Japanese agency carried out all functions of documentation, medical examination and delousing. Each repatriate was supplied with fresh civilian clothes, three days' ration and was then sent to his bombed-out home. The arrangements at Repatriation Centre, Ujina, were perfect. The repatriated soldiers did not show any sign of hostility but adopted an attitude of resignation. They were under the impression that they would not be tolerated by their own people as defeated soldiers. Hence the Japanese authorities in all towns and villages used to arrange social gatherings with light musical entertainment and refreshments to remove this impression of being " un-wanted " from the minds of the demobilised soldiers.

Ex-servicemen seemed to settle down well and never gave evidence of any subversive activities or gave trouble to the local authorities, though in many cases they had to undergo great hardship owing to scarcity of food and clothing. The pinch of winter and the shortage of housing made the problem still worse but the Japanese authorities tackled this problem bravely by rigidly rationing the housing accommodation and distributing old converted uniforms. It was necessary to keep a strict watch over the activities of ex-servicemen and to prevent them from joining hostile bodies or criminal gangs. The Japanese authorities tried to rehabilitate them and provided for their amusement and uplift through various societies for cultural instruction.

Guard duties in Tokyo: In addition to the normal guard duties in their own area Brindiv had to provide a Guard Battalion by rotation in Tokyo. This was a very important feature of the occupation and most of the units were able to mount guard at the Imperial Palace, Tokyo, twice during their tenure of duty in Japan.

Gurkhas in Tokyo: 2 Dorsets from 5 Brigade were the first Brindiv unit to mount guard in Tokyo. 2/5 Gurkhas took over the guard duties from them, and from 21 July 1946 mounted guard at:
    Imperial Palace
    Ebisu Camp Quarter Guard
    British Embassy

---

[4] "Target" meant a location of Japanese equipment of any kind for disposal.

Meiji Shrine
Empire House
Canadian Legation
Yasakusi Shrine.

During the changing of the Guard the Battalion Pipe-Band played and a large crowd of spectators with a battery of cameras witnessed this spectacle. Rifleman (64138) Budhi Bahadur Thapa had the distinction of being the first Indian soldier to be posted as a sentry at the gate of the Imperial Palace, Tokyo.

On 6 August 1946 the unit carried out a ceremonial parade at which the salute was taken by Major-General D. T. Cowan, C.B., D.S.O., M.C. The parade was followed by a massed retreat which provided a grand spectacle for thousands of Allied and Japanese nationals.

During their stay in Tokyo the Gurkhas made good contacts with the American forces. A " Country Fair " was organised for their benefit by the American Red Cross in Yokohama, where men were served with ice-cream and pop-corn.

On 2 September 1946 the Gurkhas in Tokyo were relieved by 65 Australian Infantry Battalion. The Guards at the Imperial Palace and British Embassy were changed ceremonially, and afterwards the Brass Band of the Australian Unit marched the Gurkhas to the station.

1 Punjab in Tokyo

5/1 Punjab took over guard duties from 2 Battalion Welch Fusiliers in Tokyo and the Commanding Officer reported to Brigadier General Hugh Hoffman at 2 Cavalry Brigade Headquarters. The battalion mounted guard at " Meiji Shrine " and " Akasaka Palace ". A detachment for Tokyo Guard was also selected from 429 Field Company Indian Engineers which took over guard duties at Canadian Legation, British Embassy and Imperial Palace.

On 6 January 1946, 66 Australian Infantry Battalion took over guard duties from 5/1 Punjab. On the completion of duties in Tokyo many congratulatory messages were received. General Hoffman, Commanding General 1st Brigade of 1st United States Cavalry Division wrote:

"During the recent war we read of the hard fighting engaged in by men of the 1st Punjab Regiment. Their operations at Rangoon and Ramree Island added brilliant pages to the long history of the Regiment. I consider it an honour to have your 5th Battalion of the Punjabis under my operational control during last month. The occupational duties assigned to your battalion while in Tokyo were performed in an excellent manner. The state of discipline and the soldierly appearance of your men were outstanding. We have enjoyed our association with you and when you return for another tour of duty in Tokyo we will extend a hearty welcome to the wearers of the elephant and the dragon ".

The following message was received from Major-General Chase W. Rydr, Commander United States Army IX Corps:

" It is with pleasure that I add my expression of appreciation of your fine performance of duty during the recent association of your battalion with the troops of my command ".

Mahrattas in Tokyo

On 6 March 1947, 1 Mahrattas took over guard duties from the 3rd New Zealand Battalion. The Kumaon Band was in attendance when the guard at the Plaza of the Imperial Palace took over duties from the Maori Company of New Zealand Division Cavalry. The parade was witnessed by a very large and cosmopolitan crowd, firstly because for the first time a holder of Victoria Cross was on parade, and secondly because it was also the first time that the people of Tokyo were going to witness Indian troops wearing hackles.

On 3 March 1947 the Mahrattas provided a Guard of Honour for the New Zealand Minister of Defence, Mr. Frederick Jones and the Army Chief of Staff, Major-General Weir.

The unit received great co-operation from United States 7th and 8th Cavalry Regiments. As a gesture of courtesy for their valuable help in making a loan of their parade ground and supplying transport, the Mahrattas gave them a display of " Malkhamb ", " Lezim " and wrestling at Headquarters 8th United States Cavalry Regiment lines, which was a great success.

Gurkhas again in Tokyo

During April 1947, 2/5 Gurkhas were again detailed for guard duties in Tokyo, their last turn before departure from Japan. They took over from the 4th New Zealand Guard Battalion on 30 May 1947. On 12 June 1947, the unit took part in the King's Birthday parade. A Gurkha officer described the occasion thus: " Finally 12th June arrived and a large convoy was seen to leave Embisu Camp for the Imperial Palace Plaza where we debussed and formed up. With us was a troop from 30 Field Battery RA, and as we waited for the arrival of General Robertson, we were amazed at the number of star-bearing cars which, for twenty long minutes, drew up to the spectators' stand in a continuous stream. There were Generals from all nations and even Russia put in an appearance.

At 1015 hours the Commander-in-Chief arrived, received the General Salute, and then took command of the parade. The firing of the "feu de joie" by the 25's (25-pounders) and our own rifles went off very well and the three cheers for His Majesty was as hearty as it could have been. The guns marched past to the band of the Royal Northumberland Fusiliers and were followed by ourselves headed by the Pipe Band, wearing their new Glengarries. The men marched excellently, and their arms drill left nothing to be desired".

On 24 June 1947 Gurkhas took part in a unique parade when Jemadar Gaje Ghale VC and 50 Gurkhas and a similar number of Americans carried out a combined Guard Mounting Ceremony on the Imperial Palace Plaza.

1 Punjab in Tokyo
On 1 July 1947, 5/1 Punjab took over guard duties from the Gurkhas who left for Okayama to pack and get ready for the move to India.

Guard duties at Headquarters British Commonwealth Occupation Force (Etajima): Each formation in turn provided a ceremonial guard company at Headquarters British Commonwealth Occupation Force. Due to scarcity of space and non-availability of facilities for Indian troops there was no Indian guard at Etajima till May 1947. Then the first detachment was provided by 5/1 Punjab. As this was the first time that an Indian Guard Company was mounted at British Commonwealth Occupation Force, initially serious difficulty arose about accommodation.

In June 1947, a Company of 1 Mahrattas took over Guard duties at Etajima from 5/1 Punjab. The detachment remained there for six weeks.

On 7 July 1947 the Kumaon Band played Retreat as 1 Mahrattas changed the guard for the last time at Headquarters British Commonwealth Occupation Force. The salute was taken by Air Vice-Marshal Bladin, O.B.E., Chief of Staff, British Commonwealth Occupation Force.

Guards on trains: All occupation trains carrying stores had to be escorted by occupation troops, as there was considerable pilfering in transit and strict precautions were essential.

Escorts for war Criminals: Many escorts were provided by the Indian Guard Battalion in Tokyo to convey the Japanese suspected of war crimes from Iugamo Prison, Tokyo, to Air Transit Centre, Iwakuni.

Punitive action: In order to maintain law and order punitive action had to be taken against various types of peoples and parties.

The most active party in Japan were the Communists, but they were always afraid of being " suspected " and carried out most of their activities underground. They were suspected of having direct liaison with Russian controlled Korea through Korean immigrants. But the Communists never gave any trouble and confined their activities to propaganda and electioneering campaigns and organising the dissatisfied unemployed labour. It was feared that they would gain more following and power in the future.

The ultra-nationalists who were not war criminals had adopted a non-committal attitude and had mostly retired in seclusion. The wanted war criminals were easily and quickly apprehended as they always gave themselves up.

Schools and factories were also checked to ensure that no ultra-national or underground activities were being carried out. These checks were most repugnant to the Indian troops, and when 268 Brigade Group was formed these checks were stopped.

GENERAL DUTIES

Suppression of Black-Market Activities in Japan: As food was scarce in Japanese towns, and clothing and other necessities of life were not available in the villages, there was a thriving two-way black-market trade for the exchange of village food surplus with the town manufactures. This trade was generally carried out by Koreans, who were in most cases armed. The Japanese police was at first reluctant to take action against them because the Koreans claimed to be Allied instead of Japanese nationals. But with Supreme Commander Allied Powers clarification of this point, and moral support from occupation troops, the Japanese police got to grip with the problem.

In certain cases it was found necessary to station small detachments—about one platoon in strength, at the ferry terminals or railway junctions to stop illegal movement of controlled items. In order to bring down prices to a legitimate scale all stall proprietors were ordered to display a price-card on each article for sale and these were checked by police and troops with very good results.

But as local manufactured goods became scarce another channel for black-marketing was opened by stealing and selling War Department goods. These stores had to be properly guarded but as stores were scattered over wide areas with limited manpower available to guard them, the locals with good knowledge of the layout of the camp could pilfer them at will.

Supervision of Japanese general elections: The greatest event of political importance, during the occupation of Japan by Indian troops, occurred during April 1947 when the whole of Japan went to the poll to elect a democratic Diet. The elections were covered by eighteen Intelligence teams both during the pre-election campaign and on 10 April, the polling day. One week later five officers covered the area again to make a first-election survey of public opinion and opinions of local officials. These observations pointed clearly to two distinct attitudes amongst the Japanese towards these elections. Firstly, keen interest in the Village Head and Gubernatorial election, and an even greater zeal in the Village and Prefectural Assembly elections. Secondly, almost complete apathy in respect of the House of Councillors' election, and only a little more interest in the House of Representatives' election.

An estimate of the character of elections and the feelings of the people is gleaned from the following observations of the British Commonwealth Occupation Force Intelligence Team:—

"The reason for this is clearly understandable, and was reiterated time and time again by the more enlightened people in the Prefecture, i.e. the Prefecture is inhabited by a large proportion of low-educated peasantry, whose thoughts do not go beyond the confines of their own village, Gun, or at the most, Prefecture. Consequently, the local Village Head and Village Assembly elections held for them a great deal of interest, because the candidates were all people they knew personally. In these elections, there were practically no party affiliations among the candidates, and the voters made their vote according to their own personal knowledge of the candidate's character during the past. When Election Committee chiefs were asked by Observer Teams whether Village Assembly candidates belonged to any particular political party, they were invariably surprised, or half-amused, as if to indicate that party affiliation as a qualification could be of no possible use to a candidate. The general answer was that no candidates whatever were politically attached, and even if they were, the voters, being ignorant peasants, would not appreciate the significance of this or that party.

"Consequently, the campaigns for the councillors' and Representatives' elections being based on party politics, something almost incomprehensible to the average peasant of this Prefecture—apathy was understandable. In the case of the Representatives, however, there were many candidates to each Gun,[5] which narrowed down the geographical sphere somewhat, and in some cases, candidates were personally known

---

[5] Constituency.

in various villages of the Gun. This accounted for the somewhat greater interest in the Representatives' as against the Councillors' election.

"The efforts of Election Committees in endeavouring to awaken election interest among the villagers were really praiseworthy, especially where they realised such propaganda was most required—in case of the Councillors' and Representatives' elections. Many were the posters telling women of their voting rights, and exhorting them to take an equal place with the men in the election and use some individuality.

"The conduct and dignity of responsible polling-booth officials on polling days was exemplary, judged even by our own standards. Those voters who did come to vote took the whole business most seriously from the time of entering the polling-booth until leaving it, regarding it as a duty of the utmost dignity.

"Complaints received by Field Security and Military Government teams on the whole seem to indicate, after investigation, that they were mostly unfounded, and the result of some personal feud between two people, invariably caused by the failure of someone, or someone's friend, in the election.

"Almost 100 per cent of the voters were satisfied that the election officials were doing their utmost to ensure a free and fair election, and it is also the opinion of the Observer Teams who worked in nearly all parts of the Prefecture during the month.

"To sum up—electional interest was high where the people thought they had some personal knowledge or basis on which to make a choice fairly; where they felt out of their path— especially in the case of the Councillors' election—they felt it fairer to stay at home and abstain from voting".

Because of the Social Democrat majority in the elections, Premier Yoshida resigned his post as Prime Minister and was replaced by Katayama Tetsu, the leader of the Social Democrat Party. He was the first Christian and Socialist Prime Minister in Japanese history and formed a Coalition Cabinet, with the Socialists, Social Democrats and People's Co-operative Parties. The Liberal Party refused to join the coalition.

LIAISON WITH ALLIED TROOPS

One of the imporant functions of the occupation forces in Japan was to carry out "integration". This could only be permanent and wholesome if there was proper liaison between the various contingents of the Allied forces. Though Headquarters British Commonwealth Occupation Force and the Base units were integrated and Indian ranks in these units could meet the British, Australian and New Zealanders, the units in formations like 268 Brigade had little opportunity of meeting members of other contingents. To counteract this, a method of visiting parties was found useful. 27 New Zealand Battalion which had served with 1 Mahrattas in the Italian Campaign of 1944 sent a party to Hamada to meet old comrades. Similar parties came from other formations. Indian athletic teams took part in many combined shows and gave a good account of themselves.

Liaison with United States Forces was also maintained, particularly when units were stationed in Tokyo. Officers of 7th United States Cavalry paid a liaison visit to the Indian 7th Light Cavalry.

During the visit of HMS *Aanson* and *Barfleur* to Kure, harbour parties of officers and Indian Other Ranks went on board. The reception was well organised and men had tea before leaving the ship. The crew of the ship in turn paid a return call to the units on shore.

Liaison with the Japanese

In the beginning the Japanese civil population was apprehensive of the Indian troops. They had heard much adverse propaganda, but soon learnt how false it was. It took no time for the Japanese to find out, and Indians to express, their true worth. The friendliness and co-operation shown to Indians can to a great extent be attributed to the high discipline of the troops which led to the subsequent disappearance of the initial fear which was entertained by the civil population towards the occupation forces.

The Japanese took to the Indian Sepoy with very great ease and it was common sight, in Matsue, Hamada and Tottori or, wherever an Indian unit was located, for scores of Japanese children to gather round him, take him to places of amusement and try to please him. Beyond this, fraternisation was not permitted.

The liaison with the Japanese civil officials was very satisfactory and they co-operated fully in all functions. The Japanese civil administration was conducted satisfactorily and the officials gave the impression of being both efficient and reliable.

Relations with the Japanese, both official and non-official, were very satisfactory and no cases of friction were reported. The Indians were always greeted with a smile and cheer wherever they went. On many occasions, particularly on the Independence

Day, the Indian troops contributed their sugar and chocolate rations for distribution to the Japanese children, a practice which was commonly adopted throughout British Commonwealth Occupation Force. Band displays were arranged which had great response from the music loving Japanese population. The Japanese arranged many entertainments for the troops in their lines.

CHAPTER X

Navy, Air and Divisional Troops

ROYAL INDIAN NAVY IN JAPAN

HMIS *Godavari* left Hong Kong, where she had been based, on 15 January 1946 on her first visit to Japan, and arrived in Yokohama on 21 January. The ship's cruise in Japanese waters was arranged by S.O. Force "T" in HMS *Tyne* and lasted for ten days which consisted of two days in Toba, four days in Tokyo and the remaining four days in passage. From Toba, a party of officers and men went on an excursion by train to Nagoya; and all were impressed by the standard of the dress and cleanliness of the inhabitants and their very polite behaviour to the ship's company.

The ship's company, however, was not greatly impressed by the visit to Tokyo and Yokohama both of which had been heavily damaged by air raids.

On 30 January 1946, the *Godavari* took on board Colonel Yama, under close arrest, for passage to Hong Kong. Colonel Yama was the head of the Japanese police in Hong Kong for three years during the Japanese occupation, and was classified as a War Criminal No. 1.

At Yokohama, the Captain of *Godavari* made official calls on the heads of the occupation forces including General Douglas MacArthur. She left Yokohama on 31 January 1947 and arrived at Hong Kong on 8 February, having visited Okinawa on the 3rd, 4th and 5th en route. During this passage *Godavari* escorted HMS *Tracian*, a British destroyer which had been captured by the Japanese during the war and had been used as an experimental ship by them. She left Hong Kong for India, via. the Philippines and Malaya, on 12 February 1946 and arrived in Madras on 25 February 1946.

HMIS *Godavari*, then commanded by Commander S. G. Karmarkar, Royal Indian Navy, again left Bombay for the Far East on 1 November 1946 and arrived in Hong Kong on 26 November having had exercises with HM ships off Singapore. Leaving Hong Kong on 2 December she arrived in Kure, Japan, on 7 December, from where she sailed on 11 December to carry out exercises with various HM ships, military units and Royal Marines. On 21 December 1946 Southern Japan was shaken by a very severe earthquake and the *Godavari* was detailed for duty in carrying out relief work in ports which were normally considered inaccessible to shipping.

During January 1947, the ship visited Kochi, Matsuyama, Kure and Iwakuni, and on 21 January was placed in quarantine owing to an outbreak of chicken-pox on board after which period she sailed for Yokohama, Iwakuni and Tokyo. The usual formal calls were made on service and civilian officials in each port. Visits were returned by VIPs, both British and American.

During March 1947, the *Godavari* worked with the United States navy from Sasebo on the Korean patrols for detection of illegal immigration. On 26 April, she sailed for Nanking from Kure, and arrived at that port on 1 May having brought His Excellency the Indian Ambassador from Woosung. She remained at Nanking until 7 May, and then proceeded to Shanghai. The ship's stay at Nanking was marked by intense social activity, and during this time the Captain and Officers were presented to Generalissimo Chiang Kai-shek. The *Godavari* remained at Shanghai until May when she sailed for Hong Kong. On 29 May, she sailed for Singapore leaving the British Pacific Fleet.

4 SQUADRON ROYAL INDIAN AIR FORCE IN JAPAN

The duties of No. 4 Squadron included demonstrations and reconnaissance patrols over certain areas assigned to it. The most important of these patrols were over the coastal areas of Shimane and Tottori Prefectures to prevent illegal immigration of the Koreans into Japan. These patrols were carried out at dawn, noon, and dusk, direct Radio-Telephone contact being maintained with army units at Hamada and Shimane Prefectures and Headquarters 268 Brigade at Matsue. The ground units were equipped with motor-boats to intercept Japanese shipping. The area patrolled was 15 miles out to sea along the Shimane and Tottori coasts, and all Japanese shipping in this area was reported to the above mentioned units.

The record of No. 4 Squadron's occupational tour was marred by one fatal accident in which two pilots were killed. The pilots, Flying Officers Sekhon and Martin, were briefed to do a patrol of the area between Miho and Hiroshima, weather permitting. The weather over base being good, they took off but about twenty-five miles from base it closed in completely and suddenly. The pilots decided to turn back but in doing so it was necessary to climb into cloud to avoid the hills in that region. The aircraft collided in cloud and crashed into the ground killing both the pilots. They were buried with full military honours at Okayama.

The Squadron's activities in the detection of illegal Korean immigration into Japan comprised of reconnaissance off the coast and about 50 miles inside the sea. This was carried out to the satisfaction of the authorities.

General Cawthorn who visited 4 Royal Indian Air Force Squadron at Miho in June 1946 signalled "Royal Indian Air Force Squadron is in good heart and put up an excellent fly-past. Their administration stood comparison well with that of Royal Air Force units in same station".[1]

INTELLIGENCE ACTIVITIES

Two Field Security Sections were attached to the Division, the British section operating on the island of Shikoku and the Indian in the Brindiv area of responsibility on Honshu. Field Security personnel were spread out over the area and maintained close contact with units, the American Counter Intelligence Corps organizations and the Allied Military Government.

Collation of information from the Brindiv area was carried out by Divisional Headquarters Intelligence Staff and passed to British Commonwealth Occupation Force. Information from the whole of Japan was passed in the form of fortnightly reviews to formations and units under command.

Intelligence personnel, in conjunction with Counter Intelligence Corps and Allied Military Government, investigated a number of cases, including illegal sale of Japanese army goods, contravention of Supreme Commander Allied Powers Directives covering elimination of public officials connected with specified organizations, educational subversive organizations, and kindred subjects. Careful watch was kept on certain personalities, generally with a military or official background, and on organizations and societies which appeared suspicious.

The shortage of Japanese speaking officers trained in Intelligence work hampered investigation in many cases, though a number of officers and non-commissioned officers were allotted to the Division by Combined Services Detailed Interrogation Centre. Short courses in the Japanese language were not of much use to Intelligence personnel.

[1] INDEL/83 of 10 June '46,

TRAINING

Owing to heavy duties involved in disembarkation, settling down and occupation duties, and also due to lack of training facilities, no training was carried out when Brindiv was in Hiro area. With the completion of the move to Okayama, Shikoku and the north coast, individual and company training was started in all units. The new area had better facilities for training and had a few small field firing ranges, one of which was suitable for artillery firing.

A divisional school was established in the new area consisting of a Wireless Transmission Wing and a Tactical Wing. At this school personnel from other contingents, Australian and New Zealanders, were also taken. Later this school became a British Commonwealth Occupation Force responsibility.

In addition to the above, there were schools for Physical Training, Driving and Maintenance, Signals, Cooking and Provost.

During the winter, when the snowfall was very heavy, particularly on the north coast, all training had to be carried on indoors. However, a skiing school was started at Mount Daisen which was very popular. During the good weather period, April to October, training was intensified. Each unit organised a camp where each company was sent for a week. A longer stay was not possible owing to the duties in camp.

MANPOWER PROBLEMS

Apart from the general shortage of officers and other ranks in British units there was an ever increasing demand for officers and non-commissioned officers to carry out duties normally performed by sub-area personnel in India, such as Garrison Engineers, Barrack Officers, Labour Officers, etc. A case for additional work sections was put up through Headquarters British Commonwealth Occupation Force, because the one Brindiv works section was completely inadequate to cover the very large area and cope with the enormous amount of construction and maintenance work to be carried out. Officers and non-commissioned officers were provided by RA and other units, but this left them very short of the personnel they most needed to carry out their own training and to maintain their efficiency. Requests were submitted through the usual channels for small increases to War Establishments. But it was practically impossible to cover these additional and essential personnel commitments without an increase in the overall ceiling. Owing to these shortages non-commissioned officers supervised even projects which were valued at approximately 300,000 yen.

In addition, many attempts were made to transfer Indian units to British Commonwealth Occupation Force Order of Battle, and after some discussion certain Indian units were earmarked as Headquarters and Base troops and placed under the functional control of those formations, but their administrative control remained in the hands of the Commander Brindiv.

The greatest shortage was in technical services where personnel could not be replaced from local sources. These difficulties were foreseen in India before the move of the force but increases were not accepted. In the Engineer and Signal services the position remained very critical; this was due to initial deficiencies which were never made good, recurring decreases due to repatriation and release and increased commitments which required an increase in the War Establishment.

As far as Signals were concerned the communications were extensively stretched and commitments at formation Headquarters were very much greater than normal. As a result, though the equipment was for the most part available, the personnel situation remained difficult. The establishment of Division Signals did not include teleprinter operators to operate teletype/printers between division and brigades, and with otherwise heavy commitments it was not possible to spare operators for training. A start was, however, made; three line-men with a knowledge of typing were attached to British Commonwealth Occupation Force Signals for training as teleprinter operators. Moreover, the technical personnel capable of maintaining high powered wireless sets and large switchboards was also lacking.

The units in Japan were never manned up to 100 per cent of establishment. In view of the wide dispersion of the force and its limited tactical and administrative resources it was essential to maintain these units up to the establishment, but because of manpower shortage, General Headquarters (India) decided to restrict the number of Indian Other Ranks in Battalions in Japan to 760 excluding Viceroy's Commissioned Officers and Non-Combatants Enrolled. It was also decided to send back, as soon as possible, subject to the shipping situation, before 1 April 1947, all men who had not deferred their release, even if it meant a severe reduction in numbers. Battalions were, however, assured precedence in reinforcements from India even if it meant posting men from regular battalions.

PLATE IX

Scenes of Earthquake, December 1946

PLATE X

Resettlement Training

Due to this run-down and release of personnel there was a grave shortage of mechanical transport drivers in all units. To meet this deficiency Japanese drivers were employed to run War Department vehicles.

ARMOUR

7th Light Cavalry provided the armour for Brindiv. The Regiment disembarked at Kure on 20 April 1946 and was stationed in Hiro upto 10 May 1946, when it moved to Kurashiki by rail. The main role of the unit during its stay in Japan was:
  (a) To keep one mobile column ready at 6 hours notice. One squadron at a time was detailed to deal with any eventuality. This column was called out only once to assist against some Korean illegal immigrants smuggling black-market stuff.
  (b) To reconnoitre the various routes in Okayama Prefecture. The object was to gain knowledge of the land communications in the area so that armour could be sent quickly to danger spots.
  (c) To raid dumps containing warlike stores. These raids and searches were carried out regularly to locate warlike stores.
  (d) To maintain communications between Honshu (Brindiv Headquarters) and Shikoku (5 Brigade Headquarters). A troop was permanently located at the Ferry Point at Ono.

In addition to the above tactical roles the unit sent detachments to Tokyo for ceremonial parades. On 1 April 1947 this unit, with the United States 7th Cavalry, carried out a combined guard mounting parade in front of the Imperial Palace Plaza in Tokyo. An old cavalry trumpet was presented by it to the United States 7th Cavalry who in turn presented an old troop flag.

With the dissolution of Brindiv, 7th Cavalry was sent back to India for reorganisation. On this occasion the following communique was issued:[2]

" The Governments of United Kingdom, India, Australia and New Zealand in consultation with the Government of the United States have agreed that the 7th Light Cavalry Regiment will return to India from Japan. Post-war reorganisation of the Indian Army necessitates the movement

---
[2] Tel No. COS 1458 dated 1 April 47 from File No. 6325/64 SD5 Serial No. 72A.

of this unit. In the fighting in Burma and Imphal since 1944 this unit had a distinguished record and was later prominent in the spear-head of the advance to Rangoon. Considerable Indian Army forces in 268 Indian Infantry Brigade under Brigadier Shrinagesh and in the British base at Kure together with Squadron of the Royal Indian Air Force will continue to represent India in the British force in Japan ".

ARTILLERY

30 (British) and 16 (Indian) Field Batteries provided artillery support for Brindiv. On arrival in Japan they were first located at Hiro and then moved to Okayama in July 1946. 16 Indian Field Battery later moved to Wadashima, having very good barracks by the sea near Tokushima on Shikoku island. This move, due to the necessity of finding additional accommodation in Okayama, helped to provide covered accommodation for all the 30 Field Battery vehicles.

Both Batteries had an area of Okayama Prefecture to patrol and to submit intelligence reports. This was very popular and provided excellent training in initiative and report writing by young officers and non-commissioned officers. It also enabled each man to feel that he was really taking an active part in the occupation of Japan.

Owing to lack of suitable training areas close at hand, both Batteries in the beginning concentrated on individual training, but later both Batteries used suitable ranges for course shooting and limited manoeuvre, some 30 miles north of Okayama.

Whilst at Hiro, 30 Field Battery celebrated its 150th anniversary with a *feu de joie* and a mounted parade. The salute was taken by the General Officer Commanding British and Indian Division, who complimented the Battery on the high standard of drill, turn-out and driving skill. It was witnessed by a large number of spectators from the Royal Navy, British and Indian Division and 34 Australian Brigade. With the disbandment of Brindiv, 30 Field Battery was transferred to Hong Kong and the 16 Indian Field Battery returned to India.

ENGINEERS

The original decision to send the Works Section with the Advance Party to Japan was changed at the last moment, and 429 Indian Field Company, Madras Sappers and Miners Group, RIE, was included. Unfortunately, the Mechanical Transport ship on which all the vehicles and most of the equipment was being carried broke down and was long delayed.

The shipping of the first maintenance lift of Engineers Stores was a considerable problem as no definite instructions were given up to the last moment owing to the uncertainty of the shipping position. Another difficulty was that while shipping was provided in Bombay, a very high proportion of the mechanical equipment was located near Madras and it was not possible to move it by rail with the result that it arrived in Japan very late.

The Engineer work in Japan mainly comprised the making of Japanese barracks habitable; provision of electricity and water supply, heating and cooking arrangements; road and bridge repairs, provision of messes, canteens and playing fields, the provision of light aircraft landing strips; the construction and maintenance of camp areas and installation of water-borne sewage where possible. This work was partly done by Field Companies but mostly by Japanese contractors under the supervision of 907 Indian Works Section, RIE (See Appendix "H")

The Engineer Stores Depots handled in the first three months more than 5,000 tons and in one year 50,000 tons of stores. This was done by the wholesale employment of Japanese labour under the supervision of the Field Park Company, who handled over 1,200 tons per week (mostly building materials, water and steam pipes and fittings, and electrical gear, 2,500 odd electric and kerosene stoves). The Sappers produced nearly 5,000 coal stoves with above 32 miles of flue piping for space heating.

Engineer stores from Japanese sources were in short supply and were strictly controlled by United States Eighth Army Procurement Section. The following were the most critical items, which formed a bottleneck in construction:

  (a) sawn timber,
  (b) electric stores including bulbs,
  (c) heating and cooking plant,
  (d) glass,
  (e) iron gauze and screens,
  (f) roofing material,
  (g) piping and fittings.

The general engineer policy of the division was to:
  (i) make all barracks and quarters habitable with the minimum of work consistent with a reasonable standard of comfort;
  (ii) after a careful examination of each area and the requirements of the troops occupying the area, make the finished plans for the area;

(iii) having obtained approval for the plans mentioned in (ii) above, carry out the necessary work, at the same time providing all necessary facilities such as sports grounds, leave centres, canteens, clubs, cold stores, ice plants etc.

Twenty-five per cent of the construction of housing for troops was to be new while the remainder comprised rebuilding of existing barracks. Several problems had to be faced, the chief of which were:—

    (i) *Fire risk:* All Japanese construction was of wood.
    (ii) *Heating:* The only safe way was to heat barracks by steam or electricity. Both were in short supply.
    (iii) *Cooking facilities:* Field scale of cooking equipment could not be used and engineers had to improvise and install equipment suitable for Japanese housing.
    (iv) *Sewage:* In Japan removal was mostly by hand and direct disposal on the fields. This was most undesirable but had to be accepted till water-borne sewage schemes were completed.

The Brindiv Engineers carried out many major projects, which included:

    (i) Takuma Bay Holiday Home.
    (ii) Conversion of the Matsue shipyard into an Engineer Stores Depot.
    (iii) Connecting Engineer Stores Depot to railway.
    (iv) Construction of hospital accommodation for British General Hospital.
    (v) Air-strip and hangar at Okayama.
    (vi) Okayama race course.
    (vii) Bailey Bridge at Kachimura.

The works procedure in Japan was very complicated and liable to many delays. Project plans for semi-permanent work had to be approved by British Commonwealth Occupation Force, United States Eighth Army and finally by Supreme Commander Allied Powers before work could begin. All data including costing in dollars had to be provided. It took more than two months for any project to be approved.

In order to accomplish the considerable task of reconstruction it was recommended by General Officer Commanding Brindiv[3] that the following units should be added to the Brindiv Order of Battle:

    Headquarters CRE works,
    Two Works Sections.

[3] Headquarters Brindiv letter No. 221/2G, SD dated 14 May 46.

A considerable reorganisation took place in the Engineer set-up of British Commonwealth Occupation Force and with the withdrawal of the British Brigade from Shikoku the engineer commitments were gradually reduced. With the impending withdrawal of the Indian Contingent, all construction in Brindiv area, except of permanent nature, was stopped from 1 May 1947.

The Works Section was extremely thin on the ground. Even with such assistance as was provided from other units responsibilities and tasks were abnormal, as is indicated by the following:—

(a) *Garrison Engineer, Matsue:* Responsible for Tottori and Shimane Prefectures, area of some 150 miles by 30 miles, containing two infantry battalion stations, and brigade headquarters station and the necessary medical, supply and transport, cold storage, canteen and allied facilities. To assist the Garrison Engineer there was a staff of only one Staff Serjeant and four Corporals.

(b) *Garrison Engineer, Shikoku:* Responsible for the whole of Shikoku Island, some 145 miles by 45, comprising four prefectures. The Garrison Engineer, and Assistant Garrison Engineer were both Engineer Officers provided from Headquarters Royal Engineers and 429 (QVO) Madras S & M Indian Field Company, Royal Indian Engineers, respectively. The area contained three infantry battalion stations, a brigade headquarters, infantry and armoured corps detachments, a leave centre, and allied medical, supply and transport, cold storage and canteen facilities. In addition, one infantry battalion and the brigade headquarters had to move to a new location on the island for tactical reasons. The Works Section consisted of one Staff Serjeant, two Serjeants and three Corporals.

(c) *Garrison Engineer, Okayama:* This was the main Divisional Headquarters and Divisional Troops area and had an off-shoot for the Armoured Corps station in Kurashiki. The Garrison Engineer's office was run by two officers and two non-commissioned officers lent by the RA, assisted by one Sapper Corporal. Kurashiki was run by the second subaltern of 907 Works Section, who combined this job with that of Headquarters Planning Officer. He was assisted by one Sapper Corporal.

DIVISIONAL SIGNALS

The dispersion of units and formations raised many new problems not usually met with in Divisional Signals. The distances from Brigade Headquarters to Division Headquarters necessitated the full use of existing permanent lines. These were for the most part in poor condition, being maintained by the Japanese, and were generally unreliable. Records such as route diagrams and route plans were mostly non-existent and considerable labour was entailed in compiling them from scratch. Bad condition of roads made line reconnaissance very difficult. Teletype facilities were non-existent. Additional lines with teletype facilities had to be asked for as the aim was eventually to have teletype-printers working between formation headquarters.

Moreover the additional services on the War Establishment of the division called for greatly increased telephone facilities, and though the equipment was available personnel were not fully trained in the operation and maintenance of large installations.

The poor condition of the existing permanent lines and the lack of telegraph facilities made it necessary to use wireless to a very much greater extent than usual; in fact virtually all Signal traffic to brigades was cleared by wireless. The sets proved very reliable and, in spite of the mountainous nature of the country, no difficulty was experienced in maintaining communications. In particular the SCR 399 and 76 sets gave excellent service. The sun-spot activity during monsoon (July to September) caused, however, serious fade-outs on several occasions.

To meet the manpower shortage technicians from the Japanese Communication Bureau were attached to Signal Office and proved their worth. The teletype circuit to Kure gave satisfactory service.

Indian Air Formation Signals:[4] The Headquarters of the Indian Air Formation Signals was located at Iwakuni, with detachments at Miho and Bofu airfields and worked under British Commonwealth Occupation Force being directly controlled by Headquarters BCAIR. It did most commendable work. The IAFS consisted of 233 Independent Company which prior to its move to Japan was part of No. 4 Air Formation Signal Regiment in Malaya.

Its move to Japan was carried out in stages, the first advance personnel party arriving in Kure on 11 February 1946 and the vehicles and stores arriving only in May 1946. On the setting up of the Independent Company in Japan, it was allotted the role of providing landline and signals despatch service facilities to BCAIR at Iwakuni. To meet these commitments the Company was deployed as follows:

[4] Report by Major K. D. Bhasin, Indian Signals.

Iwakuni
>Headquarters 233 Independent Company Indian Air Formation Signal Regiment.
>Headquarters 231 Tele Operating Section.
>Headquarters 220 DR Section.
>>221 (I) Line Section.

Bofu
>214 Wing Signal Section.
>228 (I) Line Section.

Miho
>217 Wing Signal Section.
>Detachment 220 DR Section.

Tokyo
>A Detachment with the British Commonwealth Sub Area Tokyo (BRICOSAT).

It was the policy of British Commonwealth Occupation Force to use existing Japanese civil and other telecommunication facilities including equipment for its own signal commitments, but this could not be effected in any considerable degree because the Japanese communication system had deteriorated for want of equipment, spares, replacements and adequate maintenance during the war. The cables, particularly on longer lines and trunk routes, had outlived their usefulness by the end of the war.

Coupled with this the ever increasing demands of the occupation forces on the Japanese communication system almost broke it down, depleted as it was already. As a long term policy it was decided that occupation signal units would be responsible for the provision of local communication, supplemented by as many available Japanese technicians and tradesmen as were available and could be trained, as opposed to reliance on the Japanese communication system. These were to be employed in existing unit War Equipment deficiencies.

With pressure on the Japanese Bureau of Communications and a small reinforcement of equipment in short supply, the efficiency of the trunk line circuits rose gradually from 50 per cent in early 1946 to 95 per cent in October 1947. These trunk lines were mostly manned and maintained by the Japanese but this marked improvement was in no small degree due to the constant vigilance of signal units. A Japanese Communication Liaison Officer was appointed with each major signal unit where his duty was to maintain liaison between the Japanese Bureau of Communications and the unit to which he was attached. The Japanese technicians once trained were reliable and efficient.

To assist the Japanese Bureau of Communications in repairing faults on trunk lines, it was found advisable to provide War Department transport, to lessen the fault-time.

The IAFS when it moved from Singapore to Japan was under the impression that Chief Signal Officers' pool of signal equipment would be available in British Commonwealth Occupation Force, from which items beyond the War Equipment Tables could be drawn for British Commonwealth Occupation Force projects, but on arrival it discovered that the available stores were entirely inadequate, particularly in heavy exchanges. This caused much delay in the initial stages, but later some Japanese automatic exchanges were discovered and the Bureau of Communications was ordered to convert the major exchanges into automatic systems with underground cables. Further planning was done by the IAFS for a 800-line auto-exchange at Iwakuni and two 400-line-auto-exchanges, one each at Bofu and Miho.

When the unit arrived at Iwakuni it maintained only a 200-line command board. Even this was faulty, over-hearing being the main fault. After a while 300-line T.C. 10 C.B. American type of board was put in, but on 25 May 1947 the exchange was gutted by fire in the Air Force Station Officers Mess. During the fire, communications were set up with the outside links including outside trunk stations with the help of a 80-line F. and F. exchange and by 0300 hours all trunk circuits and major operational subscribers in Headquarters BCAIR were put through in communication. Special mention was made of the efficiency of the unit by the Air Force Commander, Air Commodore I.D. McLachlan, who wrote:

"During such a disastrous occurrence as occurred on the morning of the 25th of May, when the Station Officer's Mess was totally destroyed it is always difficult to select any individual, or group, for special mention. From my own observation, however, and reports which I am continuing to receive I wish to place on record my appreciation of the magnificent work performed by members of the Air Formation Signals both during and after the fire.

The untiring efforts of both British and Indian officers, Non-Commissioned Officers and men of your unit were responsible for the speedy and efficient replacement of our communication with the outside world.

Would you please convey my personal thanks to all ranks under your command ".[5]

---

[5] D O to Major K. D. Bhasin from Air Officer Commanding BCAIR, Japan.

The unit was administratively under the control of Headquarters British Commonwealth Occupation Force; for operational employment it was under the command of Headquarters BCAIR, for local administration like leave, accommodation and welfare etc. it was under the respective BCAIR Stations, and for domestic purposes under Brindiv. It was a complicated business, creating many difficulties, the more so as the Air Force generally tended to regard the Air Formation Signals as an 'Army baby' which the Army was not willing to accept as the unit was not doing any work for them. The position was, however, clarified and channels of communication were laid down.

During the stay of the unit in Japan a few important lessons were brought home. These were:

(i) Due to the high incidence of fire in Japan owing to the buildings being mostly wooden structures, it is essential that all exchange buildings, and frame rooms should be housed in Nissen huts or corrugated iron sheds.

(ii) Personnel selected from overseas service should be willing and keen and have had their leave before proceeding abroad.

(iii) The correct channels for Air Formation Signals should be laid down by the higher formation in the form of an instruction.

(iv) For liaison purposes Signal Liaison Officers should be appointed and careful watch and supervision kept on their activities and the agency they represent.

(v) The need for the formation of a theatre Chief Signal Officers' Pool of Stores at an early stage.

Indian Air Formation Signals during its tenure of duty in Japan did remarkable work and was highly reported on by all Air Force Commanders wherever it functioned. General Cawthorn India's representative on JCOSA, was highly impressed by their performance and prestige and wrote to Commander-in-Chief India, " India Air Formation Signals is most highly thought of by all Air Force components and is doing excellent job at all Air Stations ".[6]

SUPPLY AND TRANSPORT

All stocks on arrival regardless of the country of origin were taken into the British Commonwealth Occupation Force Base Supply Depot and pooled. Issues were made from the British

[6] INDEL/83 of 10 June 46.

Commonwealth Occupation Force Base to supply units in formation areas.

In the beginning, the Divisional Troops Composite Platoon operated a Forward Supply Depot in Hiro supplying all units in that area and making despatches to the other two Composite Platoons, which were operating supply points at Yonago and on Shikoku island.

No foodstuffs could be obtained locally and everything had to be imported. The rations were very good indeed. The British ranks appreciated, in particular, the Australian frozen meat and beer. Although a few Indian Other Ranks accepted the offer of frozen mutton, the issue of fresh meat to Indian troops presented a serious problem, and many expedients were tried to solve it. A delegation was sent to Australia to inspect the facilities available for the preparation of meat in the orthodox way. A contract was arranged but was later cancelled as it was found that the contractor was not in fact preparing meat in the orthodox way.[7]

The main complaint of Indian troops was the quality of cigarettes which were not of the same type as issued to other British Commonwealth Occupation Force troops. This was taken up by Headquarters British Commonwealth Occupation Force but Commander-in-Chief India ruled that Indian troops would only get Indian cigarettes as a ration but could purchase better quality cigarettes through canteens.

A Pacific scale of rations was put into force on 1 June 1946. This was a good scale with full nutritive value, and where certain increases were recommended and accepted the meals became very enjoyable. The scale of rations on payment from canteens was also not meagre, though many Other Ranks did not find it quite adequate specially because nothing else was available in the form of snacks outside their barracks. To meet this difficulty an increase in staple items was later accepted.

Due to lack of refrigerator shipping some fresh vegetables and fruits were initially spoilt in transit. Another difficulty was that owing to the wide difference in season between Australia and Japan, proper fruits could not be imported. However the situation improved later with the provision of refrigerator shipping and facilities at Kure and other supply points.

Fresh items on the following approximate scales were provided in cold storage by British Commonwealth Occupation Force. All these articles were of excellent quality:

Fresh Meat ... 6 days per week for British troops.
Fresh Butter ... 3 days per week for British troops.

[7] DCGS/G/100.

Fresh Potatoes	3 days per week for all troops.
Fresh Onions ...	3 days per week for all troops.
Fresh Fruit ...	6 days per week for all troops.
Fresh Mutton	Sufficient ordinary frozen mutton for Indian Troops (not *halal* or *jhatka*) available for all troops who would eat it.

59 Indian Supply Company operated in the Commonwealth Base Supply and Petrol Depots and on the move of the division to Okayama, it moved there to operate a large Field Supply Depot and Petrol Depot from which requirements of the division were met. Supplies were despatched to Composite Platoons, which operated supply points at Yonago and Takamatsu.

The transport companies were very hard worked, carrying stores and personnel from Kure Docks to Hiro and later from Okayama to unit locations. 8 Company RASC was eventually located at Wadashima on Shikoku island and one platoon of this company went to Tokyo to provide transport for the British contingent there. 169 Indian Company concentrated at Hiro and later moved to Okayama. This was replaced by 227 General Purposes Transport Company in March 1947.

As has already been mentioned, road communications in Japan were extremely poor, and jeep was the only really practicable vehicle for general reconnaissance on country roads. The few jeeps which were brought from India proved invaluable and it was a pity that the vital necessity of a high proportion of such vehicles was not emphasised in the early stages of Brindiv organisation. It was expected that future maintenance would be based on jeeps but as this responsibility was taken over by the Australian authorities who were anxious not to spend dollars on American purchases the proportion of jeeps remained inadequate.

RIASC units also organised:
  (a) Fishing—Boats were requisitioned and enthusiastic volunteers organised a fishing fleet. Small amounts of fish were caught. Sufficient fish was obtained for issue to the troops and canteens.
  (b) Launch Service—Supply and Transport crews were trained to man procured Japanese launches. Nine boats were obtained and used extensively for patrolling and recreational trips.

ORDNANCE

A small amount of captured Japanese barrack and accommodation stores was found and issued to implement the rather meagre scales which units had brought with them. No large stocks of useful Japanese equipment were found as the American forces, which occupied the area before Brindiv, had taken what they required, and had handed the remainder to the Japanese Home Ministry.

The Ordnance Distribution Centre was first established in a warehouse and dealt with 15 to 20 3-ton lorry loads of stores daily. The fastest moving item was furniture.

Laundry contracts were made with local Japanese laundry companies, the contractor undertaking to wash and iron seven articles per Other Rank each week for the sum of six Yen. In addition, he carried out two dry cleanings (Battle Dress) per month for an additional sum of two Yen.[8]

14 (m) Laundry and Bath unit arrived in Oakyama on 19 April 1946 and took on the washing for 80 British General Hospital. The call for the bath section was not pressing as all barracks were well equipped with washing facilities.

At Okayama there were excellent sites for the laundry and for store dump. The living quarters were centrally heated and there was plenty of room to organise canteens and recreation rooms.

The supply of furniture in Japan was an Ordnance responsibility. The procurement demands were first placed direct on Prefectural Governments by the local commander concerned but with the abuse of this privilege and great scarcity of many items in Japan, Supreme Commander Allied Powers fixed the scales, though procurement was still handled by British Commonwealth Occupation Force. The quality of furniture supplied was uniformly good though the wood was not of a very strong variety.

Three sheets, two pillow slips and one case pillow were issued to each man as accommodation stores. The provision of an additional battle dress (olive green) suit was approved, raising the scale from two to three, per person.

The repair of civilian shoes by Ordnance with ordnance material was also approved but due to scarcity of grindery and material this was given very low priority.

The advent of families in Japan necessitated larger holdings in officers' shops and canteens together with a number of additional items covering the peculiar requirements of wives and children, such as clothes, medicines and furniture.

Most of the Ordnance units were located in Sanganaya, a few miles from Okayama, which was also a Japanese Ordnance Depot. The stores were placed in caves which had first to be cleared of Japanese equipment and properly rehabilitated and made secure against pilfering.

[8] Five Yens to the Rupee.

Mechanical Transport stores were always in short supply. Due to extreme wear and tear, the greatest casualty ratio was amongst the fan-belts.

ELECTRICAL AND MECHANICAL ENGINEERS

The Advance Party on arrival was allotted a site for workshops in what had been an auxiliary marine engine-erecting shop in Hiro, about seven miles inland from Kure. This required extensive clearing of machinery and junk, but it had fine possibilities as a workshop with more than sufficient space to accommodate all the R/IEME elements of the Division.

For living accommodation, EME was allotted Japanese barracks known as "Infantry Lines South". These Lines consisted of five wooden two-storyed barrack blocks in a very dilapidated state and much hard work was needed to make them habitable.

All EME units were originally located in Hiro and worked to an interim plan of maintenance and repair for divisional units. 111 Indian Infantry Workshops Company arrived on 23 April 1946 and moved direct to the 268 Indian Infantry Brigade Area.

The final locations of EME units after the move of Brindiv to Okayama were as follows:—

Unit	Location	Remarks
(i) HQ CIEME	Okayama	
(ii) Division Recovery Company IEME	,,	Responsible for divisional recovery.
(iii) Independent Section 152 Indian Mobile Workshop	,,	Maintenance and Repair for Divisional Troops Transport.
(iv) Refrigerator Repair Component	,,	Maintenance of Divisional Refrigeration Plant.
(v) 111 Indian Infantry Workshops	Matsue	Maintenance and repair for 268 Infantry Brigade.
(vi) 5 Infantry Workshops Company REME	Kochi	Maintenance and repair for 5 Infantry Brigade.
(vii) 1083 Indian Troops Company Workshops Section	Okayama	Maintenance and repair for General Purposes Transport Company RIASC.

With the withdrawal of 5 Brigade and disbandment of Brindiv, 111 Indian Infantry Workshop was moved from Matsue to Okayama and took over the responsibilities of Division Recce Company in addition to its own.

Owing to very bad roads, the amount of repair work was considerable. With the employment of Japanese drivers the accidents increased. Hence a driving school was opened to train personnel in driving and maintenance and the Japanese authorities were ordered to take up road repair as high priority.

EDUCATION BRANCH

Two considerable activities, which reached early fruition, were the provision of library facilities and a daily newspaper. A Central Library to cater for British and Indian troops alike was established. Stocked with some 13,000 fiction for British troops, reference, technical and miscellaneous sections, several thousand volumes in Hindi, Urdu, Marathi, Punjabi, Gurmukhi, Nepali, Tamil, Telugu and Malayalam for Indian troops, classical music records and Indian records, the library was capable of issuing up to 60 books a day to personal callers and supplied boxes of up to 500 books to Brindiv units, clubs, and canteens. In addition, Education Branch took on the commitment of producing "Brindiv", the daily news bulletin which summarised broadcast commentaries from Australia, Tokyo, the BBC and All India Radio. This bulletin ceased with the production of *BCON* by Headquarters British Commonwealth Occupation Force as its daily newspaper.

The educational set-up in the Okayama area included the establishment of a polytechnic, and the American Divisional School was taken over complete for this purpose. Besides courses in educational method, the polytechnic catered for training in agricultural subjects and cottage industries, instructor training for the Indian Army Certificates and technical subjects and the Forces Preliminary Examination.

Much informal education was done by the organisation in canteens and clubs of quizzes, musical shows and recorded concerts of classical music. Regular Sunday night music was organized and quiz contests were held with other contingents.

An Amateur Dramatic Society was started and two plays which were staged at four stations in the Brindiv area were a great success.

Classes in Japanese for Divisional Headquarters Officers, Warrant Officers and Viceroy's Commissioned Officers were also organised.

INDIAN FAMILIES IN JAPAN

The families of Indian officers began to arrive in Japan in December 1946. By May 1947, when an embargo was placed on the move of families of Indian Army to Japan, 96 families had arrived from India.

The maintenance of "dependents", as the families were known in United States and British Commonwealth Occupation Force circles, created a few snags as they had to be fed, allotted accommodation and supplied through British Commonwealth Occupation Force channels. However, the arrangements made were very satisfactory and it can be stated without exaggeration that they had the best of time at the least expense to themselves.

The families created a very good atmosphere all round. They not only helped to raise the morale but also the prestige of the Indian Contingent. For the first time Allied personnel and Japanese met the Indian families, saw them in their reality, examined their mode of living and realised that the impressions which they had formed before were the result of false propaganda.

The Japanese public received the families very cordially and at all detraining stations like Kure and Okayama very good receptions were organised.

Arrangements were also in hand to call forward the families of Other Ranks but these had to be held in abeyance firstly as accommodation was not available and secondly owing to the impending withdrawal of the contingent.

Educational arrangements for children were made and schools were started in Etajima, Kure and Okayama. The school teachers were provided by the United Kingdom Ministry of Education and the Australian authorities.

MORALE OF INDIAN PERSONNEL

The morale of the Indian personnel remained very high throughout the period of duty in Japan. This was exceptionally so with combatant units under Brindiv. The laxity of discipline and morale of the Indian units in Integrated Headquarters was criticised by General Haydon.[9] But that was mainly due to the lack of supervision by the Headquarters of the units concerned, and improved considerably in the Integrated Formations by the efforts of their commanders.

The introduction of the New Pay Code, which benefited the Indian Other Ranks considerably was a great morale raiser but it

---

[9] BCOF AF 16915 dated 18 November 45.

had a critical reception from the Indian Commissioned Officers, who were badly hit.

The communal riots in the Punjab, from where more than half of the Indian personnel in Japan came, were a great disturbing factor. Stories of atrocities committed by one community against the other were boldly splashed in British Commonwealth Occupation Force news-sheet *BCON* and also in the American press. It goes to the credit of Indian Officers, who had only recently assumed responsibility, that there were no disturbances or friction between the different communities in units. Brigadier S. M. Shrinagesh maintained strict neutrality and ensured that there was no discrimination or communal propaganda in the units while in Japan. 268 Brigade Group came back to India as the last undivided contingent of the Indian Army.

The Other Ranks while in Japan were greatly interested in the Japanese way of living, their education and their social system as a whole. They were greatly impressed by the universality of education and taking this as an example almost all Indian Other Ranks became keen enthusiasts of education. All ranks showed great keenness and interest in the country and its people.

LEAVE

No leave ex-Japan to India was allowed except in extreme compassionate cases. Leave ex-Japan for British Other Ranks was according to existing rules regarding leave from overseas. But shipping was the limiting factor.

Leave in Japan was eight days in a year which the troops generally spent in one of the many leave centres. Later on this was increased to two periods of eight days.

MEDICAL

Medical Layout: Hospitalisation for Indian personnel was provided by 92 Indian General Hospital at Kure while the British personnel were covered by 80 British General Hospital at Okayama. With the opening of the Australian General Hospital at Etajima, all surgical and infectious cases were transferred there. It also provided hospital cover for the families.

5 (British) Field Ambulance and 9 (Indian) Light Field Ambulance provided medical detachments for the troops in Shikoku island and North Coast respectively. The medical layout was:—

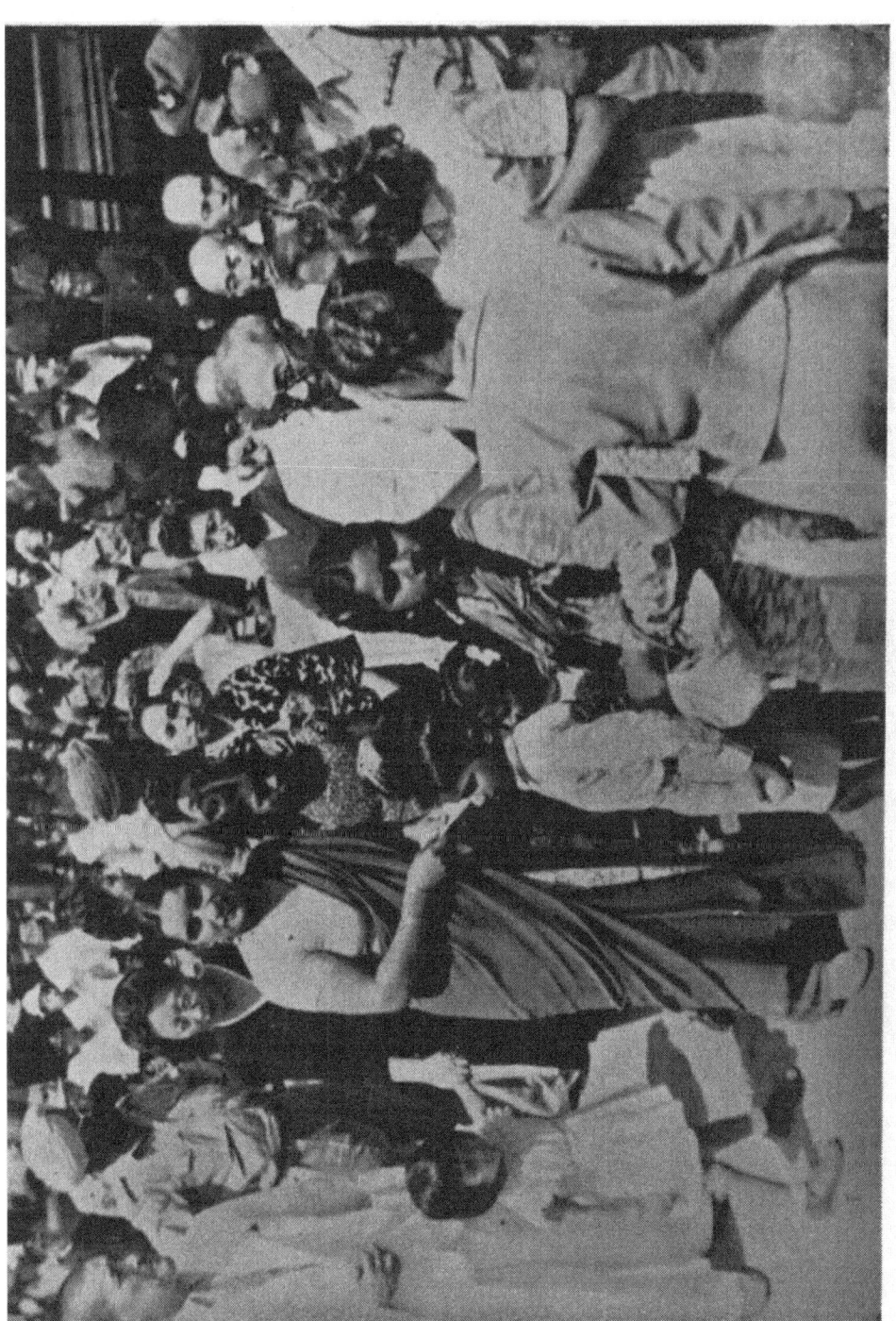

Japan meets India

Plate XII

Indian Troops in Etajima

92 Indian General Hospital (C) 300 Beds at Kure.

92 Indian General Hospital (C) 150 Beds at Kegoya (VD Centre and Isolation Hospital).

80 British General Hospital, 200 Beds at Hiro (moved to Okayama).

5 British Field Ambulance Headquarter and 1 Company at Hiro (moved to Kochi).

9 Indian Light Field Ambulance at Hamada (moved to Imaichi).

1 Company 5 British Field Ambulance at Matsue (20 Beds).

Dental Centre British / Dental Laboratory } at 80 British General Hospital.

Dental Centre Indian at 92 Indian General Hospital (C).

Evacuation from Shikoku was to Okayama or to Etajima depending on the case. As the evacuation to Okayama required transhipment at two places, the evacuation to Etajima by sea was speedier and more comfortable. Evacuation from 268 Brigade Area was by rail. Evacuation by air for emergency cases was available at all centres.

HEALTH OF THE TROOPS

Japan has extremes of climate, the winter is very cold while the summer is humid and hot. Considering the poor initial accommodation it was anticipated that Indian troops would have many cases of frost-bite but there were only a few cases of chilblains and the Indian troops stood the rigors of winter very well.

The summer is the most dangerous period when epidemics break out in Japan. The diseases spread very quickly because the Japanese use fresh night-soil in the fields. This not only generates bad odour but also intensifies the distribution of germs. Most of the areas in close proximity to the troops were air sprayed with DDT with good results. Inoculation against cholera and all communicative diseases was essential. All men had to be inoculated against B-Encephalitis in three doses as this disease is endemic in Japan.

The incidence of venereal diseases in British Commonwealth Occupation Force was great but the Indian Contingent had a very low percentage (as low as in India itself). Instructions were given to all ranks regarding its prevention.

Extensive screening of barracks and drainage was carried out to combat mosquito borne B-Encephalitis which was endemic in the Okayama area. There were only three cases reported in Brindiv.

Local Prevalent Diseases

Typhus—In 1947 there was a very extensive outbreak of this disease among the civil population. Allied Military Government carried out large-scale dusting and the epidemic soon declined. Indian force was 100 per cent protected and had no casualties.

Small Pox—A fairly large number of cases among civil population were reported. Allied Military Government arranged for vaccination by preparing lymph in Japan. Period of revaccination in Brindiv was reduced to 12 months.

Hygiene and Sanitation

Latrine and disposal of contents—
This was a complicated problem because of
(a) high water level (in many parts 1-3 ft. below surface) which ruled out deep trench latrines;
(b) very few latrines being fitted with water carriage system;
(c) free use of human faeces in Japan as manure.

Two types of latrines were mainly used:
(a) Japanese (squatting type) with a pit underneath. This was the commonest type of latrine. Practically all houses were fitted with this type. The pit was emptied by scooping out contents once a week or fortnight. Those used by troops were emptied every other day by local labour;
(b) Bucket removal type with seat. These were largely constructed by Brindiv, and were emptied daily.

Emptied contents were taken away by farmers in wooden buckets with closely fitting lids and were used to fertilize crops.

Water: Two sources of supply were available:
(a) pumping from ground,
(b) collection in a catchment area.

Water supply on the whole was good, but as a precaution drinking water used by troops was chlorinated.

WELFARE

The maintenance of morale, discipline and health depended mostly on welfare facilities available within the area. As fraternisation was not allowed, with meagre recreational facilities and with poor initial accommodation and severe weather conditions it was essential to divert the attention of men into healthy channels. In view of the lack of indigenous amusements and amenities in

Japan, every effort was made to improve all forms of welfare, so that troops could have comfortable clubs etc. to visit and have adequate amusement in their free periods.

After careful planning and hard work by welfare services a very high standard was reached, and General Scott who visited units in February-March 1947 wrote, " The men are having the time of their lives ".[10]

The following were some of the items of welfare provided:—

(a) *Canteens/Clubs*

Separate canteens both wet and dry were established in the majority of units. Certain difficulties in the beginning were experienced over the question of supplies, but with Australian Canteen Services taking over the overall responsibility of Canteen Services, the supplies became adequate. Indian Other Ranks could have English cigarettes and two bottles of Australian beer a week, besides chocolates and other delicacies at very low price. The following Central Clubs were established and catered for a large number of troops both day and night:—

(i) Wavell Club—British and Indian troops.
(ii) Auchinleck Club—Indian troops.
(iii) YMCA—British troops.
(iv) YMCA—Indian troops.

Such clubs were established at Okayama, Matsue, Hamada and Kochi.

(b) *Entertainments*

The following entertainments were provided and were widely attended:—

Films:

The supply of films in the beginning only allowed one 16-mm. and one 35-mm. film for British troops each week and a similar allocation for Indian troops. In view of the complete lack of local entertainments or amenities, two films per unit per week were found to be insufficient. The Army Director of Service Kinematography from Supreme Allied Commander, South-East Asia, visited Japan in May 1946 and stepped up the film supply per week which was:

Two 35-mm for British troops.
Two 16-mm for British troops.

---

[10] 2504/B/DCGS(B) dated 5 February/1 March 47.

One 35-mm for Indian troops.
One 16-mm for Indian troops,
One 35-mm film per week was also provided from stocks withdrawn from general circulation.

In view of the extremely poor state of the roads, mobile projectors could not be used except where rail journeys were involved; consequently they were used in a static role. For that role thirteen 35-mm projectors were required. Out of this only two 35-mm projectors were available with 9 Kinema Section. Five more were received from Australian sources and with the withdrawal of 5 Brigade they proved adequate.

ENSA Concert Party

The above party did a circuit of Brindiv units and was withdrawn on 4 May 1947, after which ENSA parties were not available. Australian Services organised many concert parties which visited all the units in rotation.

Fauji Dilkhush Sabha

No. 83 Fauji Dilkhush Sabha Concert Party gave a few concerts to Indian troops but was returned to India owing to its proving unsatisfactory.

Kumaon Band

The Kumaon Band played numerous programmes of light, orchestral and dance music both for British and Indian troops of Brindiv and other formations and had very good reception.

Local Entertainments

In addition, the following entertainments were provided periodically and proved very popular:—
  (a) Dances
  (b) Concerts
  (c) Whist Drives etc.

Ladies Services

Detachments of FANYs, WAS(B), WVS(UK) and WVS(I) which accompanied Brindiv to Japan assisted in all welfare projects. They rendered considerable assistance in the running and furnishing of unit and central club/canteens. The majority of ladies had to be concentrated in Division Troops and 5 Infantry Brigade Area, but small detachments were despatched to live in the unit areas to assist in the canteens and the running of all forms of entertainments. Their help was invaluable. Representatives of SSAFA and SSAHA were fully occupied with the various family and home problems of the troops.

The YMCA ran a mess for members of the Women's Service. This proved a most comfortable mess run on most efficient lines.

The withdrawal of the FANY from Japan created a difficult situation. Members of the Women's Voluntary Service were required to run the welfare centres and canteens, and they rose to the occasion by making the centres efficient and attractive. Six members of WVS(I) were insufficient for the purpose and it was strongly recommended to GHQ(I) that Indian ladies should be sent to look after the welfare of Indian troops. This was an urgent requirement which was never fulfilled.

Takuma Bay Holiday Home

A first class Holiday Home for British and Indian troops was opened at Takuma Bay on the island of Shikoku on 1 September 1946. This home was very popular with troops who spent ten days holiday by turn.

Shimatsue Leave Centre

The Cherokeon Hotel on the beach near Shimatsue was converted into a Leave Centre where 70 men could stay for short periods upto three days. As it was only 20 miles from Okayama by good road and could be reached by sea in a few hours by Inland Sea, it was a very popular summer resort. All arrangements were made by Women's Voluntary Service.

Ebisu Leave Centre in Tokyo

Leave in Tokyo was very popular and during the tour of duty of an Indian unit there 50 leave vacancies were provided. From there trips were arranged to Nikko, Kamakura and other places of interest.

Ujji Leave Centre

A British Commonwealth Occupation Force Leave Centre was opened on 1 October 1947 for Indian troops ten miles from Kyoto. It was a luxurious place and arrangements were comparable to those in the best hotels in India. Its proximity to such famous places as Nara, Kyoto and Kobe made it very popular.

Other Leave Centres

British Commonwealth Occupation Force had holiday homes at Kyoto, Kawana, Nikko and Beppu and the trips to these places were very popular. Every one had an opportunity to visit one of these centres twice during his stay in Japan.

Recreational Trips

Tours and welfare parties were organised to visit atom-bombed Hiroshima and the blasted docks of Kure. As an antidote to war memories, trips were organised to various beauty spots; Miyajima Island, known as, " Paradise Island ", being the most popular.

All the roads of Miyajima were lined with souvenir shops full of many interesting toys, mementos and junk. The main road which ran from the wharf south of the shrine ended on the west side on a small beach near which was located a small hotel, which was converted into a Convalescent Depot for British Commonwealth Occupation Force. Every Sunday and on holidays many British Commonwealth Occupation Force personnel used to visit Miyajima to enjoy the beautiful scenery and to be photographed with the sea-Torii in the background.

Indian troops had a good look at the destruction and reconstruction of Hiroshima. They were told by those who were fortunate enough to survive that when the town was burning there was no panic, there was no crying and cursing. How like the Japanese to suffer with patience. It was these qualities of character, patience and perseverance which were helping them to rise again. Indians could profit by the good example of the Japanese and help in the rise of their country to greatness.

Okayama Race Course

To provide some amenities to troops it was decided to use the Okayama Race Course, which lay on the main road from Okayama to Kobe via. Himeji. It was about three miles from the town and was patronised by the Japanese before the war, but during the war, horse racing was stopped by law and the race course had fallen into decay. The first race of the season was organised on 10 August 1946. It was a great success.

British Commonwealth Occupation Force Sports and Amusements

On 29 October 1946, British Commonwealth Occupation Force sports were held at Kure. The Indian athletic team was selected from the persons taking part in the Brigade sports held at Matsue on 9 October. 268 Indian Infantry Brigade came out third, losing to 34 Australian Infantry Brigade and BCAIR Group.

A grand musical display by British and Indian Military Bands was given in the Okayama Park on 16 November 1946 at 2-30 p.m. Major-General Cowan was present on the occasion. An extract from the Japanese press reads:—

"The paper mulberry trees were beginning to bloom and the impressive array of the bands arrested the attention of the crowds.

Firstly the Band of the Cameron Highlanders marched around the lake with the ribbons of their dark blue hats trailing and their golden hair glistening in the sun. The marching was spirited and courageous and in perfect time.

Continuing, General Cowan's Headquarters Band gave a solemn marching display. Their coloured coats painted a beautiful picture in the sun. After half circling the lake and following a brilliant musical display they returned to their base.

Soon afterwards the band of the Gurkhas, marching with dauntless carriage and full of strength marched around the lake playing their bag-pipes. As they returned to their base the main part of the musical performance came to an end.

The Headquarters Band marched once more around the lake and finally as a present for the people of Okayama, the "Apple" song was played and amid the applause of the large audience the display was concluded at 3.30 p.m."[11]

Pay

The pay organisation began to function in Japan from 17 February 1946, when the Air Advance Party arrived at Kure. Supply of cash and exchange of currency, the main things aimed at, were achieved smoothly in spite of the large volume of currency to be dealt with and the fact that British personnel at Headquarters British Commonwealth Occupation Force as well as Royal Navy, Royal Air Force and Royal Indian Navy requirements had to be attended to. This involved a great deal of work but was carried through satisfactorily. The currency question was complicated by the fact that the Japanese Government introduced a new currency and commenced a system of restrictions on bank drawing at the same time as the Sea Advance Party arrived in Japan.

It was thus necessary to collect non-Japanese currency from personnel on board without giving Yen in return. This latter had to be deferred for two days owing to the late arrival of the " New " Yen notes and Military Issue Currency. The " New " Yen notes were reissued and consisted of old Yen notes with adhesive stamps affixed to the top right hand corner. These stamps were printed to show the denomination to which they referred.

Various complications followed, such as the adhesive stamps becoming " non-adhesive " and the 100 Yen notes being tendered

---

[11] From Japanese press.

with 10 Yen stamps affixed. This of course rendered them valueless.

Further currency restrictions were introduced with a view to eliminating black-market transactions and proved effective. Supplies of New Bank of Japan notes were circulated in October 1946.

Contacts had to be made with Headquarters British Commonwealth Occupation Force, Royal Navy, Royal Indian Navy, Royal Air Force bodies, as well as other components of the force and cash supply to them was co-ordinated. The Staff Paymaster Japan was the sole channel of currency supply to all British formations in Japan.

The move to Okayama involved some alteration in the Pay "layout". One cashier was sent to Shikoku with Headquarters 5 Brigade and one for 268 Brigade. Owing to the small strength of this unit, it was necessary for units to be supplied by cashier's visits till additional paymasters were made available. Time and distance were great factors in cash supply and efforts were made to arrange transfers from British Commonwealth Occupation Force to Royal Navy and Royal Air Force by cheque. Till this was arranged, bulk supplies had to be collected and delivered by the cashier.

It is considered that a civilian with banking experience would have done better owing to the pressure of work and volume of currency to be dealt with.

Despite many reminders to FCMA regarding the correct exchange rate between £/Rupee/Yen, the Military Accounts continued to deduct at the pre-war exchange rate of 1s 2d to the Yen. This eventually necessitated the review of all accounts.

Public Relations

The Public Relation Detachment originally consisted of DADPR and one Cine Photographer at Brindiv Headquarters. GHQ(I) later agreed to appoint one officer with each brigade.

At Nasik it was decided to give the fullest publicity cover possible to every contingent of Brindiv leaving India. As a result it was decided to divide the Public Relation Detachment into three different parties.

An All India Radio correspondent was attached to the first party with Brindiv Headquarters which included DADPR and one Cine Photographer. One observer was attached to 5 Infantry Brigade to cover its departure. One Cine Officer was attached to 268 Indian Infantry Brigade, to travel with the Brigade, cover its departure from Bombay and on its way, with the help of PROs Bombay and Singapore.

The work of the Public Relation Detachment was handicapped by shortage of officers and consequent lack of personal contacts with the scattered units.

Before departure, a feature broadcast on the Brindiv force was arranged through All India Radio correspondent from Bombay Radio Station. Major-General Cowan took part in the feature. The Camerons' Band and the Kumaon Band were included in the programme.

In the evening an informal tea party was held on the ship HMT *Dunera* to enable Bombay Pressmen to meet Major-General Cowan and other officers and men proceeding to Japan. Thirty Pressmen representing English and Indian papers and News Agencies attended the party.

Another feature broadcast on Brindiv was arranged by All India Radio correspondent on board the ship *Dunera*, through All India Broadcast Recording Unit in Singapore. The parade through Singapore, at which Lord Louis Mountbatten took the salute, was covered by representatives of *SEAC* and other local papers and also by the Recording unit of Singapore Radio.

In Hong Kong the local press was very hospitable. Posters bearing headlines " British and Indian troops, here on way to Japan ", heralded the arrival of Brindiv in Hong Kong.

In Japan the arrivals of various contingents, receptions and subsequent functions were reported and photographs and material were despatched to GHQ(I) and other countries for distribution.

2 Dorset taking over guard duties in Tokyo was fully covered by news agencies and correspondents there. The departure of 268 Indian Infantry Brigade from India received full coverage with the help of PRO Bombay and was filmed.

2/5 Royal Gurkha Rifles taking over guard duties in Tokyo was covered by PR Photographic Team and also news agencies and correspondents in Tokyo. Brindiv Retreat ceremony in Tokyo was also successfully covered by PR Photographic Team and a dozen other photographers and correspondents representing news agencies in Japan.

Various correspondents, both British and American, visited and wrote about Brindiv. Among them were Mr. Jack Potter of *Daily Express*, Mr. Morris of BBC, Mr. Massey of *Telegraph* Sydney, Mr. Eston of *Illustrated London* and Mr. Brian of A. P. America. Mr. John Ulm paid a visit to Brindiv where he conferred with the General Officer Commanding and Staff Officers.

Photographers of *Nippon News* paid a visit to film VJ Day celebrations.

The Retreat Ceremony was broadcast throughout Japan by American Forces Radio with a complete commentary on Brindiv. Recordings of the ceremony were also made and copies sent to the BBC London for broadcast. The other two copies were sent to Melbourne and India.

Arrangements were made with the *Nippon News*, Tokyo, to show the Retreat Ceremony film, taken by them, to the troops at Brindiv Headquarters. The film was shown to the troops at Okayama for three nights and was a great success.

Mr. Collings and Mr. Pearce of the Department of Information, Melbourne, paid a four day visit to Brindiv to make a documentary film. For this purpose—

(a) A motorised march past by Brindiv units was held at Okayama.

(b) At Matsue, Headquarters of 268 Indian Infantry Brigade, some Indian folk dances and wrestling were arranged by 5/1 Punjab.

(c) 1 Mahrattas at Hamada organised some very colourful national dances.

Stars and Stripes, the official newspaper of the United States army, *BCON*, the official paper of BCOF and both Japanese English and vernacular press showed great interest in the Division. *BCON* gave generally one full page for Indian news exclusively and printed a large portion of it in Urdu.

The literature produced by PR India and Information Department of Great Britain was published through the agency of the Japanese press. It was important to tell the Japanese people of our contribution in the war. A steady flow of stories was also maintained. These stories were released to the local press, sent to Public Relations, India Office, London, and DPR India.

On Empire Day, literature on the Force was distributed to the American troops through Information and Education Department of the United States Army. It included 'Brindjap' booklets, *Fighting Men of India*, *Three Famous Divisions*, and *Indian VCs in two World Wars*. These helped to dispel many doubts and misunderstandings from the minds of American troops about the British and Indian soldiers.

The photographic situation in Brindiv improved with the arrival of a PR Photographer. Brindiv dark room catered for the needs of local papers, but owing to the shortage of paper it was impossible to meet the demand of various units. Military History Section, Melbourne, with British Commonwealth Occupation

Force, covered nearly every Brindiv function and sent pictures of prints to every Brindiv unit. The situation regarding cine film remained unsatisfactory. Cine film brought from India was either exhausted or stale. Brindiv required ten thousand feet of 35-mm film in 200-feet spools and ten thousand feet of 35-mm film in 100-feet spools during six months.

During the earlier period of its duties in British Commonwealth Occupation Force the Indian Contingent did not get very good publicity in Japan or abroad. This was partly due to an initial lack of PR arrangements with JCOSA and British Commonwealth Occupation Force and partly due to the hostile attitude of the Press in general about happenings in India. In India " it was extremely difficult to get any publicity about British Commonwealth Occupation Force because Indian editors were convinced that conditions were bad and that the Indian Contingent in particular was regarded as inferior to the other Contingents and was so treated".[12] After the disbandment of Brindiv and formation of 268 Indian Infantry Brigade Group, as a separate entity, the position of Indian *vis-a-vis* other contingents was one of equality and what little doubts remained in the minds of the few were removed after the declaration of Independence on 15 August 1947. While important political and civilian Heads of the United Kingdom, Australia and New Zealand visited their contingents in Japan, no senior Government representative from India or Indian newspaper correspondent visited the Indian contingent in Japan. Their attitude may be gleaned from this communication: " Government of India appreciate Robertson's desire for visit of senior Government representative and are now considering the matter but I anticipate their refusal owing to uncertainty regarding future ".[13]

[12] INDEL/45/11/1 dated 8 October 46,
[13] Armindia signal 245247/SD5 dated 14 January 47.

CHAPTER XI

Withdrawal of the Indian Contingent from Japan

NEGOTIATIONS FOR WITHDRAWAL

The rumours about the withdrawal of the Indian Contingent from Japan were afloat from the beginning of 1947, and with the withdrawal of 5 (British) Brigade it became obvious that the withdrawal of Indian Contingent was a matter of time; though the two had no connection whatsoever. The British withdrawal was essentially governed by conditions of manpower, and United Kingdom had still a fair size contingent in Japan. The Indian withdrawal, however, was the result of the principle enunciated by the Prime Minister of India, viz., " We have to bear in mind the strong feeling in India about the use of Indian troops abroad and because of this we should not retain any troops in foriegn countries unless there are imperative reasons for doing so ".[1]

It is not unlikely that for prestige considerations the Government of India might have preferred to retain the contingent in Japan. But the impending constitutional changes prompted the Indian Interim Government to finalise their views in March 1947, when they stated: " In view of the constitutional changes which will be put into effect by 1 June 1947 and consequent reorganisation within the Indian Army, the Government of India now wish to withdraw all Indian troops serving overseas by end of 1947 ".[2]

According to the MacArthur-Northcott agreement it was necessary for Australia to give six months' notice to the United States to withdraw this contingent. Australia was not keen to forward this request and was still hoping that India might change her views on further consideration. She felt that the withdrawal of the Indian Contingent " will not only destroy the representative character of the Commonwealth Force but create many administrative difficulties for the forces remaining behind in Japan ", most of the installations and integrated administrative units being of Indian origin. It was urged that their complete withdrawal would cause a breakdown, as replacements could not be easily provided from Australian or New Zealand sources.

Dr. Evatt, Minister of External Affairs, Government of Australia, informed General Cawthorn, Indian Representative on JCOSA, that he was holding up the despatch of notice to America " pending a further official Australian request to Pandit Jawahar

[1] EAD u/o No, D729-ME/47 dated 11 February 47.
[2] Telegram No. 1164 dated 22 March 47 in File FUO/47/D7.

Lal Nehru, Prime Minister of India, to reconsider his decision ".[3] But it transpired later that the Australian Cabinet decided not to send an official request but authorised Dr. Evatt to write to Pandit Nehru urging reconsideration of the withdrawal or at least to leave a small token force in British Commonwealth Occupation Force. On 9 April 1947, however, the Australian Government sent the following notice to the United States Government:

"At the request of the Government of India the Australian Government gives formal notice to the United States Government in accordance with Paragraph 3(B) of the MacArthur-Northcott Agreement, of the intention of Government of India to withdraw the whole of the Indian Contingent from the British Commonwealth Force in Japan.

At the same time the Government of India would be grateful if the United States Government could see its way clear to agree to the withdrawal being effected earlier than the date of expiry of the formal six months' notice ".[4]

Head of the Indian Liaison Mission in Japan signalled to the Government of India on 14 February 1947, " General MacArthur would not object to the withdrawal of the Indian troops if the Government of India so decided although he is very proud of Indian troops and highly praised them for their excellent work in Japan ".[5]

Not only India but New Zealand also expressed her desire to reduce her contingent. Dr. Evatt, who had done so much for the establishment of British Commonwealth Occupation Force deplored the attitude of both the Indian and New Zealand Governments. He was under the impression that these Governments were not acquainted with the value of British Commonwealth Occupation Force and asked JCOSA to prepare a paper on the subject for the information and enlightenment of the various Governments, which might induce them to change their decision.[6] Dr. Evatt was keen that India as an interested power in the Pacific should maintain her contribution to British Commonwealth Occupation Force. In his opinion, " the Indian withdrawal and the reduction of the New Zealand Contingent will be detrimental to Australian Forces, as it will raise a public demand for their withdrawal ".[7] Dr. Evatt had various interviews with General Cawthorn, and Dr. Paranjpye, Indian High Commissioner in Australia, who on 28 April 1947,

---

[3] Signal INDEL/287 of 28 April 47 and INDEL DO192/2 dated 29 April 47 from Cawthorn to Smith.
[4] Signal 134 dated 14 February 47 in File No. 6385/120/SD5 Serial No. 50-A.
[5] Ibid,
[6] Lessons of British Commonwealth Occupation Forces File INDEL/98.
[7] INDEL DO 192/2 dated 29 April 47 from Cawthorn to Smith.

wrote to Pandit Jawahar Lal Nehru urging him to consider the retention of a token Indian force in Japan to maintain Indian prestige. The Government of India were not prepared to alter the decision and informed him that " the decision to withdraw the Indian Contingent of British Commonwealth Occupation Force was taken in the Cabinet after fully considering all aspects of the question. Defence Department do not consider that any new points have been raised which would justify a revision in policy. The reversal of previous decisions will interfere with the nationalisation of the Armed Forces".[8] Due to the political developments, the partition of India into the two Dominions—India and Pakistan, and the consequent division of the Armed Forces, such a course had become inevitable.

On 16 July 1947, therefore, the following communique was issued with the concurrence of SCAP:—

> " The following announcement has been made by Headquarters of the British Commonwealth Occupation Force in Japan. During the period from July to September this year, with the concurrence of the United States Government and of the British Commonwealth Governments concerned, there will be a gradual reduction in the strength of the British Commonwealth Occupation Force in Japan. The whole of the Indian Contingent will be withdrawn and a reduction will be made in the New Zealand Army component. There will however be no alteration in the areas occupied or the responsibilities allotted to British Commonwealth Occupation Force. The withdrawal of the Indian Contingent is necessary in view of the constitutional changes and consequent reorganisation of India's Armed Forces. The RNZAF Squadron in Japan will continue to be maintained at its present strength ".[9]

Warning Order and Plan of Withdrawal

At the end of May 1947, warning orders were issued for the withdrawal of the Indian Contingent to be completed by the end of December 1947.

The original plan envisaged the withdrawal in three stages by the end of December 1947. Orders to this effect were issued by the Headquarters British Commonwealth Occupation Force on 30 May 1947. 268 Brigade Group was made responsible for the withdrawal

---

[8] DO No. 302-AA/47 dated 4 June 47 from A. V. Pai to Paranjpye.
[9] British Commonwealth Occupation Force Signal No. COS 1585 dated 14 July 47.

of the whole of the Indian Contingent and this had to be carried out in the following phases:—

Phase I — 1 Mahrattas.
2/5 RGR.
4 Squadron Royal Indian Air Force.
Phase II — Ancillary Base troops followed by Base troops.
Phase III — 5/1 Punjab.
Headquarter 268 Infantry Brigade Group.
Administrative details.

The plan was later slightly modified in detail due to the pressure from India to accelerate withdrawal and the consequent changes in the administrative plan.

1 Mahrattas were completely nationalised on 17 May 1947, and as there was still hope that a token contingent might be retained in Japan, 1 Mahrattas were scheduled to move last to obviate the Defence Department objection about the difficulty of nationalisation.

2/5 Gurkhas were stepped up to move first so that they could go straight to Kure after completion of their guard duties in Tokyo. They were to be reinforced by the rear details of Brindiv units and such 268 Brigade units as were not needed for the maintenance of the remaining Phases.

Considerations affecting withdrawal of Indian Contingent

Units of the Indian Contingent formed part of many administrative units of British Commonwealth Occupation Force, which not only provided for Indian needs but also for other elements. Their withdrawal was possible either when replacements were received from Australia or a complete reorganisation of the supply and maintenance system had been effected. In any case these units had to remain *in situ* till the last to look after the Indian Contingent, which could not be administered or maintained by British Commonwealth Occupation Force sources, as it was outside their jurisdiction and beyond their means.

268 Brigade Headquarters therefore had to be broken up into four echelons:—
  (i) Advance Headquarters for establishing the Force in India. As it turned out later this party was completely wasted because 268 Brigade Group was never formed in India and the advance elements were dispersed, thus causing serious administrative dislocation.
  (ii) Main Headquarters to leave with the main body. It was expected that before the departure of this group, three-fourth of the troops and stores must have been withdrawn.

(iii) Rear Headquarters to arrange for the withdrawal of the remaining force and stores.
(iv) Rear party to arrange for the liquidation of any outstanding items which could not be cleared by group (iii). This party was to consist of a couple of officers.

The priority of withdrawal of administrative units of the Indian Contingent in Integrated Headquarters and Base installations was to be determined by those formations and they were not keen to let them go till the very last. Their retention meant a further retention of more administrative units to look after them. This situation was explained to British Commonwealth Occupation Force, who were helpless in the matter because of replacement difficulties. To fill the shipping space it became necessary to break up units and send unessential personnel under command of other units. This created many difficulties during the voyage and on arrival in India. The broken up units were not self-contained and in many cases did not have their own officers, and on arrival in India did not find, as they had been led to believe, their own formation to look after them. They were dispersed to their Depot/ Regimental Headquarters in India waiting there for many months for their main body to arrive.

The position of the British officers of the Indian Army on integrated and national headquarters was never clarified. It was quite obvious that all British officers of Indian units could not be withdrawn without creating chaos and the majority of them desired to remain behind in Japan.

Another difficulty was that the Indian units were dispersed over a wide area, where they were responsible for occupation duties. These units could not be withdrawn unless their responsibilities were taken over by other units, which were not then available from British Commonwealth Occupation Force.

On the withdrawal of Indian units it was decided that Okayama and Tottori Prefectures were to pass to 34 Australian Infantry Brigade and Shimane to 2 New Zealand Expeditionary Force. It was easier for 2 New Zealand Expeditionary Force to take over the additional responsibility as it was adjacent to their existing area but 34 Australian Brigade could not administer detachments in Tottori without occupying Okayama, which was to remain under 268 Brigade control till their final departure. It was therefore necessary to withdraw the Tottori garrison last of all.

The smaller detachments of the contingent had, moreover, to be concentrated at a central place to facilitate their administration and maintenance before embarkation.

CONCENTRATION AREA

There were two possible concentration areas in British Commonwealth Occupation Force, Kure Base and Okayama city. To make the selection it was necessary to take the following factors into consideration:—
- (i) accommodation for troops awaiting embarkation;
- (ii) maintenance facilities during detention;
- (iii) transport facilities from concentration area to port of embarkation;
- (iv) covered accommodation for stores;
- (v) space for vehicles and engineer stores;
- (vi) facilities to guard (iv) and (v);
- (vii) transportation to carry stores and equipment to the point of embarkation.

It was considered a waste of effort to transport large quantities of stores and equipment from Okayama to Kure and then move them again for transhipment. As the great majority of stores was already at Okayama it was decided to make a central dump there instead of sending out-station stores direct to Kure. The latter would have meant creation of another detachment and consequently further dispersion.

Surplus accommodation was available in Okayama, but was not available in the close vicinity of Kure.

Depending on the shipping information, troops and stores could be moved from Okayama to Kure within 24 hours and embarked direct. In case of any unforeseen event a small escort party was made available from local Indian units in Kure to guard the stores which could not be loaded.

The main problem was manpower; with dwindling resources, the mounting stores had to be guarded, loaded and escorted. This was a formidable task, considering the desire of all to take what could be taken. It was therefore decided to make the concentration area at Okayama under 268 Brigade control and to concentrate all Rear Parties there and to move all units except those in closer proximity of Kure, the port of embarkation, through Okayama.

Shipping Position

There was no proper forecast about shipping. Headquarters British Commonwealth Occupation Force was asked to arrange for two store ships to precede each personnel ship. As Headquarters British Commonwealth Occupation Force did not control any shipping they could not arrange this. Unfortunatey the attitude of General Headquarters (India) did not smooth matters as they declared that they were not responsible for the provision of shipping for stores and vehicles[10] and kept on insisting that personnel must be withdrawn by 15 September 1947, without taking into consideration that they would be leaving behind stores worth many thousands, to the mere mercy of adverse elements.[11]

The withdrawal of the personnel did not involve great difficulty and by 25 October all Indian troops were withdrawn along with five ship-loads of stores.

Time Factor

Considering the amount of stores to be shipped it was necessary that the withdrawal should be spread over six months. The original plan was to complete withdrawal by 31 December 1947, but on 22 July 1947 General Headquarters (India) signalled, " For political reasons must plan for all Indian troops to leave Japan by 15 September 1947 ".[12] This upset the whole applecart; the stores, equipment and vehicles of Brindiv, which were moved in April, were still lying in Okayama, while the personnel of 268 Brigade Group had begun to move out and there was no news of the store ships.

It was again represented to India " that British Commonwealth Occupation Force would not undertake responsibility for stores and equipment left behind by Indian Contingent not required for British Commonwealth Occupation Force purposes ".[13] Supremind who had taken over the control of overseas contingent signalled that " all personnel must be withdrawn by 1 October 1947 the latest, and no Rear Party will be left behind ".[14] This meant " that stores left behind would become virtually dead loss to India unless shipment could be arranged before last phase sailed ".

There was no relaxation in the time limit and the last Indian soldier left Japan by HT *Dilwara* on 25 October 1947. The result of this acceleration and the uncertainty about the title to the stores was that much valuable store had to be left behind without any financial adjustments about its value.

Departure of Units

The first unit to leave Kure was 2/5 Gurkhas and Rear Parties of Brindiv. The Gurkhas left Fukushima in the early hours

[10] Armindia 24588/1 SD5 dated 17 July 47.
[11] BIE JCOSA INDEL/368 dated 1 September 47.
[12] BIE JCOSA INDEL/368 dated 1 September 47.
[13] BIE JCOSA INDEL/364 dated 1 September 47.
[14] Army Melbourne 4/M. G. O. dated 13 August 47 and BCOF QG/7974, dated 12 August 47.

of 17 July, and the special trains were met at Kure station by Brigadier Shrinagesh, the Commander of Kure Base and the Band of 4 New Zealand Battalion. The whole Battalion was embarked on HMT *Devonshire* by 1300 hours. In the evening 2/5 Gurkhas Pipe Band with the Kumaon Band played a final Retreat at the Kure sports stadium; many spectators said it was the best Retreat the two bands had given. The applause given by a very large crowd at the end was indicative of the great appreciation of the combined efforts of the bands. General Robertson, Commander-in-Chief, British Commonwealth Occupation Force, sent the following message:—

"The departure of the Kumaon Band brings to a close a period of one and a half years service in Japan. During this tour of duty the Band has served with distinction in the British and Indian Division, at my Headquarters at Etajima, at Tokyo, at Kure and also with the military and air components of the National Contingents, comprising the British Commonwealth Occupation Force in Japan.

Before they embark for India, I desire to express my thanks to Jemadar Abdul Ghafur, OBI. and members of the Kumaon Band for their willing response to the many calls made upon them and for the valuable welfare services they have rendered".

Many messages of goodwill were sent by various commanders. The Head of the Allied Government Team at Okayama wrote to Brigadier Shrinagesh: "As the first echelon of the Indian troops of your command depart from Okayama on the journey back to India, we wish to express to you, and through you to all ranks, our deep appreciation for the splendid co-operation this command has received from 268 Indian Infantry Brigade Group.

"The entire period of our relationship has been singularly marked by a complete absence of differences of opinion, by mutual trust and assistance, and by superlatively cordial and harmonious professional and social dealings.

"Our military government duties have been made easier and pleasanter by the understanding of our problems in relation to the Japanese people that has been displayed by you and your staff. Our surroundings have been made much more home-like by the interest shown in improving our military and personnel quarters. Our social lives have been expanded by the whole hearted welcome we have received in the Okayama Officers' Club and in the several Indian messes, and our understanding of India, it's customs, people and ideals increased far above the average by the friendships we have made among your people.

"You have been personally most gracious in your dealings with the American contingent in Okayama. We will recall in later years with great pleasure, our acquaintance with you and your family. It is a distinct pleasure to serve with senior officers who are as completely harmonious as you have been ".[15]

Departure of Brigadier S. M. Shrinagesh

On 17 August 1947, orders were received for Brigadier Shrinagesh to proceed to Australia as the Indian representative on Japanese Peace Conference to be held in Canberra. The orders were very sudden as they were received so soon after the Independence Day celebrations. In view of the fact that the withdrawal of the Indian Contingent was speeded up, it was arranged for him to return to India direct after completion of his task in Australia.

On the departure of Brigadier S. M. Shrinagesh the command devolved on Lieutenant-Colonel J. A. C. d'Apice, O.B.E., of 5/1 Punjab Regiment. It was decided that the Main Headquarters of 268 Indian Infantry Brigade Group would close at Okayama, at 0001 hours on 25 August 1947 and Lieutenant-Colonel D. A. Surve, Commander 5/1 Mahrattas would take over the command of 268 Brigade Group Rear Headquarters.

On his departure from Japan on the midnight of 18 August 1947, Brigadier S. M. Shrinagesh sent the following message to all ranks—

"On my departure from Japan, I want you to know that I have appreciated deeply your very loyal support, co-operation and hard work. As a result of our team work, we have:—

(a) represented worthily the British Commonwealth in the eyes of her Allies,
(b) consolidated and enlarged, during our time of duty in Japan, the fellowship and unity of effort which were forged in war.

I am convinced that the effect of the Indian Occupation on the Japanese people will prove beneficial to both the Dominions of India and Pakistan.

I wish most sincerely all members of 268 Indian Infantry Brigade Group all good wishes in the future, wherever they may be ".

The sudden departure of the very popular Commander was a great shock to all concerned who only learnt of his departure

---

[15] DO from Lieutenant-Colonel Karl. L. Springer, Commanding Allied Military Government team Okayama to Brigadier S. M. Shrinagesh, Commander 268 Brigade Group.

the next morning. But the news had trickled through and hundreds of Japanese and a large number of troops came to wish him " *Bon Voyage* " at the Okayama Railway Station.

Departure of 268 Brigade Headquarters

Units, one after the other began to leave Japan. The main body of Brigade Headquarters with all the families and 5/1 Punjab left in the second Phase. The remaining personnel were cleared in H T *Talma* and *Dilwara* on 25 October 1947. On that occasion Commander-in-Chief British Commonwealth Occupation Force, Lieut.-General H. C. H. Robertson sent the following signal to Lieutenant-Colonel Rajendra Singh. " On the eve of your departure from Japan I wish to express to you and to all ranks under your command my deepest regret that the time has at last come to say farewell. It has been a great privilege to have had you under my command and I wish you all the safe voyage, happy home coming and all good fortune in the future ".[16]

In reply Lieutenant-Colonel Rajendra Singh, sent the following message:

" On behalf of myself and all ranks Indian Contingent I thank you for your kind farewell message. During our time of duty in Japan we worked together with forces of other Dominions and United States of America; the ties of comradeship born out of this association, I am sure, will endure for ever. We have gained valuable experience, we had the best of time with British Commonwealth Occupation Force and thank you and your staff for all they did for us. We are proud of having served under you ".[17]

As the ships carrying these Indian stalwarts sailed down the Inland Sea, the memory of their stay in Japan must have reminded them of the hectic and trying days, pleasant and cheerful time, dull and boring periods, but none regretted his stay in Japan.

As *Dilwara* carrying the last Indian soldier left Kure a loud roar arose:

" GOODBYE "—" SOYA—NARA "—" GOOD LUCK ".

---

[16] British Commonwealth Occupation Forces Signal 20505 dated 24 October 47.
[17] Rear 268 Brigade Group Signal Q S 140 dated 27 October 47.

South–East Asia

CHAPTER XII

The Overall Plan

INTRODUCTION

Many months before the Japanese had actually surrendered, Lord Mountbatten had ordered the preparation of plans for liberating the territories in their occupation in South-East Asia. This work was taken up by the Joint Planning Staff, whose appreciation was that for obtaining immediate control of the territories under Japanese occupation, it would be necessary to use their chain of command till such time as direct control over these areas had been established by the Allied troops. It was therefore of the utmost importance to seize control of the Headquarters of the Japanese *Southern Army* at Saigon, as quickly as possible.

The plan adopted was to send a control party with suitable escort to take over this Headquarters for the purpose of obtaining information and intelligence by gaining access to all Japanese files, records and confidants, and ensuring that the terms of surrender were carried out, and that all orders of the Supreme Commander and his subordinate commanders were correctly transmitted to subordinate formations of the Japanese Army. The primary duties of the escort were to ensure the personal safety of the control party and to disarm and take over control of Japanese troops at their *Southern Army Headquarters* and in its immediate vicinity. The escort of at least a brigade strength was to be flown to an air-field in the Saigon area where it might be raised up to a division, at the earliest possible moment.

For this purpose it was necessary to use naval ships in the Saigon river, but in the existing situation of air and naval resources it was difficult to provide a suitable escort early enough. However, it was expected that the commanders of China and South-West Pacific Area theatres might also like to send control parties to the Headquarters of Japanese *Southern Army*.

PRIORITIES FOR DESPATCH OF TROOPS TO THE OCCUPIED AREAS

In addition to the seizure of the Japanese Headquarters in Saigon, there were other regions to which troops had to be sent for liberation purposes. The following priorities were, therefore, laid down:—
    (1) Singapore and Penang (Butterworth area)
    (2) Southern Army Headquarters at Saigon

(3) Remainder of Malaya
(4) Batavia and Sourabaya
(5) Hong Kong after its initial occupation by British Pacific Fleet and Australian forces
(6) Remainder of South-East Asia Command (SEAC) area.

In addition there were two other tasks, viz., participation in the occupation of Japan and the occupation of main ports on the coast of China, other than Hong Kong, which were assigned to the SEAC. The liberation of Andaman and Nicobar islands which were Indian territory, was entrusted to the Commander-in-Chief of India.

Allotment of Areas for Liberation

The areas for liberation were allotted as follows:—
(a) Twelfth Army Headquarters—Burma, Siam and southern French Indo-China
(b) Fourteenth Army Headquarters—Singapore, Malaya, Java and Sumatra.

It was accepted in principle that the bulk of the Twelfth Army would be lifted by air, while the Fourteenth Army would move by naval transport. It was further expected that the Twelfth Army would get assistance from the Siamese army, while the Fourteenth Army expected the collaboration of the Dutch Civil Affairs (NICA) staffs direct from Australia.

DISTRIBUTION OF FORCES AT THE INITIAL STAGE

Tasks	Location	Army	Air Force
First priority task	(a) Singapore	2 divisions with armour	6 squadrons
	(b) Saigon	1 brigade to be raised to one division	1 squadron
	(c) Bangkok	1 division	2 squadrons
Second priority task	(a) Port Swettenham area	1 division	1 squadron
	(b) Java-Batavia	1 division less 1 brigade	2 squadrons
	(c) Sourabaya	1 infantry brigade	1 squadron
	(d) Hong Kong	1 brigade group	1 squadron
	(e) Northern Siam	1 division less one brigade	

Tasks	Location	Army	Air Force
	(f) Sumatra and other off lying islands:		
	Padang etc.	1 division less one brigade	1 squadron
	Medan etc.	1 division	1 squadron
	Palembang etc.	1 infantry brigade	1 squadron
	(g) Kra Isthmus	2 brigades	
	(h) Japan	2 brigade groups	2 squadrons
	(i) Chinese ports	1 brigade group	

It was noted that Burma would require not less than two divisions, while a brigade would be adequate for Andamans and Nicobars. It was expected that in French Indo-China and Netherlands East Indies, French and Dutch forces would be available for carrying out liberation duties.

Naval forces were available, as required, for support and protection of operations, for mine-sweeping and other escort duties.

While the plans for the liberation of these territories were being formulated, it was decided that the Supreme Allied Commander would accept the Japanese surrender and the commands were to be kept informed of the whole process and of all instruments of surrender.

Concurrently with the acceptance of the surrender of Japanese troops in Burma, it was planned that the South-East Asia Command would seize strategic areas with utmost speed and subsequently reoccupy the remaining parts of that expansive region.

To carry out the above policy the following tasks were assigned to the commands:—

(a) disarm and concentrate all Japanese forces;
(b) protect, succour and subsequently evacuate Allied prisoners of war;
(c) establish and maintain law and order;
(d) introduce food and other civil supplies;
(e) set up the appropriate civil administration in accordance with the wishes of the people, if possible, but consistently with the honour and dignity of the United Nations, everywhere without exception.

In accordance with these general directions each Force Commander prepared a plan to carry out his assignment. The South-East Asia Command prepared outline plans for each area for the guidance of the local commander. Instructions were prepared for division, brigade and down to the lower units.

All the details of the plans for liberation had been formulated by the time that the Japanese decided to lay down their arms. On 20 August 1945, All India Radio established communications with Field-Marshal Terauchi, commander of the Japanese *Southern Army* at Saigon, and the Supreme Allied Commander ordered him to send a delegation by air to Rangoon to sign a preliminary agreement prior to a formal instrument of surrender to be signed at Singapore.

At the same time the following troop movements were ordered[1]: —

(a) to fly in the 7th Indian Division from Burma to Bangkok, to seize Don Muang air-field as a staging post and carry out Allied tasks in Siam (including recovery of Allied Prisoners of War and Internees (APWI);

(b) to fly in the 20th Indian Division from Burma to Saigon via the staging post in Siam and to control the Headquarters of Field-Marshal Terauchi;

(c) to carry out by sea the build-up of the 7th and 20th Indian Divisions, as soon as lift should be found and channels and ports had been swept;

(d) to reoccupy Penang with the Royal Marines of the East Indies Fleet; with one brigade from the 5th Indian Division (destined for Singapore) in case of any local resistance beyond the capacity of the Royal Marine force;

(e) to reoccupy Singapore Island from the sea with the 6th Indian Division as soon as a channel could be swept;

(f) to despatch the Commando Brigade to Hong Kong in order to take over occupation duties from the British Pacific Fleet and the Australian contingents;

(g) to carry out Operation Zipper;

(h) to despatch the 26th Indian Division to either Java or Sumatra, as soon as channels had been swept and lift found; and

(i) to reoccupy Lower Burma and the Andaman Islands at a later date, when the approaches and ports of these areas had been cleared.

[1] Mountbatten's *Report*, p. 226, para 640.

PLATE XIII

Admiral the Lord Louis Mountbatten, Supreme Allied Commander SEA, reading a message from His Majesty the King after the surrender of Japan

PLATE XIV

Lieut.-General Sir Philip Christison,
Allied Force Commander in
Netherlands East Indies

Lieut.-General E. C. Mansergh,
Allied Force Commander in
Netherlands East Indies

On 26 August 1945, Field-Marshal Terauchi's delegates arrived at Rangoon and signed the preliminary agreement on the night of 27 August 1945. Operations for the recovery of APWI began on the following day. The operations for landings of the forces in South-East Asia began on 2 September, as soon as news was received of the formal signature of Japan's unconditional surrender to General MacArthur in Tokyo. The interval was spent in distributing stores and relief to APWI and in mine-sweeping and buoying the channels. On 12 September, the Supreme Allied Commander accepted the surrender of the Japanese *Expeditionary Forces* of the Southern Regions in the Singapore Council Chamber, in the presence of the representatives of the armed forces of India, United States, Australia, China, France, Holland and Great Britain.[2]

[2] Mountbatten's *Report*, p. 229.

CHAPTER XIII

Recovery of Allied Prisoners of War and Internees

In the course of their conquest of South-East Asia in 1941-42 the Japanese had captured many thousands of British Commonwealth and Allied servicemen and kept interned a large number of civilians residing in those countries. Owing to the vastness of the area, the speed of the Japanese advance, the unprecedented quick capitulation of the British forces and the non-availability of records it was not possible to make accurate documentation about the number of prisoners or the places where they were kept. Many units or their sub-units, which had been cut up by the Japanese advance, had drifted to areas different from the place where they were supposed to have surrendered. Moreover, no information was obtained from the Intelligence sources as no underground intelligence organisation had been established during the quick capitulation of the Allied forces. Further, no notification was made by the Japanese authorities about the prisoners they held, which was required under the Geneva Convention. However, during 1944, some information about the prisoners had trickled in from various sources, particularly the clandestine forces operating in the Japanese occupied territory. These scraps of information made it possible to reconstruct a picture of the distribution of prisoners between areas and camps and the following figures were assembled according to the distribtion, countrywise, of the prisoners of war:—

Country	Prisoners	Internees	Total
Burma	1,100	102	1,202
Siam	28,639	171	28,810
Singapore Island	13,000	3,334	16,334
Malaya	3,940	...	3,940
French Indo-China	6,150	35	6,185
Sumatra	7,700	1,700	9,400
Java	27,000	28,840	55,840
	87,529	34,182	121,711

These men were distributed over various camps of which 227 were then known to exist. These figures became the basis for the planning of evacuation of the prisoners of war.

PLANNING AND ORGANISATION

In the month of February 1945, the War Office, London, issued an instruction directing plans to be prepared for the recovery and evacuation of the Allied Prisoners of War and Internees. The Supreme Allied Commander assigned this duty to the Commander-in-Chief, Allied Land Forces South-East Asia (ALFSEA). The sudden surrender of the Japanese demanded quick evacuation of nearly 100,000 men, who were scattered all over South-East Asia.

A new organisation was therefore set up to deal with this immense problem. On 18 August 1945, a special section of the Adjutant General's Branch of the Headquarters ALFSEA, comprising 16 officers, was set up under the Director of Organisation to deal with it. The principal subjects to be dealt with by this organisation included:—

(a) plans and operations in connection with repatriation of Recovered Allied Prisoners of War and Internees (RAPWI);
(b) RAPWI intelligence and dissemination of information;
(c) RAPWI stores;
(d) statistics.

This organisation incorporated the Searcher Clearing House which undertook the responsibility for the collection and distribution of nominal rolls of all prisoners of war and internees.

However, it was soon realised that for rapidity of execution of the plans, a greater degree of co-ordination would be required between the three services and the various Commonwealth and Allied Missions and Governments. Hence a 'RAPWI Co-ordinating Committee', with representatives of the three services and of some Allied Missions, was set up at the Headquarters SACSEA, on 22 August 1945, under the Principal Administrative Officer. This committee acted as a clearing house for information and gave decisions on policy, priorities and allocation of responsibility. Decisions on day to day problems, which were numerous, were also made by this committee, which became the nerve-centre of the whole RAPWI organisation.

In addition to the establishment of this high level organisation, the Headquarters SACSEA, in conjunction with the Commander-in-Chief, prepared a plan outlining the mode of operation. This was divided into the following four phases:—

(a) establishment at the earliest possible moment of initial contact and communication with the prisoner of war camps throughout the SEAC, and the immediate provi-

sion of medical attention and urgently required supplies there;
(b) the delivery to camps of bulk-supplies of food, medicine, clothing and other requirements;
(c) the documentation and movement of prisoners of war to the centres of evacuation; and
(d) the final evacuation of the Allied Prisoners of War and Internees outside the SEAC.

An immediate need was to prepare and position the contact teams, medical stores, clothing and food adequate to meet the requirements. This was made the responsibility of General Headquarters, India. Many of the requirements were special items, not normally carried in the field and had to be specially packed in India for the purpose. The lack of definite information as to the numbers of RAPWI in each area made the task rather difficult.

Although the Japanese intention to surrender had become definitely known on 15 August 1945, RAPWI operations were not started immediately, because, firstly, the reaction of the Japanese in the SEAC to the surrender was not definitely known, and, as such, there was the likelihood of undertaking an assault operation for the reoccupation of Malaya; and, secondly, General MacArthur had definitely laid down that no occupational forces were to land in the SEAC until the unconditional surrender had been signed.[1]

INITIAL OPERATIONS TO CONTACT AND SUCCOUR RAPWI

At the outset it was necessary to gain contact with the many RAPWI camps. However, before any such action was initiated, it was essential to drop warning, instructional or informative leaflets in the camps for the guidance respectively of Japanese guards, prisoners of war and the civil population in major towns. But the task of preparing and dropping different types of leaflets was not an easy one. The difficulty was heightened by the number of languages involved and by the fact that only two printing presses were equipped with Japanese type, and these were located only in Calcutta and Colombo.

These preparatory operations were given the code-name 'Birdcage' which started on 28 August and were completed in three days.

After the leaflet operation, the next task was to ascertain the number and condition of the prisoners in each camp and to meet

---

[1] The surrender was signed on 2 September, 1945.
This ruling was subsequently modified to allow all the contact teams to be parachuted into camps before that date.

their urgent requirements. It was essential that medical aid, comforts, food, clothing and, where necessary, RAPWI control Staffs, and other preliminary needs were provided in the camps, as early as possible. The known 227 prison camps were widely scattered throughout the whole of South-East Asia. If normal ground resources were employed it would have taken considerable time, hence air resources had to be used to the maximum extent to contact camps not within the immediate range of the ground forces. Operation Mastiff covered the initial phase until control and administration of RAPWI by land and sea became practicable.

The following resources were available for this initial operation: —

(a) *Personnel:* There were in the SEAC two clandestine forces (Force 136 and 'E' Group) whose organisation, training and equipment made them particularly suitable for the task of establishing contacts. Many men of these forces had operated, or were then operating, in the Japanese occupied territory, and were familiar with local conditions, in the various territories. Some, notably in 'E' Group, had been in contact with the prisoners of war in Japanese hands for some time. Hence, till such time as the ground forces might establish contact, the services of 'E' Group and Force 136 were utilised to render succour to RAPWI. Forty contact teams were formed from these forces, and from the 44th Indian Air-borne Division, of which thirty were parachute teams. These teams comprised one officer and one non-commissioned officer as Control Staff; one medical officer and a medical orderly with medical stores, special foods and comforts.

(b) *Aircraft:* Owing to the distances involved the long-range aircraft had to be employed. The following forces were available: —
   9 RAF Liberator Squadrons
   4 RAF Sunderland Squadrons
   1 RAF Dakota Squadron
   1 RAF Liberator Squadron.

(c) *Stores:* Various types of stores were made available from the army, Red Cross, Force 136 and 'E' Group resources.

CONTROL ORGANISATION

To achieve the purpose in view and execute the various operations, a control organisation was evolved, and orders for setting it up were issued on 17 August 1945:

(a) *Main Control:* This was located at Headquarters SACSEA. It consisted of staff officers of Headquarters SACSEA, ALFSEA, Force 136, 'E' Group and ACSEA. Its functions were:
  (i) to receive, collate and disseminate information;
  (ii) to allot priorities for the flying in or parachuting of personnel, stores etc.; and
  (iii) to arrange the bulk provisioning and positioning of stores at the air-fields.
(b) *Sub-controls:* These were located at Calcutta for French Indo-China, and at Rangoon for Siam, and acted, in the same manner as the Main Control, at the local air-fields. These sub-controls consisted of representatives of ALFSEA, Force 136 and 'E' Group.

Later a sub-control was also established at Singapore to co-ordinate supply-dropping operations in Java and Sumatra from the Cocos Islands.
(c) *Despatch Organisation:* This was located at Colombo and consisted of an ALFSEA representative and the existing organisation of Force 136 and 'E' Group. Its function was to work out flight plans and to pack and position containers for dropping.

The provision of personnel and stores by ALFSEA and their positioning at appropriate air-fields by ACSEA was well in hand before operations commenced on 28 August 1945.

The control system described above came into operation on 22 August 1945. On 28 August, the Supreme Allied Commander authorised operation Mastiff to begin. Pamphlet dropping on camps was started at once and was completed by 31 August 1945.

CONTACTING THE RAPWI CAMPS

Meanwhile clandestine contact teams in Siam had gained contact with the local Japanese authorities. With the arrival of further teams and Japanese co-operation the situation was well under control.

No. 5 RAPWI Control Staff arrived with the leading elements of the occupying troops. In French Indo-China it was not until 5 September that control of RAPWI by clandestine forces became effective, because five out of the eight parachute teams were unfortunately interned on landing.

No. 3 RAPWI Control Staff arrived at Saigon with the SACSEA Control Commission on 6 September 1945. In Malaya clandestine forces commenced gaining contact on receipt of orders on 30 August 1945. RAPWI Control Staff disembarked at Singapore on 5 September and at Port Swettenham on 9 September 1945, and took over from the clandestine forces.

From the beginning of September, teams and stores were dropped regularly, an average of thirteen sorties a day being flown. The actual situation in Java and Sumatra became known by mid-September and operations commenced from Singapore. Some assistance was obtained from the Australians (operating from Darwin) and a little from the Dutch (operating from Balik Papan), and the activities of Mastiff were extended to Java.

It may be emphasised that it was not until 15 August that responsibility for Java was transferred from SCAP to SACSEA; and this sudden and heavy increase in commitment introduced a new problem in the production, positioning and carrying in of large quantities of additional stores. By the end of September the arrival of occupying forces had reduced the commitments for which this operation was planned and the controls began to close down except the one at Singapore, which continued to function under the control of advanced echelon, RAPWI, HQ ALFSEA, until November, dealing with RAPWI in Java and Sumatra.

CARE OF RAPWI PRIOR TO EVACUATION

Operation Mastiff covered the movement by air of medical staff, RAPWI control staffs and urgently needed supplies of all natures to the prisoners of war and internment camps. Once RAPWI control staffs were established and supply by air to camps ceased to be essential, operation Mastiff was completed. Thereafter RAPWI were to be administered by the control staffs directly.

Immediately the Japanese capitulation became known, Headquarters ALFSEA raised more RAPWI control staffs to accompany the Allied forces going into Siam, French Indo-China, Hong Kong and Java and provided additional officials for the staff of the Twelfth Army at Rangoon. No Allied force was at that time detailed to occupy Sumatra. Hence No. 1 RAPWI control staff accompanying the Allied force occupying Malaya was earmarked, after completing its task in Malaya, for diversion to accompany such forces as might be sent to liberate Sumatra. By early September the six control staffs had been established in Malaya, Singapore, Bangkok, Siam, Hong Kong and Batavia. The flow of RAPWI from Siam and French Indo-China was handled by the RAPWI staff with the Twelfth Army at Rangoon.

The situation in Singapore demanded a different treatment. There were 35,000 RAPWI as against the earlier report of 16,000. It was also the focal point for evacuation of all RAPWI from the

Netherlands East Indies, Borneo, Hong Kong and even the Australian areas in New Guinea, as far as the British and Indian RAPWI were concerned. As the staff attached to the formations sent to Malaya was inadequate to handle this large number of RAPWI, the ALFSEA established an Advanced Headquarters RAPWI under the Director of Organisation. This formation utilised the APWI themselves and local civilians, and formed them into an organisation which controlled the RAPWI operations in Singapore, the Netherlands East Indies and Borneo, and assisted the Hong Kong and the Australian RAPWI coming by air from Siam and French Indo-China.

The Advanced Headquarters obtained representatives from the Royal Navy and Royal Air Force, and set up a staff which represented various branches and services. It defined policy, seeking guidance from the Headquarters SACSEA, through the Headquarters ALFSEA, when necesary. It organised the entire feeding, clothing, transport, embarkation and evacuation of RAPWI in Singapore and of those coming into that place. It co-ordinated all RAPWI air operations and set up an Air Maintenance Organisation for the air supply of RAPWI in Java and Sumatra. Its Medical Section was responsible for the entire hospital arrangements in Singapore and directed and supervised those in Java and Sumatra.

The problem of Sumatra was, however, peculiar. No occupying force was included in the initial contingent entering Malaya. The Japanese were in complete control there, and all Dutch subjects were in the prisoners of war or internment camps. It was observed from air reconnaissance that there were nearly 21,000 RAPWI scattered in camps throughout the country and living in a wretched condition of existence. A party from the Advanced Headquarters RAPWI ALFSEA, therefore, flew to Medan and collected together a few Dutch officers and civilians of standing from the RAPWI camps. A meeting was then held, and plans were suggested to the Dutch for the evacuation of all sick prisoners of war to Singapore, and for the settlement of the Dutch in the towns of Medan, Padang and Palembang. This was gratefully accepted by the Dutch authorities.

Internal communications in Sumatra were completely non-existent. The whole operation therefore had of necessity to be directed from Singapore, and communications were made by wireless to the clandestine personnel in Sumatra who had a few receiving sets with them, and messages were also sent by the daily supply aircraft which carried in food and clothing and brought out RAPWI to Singapore.

RECOVERY OF ALLIED PRISONERS OF WAR AND INTERNEES

There was at that time little political trouble in Sumatra and the resettlement of all RAPWI in the country into reasonably comfortable conditions in the towns was virtually completed when the first occupying forces arrived.

It had been estimated, prior to the Japanese surrender, that 88,530 prisoners of war and 34,170 civil internees, all of whom were in camps, would be recovered, making a total of 122,700. At that time the subsequent trend of events in the Netherlands East Indies, which was not then part of SEAC, could not be foreseen. Later their numbers considerably increased and many of them were not strictly RAPWI in the sense that they were not prisoners of war or had been interned, but in fact they were only refugees.

The statement of prisoners and internees recovered in SEAC shows a total respectively of 80,419 and 16,156, making a grand total of 96,575, but this does not include some 110,000 Dutch and Indonesian civilians recovered from Java and Sumatra and for whose well-being also the Supreme Allied Commander ultimately became responsible. Nor does it include 245,000 displaced persons of Asiatic origin.

The problems which faced the control staffs were many and varied in each area. The principal ones may be outlined below:

(a) The number of different nationalities involved, with their different languages, customs and needs—nationals of seventeen different countries were evacuated from Singapore alone.

(b) The number of civil internees permitted to defer their repatriation for various reasons—until they could be disposed of they remained a RAPWI commitment.

(c) The problem of accommodation and provision of staffs for RAPWI camps—although ultimately it was the responsibility of the Force Commander, the whole task fell to the RAPWI control staffs.

(d) Documentation and distribution of nominal rolls in accordance with the movements of RAPWI.

(e) The medical treatment of sick RAPWI.

(f) The speed with which RAPWI were being evacuated and the carrying out of certain administrative functions with small staffs.

MOVEMENT OF RAPWI

At the time of Japanese surrender there were in the Indian Ocean approximately fifty-two personnel ships with a trooping capacity of 95,000 and also six hospital-ships with a carrying capacity of 3,050. This shipping had been assembled in the ports of India and Burma for the purpose of assault on Malaya; and the movement and sea transport authorities were thus able to make a very early start in transferring the recovered prisoners of war to their ultimate destinations. In addition to the Red Ensign shipping available, every advantage was taken of White Ensign lift which was immediately offered by the Commander-in-Chief of the British Pacific Fleet and East Indies Fleet. The Royal Navy rendered all assistance in the movement of RAPWI and converted even some aircraft carriers to remedy shipping difficulty, for these vessels with their large capacity and speed made a very considerable addition to the shipping lift otherwise available.

Movement of the recovered prisoners of war involved two definite stages, one from the camps to collecting centres or hospitals within SEAC and India, and the other their evacuation from collecting centres to the ultimate destinations within or outside the SEAC. Both these operations had their peculiar administrative aspects. In addition there was the problem of evacuation from Netherlands East Indies to Singapore.

The principal collecting centres within the SEAC were Rangoon, Singapore and Hong Kong. The majority of the prisoners recovered in French Indo-China and Siam were moved to Rangoon, with the exception of Australians, who as far as possible were concentrated in Singapore. Those found in Netherlands East Indies and Malaya were concentrated in Singapore, except for those who were evacuated by Zipper shipping from Port Swettenham, Port Dickson and Penang. Others recovered from the territories controlled by the Commander-in-Chief, British Pacific Fleet or South-West Pacific Area were normally concentrated in Hong Kong.

These men were moved to collecting centres by all means of transportation available except that the movement to Rangoon from French Indo-China and Siam was exclusively by air.

The plan had to provide for a double process, maximum evacuation of RAPWI and simultaneous movement of the British occupying forces into the countries liberated within the SEAC. The latter task, although of lower priority than the former involved the transportation of a vast number of men and their equipment to the various countries to be occupied. Bearing in mind that the maximum personnel shipping had already been allocated to the theatre for many weeks, it was essential to prepare very carefully the plans to ensure the utmost economy in both White or Red Ensign personnel shipping.

Several plans were worked out and eventually a finally agreed detailed plan was produced by SACSEA which had the agreement of the movement and shipping authorities in London, India and Australia and also that of Commander-in-Chief, British Pacific Fleet.

Once the overall plan had been agreed to, the broad allocation of shipping was relatively a simple affair and was done in the following manner:—

    (a) Certain ships were allocated for repatriating to the United Kingdom, from Rangoon and Singapore; and subsequent to their leaving Colombo these were lost to the SEAC pool.

    (b) Certain ships were allocated for the repatriation of Australians from Singapore to Australia and on their return voyage were utilised to repatriate Indian prisoners of war from the South Pacific to India or to assist the Commander-in-Chief, British Pacific Fleet in moving personnel from the areas under his control.

    (c) The remainder of the personnel shipping lift was occupied in building up the occupation force in Malaya, and on their return journey to take Indian prisoners of war back to India.

    (d) All sick RAPWI, other than Australians, were evacuated to India apart from a small proportion who were moved to Ceylon by air. These were carried by Sunderland Squadrons which had carried Red Cross parcels to Singapore. Australian sick were evacuated direct to Australia or staged through Labuan. To assist such movement the Australian authorities had provided some hospital-ships.

From the information available from medical sources, it was obvious that the condition of many RAPWI prevented them from being embarked at full trooping capacity. Ships were therefore carefully classified as to accommodation, and allocation of capacity was made as follows:—

    Cabins ... ... 100 per cent of normal
    Standees ... ... 70 per cent of normal
    Troopdeck ... ... 50 to 60 per cent of normal.

This schedule was communicated to embarkation ports to operate as a guide. The medical authorities at these ports were allowed discretion as to the actual numbers which might be embarked, and that depended on the condition of recovered prisoners as also the number of women and children among the internees.

Reception centres had to be staffed and equipped. This involved a movement of administrative and medical units, with supplies of equipment to reception centres, before full-scale concentration of the prisoners and internees was undertaken.

All ships had to be victualled with special food. Additional staff including medical and nursing personnel, and welfare workers had to be provided; ships had to be equipped with blankets, clothing, knives, forks, spoons and many other items because the recovered prisoners, unlike the normal soldier, had not been provided with these at the time of their recovery. There was variation in items provided depending on whether the ship was allocated to carry British or Indian prisoners of war.

The various authorities at the ports on the route were kept informed of the overall plan as it developed. They were thus in a position to handle ships expeditiously as these passed through. The principal ports affected were Colombo and those of the Middle East where ships were watered, refuelled, or took on special supplies; as, for example, in the Middle East where the recovered prisoners were equipped with warm clothing prior to their entering the European waters.

From the two ports of embarkation, under the organisation outlined above, a considerable number of repatriated persons were sent to India or the United Kingdom. The figures are given below:—

(a) *Rangoon:* Repatriated Allied Prisoners and Internees began to arrive from Siam and French Indo-China by air on 26 August 1945, and by 30 September 9,700 had left for the United Kingdom by sea. During this period 1,600 had sailed for India including 750 invalids; and 157 had been moved to India (including those for onward passage to the United Kingdom) by air. In all 19,543 were brought into the Rangoon area by air.

(b) *Singapore:* The first troops entered on 5 September 1945. The first RAPWI vessel sailed for India on 10 September, for the United Kingdom on 11 September, and for Australia on 15 September 1945. By 30 September 1945, 33,000 prisoners and internees had been evacuated by sea (8,000 to United Kingdom, 7,000 to Australia, and 18,000 to India). Air evacuations during this period were 526 to Australia and New Zealand and 723 to India and Ceylon. By 30 September 1945, in all nearly 54,000 prisoners had been evacuated out of the SEAC from these two stations—Rangoon and Singapore, of which 2,216 were moved by air. By the end of October 1945, the figure had risen to 71,000. Thereafter the process became slow depending on the availability of RAPWI after their release from the hospitals. Many had deferred repatriation.

RED CROSS ORGANISATION

The Red Cross also collaborated in the schemes of repatriation. Its activities were directed throughout the Command by the Red Cross Co-ordinating Committee at the Headquarters of the SACSEA. This committee, which was formed in May 1945, consisted of the Director Medical Services HQ SACSEA as Chairman, assisted by members of the Red Cross organisations of Great Britain, Australia, India, Burma, France and the Netherlands.

The principal functions of the committee were to co-ordinate the requirements of Red Cross aid throughout the Command and the allocation of the available resources to meet a constantly changing situation. Necessary resources for implementing the policy outlined by the Co-ordinating Committee were under the general control of the Commander-in-Chief ALFSEA. All executive action was undertaken by the Red Cross representative at that Headquarters, who worked under the DMS there.

Red Cross aid to the prisoners of war and internees included:—
(a) the affording of moral and material assistance at the earliest practical moment to the camps and hospitals where these people were located;
(b) the location of reception parties at overseas ports to assist RAPWI before and during embarkation;
(c) the provision of assistance in hospital-ships and transports during the voyage;
(d) the distribution of enquiry messages from their relatives in the United Kingdom and other countries which were sent out under Red Cross auspices.

From the very beginning it was evident that this plan would strain the existing resources of the Red Cross to the full, and would involve augmentation, particularly in the matter of personnel. This was achieved by organising teams of Red Cross workers in the localities where prisoners were recovered and a suitable leader for each team was appointed, regardless of the community to which he or other members of his team belonged. These teams visited camps and hospitals regularly, and distributed comforts including food and cigarettes. Similarly teams were formed at the ports used for purposes of evacuation. These teams provided reception parties who served tea and administered comforts at the docks or at the air-fields. The teams also received Red Cross stores at ports and distributed them to the various parties working at the camps, hospitals and in the reception organisation.

Red Cross personnel met each hospital-ship and workers accompanied every transport on its way to the United Kingdom or Australia. In addition, all the ships arriving at Colombo and at the Indian ports were met by Red Cross parties. RAPWI hospitals in India were visited regularly by Red Cross personnel who distributed comforts. In the early stages a large number of gift parcels were delivered to the camps by the Royal Air Force, whilst more parcels were provided at Singapore and Colombo for such of the prisoners as had not formerly received them.

Lady Louis Mountbatten (Chief Superintendent, Nursing Division, Joint War Organisation St. John's Ambulance Brigade) toured all the recovering areas immediately after RAPWI Control Staffs had been set up and visited the prisoners in the camps and hospitals. She also assisted local Red Cross workers in obtaining their requirements by the most expeditious means and did much to improve the morale of RAPWI.

Enquiry bureaux were formed in Singapore and Rangoon to answer enquiries received from the United Kingdom and other countries.

In all, between August and November 1945, 294 Red Cross workers were in action in the areas outside India. Another 361 of them were employed in India in connection with RAPWI hospitals, the Red Cross depots, port parties and the searcher organisation.

A total of 1,200 tons of Red Cross stores to the value of £300,000 was despatched from India. Additional 5,000 tons, of the value of £800,000 were provided by the Australian Red Cross. The gift parcels issued totalled 120,000.

THE INDIAN PRISONERS OF WAR RECOVERY MISSION

The ALFSEA directive on the " Treatment and Evacuation of Recovered Allied Prisoners of War and Civil Internees " had been drawn up in consultation with the General Headquarters, India. When the war suddenly ended, the Viceroy and the Commander-in-Chief in India decided that it would be desirable to send an Indian Army Mission to advise and help the ALFSEA RAPWI Control Staffs, for it was presumed that many of these would have little experience of Indian troops. The proposal was agreed to by the SACSEA and the ALFSEA. A similar mission was sent to the American Zone while one had been established at

PLATE XV

Lady Mountbatten, Chief Superintendent, Nursing Division St. John Ambulance, talking to some ex-prisoners of war

PLATE XVI

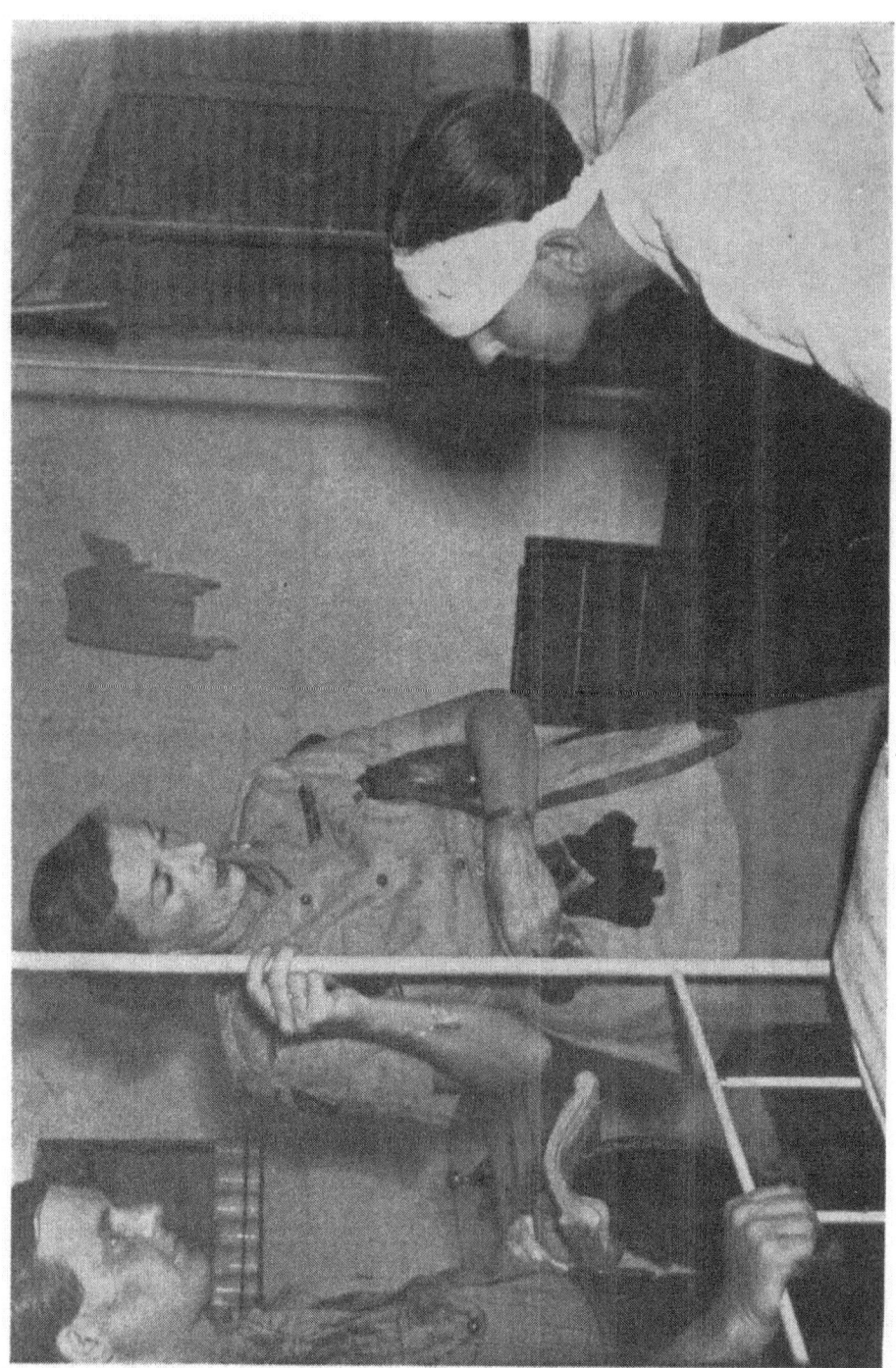

Lady Mountbatten talking to a patient in a hospital in Saigon

Brisbane, and was dealing with the Indian prisoners of war recovered by the Australians in New Guinea.

The object, as defined in the directive issued to the Mission, was to give advice and every possible assistance to the ALFSEA RAPWI Control Staff in the recovery and disposal of prisoners of war of the Royal Indian Navy (if any), Indian Army, Royal Indian Air Froce (if any), and of the Indian personnel of the Burma Army and Hong Kong—Singapore Royal Artillery as also Indian merchant seamen, who all had the status of prisoners of war, and Indian civilian internees. Their co-operation was, in particular, to extend to the following operations:—

    (a) collection;
    (b) sorting of JIFs (members of Indian National Army) from the other prisoners of war;
    (c) sorting of the latter by Regiment/Corps;
    (d) documentation, pay and fitting out with clothing;
    (e) despatching these to India:—
        (i) in the best conditions possible as to travel;
        (ii) well-primed as to conditions to be expected in India;
        (iii) rehabilitated both mentally and physically to the utmost extent that circumstances and time available permitted and instilled with the idea that they were still soldiers.

Perhaps the most important of the Mission's duties was personal contact and by that means to show to the recovered prisoners of war that they had not been forgotten and that the government wanted to help them in every way possible; to tell them that their regiments and relations were eagerly awaiting their return; to explain to them the changes in pay that had taken place in their absence, and how their pay had been accumulating for them, details of which they would receive on arrival at their depots; and to explain the political and economic situation (including such matters as food and cloth rationing) that they must be prepared for on their arrival in India.

The Mission worked with, but under the command of, the Headquarters ALFSEA, or of any subordinate ALFSEA formation with which it, or any part of it, happened to be located. It consisted of a commander, with the rank of brigadier, two deputy commanders as colonels and a staff captain, with small staff, and two contact teams (later four), each consisting of one lieut-colonel, two majors, two captains, eight VCOs, and a number of clerks, drivers, batmen and followers.

The commander and his two deputies arrived at Rangoon by air on 29 August 1945, when Operation Mastiff had begun, and the first batch of recovered prisoners of war was already arriving from Bangkok. Tactical Headquarters of the British Forces in Siam and in South French Indo-China, and the RAPWI Control Staffs, were about to fly in. One of the deputies was left, therefore, at Rangoon as the Mission's representative in Siam and South French Indo-China and for liaison with the Headquarters Twelfth Army at Rangoon.

A signal was also sent to the General Headquarters India for a third and fourth contact team, for Siam and French Indo-China respectively. The commander and the other deputy sailed by the second convoy to Singapore arriving on 7 September. There the Mission Headquarters was established with No. 2 RAPWI Control Staff (and Advanced Headquarters ALFSEA RAPWI when it was formed), at Goodwood Park Hotel, the deputy being responsible, pending the arrival of 1 and 2 Contact Teams, for Singapore, Malaya, Sumatra and Java.

1 and 2 Contact Teams were held up at Madras through lack of shipping space and eventually landed at Port Swettenham on 20 September. Their transport did not arrive until 20 October. The commanders of 3 and 4 Contact Teams, with nearly half of their officers, arrived by air at Bangkok and Saigon, respectively, on 23 September. The remainder of their personnel arrived at Rangoon early in October. But their transport never reached them.

The number of Indian Army RAPWI in South French Indo-China was small (107) and by the time No. 4 Contact Team arrived at Saigon, all had been evacuated.

The problem of the Indian National Army in South French Indo-China also was not a major one, and was well under control of the British Mission. No. 4 Contact Team was therefore brought into reserve, first at Rangoon, and later at Singapore whence it was sent eventually to deal with the Indian RAPWI at Rabaul and Morotai and in Borneo.

In Siam, also, the number of Indian prisoners of war was comparatively small (760) but there were over 300 British officers of the Indian Army. These officers and men were soon evacuated to Rangoon. Commander ALFSIAM put the Mission's representative in complete charge of the Indian National Army personnel in Bangkok, numbering about 2,000. The work combined with liaison on behalf of the Mission with Headquarters Twelfth Army in Rangoon and with the British troops in South French Indo-China, kept him fully occupied until he handed over the INA men to the 89 Indian Infantry Brigade (of the 7th Indian Division) in November 1945, and returned to India.

No. 3 Contact Team arranged, with the local Headquarters, for the administration, accommodation, interrogation (by CSDIC), and eventual despatch to Rangoon, of the prisoners of war (distinct from the INA) and stragglers, as they came in. Searcher parties were sent out to comb Siam for more stragglers, who brought in a considerable number of them.

Records of those already evacuated were collected and despatched to the General Headquarters India. Assistance was given to the British Mission in Siam in reconnoitring and organising camps for displaced coolie labour that had been working under the Japanese on the Siam—Burma Railway. No. 3 Contact Team completed its work and returned to India towards the end of November 1945.

For evacuation from Singapore, Sumatra and Java, the commander with one of his deputies, as the sole representative of the Mission, arrived at Singapore on 7 September. Arrangements had already been made for the evacuation of RAPWI to India from 9 September 1945 onwards. British officers of the Indian army had been separated from their men during their captivity and had just rejoined them in the Indian camps. All the detailed work involved in running these camps, such as the issue of food, clothing, pay etc., and all the work of selecting and preparing men for evacuation, and making out their embarkation rolls, had to be done initially by these officers and the prisoners of war themselves. Gradually the work was taken over by the officers of the XV Corps and by locally employed clerks. If arrangements could have been made for 1 and 2 Contact Teams to arrive at the same time as the commander of the Mission, their assistance would have been invaluable during this rush period.

Besides the above activities the Mission's representatives had personal contact with the recovered prisoners of war and assisted in separating their own prisoners of war from the INA men. The latter were already living in separate camps at Bidadari Road, but, on the capitulation, the Japanese had mixed up the " Changi Guard " with the prisoners of war. But these could not be allowed to get back to India along with the others. A plan for their separation was worked out with the Headquarters XV Corps. The deputy commander of the Mission continued to work with the Headquarters ALFSEA, Fourteenth Army, XV and XXXIV Corps on matters relating to the Indian National Army, until he returned to India in November 1945.

The rush period of evacuation from Singapore to India ended about 20 September, and the chief task of the detachment of the Mission in Singapore then came to be the accommodation, administration, and despatch (after interrogation) of Indian prisoners of war passing through Singapore from other areas such as Sumatra, Java, Sumbawa, etc.

A staging camp was established at Buller Camp and administered by the contact team which had arrived just in time to take over this work.

Liaison parties went by air to contact RAPWI control staffs throughout Sumatra and Java, and to confirm that no Indian prisoners of war remained in those islands.

Turning to Malaya, the personal contact between the Mission and the Indian RAPWI camps in Kuala Lumpur and Port Dickson was established by the middle of September. When 1 and 2 Contact Teams arrived on 20 September, the former remained at Kuala Lumpur and the latter moved to Penang to deal with the mainland. Searcher parties were also sent out to comb the mainland from Alor Star and Kota Bharu in the north to the Johore causeway in the south, and they brought back considerable numbers with them.

Most of the later evacuations to India of small parties of stragglers, including a few Indian prisoners of war who had married local wives, were brought by air from Penang to Madras. No. 1 Contact Team handed over to the Headquarters Fourteenth Army in the middle of November 1945.

It had been intended originally that the Indian prisoners of war from Borneo, Morotai and Rabaul areas should be evacuated to India via Australia. The end of the war made this no longer necessary, and HQ SACSEA became responsible for the evacuation direct to India.

After a liaison visit by the commander of the Mission to all the camps, and to the various Australian Headquarters concerned, detachments (mostly from No. 4 Contact Team) were flown from Singapore, to assist in the administration of the camps and the evacuation of the prisoners of war, and to accompany them as Draft Conducting Officers.

Following RAPWI including the sick, of whom there was a large number in Rabaul, were evacuated by the end of November:

Place	British	Indian
Borneo (Labuan)	5	90
Borneo (Balik Papan)	...	190
Morotai	...	390
Rabaul	...	5,674

The Mission closed down and left the SEAC by the end of November 1945.

Altogether about 600 British officers of the Indian Army and 19,677 Indian prisoners of war were evacuated from the SEAC (excluding Burma and the Andamans, which were not touched by the Mission); and 5 British officers and 6,344 Indians from Borneo, Morotai and Rabaul.

The members of the Mission were very greatly struck by the high morale of the Indians, their discipline and patience, their pleasure in finding somebody who could tell them in their own language the latest news from India, and their gratitude for anything that was done for them.

CHAPTER XIV

Restoration of Law and Order in French Indo-China and Thailand after the defeat of Japan

After the defeat of Japan the French dependency of Indo-China was divided into two parts by the 16° north latitude, the northern portion becoming the responsibility of Nationalist China of Generalissimo Chiang Kai-shek and the southern half falling under SACSEA. It is with the latter portion that we are mostly concerned in this narrative; but some knowledge of the basic problems of this region is essential to understand the course of events which followed the defeat of Japan.

French Indo-China is a mass of fertile land sandwiched between the land-masses of India and China. With India it is not directly connected because of the interposition of Burma and Siam, but it is an adjacent neighbour of China and that is how its policies and problems got connected with the Chinese. Before World War II, the French had divided their colony into five regions of Tonkui, Laos, Annam, Cambodia and Cochin-China. The SEAC was concerned generally with the last three, though mostly with the Saigon area, bounded on the south by the northern channel of the Me-kong river from Mytho and on the north by an arbitrary line of Mytho—Thu Dau Mot—Nha-trang.

Topographically the region was a mixture of delta land, coastal low-lands, low plateaus and jungle-covered mountains. It has fairly good communications; roads connect the important towns, the railways though few converge on Saigon, telephone and telegraphic lines run along railways and principal roads, all focussing on Saigon, the capital of Cochin-China, which also boasts of the air-field of Tan Sun Nhuat just outside the town.

The climate of south Indo-China is tropical, subject to the seasonal influences of the Asiatic monsoon circulation. From May or June the south-west monsoon continues for many months and renders the climate of Cambodia and Cochin-China hot and humid, and from November the north-east monsoon fills Annam with a wet misty weather. But the peculiarity of weather is the variation in visibility. At Saigon, for instance, the clouds are below 1,000 feet and visibility is less than one and half miles for some time during the day, particularly during September. Flying on those days is possible only in the mornings when there is generally a short spell of fair whether. But flying at night is undoubtedly dangerous not only because of the turbulent clouds but also due to the mist over the delta.

The region is self-sufficient in food-stuffs, with a surplus produce of rice. Its economy is based entirely on agriculture and export of rice. In 1945, the rice surplus was very small for distribution to civil population and it could not be augmented till the harvest of 1945.

The most important towns are Saigon, Bien Hoa, Dalat, Mytho, Jiring and Phan Rang. Cholon is the commercial and Chinese quarter of Saigon. The important ports and anchorages in the area, which came under the British control, were, Tourane, Kwinton, Kam Ranh Bay and Nha-trang. Saigon was largely built by the French to a standardised rectangular street pattern and contained several fine buildings and boulevards with attractive names. During the period of Japanese administration post and telegraph facilities had increased and the wireless transmitting station was considerably improved.

French Indo-China below 16°N may be divided into three parts:—

(a) *Cochin-China*, which was a French colony and administered as such in normal times by the French colonial authority;

(b) *Cambodia*, which was a kingdom under the French protectorate, administered by local officials but closely supervised by French residents; and

(c) *Annam*, which was like Cambodia in all respects.

The political history of Indo-China ran on parallel lines with those of other nations in South-East Asia, but it was mainly Annam with some support of Tonkin which bore the brunt of the struggle with the French. A strong independence movement existed before the war and had been a problem for the French authorities. When the Japanese occupied the country they fostered the movement and the Vichy administration in Indo-China looked on helplessly. In March 1945, when Germany and the Vichy regime were about to collapse, the Japanese decided to assume complete control of the state. This led to resistance by the French army in Indo-China, but the opposition was suppressed and the bulk of the army and civilian French personnel were interned or placed under severe restrictions. In August, Japan itself was defeated. There was a hiatus in the general administration of the country. The Annamite independence movement at once grasped the opportunity thus offered and drove Bao Dai, the emperor, from the throne and set up a republic at Hanoi, under the very nose of the Chinese, who were in occupation of North Indo-China. This movement was known as Viet Minh. It was in possession of arms, was anti-French and during the post-war period became also anti-British.

From the stand-point of the SACSEA there were three organisations, besides the Annamites, which caused uneasiness to the British military authorities. The Baodaists, whose field of work was mainly in Cochin-China, were most active in Saigon uptil the end of March 1945, and their aim was to eliminate the white man from Indo-China. When in August 1945, Japan was about to surrender they formed the National Front with other pro-Japanese elements to take over the civil administration from the Japanese. Unfortunately for them, the National Front was overthrown by the Viet Minh and its members were absorbed into the latter party. It is most probable that it were the Baodaists, armed by the Japanese, who led the demonstrations on 2 September 1945, when a number of French and Allied prisoners of war were killed and wounded and several European houses were sacked.

The second group was the Dao-Xen, founded in 1939, in the western provinces of Cochin-China, with the object of overthrowing French domination by resort to terroristic activities. But they joined the Viet Minh party at the end of August 1945. It is stated that after the lapse of a few months they became hostile to the Viet Minh and attacked its troops in the Cantho province.

The third party was the Voluntaires de la Mort, which was a terrorist body, pure and simple. Its aim was looting and murdering and sabotaging in the Allied territory. But like the Dao-Xenists, the Voluntaires were suspected by the Viet Minh to be its enemies and were therefore suppressed by the latter at an early date.

At the Potsdam Conference, the Combined Chiefs of Staff had allotted to the SEAC the part of French Indo-China lying south of 16° north and instructed Lord Louis Mountbatten to secure control of the Supreme Headquarters of the Japanese army in the south, which was then in Saigon, under Field-Marshal Count Terauchi. This objective was superimposed by the restriction: " that not more than what was required to ensure control over the Japanese army was to be occupied in southern Indo-China, that the British occupying force must be withdrawn as soon as its military task was done, and that the French be responsible for all political and administrative key-areas in which the SEAC army would be operating as well as in Indo-China in general by virtue of their historical position in the country ".

The Supreme Commander prepared his plans according to this clear-cut policy. He stated the object of reoccupation as 'to introduce a force into French Indo-China south of 16° north in order to control Japanese *Southern Army Headquarters*, to concentrate and evacuate Allied prisoners of war and internees and to disarm Japanese forces'[1], and added that the eventual reoccupation of Indo-China was a matter for the French; and all matters affecting the civil population would be dealt with through the French representatives on the Control Commission, while the British Foreign Office representative on this commission would direct by advice the French handling of the political affairs of Indo-China.

The strength of the British force depended on two factors: the strength of the Japanese army and the adequacy of the French resources to support their general responsibilities. It is on record that for six weeks from the middle of September 1945, the only troops available to the French authorities outside the key areas were 1,000 men of 5 Colonial Infantry Regiment (5 RIC) in Ceylon, 500 French released prisoners of war and local inhabitants and certain warships, one of which was *Richelieu*. The 9th and 3rd Colonial Infantry Divisions (DIC) were still in Europe and inadequately equipped. The 1 Far East Brigade could not come safely into Indo-China until the 9th DIC had arrived which was due only in the first week of November. The British had, therefore, to bring a larger force into Indo-China than was necessary for a more restricted task, like that of merely controlling the Japanese and evacuating the RAPWI.

The strength of the Japanese army was still unknown; its morale after surrender was not gauged; and its dispositions were not easy to trace. It was therefore decided to control the whole of Japanese army through Field-Marshal Count Terauchi and make him responsible for its loyal and proper conduct. The chain of command was helpful as all services, land, sea and air, were directly controlled by the Japanse *Southern Army HQ* from Saigon. The total strength of the Japanese forces was established at 71,000, with 31,000 in the north and 40,000 in the south. The latter figure was made up mainly of three divisions, the *2nd*, the *22nd* and the *55th Divisions*, distributed in Saigon, Phnom Penh and Tourane areas. Besides these there were a number of non-divisional ancillary units of air, ground and naval forces and other unidentified troops. There were about sixty-seven aircraft of both army and navy, with 5,880 men attached to them, the

---

[1] Force Plan No. 1 'Occupation of French Indo-China', 31 August 1945, para 2.

majority of the aircraft being based on air-fields in Cambodia.

BRITISH FORCES IN FRENCH INDO-CHINA

Lord Louis Mountbatten decided to move into Indo-China the following units, personnel and vehicles:—

	Personnel	Vehicles
Royal Navy	140	30
20th Indian Division and attached troops	22,287	2,036
Royal Air Force	2,250	320
One Company SAS 5 French Colonial Regiment	178	4
One Light Commando 5 French Colonial Regiment	623	10
SACSEA Control Commission ...	260	...
Public Relations	10	...
Total ...	25,748	2,400

He also resolved to continue liaison with the old clandestine organisations, and for that purpose he included an officer in the Control Commission. The policy behind this move was to keep these forces concentrated in their areas to perform the following duties under British direction:—

    (a) to provide local intelligence particularly about the actions taken by the Japanese, to comply or otherwise, with surrender orders;

    (b) to give topographical and other local information to the Allied occupational forces when these arrive;

    (c) to supply guides and interpreters to Allied occupational forces;

    (d) to establish contact with the Allied prisoners of war camps in certain cases; and

    (e) in the event of continued Japanese resistance in certain areas or of their failure to comply with surrender orders, to join the army in a common operation against the enemy.

It may be repeated that the naval and air forces were very meagre and their roles minor. The naval forces swept the channels for shipping, organised port services and imposed surrender terms on the Japanese naval surface and naval air forces, while the air forces lent a 'show of force', provided air lift to Saigon and air supply to the Allied troops of occupation.

Lord Louis Mountbatten warned his officers in good time that they should not become involved in Indo-China politics and that their sole duty was the maintenance of law and order. But he advised them, at the same time, that they must keep themselves well-informed about political happenings in order to avoid all politics. The Viet Minh party promised to co-operate with the Supreme Commander as long as the above policy was strictly adhered to.

On 2 September 1945, before the SEAC forces had arrived, a serious riot broke out against the French authority. It was suppressed by the released British and Australian prisoners of war, who were without arms and by a RAPWI control officer who had just been flown in.

On 17 September, the day on which the independence of the Viet Nam republic was declared, the Viet Minh organised the closure of markets in Saigon and enforced a boycott of all French employers. Also sporadic fighting took place in the town, and there were riotous conditions all over the place. For a few days no legal writ ran, and no steps were taken to restore law and order. Mob violence had spread all over the country, and armed bands had resorted to killing the French and terrorising the neighbourhood.

OCCUPATION OF FRENCH INDO-CHINA

The post-war occupation of French Indo-China lasted for five and a half months. It began on 12 September 1945. Lord Louis Mountbatten could not, however, send an adequate force there before the middle of October. Consequently, he had to make use of the Japanese army to maintain the minimum of control over the people there. "For this purpose," the Supreme Commander reported, " I maintained the existing Chain of Command, through their Supreme Commander, to publish and enforce my orders. I consider that if the Japanese Chain of Command had been disrupted for fear that it might provide the enemy Commanders with a means of controlling their forces in resisting us before we had fully replaced it with our own, it would have been impossible for us to use their forces for our own purposes as effectively as we did "[2].

The units which were moved into Indo-China were informed exactly about their duties. They were told: " Our task is not yet

---

[2] Mountbatten's *Report*, p. 257.

FRENCH INDO-CHINA
SCALE OF MILES
100 0 100 200 300 400 500
KILOMETRES
100 0 100 200 300 400 500 600 700 800
CHINA
KAO-BANG
LANG-SON
Song bo
HANOI
M. HET
Song ma
N. Hu
BAN HWEI SAI
LUANG PRABANG
GULF OF TONG-KING
HAI-NAN
N
Song ka
FRENCH INDO CHINA
VINH
HATINH
TURAKOM
THAKHEK
DONG HOI
HUE
M. SAVANNAKET
THAILAND (SIAM)
KWANG NGAI
R. MUANG
Se khang
QUI-NHON
STUNG-TRENG
KRATIE
KOMPONG CHHANG
Me kong
PHANG RANG
GULF OF SIAM
PHNOM PENH
THU DAU MOT
THU DUC
SAIGON
MYTHO
CAP St. JACQUES

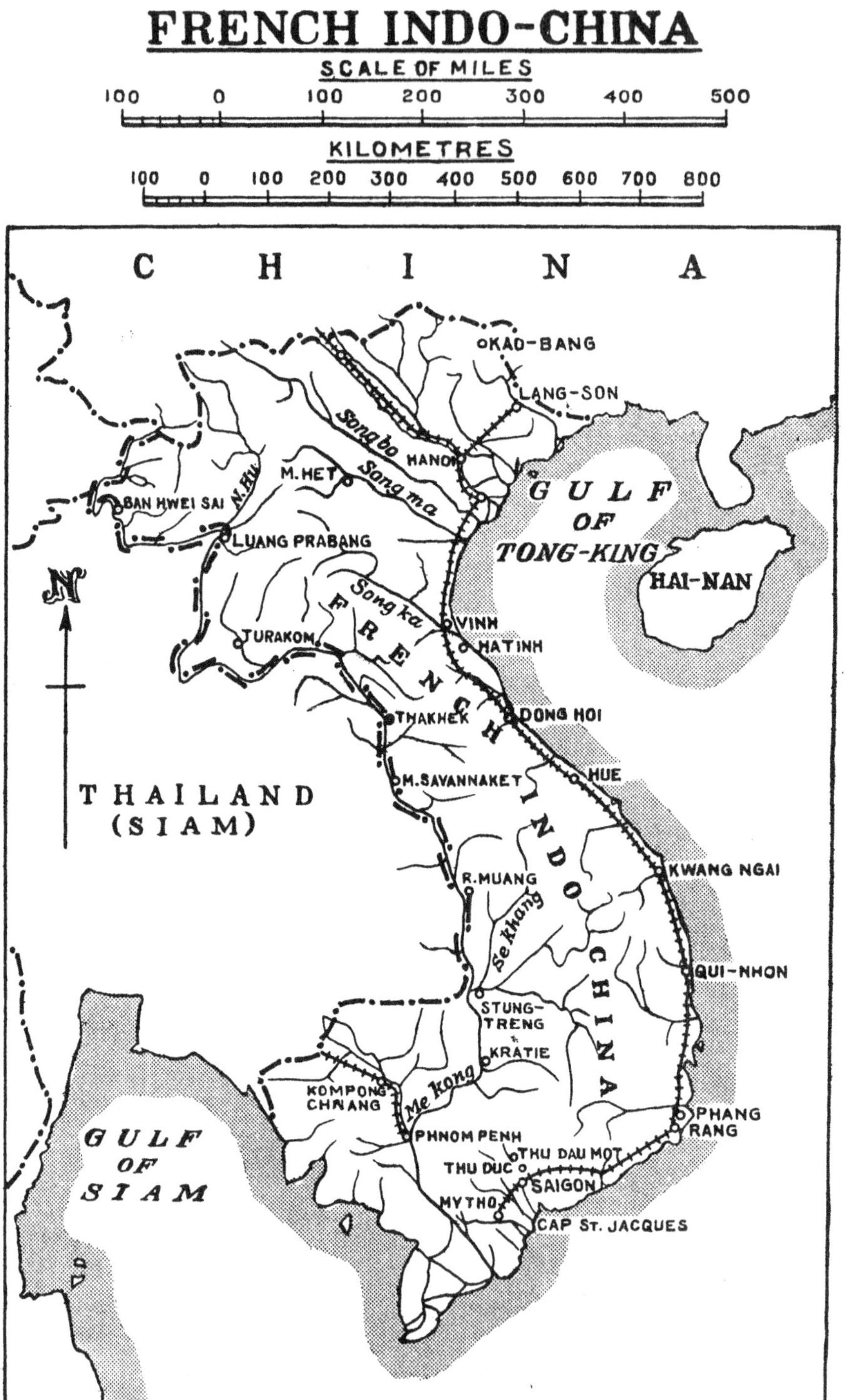

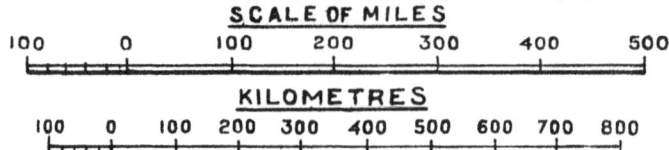

RESTORATION OF LAW AND ORDER IN FRENCH INDO-CHINA

over. Countries occupied by Japan earlier in the war have still to be reoccupied, prisoners of war have to be freed, fed and rehabilitated, civil administration of these countries has to be restored, buildings, railways, ships, roads, all these and many more have to be restored and repaired. It is no easy task and will take time. We must now even more than before maintain that discipline and bearing which have been the bed-rock of success. Much of the future will depend on the way we conduct ourselves in reoccupied countries. We may still have to use force of arms to clear these countries of the Jap".[3] General Douglas Gracey, the commander of the 20th Indian Division, was appointed to command the Allied Land Forces in French Indo-China south of 16° N and was instructed to:

(i) secure the Saigon area including the Headquarters of the Japanese *Southern Army*;
(ii) disarm and concentrate all Japanese forces in accordance with policy;
(iii) maintain law and order and ensure internal security;
(iv) protect, succour and subsequently evacuate Allied prisoners of war and civilian internees; and
(v) liberate Allied territory so far as resources permitted.

The 20th Indian Division was warned that it was not entirely an operation of peace and that resistance might be met. They were to take all precautions of war and observe the principles of warfare. "There is no front in these operations: we would be dealing with bands of guerillas and are likely to meet opposition on flanks and from rear; we may find it difficult to distinguish friend from foe. Same vigilance against ambushes and doubtful friends as one observed in North-West Frontier of India, would be required all over. Also beware of 'nibbling' at opposition. Always use the maximum force available to ensure wiping out any hostiles, we may meet. If one uses too much no harm is done. If one uses too small a force and it has to be extricated we will suffer casualties and encourage the enemy"[4]. All the units were also given full information about the political situation in the land and also maps of Japanese concentration areas.

MOVE-IN OF TROOPS

The 20 Indian Infantry Brigade with elements of 1/1 Gurkha Rifles and the Control Commission were the first to arrive from

---

[3] War Diary, 14/13 Frontier Force Rifles, 15 August 1945.
[4] War Diary, the 100 Indian Infantry Brigade, 27 October 1945. Operation Instruction No. 220, October 1945.

Rangoon by air and landed at Saigon on 11 September 1945. They occupied vital points such as the airfield, the banks, the powerhouse, the police stations, and relieved the Japanese guards there. Later they occupied the jail and the Post and Telegraph offices. This quick action deprived the Annamites, who were in administrative control of Saigon, of their hold over the capital and forced them into opposition to the Allied army.

On 17 September 1945, the Annamites celebrated their Independence Day when disorder prevailed in Saigon, which made the position of the Allied army extremely delicate, if not difficult. Hence Major-General Gracey issued a proclamation on 21 September 1945, in the languages[5] of the people, that it was his firm intention to ensure with strict impartiality peace throughout southern Indo-China and to dislocate public services and legitimate business and trade as little as possible so that peaceful citizens might carry on their normal occupations without any interference from anybody. Calling on all citizens to co-operate to the fullest extent the proclamation warned all wrongdoers (specially looters of public and private property and saboteurs) that they would be summarily shot. No demonstrations or processions, it stated, would be permitted; no arms of any kind including sticks, staves, bamboo-spears etc. would be permitted to be carried except by the Allied troops and other authorised persons.

The Annamites demonstrated against this order on the ground that it interfered with their relations with the French and stifled their political aspirations. Lord Louis Mountbatten also instructed Major-General Gracey to confine himself and the forces under him to those limited tasks for which he and they had been appointed. The Chiefs of Staff agreed in this warning but added, with due regard to the sentiments and sovereignty of the French in Indo-China, that the Indian troops should assist the French everywhere south of 16°N, as long as this did not prejudice the Allied primary responsibility for Saigon. In the meantime, Lady Mountbatten toured Saigon on 20 September in her capacity as Chief Superintendent, Nursing Division, Joint War Organisation, St. John's Ambulance Brigade, and she assisted the local workers in doing their work expeditiously and enthusiastically with the RAPWI, many of whom were evacuated by the returning planes from Saigon.

On 23 September, the French under their military commander General Leclerc took Major-General Gracey's permission and seized control of the administration of Saigon wholly, and

---

[5] According to War Diary of the 80 Indian Infantry Brigade the date is 19 September.

installed their own government in the state. This led to bitter fighting with the Annamites for nearly one week.

The military position in Saigon was deteriorating and the appreciation was that soon it might well prove beyond the capacity of the only brigade of the 20th Indian Division to tackle it. Hence Lord Louis Mountbatten called a meeting on 28 September, which was attended by Major-General Gracey and Colonel Cedille in Singapore. The British Secretary of State for War, who was visiting the British troops in India and SEAC, was also present. The Supreme Commander told the French colonel that the French and the Annamites should meet and come to an amicable settlement of their outstanding differences. The Secretary of State for War also added that it was the policy of the British Government not to interfere in the internal affairs of Indo-China but to encourage mutual understanding between the rulers and the ruled.

From 1 to 10 October, the British encouraged the holding of a conference between the French and the Annamites with a view to bringing about reconciliation between them. On 1 October 1945, Major-General Gracey and Mr. H. N. Brain, his political adviser conferred with the Viet Minh party leaders and enunciated the British policy. A cease-fire followed and an armistice was declared during the period of the conference between the French and the Annamites. But the discussions bore no fruit. The Annamites broke the truce on 6 October by firing on the British and Indian troops in Saigon. Major-General Gracey thereupon warned the Annamites, that " maximum force would be used in the event of further disturbances "[6]. Fortunately the remaining formations of the division had arrived in Saigon and it was possible for Allied Land Forces French Indo-China (ALFFIC) to carry out the warning if it was necessary.

On 9 October 1945, Major-General Gracey, General Leclerc and Colonel Cedille met Lord Louis Mountbatten at Rangoon to discuss the situation. During the meeting the news came that the Annamites had again broken the truce by ambushing and killing one officer, one Viceroy's Commissioned Officer and two Indian Other Ranks and wounding others of an engineer reconnaissance party, and it became clear that the Viet Minh spokesmen were incapable of guaranteeing the terms of the armistice. Lord Louis Mountbatten, therefore, ordered that strong action must be taken by the Indian forces to secure further key-points, and to widen and consolidate the perimeter of these areas, while the efforts to negotiate peace with the Annamites might continue. The Annamites

---

[6] War Diary, the 20th Indian Division, G. Branch, 8 October, 1945.

begged for extension of truce; their leaders 'came in to HQ 20th Indian Division to say that they would *not* oppose the British entry into Gia Dinh but that any movement of French troops would be resisted to the utmost. It was accordingly decided not to employ French troops in the operations planned on 11 October 1945.'[7] But these assurances proved futile and led to the negotiations being broken.

There was at this time some cause for anxiety about the surrender of the Japanese forces in Cambodia. The establishment of the Annamite regime in Cochin-China, Annam and Tonkin had its repercussions in Cambodia, and the Japanese were behaving rather funnily. The SEAC, therefore, sent the Officer Commanding 4/10 Gurkha Rifles to Phnom Penh, the capital, and at the same time General Leclerc arrested the pro-Japanese Prime Minister and took him to Saigon. These two measures helped to make the Japanese in that area observe the terms.

DEVELOPMENTS IN SAIGON—CHOLON AREA

Meanwhile, the situation necessitated a few engagements between the Allied troops aided by the Japanese and the Annamites, in particular in north-western Saigon. Also a successful sweep was made through Gia Dinh, which demonstrated the British potentiality to move troops out of Saigon whenever they wished. This made the Viet Minh leaders agree to an armistice from 1800 hours on 2 October. The following day was quiet and a certain influx of Annamite population from north of the Arroyo de l'Avalanche gave rise to the hope that negotiations for peace would be successful. On 4 and 5 October, however, the truculent attitude of their rank and file gave the lie to the pacific assertions of their leaders. Grenades were thrown at the sappers guarding artesian wells, crowds demonstrated in front of the British positions on Khanh Hoi island and in the Rue de Verdun and subversive leaflets were distributed. On the night of 6 and 7 October, the evacuation of civilians started again and concentration of Annamite troops was reported in Gia Dinh and to the south of Khanh Hoi. On 9 October, British troops were snipped at at the Tan Sun Nhuat airfield. On 10 October, as stated earlier, an engineer reconnaissance party was ambushed. Consequently, Gia Dinh was occupied by the 32 Indian Infantry Brigade on 10 October, and Go Vap was taken on 11 and 12 October 1945. For the first time, armoured cars were used. By 13 October the 32 Indian Infantry Brigade had established itself on all the bridges across the river Cho Moi.

---

[7] War Diary, 16th Light Cavalry, B Squadron, 10 October 1945.

PLATE XVII

Major-General G. C. Evans,
Commander 7 Indian Division

Major-General O de T. Lovett,
Commander 7 Indian Division

Plate XVIII

Major-General D. D. Gracey,
Commander 20 Indian Division

Major-General D. C. Hawthorn,
Commander 23 Indian Division

Meanwhile, the Annamites in Cholon and Khanh Hoi made strenuous attempts to destroy European stores and installations and to gather arms. On the night of 13/14 October 1945, an abortive attempt was made to storm the docks and to attack a Japanese position at Phu Lam. On 16 October, a resin factory in Khanh Hoi was gutted by fire, and numerous other attempts at arson were reported. An attempt was also made by a crowd of four hundred men armed with rifles, spears, bows and poisoned arrows and even a mild type of tear gas to capture a bridge on the 32 Indian Infantry Brigade perimeter. But the attempt failed and with it the Annamites ceased to fight openly and began a guerilla warfare.

DEVELOPMENTS IN THU DUC—BIEN HOA—THU DAU MOT AREA

The Annamites were collecting large forces in the area, between Thu Duc and Dian, with the intention of opposing the British advance along the railway. There was also a report that there were several huge non-violent demonstrations in Thu Dau Mot. But with the liquidation of Annamite trouble at Saigon the opposition in this area subsided by itself.

BARIA-CAP. ST. JACQUES AREA

The fortifications in the Baria-Cap. St. Jacques area were held by the Japanese, who were reported to be negotiating with the Annamites. An attempt to barter 107 rifles for food was forestalled by an order from General Manaski. Surrender discipline was enforced.

DEVELOPMENTS ON THE EAST COAST

The coastal area as a whole continued to be disturbed. A patrol from Phan Rang to Dalat on 10 October 1945 was ambushed. One man returned to tell a sorrowful tale that a thousand Annamites had congregated at Phan-thiet and ambushed the patrol. The real centre of disturbance was Nha-trang where again the Japanese had compromised with the Annamites with the result that the latter adopted a threatening attitude towards the European population. They demanded the handing over of public buildings. But the situation was brought under control by the Japanese ordering their nationals to observe surrender terms and by the landing of seventy French marines.

TAY NINH AREA

During October 1945 the Tay Ninh area remained inactive. The insurgents, estimated at 10,000 assisted by 1,000 deserters, who were natives of Cambodia were believed to be planning an offensive. But this estimate was not accepted by the Japanese who placed the figures at 500 Baodaist troops and a few Viet Minh regulars and irregulars. Their conjecture was correct and no trouble took place.

PHNOM PENH AREA

There was little difficulty in establishing a friendly government in the Phnom Penh area. Siamese and Annamite influences were very strong in Cambodia. The Prime Minister was anti-French. Following his arrest there were one or two signs of unrest, mainly Annamite inspired. The railway employees, for instance, went on strike for a few days. But the Cambodian element returned early to work, with the result that the Annamites were arrested. Further the whole police force was de-Annamitised and brought under the control of the commander of the Allied Land Forces in Phnom Penh. One consequence of this strong measure was that the small Annamite community in the outskirts of Phnom Penh became very demonstrative in their loyalty to the Allies and accepted the situation without demur.

DEVELOPMENTS IN MYTHO-GANTHIO AREA

Public opinion in the Mytho-Ganthio area was highly excitable but the Japanese acted more vigorously here than in other districts. They removed road-blocks on the Cholon—Mytho road and secured important bridges. The Viet Minh party also was not strong in this area.

VIET MINH ACTIVITIES

The main Viet Minh strength was in the area Thu Duc—Bien Hoa—Thu Dau Mot area. Whether it was being reinforced from the north of 16°N remained to be confirmed. The Annamite forces were better organised and disciplined in this area than elsewhere and it was feared they might attempt organised warfare as opposed to mere guerilla tactics.

All the dirty work, to fight and disarm the Annamites, was assigned to the Japanese troops. Order No. 1, dated 25 October

1945, by Lieutenant-Colonel E. C. Pickard, Commanding 14 Frontier Force Rifles, to Colonel Miyake illustrates this point. The effect of this system was that the British troops had nothing to do and so became irresponsible and idle. One unit confessed that 'with the rest of the 100 Brigade arriving the battalion was in the fortunate position of being responsible to no one (except the Mission for guard duties)'[8]. Lest the Indian element of the British force might be seduced by Annamite propaganda, which was strong and persistent, a warning was given about the Annamites being treacherous. It was also announced that 'the answer to this (Propaganda) is that if they (Annamites) obstruct our disarmament of the Japs, as they are doing, they will be dealt with by force of arms'[9].

The last week of October 1945 was comparatively of less anxiety for the Allies. The 'hostile acts of Annamites to a large extent receded from our expanding perimeter within and on the edge of which they have now confined themselves to minor guerilla tactics'[10]. Thu Duc, Bien Hoa and Thu Dau Mot were occupied by 4/10 Gurkha Rifles, 14/13 Frontier Force Rifles and 1/1 Gurkha Rifles, respectively, and pending the arrival of Japanese reinforcements Dalat area was guarded by strong, offensive reconnaissance by air. President Hala of Chinese Chamber of Commerce was arrested and the Foukien Boy Scouts were banned. All British units commenced systematic patrolling beyond the existing perimeter on the principle that offensive is the best form of defence. Peaceful inhabitants who were ready to carry on their normal occupation wanted also evidence of the superiority of the Allies over Annamites which they were now assured of.

On 30 October, Vice-Admiral d'Argenlieu arrived in Saigon to take up his appointment as High Commissioner for French Indo-China and nominal Commander of the French forces in the theatre; in the latter capacity he was subordinate to Major-General Gracey.

If October was a month of strain attended with success, November was one of success without strain. The Chinese were helpful with useful information, French troops arrived from outside, and the Japanese were willing to do their task. There was little for the British troops to do. They searched Long Kisen, a forest village, arrested and jailed a hundred and sixty-six men of the Kempei Tai (Japanese Gestapo), and searched the Coast

[8] War Diary, 1/1 Gurkha Rifles (King George V's Own) 17 October 1945.
[9] War Diary, 4/17 Dogra Regiment 9 October 1945.
[10] War Diary, the 80 Indian Infantry Brigade, Operation Instruction No. 33, 25 October 1945.

Church for the arrest of a priest. And then started the pictorial ceremony of Japanese surrenders, the best of which was the one at the Mission Headquarters on 1 December 1945 at which Lord Louis Mountbatten ' accepted the personal surrender of Field Marshal Count Terauchi's family swords '[11].

The logical result of the expansion of the perimeter was the formation of the occupied area into inner and outer zones, for the latter of which the Japanese were made responsible. Ben Cat was considered as being vital to the Annamite defence, and so it was attacked by a special column known as Clarkol, with the intention of encircling and destroying the Annamites in the area. While the French established a firm base in Tay Ninh and drove the Annamites eastwards to Ben Cat, the Japanese at the same time moved south of Loc Ninh and established a block at Chon Thanh. The plan succeeded.

In spite of the decrease in the disturbances, the animosity of the local population towards the British forces had increased. It was reported that: ' During the period under review, the civilian disturbances have decreased, and this coupled with the arrival of more French troops etc. has enabled a start to be made with the formal surrender and disarmament of the Japanese. Although disturbances have decreased, there is, however, still an atmosphere of animosity towards us among the indigenous population and there has been no improvement in our relations with them '[12]. This was mainly due to the indifference of the commanders to the complaints of the people against the units or individuals, and even if the pretence of investigation was made the offenders were let off. Moreover, the conduct of some of the Allied commanders towards the Japanese commanders was not proper.

FIGHTING IN SAIGON AREA

28 October was the quietest day for some time in the stormy area of Cholon, Gia Dinh and Go Vap. This lull was used by the British to do propaganda in the villages. 29 October saw the establishment of an armoured column base at Xuan Loc and the patrolling of the route Baria—Dalat—Nha-trang.

On 1 November, however, fighting started in the area north of Saigon. During the night of 2/3 November the British positions in Gia Dinh area were attacked with light machine-guns, grenade discharger and tear-gas bombs. At the same time a bridge between

---

[11] War Diary, the 23rd Indian Mountain Regiment, 1 December 1945.
[12] War Diary, the 32nd Indian Infantry Brigade, Annexure for November 1945, No. 43/1/A. HQ 32nd Indian Infantry Brigade. SEAC 22 November 1945.

Go Vap and Gia Dinh was attacked. The fighting lasted two days.

Thereafter firm action was taken to search and recover Annamite arms and to prevent grenade throwing and sniping. A large part of the male population was rounded up and subjected to a severe security check. Sweeps were carried out extensively in the 100 Indian Infantry Brigade area, and roads were cleared of all obstacles. Thus the key-area was well secured against organised opposition. The arrival of more French troops facilitated the task of the British and they took over certain sections, extending southwards into the Mekong delta, relieving the Japanese forces to be withdrawn.

DEVELOPMENT IN BARIA - CAP ST. JACQUES AREA

Until 29 October, the Japanese had an extremely anxious time owing to the presence of a large number of armed Annamites in the Baria area. They first tried to pacify them, but the senior British naval officer attached to the area ordered a firmer policy. The Japanese carried out his instructions and rounded up and disarmed a large number of Annamites at Baria. They also cleared the roads Baria—Long Thanh and Baria-Xuan Loc and reduced Annamite influence to a great extent.

DEVELOPMENTS ON THE EAST COAST

The east coast was the play-ground of Viet Minh forces who had reduced the isolated Japanese garrisons to a state of helplessness. All Annamite troops were trained here and also in Dalat and Ban Me Thout area. The hill tribes of this area, the Mois, who were under the influence of the French, were reconciled to the Annamite control; their hills and jungles offered a splendid refuge to the Annamite guerillas when pursued by the Allies.

The largest concentration of the Annamite troops in this area was at Phan-thiet, where the forces driven from Xuan Loc and Bien Hoa had also collected. The Japanese garrison in this place was threatened and asked for further reinforcements. The Annamites attacked the French marines at Nha-trang on 22 October, and this developed into a serious fight. On 27 October the town was cleared of all Annamite forces.

During November there were reports of Annamite reinforcements for Nha-trang area from the north and from Phan-thiet in the south. But the area remained uneasily quiet, perhaps due to the landing of 1,200 men on 19 November from the French battleship *Richelieu*.

DEVELOPMENTS IN LOC NINH—BEN CAT—TAY NINH AREA

During October the withdrawal of Viet Minh forces from Bien Hoa to Loc Ninh—Ben Cat area caused anxiety. The Japanese were ordered to take strong action against this concentration. They had swept the area on 25 October and encountered some opposition. By 30 October the situation was under control but within a week the trouble started again. A combined British and French operation to clear the triangular area made up of Loc Ninh, Tay Ninh and Saigon commenced on 8 November. A mobile column of armoured cars and Indian and Japanese infantry occupied Ben Cat without opposition. Tay Ninh was occupied by a French armoured column from Saigon in the evening of the same date while a river-borne force moving on the Vacio river arrived at Tay Ninh on 9 November.

Both these forces encountered opposition *en route* although Tay Ninh itself was found deserted. The British column from Ben Cat occupied Chon Thanh on 9 November without opposition, but on the following day a six hour battle was fought with the Annamites at a road-block (RD 158870). A French column from Tay Ninh reached Loc Ninh unopposed on 11 November, while Budop, to the north-east of Loc Ninh, was occupied on 12 November.

THE FRENCH TAKE OVER

The Viet Minh resistance in the Allied occupation areas was broken. They had either withdrawn into Annam in the south-east or behind the Song Bo in the north or retreated into the 'Plain des Jones' in the west. They were also trying to enter Cambodia. In Cochin-China, therefore, there was only guerilla activity left, which even at best did not profit the Annamites in any way.

The French thereupon endeavoured to take over responsibility for the area as quickly as possible. On the political side, Admiral d'Agrenlieu repeated his country's intentions to pacify the hostile elements in the population. On 1 November, he addressed the public in Saigon to say that France would give autonomy, not independence, with suitable reforms in the economic, political and financial spheres of government. The Annamites did not accept this offer and replied that they would attack the French only and, if necessary, their new allies, the Japanese, but would spare the British who were mere birds of passage.

On 14 November again, the Admiral broadcast on the same subject and stated that the programme of the Government of France included the setting up at the earliest moment of 'a very broadly conceived political and administrative economy, with the assistance of counsellors and experts, as required, in every one of the Indo-Chinese countries'. The Annamites responded to it by a rebellion in the south of Saigon which called for 'Can Gioc' action on 16 November and for an armed offensive on the 18th. A third time, on 23 November, the High Commissioner repeated the policy of his government of granting internal autonomy to all provinces and protectorates in French Indo-China and added that he was still maintaining contact with Viet Minh representatives and hoping for good results; to which the Annamites answered with isolated attacks on the French and the Japanese. Lord Louis Mountbatten was pressing for more substantial changes in the French policy, and this may account for the new attitude of the French shown in a press conference held at the end of November. This attitude favoured the creation of a 'Federation of Indo-China' with freedom in economic affairs, abolition of race distinction, educational reform and development of national culture. The High Commissioner also gave an assurance that the revolutionary members of the Annamite population would not be touched by officers of law and order. This produced a slightly better effect on the other party.

On the military side, too, the French made much progress in taking over responsibility. In the first week of November their forces were well established in the delta up to a point eighty miles from Saigon, after replacing the Japanese troops stationed there. In the next two weeks the French assumed real responsibility for the east coast with two battleships ready for action. The last week saw the extension of French control in the north-easterly direction from Cochin-China to Annam, although many tracts in the former still remained unpacified. On 29 November Lord Louis Mountbatten discussed with Admiral d'Argenlieu at Saigon all problems relating to the ultimate assumption of control by the French troops and the subsequent departure of the 20th Indian Division. He even hoped that the withdrawal of his troops might possibly begin within two or three weeks in view of the steady progress in disarming and concentration of the Japanese troops. The French also thought likewise as their military strength and experience of warfare with the Annamites was gradually improving. They had in the city the 2nd Armoured Division, two regiments of colonial infantry, 300 Marines and 1,500 locally recruited troops. The elements of the 9th Colonial Infantry Division arrived in Saigon on 25 November and greatly improved their morale.

The disarming and concentration of the Japanese forces went on according to programme. They had been fulfilling their responsibility fully and correctly.

By 24 November nearly half of the total service personnel of 65,000 had been disarmed and concentrated in different places, before the French took over from them on 25 November 1945.

The expansion of the perimeter hastened the work of the Allies. This quickened activities in Cambodia and in north-eastern Cochin-China. But every time Cambodia or the east coast was brought under control, there were fresh disturbances, within a few days owing to their being close to Loas and Annam. So full and definite control of Cambodia and east coast was only possible after strong action both in Cambodia and Laos and by concentration of troops in Nha-trang and adjacent areas in the interior. These were achieved by a formal expansion of the Allied perimeter around Saigon.

The French forces assumed responsibility on 6 December for the area immediately south of Saigon, formerly held by the 80 Indian Infantry Brigade, but this brigade did not leave French Indo-China until the next month and stood by the French for any emergency. In the first week of December, the French were still anxious to decimate the rebels. They encountered resistance to the south-west of Saigon in the Mekong delta and also in the most westerly part of Cochin-China and north-east of Cantho. The French won in every place, occupied Tra-vinh on 6 December and cleared Cantho on the 8th. The result of this was that the next week was quiet, except for a grenade-throwing incident on 14 December when ten Gurkhas were killed, during a football match in Saigon. Some casualties were inflicted at Mytho and Gia Dinh on the 15th and in Vinh Long—Cantho sector on the 17th. These provoked the local Annamite partisans to fresh hostility, and the French retaliated by sweeps of coastal areas at the mouth of the Mekong. This action and reaction process continued until the end of the month, but all actions ended with the extension and consolidation of the French control in the area west of Mytho, where important resistance centres had been located.

The French took over also the responsibility for the centre on 19 December from the 32 Indian Infantry Brigade, partly because this brigade had to go to British North Borneo, about 25 December, for the relief of Australian troops stationed there, and partly because the Annamite stronghold of Han Phu island in the Cho river, five miles north-west of Saigon, was captured by 4/2 Gurkha Rifles, assisted by 9/14 Punjab Regiment on 15

December.[13] Following a concentration of mortar fire, landings were made on the island against fairly light opposition; 31 Annamites were killed and 415 were captured, together with a large arms dump, a radio station and a printing press. There were also a hospital, a kitchen, a telephone exchange and an armoury in that place.

As a result of the French taking over, the 32 Indian Infantry Brigade left Saigon in the middle of the last week of December, while the 80 Indian Infantry Brigade was waiting for orders to move out. But the 100 Indian Infantry Brigade continued to be active. The operation instructions of this brigade repeated that the hostile elements were increasing, their attacks were serious and they were planning a co-ordinated offensive between the end of December and 10 January. Instruction No. 63 of 31 December stated that the Viet Minh bands had been placed under the control of one man and he was said to have stated that this would be 'the last grand offensive before the British leave'. The opposition concentrations were four in number, viz., between the Thu Dau Mot and Ben Cat, west and south-west of Bung, Ben Go area and north-east of Bien Hoa. The Allied army was to strike at these areas and demoralise them even at the starting point. But at the same time the commander recognised the difficulties of the actual fighters. He said as follows: 'The difficulty is to select him (the enemy), as immediately he has had his shot or thrown his grenade he pretends to be friendly. It is, therefore, perfectly legitimate to look upon *all* locals anywhere near where a shot has been fired as enemies, and treacherous ones at that, and treat them accordingly. Similarly if, when following up a report, no enemy are met with suspects must be brought in from the area concerned. They are probably the hostiles reported, who have for the moment become friendly villagers'. This special warning was considered necessary, because Lord Louis Mountbatten's idea was not to terrorise but to reconcile authority with the Annamites. The brigade had to spread itself out over the whole area to inspire the peaceful citizens with confidence in the fairness of the British officers and thereby to secure their co-operation in the restoration of law and order on the one side and the disarmament and evacuation of the Japanese on the other.

The record of the 100 Indian Infantry Brigade during December 1945 was as follows: Taking the units one by one, 14/13 Frontier Force Rifles was ordered on 2 December to 'encircle and clear the forest area between Tan Phong and Ben and prevent the

---

[13] War Diary, the 20th Indian Division, 11 December 1945.

escape of 20 Viet Minhs presumed to be encamped there'. The operations were carried out on 3 December[14], and the battalion did its work thoroughly on the next day and returned to its Headquarters. 1/1 Gurkha Rifles was busy in Bung area, and the greatest achievement of 4/10 Gurkha Rifles was the detection of a quantity of opium worth approximately £2,000 sterling and the back-loading of ammunition. This brigade also carried out patrolling against harassing opposition in Bien Hoa—Thu Dau Mot (3 January), Thu Duc and Tang Phu areas with remarkable success.

The Saigon radio station passed from the British to the French control on 9 December. Figures given on 17 December revealed that 42,254 Japanese army and air force personnel had been disarmed and concentrated in south French Indo-China, leaving 15,020 to be dealt with later. The latter were still required for garrisoning outlying areas, but in view of the rapid progress in pacifying local population it was expected that these remaining personnel would be disarmed and concentrated by the end of December 1945. The surrender of the last 7,988 Japanese naval personnel in south French Indo-China was accepted at Saigon on 15 December. About 5,000 Japanese were expecting to be repatriated by the end of the year if shipping could be made available. Interrogation of RAPWI had enabled the British military authorities in Saigon to draw up a list of 400 Japanese war criminals and Indo-Chinese collaborationists, 20 of whom were accused of mass murders.

The year 1946 started therefore with everything moving quickly towards the firm establishment of the French authority in southern French Indo-China and the withdrawal of the British occupation forces in the first month. Lord Louis Mountbatten gave the following account of the situation:—

" Outside Java the state of affairs in South-East Asia gave no cause for anxiety. In French Indo-China the situation had cleared up by the end of the year; the 9th DIC had arrived, and the 3rd DIC was expected to arrive soon......... On the 1st January, Vice-Admiral d'Argenlieu and I issued a joint statement, announcing that the French authorities assumed full responsibility for military commitments in FIC and on the 28th January, command of all French forces in the country passed from Major-General Gracey (who then left French Indo-China) to General Leclerc; while command of the British/Indian forces which remained passed to a reduced SACSEA Inter-Service Mission established under

[14] War Diary, 14/13 Frontier Force Rifles, Operation Order No. 3, 3 December 1945.

PLATE XIX

Major-General Cawthorn, representative of C-in-C India on Joint Chiefs of Staff, Australia

Major-General H. M. Chambers, Commander 26 Indian Division

PLATE XX

Resettlement Training of Repatriates

Brigadier M. S. K. Maunsell, late Chief of Staff of the SACSEA Commission No. 1. The commission itself ceased to exist"[15].

On 11 January 1946, the 80 Indian Infantry Brigade was relieved of "all operational commitments by the French forces from 1600 hours"[16]. On 12 January it came under the 20th Indian Division for administration and under ALFNEI for operations[17]. Between 10 and 18 January, 23 Mountain Regiment, 114 Field Regiment and 16th Light Cavalry left French Indo-China. The 80 Indian Infantry Brigade sailed for Makassar in the last week of the month.

The 100 Indian Infantry Brigade was still left in French Indo-China. Its responsibility was not confined to any town or compact area but spread over an undefined space in north-eastern Saigon in which the French had not been able to attain mastery. This population was in no mood to be friendly to either the British or the French. "There is no contact as yet between the troops and civilian population either Annamite or Chinese. The troops .... view them with suspicion......... (and) friendly Annamite and Chinese are still frightened to co-operate to any great extent for fear of possible reprisals"[18].

The patrols of the 100 Indian Infantry Brigade, in Thu Dau Mot and Thu Duc areas, were still subjected to sniping, grenade throwing and light machine-gun fire. An unusually heavy action took place in 14/13 Frontier Force Rifles area near Bien Hoa during the night of 2/3 January when a force of 200 men, armed with heavy and light automatics, rifles and grenade-dischargers attacked two bridges and tried to wreck the railway. The attack was repulsed without any loss to the Indian troops but with a loss of 33 dead to the other side. There was heavy sniping in the brigade area on 4 January. 4/10 Gurkha Rifles was warned that the Viet Minh all-out offensive was expected between 2 and 10 January, and that besides arresting every male the regiment must hit hard and discourage the opportunists from the very start. The unit carried out this operation effectively on 10 January, it killed 7 and arrested 120 Annamites in Thu Duc area. The brigade commenced operations on 10 January, in conjunction with the French forces, to establish posts on the east bank of the Saigon river. The French cleared the area between Saigon and Thu Duc Mot and swept the area in the north up to Ben Cat. These operations continued for over two weeks with good results, and

[15] Report to the Combined Chiefs of Staff by the Supreme Allied Commander, South-East Asia, 1943-46, pp. 278-79, para 83.
[16] War Diary, the 20th Indian Division, 11 January 1946.
[17] War Diary, the 80th Indian Infantry Brigade, 12 January 1946.
[18] Monthly Summary Security Intelligence, 20 January 1946.

had to be repeated in the area between the Saigon and Don-nai rivers.

The last week of January saw the passing of military control to the French. The Headquarters ALF FIC closed on 20 January after the embarking of the main Headquarters of the 20th Indian Division the previous day.

REPATRIATION OF JAPANESE

During January 1946 the Japanese were asked to leave Bien Hoa for Cap St. Jacques. By 15 January, 21,150 disarmed Japanese were concentrated at that place.[19] About 25,000, similarly, arrived at Saigon and Thu Dau Mot. By 18 January, about 70,000 Japanese were disarmed and concentrated in southern French Indo-China. There were still 3,000 on garrison duty, and they were expected to be concentrated at Cap St. Jacques by the end of February.

WITHDRAWAL OF INDIAN CONTINGENT FROM FIC

Nothing of importance occurred in February 1946. Between the 1st and 7th, all matters relating to French Indo-China were handed over to the SACSEA Inter Service Commission. On 8 February, the rear headquarters of the 20th Indian Division closed, and command passed to the Mission. On 9 February, the Headquarters of the 100 Indian Infantry Brigade, 14/13 Frontier Force Rifles and remainder of 1/1 Gurkha Rifles (half of this regiment having left on 27 January 1946) left Saigon for India. The rear headquarters of the 20th Indian Division, 9 Jat (MG Battalion) and 4/10 Gurkha Rifles left for India on 12 February.

On 1 March, the SEAC received the approval of the Combined Chiefs of Staff for its proposal to exclude French Indo-China south of 16° N from SEAC. This was given from the midnight of 4/5 March 1946. Thus Lord Louis Mountbatten's responsibility to the General of the Army, MacArthur, was limited to the repatriation of the Japanese and for this the Inter Service Mission was detailed. On 13 February, the SEAC transferred Field-Marshal Terauchi with a skeleton staff to Singapore; two days later he bade good-bye to Admiral d'Argenlieu and concluded with him the arrangements for handing over to the French authorities 68,000 Japanese still in the country. By the end of the month the remaining two battalions of the British army left for

---

[19] Weekly Intelligence Summary No. 221.

India. The phase-out of the Royal Air Force had already been completed, only one small staging-post being left behind in Saigon.

On 3 April 1946, the Chiefs of Staff transferred all the SEAC's remaining duties to the French military commander, who alone was thereafter responsible to the General of the Army, MacArthur, for French Indo-China. Lord Louis Mountbatten relinquished his responsibility at midnight on 13 May 1946.

THAILAND

The reoccupation and liberation of Siam or Thailand had a course different from that of French Indo-China, particularly in so far as there was no Chinese intervention or responsibility anywhere in the country. The Siamese Government welcomed the Supreme Allied Commander's authority and co-operated with him at every stage. Their problem was essentially economic, and their policy was the earliest elimination of foreign elements and strengthening of internal administration so as to establish peace and prosperity for the state.

Siam stretches from 6°N to 20°N latitude and from 97°E to 106°E longitude, and consists of an almost square mass of continental land, with a peninsula running south into Malaya. At its broadest Siam is about 500 miles, but in the Kra Peninsula it is only about ten miles in width. The coast-line is immense, 1,200 miles along the Gulf of Siam and 300 miles on the Indian Ocean. During the Japanese regime, between 1941 and 1945, two Shan and four Malaya states were included to enlarge the area.

The railways and roads were fairly good and had mostly replaced river and canal communications, which had been the sole effective means of communication in the historical past. In the central plains through which the Menam Chao Bhraya (the most important river in Siam) flows the waterways still constitute the normal means of communication. For about sixty miles north of Bangkok the rivers and the canals provide, besides irrigation, navigation by poled or towed lighters.

Strategically the country can be divided into five broad zones; mountainous north, Karat basin of the east, south-eastern Siam, Karat peninsula and the central plains. The first three important towns of the state were Bangkok, Chiengmai and Puket, with a total population of 7,60,000, with Bangkok alone accounting for 7,00,000. In 1941, the total population of Siam was estimated at 16,367,000.

Until 1936 the Siamese Government had discouraged road construction for fear of competition with railways, which were state-owned. Although the Japanese opened new routes they were in a neglected condition at the time of their surrender. The Japanese during their occupation had constructed railways to connect lower Burma, and through Kra Peninsula to join with the Malaya railway network.

The temperature is hot and humid throughout the year, with south-west and north-east monsoons in the two seasons into which the year is divided. Troop movements from Burma to Siam and from Bangkok or Muang Don or to any other town had to be regulated according to rainfall at any particular place and time. Air-lifts were a real problem; the air distance from Rangoon to Bangkok is about 380 miles, but it involves the crossing of hills with an altitude of 5,000 feet and covered with thick clouds. The time for safe flight is between 1000 and 1300 hours. A light rain would spoil the airfield; a prolonged spell of bad weather makes the airfield unfit for use for many days.

Since 1932 the Government in Siam was a constitutional monarchy, but as the ruler was a minor, a council of regency performed these functions. The Regent, Luang Pradit, was friendly to the Allies even during the war, and on the defeat of Japan he had overthrown the pro-Japanese Government and announced his intention to try its leaders as war criminals. The local administration in Siam was generally troublesome due to poor communications and inefficient police force. This involved avoidance of interference with local politics for which strict instructions were issued to the unit commanders of the occupation force. Lord Louis Mountbatten, therefore, decided to treat Siam as a friendly power for military purposes and invited a Siamese military mission to his headquarters at Kandy. Led by Lieutenant-General Sena Narong, it arrived on 3 September 1945[20], and signed a military agreement relating to 'details of Allied military operations in Siam for surrender and disarming of Japanese[21].

In September 1945, the post-war reoccupation of Siam began. The South-East Asia Command had planned to employ two full divisions, but as the Siamese had promised full co-operation as a friendly power and there were also clandestine forces favourable to the Allies (through Allied Force 136 and OSS) it was decided to send only one division from Rangoon. The 7th Indian Division was chosen for this purpose, while the 26th Indian Division was kept in reserve. The 207 Military Mission was attached to the division selected for liaison with the Siamese army, and Royal Air

[20] '1 September' is another date. Vide page 279, para 87 of Mountbatten's *Report*.
[21] Tel. No. SEACOS 466, SACSEA to AMSSO, 5 September 1945.

RESTORATION OF LAW AND ORDER IN FRENCH INDO-CHINA 217

Force support, at the estimated strength of 1931 personnel, was also provided.

The South-East Asia Command's task, throughout the first month of reoccupation, was organisation and negotiation of a treaty of peace and friendship with Siam. With a view to helping the subordinate commanders to grasp the complete picture of his plan, Lord Louis Mountbatten prepared instructions pertaining to all major tasks. There are three such documents which may serve as illustrations of the South-East Asia Command's method of work. The first is Force Plan No. 2, dated 2 September 1945, the second is Detailed Order, dated 8 September 1945, for the concentration of the 18th Area Army, while the third is 'Notes by General Officer Commanding ALF Siam, dated 19 November 1945, on the post-war surrender tasks in Siam'. The administrative instructions of ALF Siam gave considerable latitude to the subordinate commanders as it was admitted that, owing to the large number of additional troops allowed to this formation (ALF Siam) and the size of the country to be controlled, it was necessary to decentralise responsibility to a greater extent than elsewhere[22].

The Order of Battle in Siam was as follows:—
   7th Indian Division
   136 Field Regiment
   30 Indian Mountain Regiment
The Division had three brigades with the following infantry battalions:—
   33 Indian Infantry Brigade
      1 Queens
      4/15 Punjab
      4/1 Gurkha Rifles
   89 Indian Infantry Brigade
      1 Sikh
      3/6 Gurkha Rifles
      4/8 Gurkha Rifles
   114 Indian Infantry Brigade
      1 Royal Jat
      4/14 Punjab
      4/5 Royal Gurkha Rifles

On 5 September 1945, the King of Siam returned from Switzerland at the request of the Regent. On the 20th, Seni Pramoj (former Siamese Minister in Washington and leader of the Free Thai Movement abroad) was appointed as Prime Minister. On 24 September, the Siamese delegation arrived at Kandy,

[22] War Diary (A/Q and G Branch), the 7th Indian Division, 29 September 1945.

headed by Prince Viwatcha Chaiyant, at the invitation of Mr. Dening, the British plenipotentiary for negotiating the treaty with Siam. The discussions started well but proceeded rather slowly for, among other reasons, lack of instructions from Bangkok. No conclusive agreement was therefore reached until the close of the year.

The new year 1946 opened with the signing of a treaty between the United Kingdom and Siam. Consequently the whole of January was spent in rejoicings, ending with the bestowal of Siam's highest honour on Lord Louis Mountbatten. Australia followed the United Kingdom in making a similar treaty with Siam. China too sent a good-will mission and signed a treaty with Siam in Bangkok. Elections took place in Siam on 6 January, and within a few weeks a new government was installed. Meanwhile, the recovered prisoners of war had been sent to Rangoon, and the members of the Indian National Army were sent by sea to Calcutta. A part of their work being completed on 14 January, the 33 Indian Infantry Brigade left Siam, and the Headquarters of the 7th Indian Division was closed on 26 January. French observers were attached for the first time to ALF Siam for the mutual benefit of the French, the British and the Siamese. The demobilisation of the Siamese army continued which ceased to be a tool of unscrupulous politicians.

Normal conditions were now re-established in Siam, which reverted to its status as a sovereign power but for certain undertakings relating to restitution and readjustment to security and commercial and economic collaboration..........[23] She had to pay as reparation 1,500,000 tons of rice out of her old savings and the 1946-47 crop which was to be sold. United Kingdom and India promised to help Siam to become a member of the United Nations Organisation.

By the third week of January 1946, 1,12,630 Japanese had been disarmed and only 600 remained at Nakhon Nayok for similar disposal. A formal surrender parade was held at Bangkok on 11 January, when two admirals and eighteen generals surrendered their swords. On 8 February, the Chiefs of Staff delegated the authority to the French, Dutch and Siamese to hold surrendered Japanese troops[24]. Thereafter the occupation forces were free to leave Siam.

In March 1946, the 207th Military Mission was disbanded. In April, the 114 Indian Infantry Brigade left for Malaya, and by 31 May all British forces had left Siam, with the exception of the

[23] War Diary, the 7th Indian Division, 5 January 1946.
[24] Telegraph No. COSSEA 473, Combined Offices to SACSEA, 8 February 1946.

naval officer in charge at Bangkok, the Royal Air Force Transport units and two battalions. The repatriation of the Japanese surrendered personnel and of the few RAPWI was the only responsibility of SACSEA in Siam thereafter which was accomplished smoothly as troop-ships became available.

CHAPTER XV

Restoration of Law and Order in the Netherlands East Indies

INTRODUCTION

The British Government had no idea that the responsibility for the restoration of law and order in the Netherlands East Indies would fall to them. But a month after the Japanese surrender the situation in that country was reported to be one of anxiety, hence the restoration of law and order there was assigned to the SACSEA, with effect from 15 August 1945. The estimate of forces to be employed under the Joint Planning Staff was that for this task a division less two brigades would be required at Batavia, to be in position there by 4 October, and that a brigade group should reach Sourabaya by 16 October. However, the problem there ceased to be an easy one, owing to its complicated political background.

POLITICAL BACKGROUND

Before World War II, the large number of islands which string like beads between Malaya Peninsula and Australia were subject to the Dutch colonial domination. There was a growing movement for national emancipation in these lands, which the Japanese did not fail to exploit. They had defeated the Dutch easily and promised freedom to the people. Their policy of appeasing the nationalists and employing Indonesians in large numbers in the administration and the exclusion of the Dutch, provided further strength to the independence movement.

The Dutch had lost heavily in Europe and were not able to recover completely by the time the Japanese surrender came about. None-the-less, they dreamt of restoring their lost authority and regaining their former possessions. They naturally found themselves in a dilemma because they could find neither men nor material to reoccupy the Netherlands East Indies immediately after the Japanese surrender. The gap of time which thereby intervened was their undoing because in the interval the Indonesians prepared themselves for a fight against the Dutch, the war of liberation which many nationalist Indonesians had been contemplating for a long time. On 17 August 1945, the Indonesians under the leadership of Dr. Soekarno and Dr. Hatta, declared a Republic in spite of the Japanese opposition to it, and thereby united the

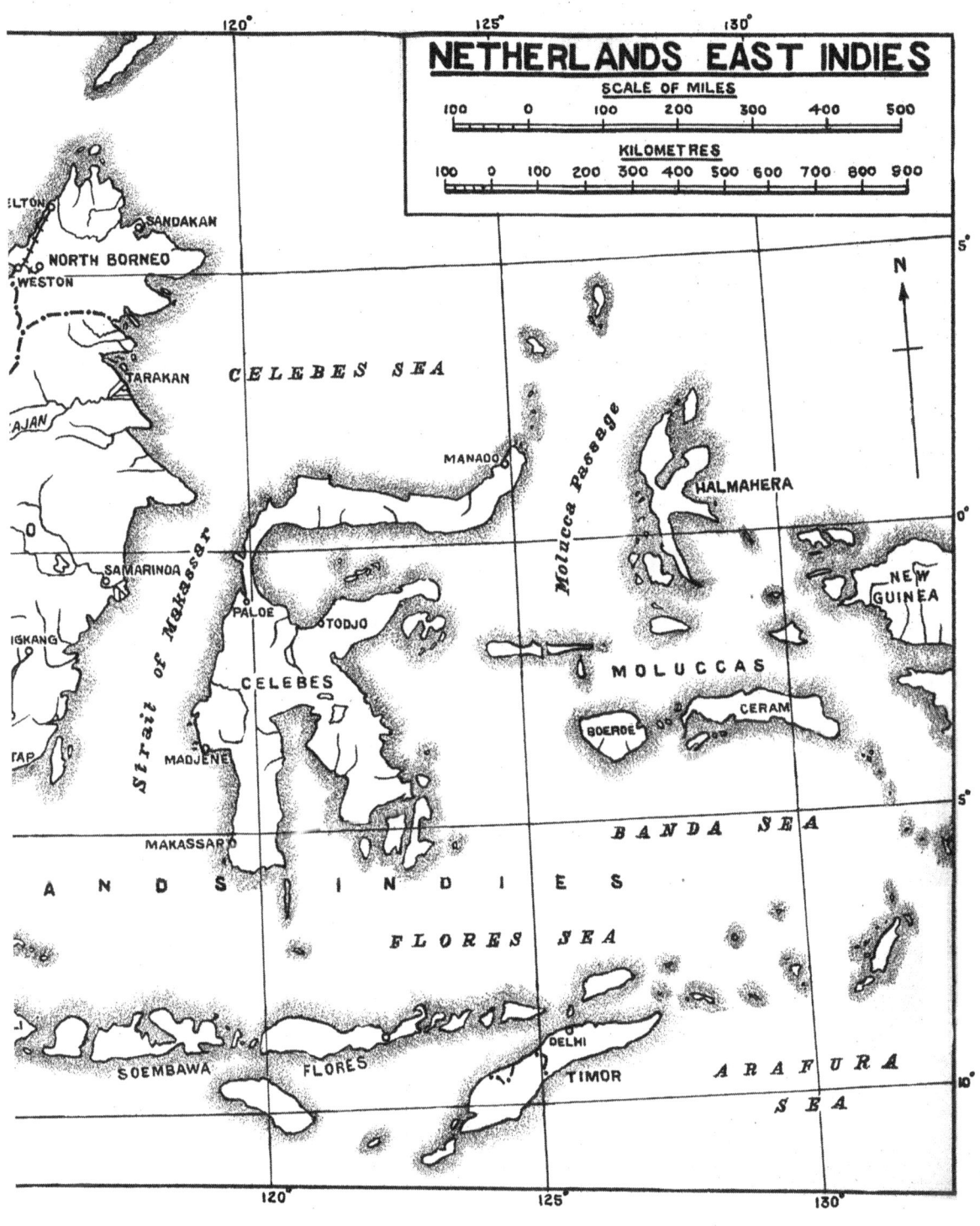

diverse elements of public life, the nationalists and underground extremists. Dr. Soekarno, the pride of the Indonesian people, headed the government, and they organised the country to resist the restoration of colonialism, which the European powers were not yet prepared to relinquish.

It was at this stage that the South-East Asia Command was assigned the responsibility of maintaining peace in that country. The main tasks were defined as, firstly, the enforcement of the surrender of the Japanese troops and their disarmament; and secondly, the release of British and Indian prisoners of war there. Lord Louis Mountbatten appointed General Christison as the Allied Force Commander in Netherlands East Indies and to him were given detailed instructions which ran as follows:

"(a) to take such measures as you consider necessary to ensure the effective control of Japanese headquarters within your command;

(b) to disarm and concentrate under Allied control all Japanese forces within the area under your command;

(c) to arrange for the care and disposal of all APWI in accordance with instructions which have been or may be issued to you separately."

"In the execution of your role you will be guided by the principle that operations undertaken by British troops are confined as far as possible to the immediate areas in which they land."

The Supreme Allied Commander also wrote privately to General Christison, as he had written previously to his other generals in South-East Asia Command, to restore confidence in the people.

The British Government concluded a Civil Administration Agreement with the Dutch Government on 24 August 1945.[1] According to this document, the Supreme Allied Commander was empowered to exercise final local authority over every branch of the Indonesian Government in all matters of a military nature. In purely civil matters the Dutch Lieutenant-Governor-General continued to be the supreme authority, but his actions were required to conform to military orders. Furthermore, it was up to the Allied Force Commander to note the changes in the military situation and to notify the Governor-General of the extent to which responsibility for the civil administration might be resumed by the Netherlands East Indies Government. As military situation became quieter and happier, the Dutch civil administration would enlarge its scope of authority.

[1] Van Mook: *The Stakes of Democracy in South-East Asia*, pp. 186-87.

In September 1945, the month after the surrender, all the parties concerned were making hectic preparations. The British were preparing to land to restore the military situation, the Dutch to restore their empire and the Indonesians to fight the Dutch and the Allies if they obstructed their path in their march for freedom.

BRITISH LANDINGS

After the Japanese surrender on 2 September 1945, British landings became possible. But preparatory work was necessary. Mines had to be cleared to let the ships sail safely up to the coast. Between 5 and 10 September, only a few detachments were landed in Java and Sumatra to 'show the flag and symbolise the reconquest' and to release the prisoners of war. But full landings at Batavia were scheduled for 4 October 1945 (one month later) and afterwards. On 16 September, four days after the Japanese surrender in Singapore, and thirteen days before the arrival of the expected British force, one advance battalion of the Seaforth Highlanders and a few other detachments from the British cruiser *Cumberland* and the Netherlands cruiser *Tromp* reached Tanjong Priok (the port of Batavia).

The Dutch preparations were visible not in Java but in Australia, where they had a camp-government, and in Holland where the government was straining itself to fill the vacuum of colonial administration. Until October 1945 there was not much evidence about Dutch ability to restore authority in the country.

By far the best preparations were made by the Indonesians. During the six weeks between the declaration of independence and the landing of the British force, the nationalists had worked day and night to create a government of their own. They brought about essential unity among themselves for the achievement of independence, collected arms from every conceivable source and created a nucleus of Indonesian state army. The Independence Preparatory Committee met from 18 to 29 August and filled all appointments in the state with suitable personnel and drafted the Indonesian Constitution which was promulgated. It prepared a blueprint for the administration. On 29 August 1945, the Independence Preparatory Committee was dissolved and in its place the Komite Nasional Indonesia Poesat (KNIP) was established as an advisory body to the President without legislative functions. Batavia was selected as republican headquarters and named Djakarta. In quick succession, regional governors for the eight provinces (west, central and east Java, Sumatra, Borneo, Celebes, the Moluccas and the Lesser Soendas) were appointed.

Dr. Soekarno chose his cabinet. The Sultanates of Djakarta, Soerakarta, Mang-Koenegearan and Pakoelaman announced their support for the republic. The Japanese-raised puppet Hei-Ho was disbanded. All buildings flew red and white merdeka flags, sign-boards in Javanese were placed outside the offices, and posters with quotations from Lincoln's Gettysburg address were pasted. Indonesian civil police began regular rounds of the streets of Batavia, and life slowly became peaceful and normal. Also, fitful fighting continued between the Republicans and Japanese forces, for the former sought Japanese arms and the latter contested the new civil authority.

Lord Louis Mountbatten was not well informed about the developments in the Netherlands East Indies; hence he decided to send a mission to report upon the actual conditions there. The advance party of this mission of observers was literally dropped on the Republic of Indonesia by parachutes on the Kemajoran aerodrome as also on Batavia, on 8 September 1945. They were seven officers and were sent in advance of the main Allied party which sailed by HMS *Cumberland*, arriving a week later. The observers, contrary to facts, reported, on 12 September, that the bulk of the population in Java was indifferent to all political movements, that the nationalist movement was the handiwork of the intellectuals, and that once transport and security problems were solved other tasks would be comparatively simple[2].

With a report of this kind in his hands, it was only natural for the Supreme Allied Commander to feel highly optimistic about the successful accomplishment of his assigned task. He gave orders to the Japanese Command to maintain law and order, and on 3 September 1945, desired them to dissolve the Republic unconditionally. Three days later he further warned them not to hand over the administration to any political party in the country. But all these orders could not be carried out by the Japanese, because they were not in control of events. In some places they did check nationalist opposition with conscientious efficiency, in other places they relapsed into an attitude of listless indifference, while at some places they voluntarily interned themselves in camps awaiting the arrival of the Allied troops, and in other places they joined the Indonesian extremists. The whole situation was in a flux. In these circumstances, on 28 September 1945, Lord Mountbatten reversed his former order of the non-recognition of the Republic. When General Christison was appointed Allied Commander, on 27 September 1945, with no knowledge of Indo-

---

[2] David Wehl: *The Birth of Indonesia*, pp. 37-38.

nesian country and people and with only two days to join his post in Batavia, the BBC announced that he was going to hold a round table conference of the British, the Dutch and the leaders of the Indonesian Republic. He declared that ' The Indonesian Government will not be expelled and will be expected to continue civil administration in the area outside those occupied by British forces. We intend to see the leaders of the various movements and shall tell them what we are coming for. I intend to bring Dutch representatives and Indonesian leaders together at a round-table conference which the Dutch have steadfastly refused to do hitherto'.[3] In other words, the General recognised the nationalist leaders as a *de facto* political power, gave them an international status and invoked their assistance in the solution of the problems of that country. He also refused to keep the Indonesians out of the administration of the country, whether it was occupied or not by the British forces for the time being. In fact he asked the party leaders to treat him and his troops as their guests and make themselves responsible for the distribution of supplies in the area which were controlled by them. Thus was Lord Mountbatten's policy expressed in effect, which did not coincide with the expectations and objects cherished by the Dutch. Hence Admiral Helfrich protested to the Supreme Allied Commander, on 30 September, against his policy which he termed a betrayal. Dr. Van Mook joined him in it. But Lord Louis Mountbatten refused to crush the Indonesians. He was supported by the Rt. Hon. J. J. Lawson, the Secretary of State for War, who declared on 30 September that 'although he understood the Dutch attitude, British forces would not be allowed to become involved in political strife '[4].

The troops used by the South-East Asia Command in the Netherlands East Indies were mainly troops of the Indian army and quite a large number of them subscribed to the same faith as the Indonesians. Moreover, Java had been made over to this Command to be treated on the principles of the United Nations Charter, which assured the people sovereignty and freedom. The United States had assured the Japanese that they would be released and repatriated, and not massacred at the altar of Dutch imperialism.

The situation in the Netherlands East Indies presented a contrast to that in French Indo-China or Siam. In the former, the French had sent in several divisions and had saved the British troops from being implicated in local hostilities, while the govern-

[3] Gerbrandy, P. S.: *Indonesia*, p. 99.
[4] Mountbatten's *Report*, p. 270.

ment in Siam had assumed responsibility for administration quite readily. But the position of Holland was quite different. She was not in a position to take over control, yet wanted Java back as part of her empire immediately, and like the Bourbons of France had learnt or forgotten nothing. The people of Indonesia feared the revival of the hated imperialism. Consequently their pent-up emotions, the accumulated hatred of the oppressor, vented themselves in violence against the Dutch, the Chinese and the Ambonese, who, in the eyes of the people, symbolised the institutions of colonial government.

The disposition of troops sent by the South-East Asia Command aggravated suspicion and heightened the alarm and anger of the people. The only troops that arrived were three Indian divisions, which were located separately at Batavia, Sourabaya and Sumatra. The South-East Asia Command's policy in this disposition of the troops was, as in French Indo-China, to station them at strong-points in the country, in order to round up the Japanese, liberate and repatriate the Allied prisoners of war, and to maintain law and order. Though Dr. Soekarno had issued general orders against interfering with the British, the Indonesians suspected that the presence of these troops was only a preliminary to the return of the Dutch. They were strengthened in this belief by the protected landings of Dutch troops. Whatever the British professions, the Indonesians felt that the practical effect of British policy would be to hold the ports until the Dutch could amass enough troops to return to Java in force. This apprehension influenced the views expressed by the nationalist leaders in India also.[5]

The proclamation issued by Rear-Admiral Patterson and Lieut.-General Sir Philip Christison, as well as the activities of the Dutch and their colonial troops further confirmed the apprehensions of the Indonesians. Patterson had announced on 29 September that the Allied troops were there " to maintain law and order until the time that the lawful government of the Netherlands East Indies is once again functioning ". And the commander of the land forces indiscreetly proclaimed that the Japanese forces in Java would be used to maintain law and order as a temporary measure—the Japanese who had created so much hatred for themselves. To cap all this came the almost insane military operations of General Van O Yen, whose " trigger-happy Dutch and Ambonese soldiers shot at anything that looked suspicious, and when hunting was poor, they were not above forcing an

[5] Armindia to SACSEA on 18 October 1945.

Indonesian's house and dragging off, without charges or warrant, some or all of the inhabitants"[6]. As a result of all these political, military and psychological factors, October 1945 began with horrible scenes of violence and ugly expressions of mass hysteria against the British forces. An explanation of this may be found in the statement of Lord Louis Mountbatten that ignorance of British motives and methods was responsible for the attacks by Indonesians. Major-General Hawthorn, commanding the 23rd Indian Division, issued printed leaflets on 14 October 1945, to inform the citizens of Batavia about the objects of the British occupation of Java and seeking their co-operation. This was perhaps a rejoinder to a proclamation issued by the nationalists on 11 October 1945, that guerilla warfare would start in Batavia and the city had been put in a state of siege. Lord Louis Mountbatten has hinted also on a second cause of opposition by the Indonesians to the British force. The Dutch troops associated with the British unit " created a number of incidents which though in themselves of minor importance had the cumulative effect of provoking the Indonesians............ I directed, at Lieut.-General's request that no more Dutch forces should be brought into Java until the situation was clearer and the risk of insurrection less acute"[7]. The British attitude towards the Indonesians was one of readiness to meet the situation at any cost and at any moment, but only in defence of their position and power. They, therefore, built up their military strength as quickly as they could. Having selected certain key-positions in Java they sent their troops only to those places and maintained communications with them[8]. On 29 September, as stated already, Batavia was occupied, and between 2 October and the end of the month, sufficient force was collected at that centre. One brigade arrived on 2 October and started building up the divisional headquarters there. Together with seven Netherlands East Indies army companies and one ex-prisoners of war battalion, both of which arrived on 4 October, and with an advance Royal Air Force Headquarters, which arrived on 7 October, the brigade constituted adequate force for the time being. By the third week a second brigade of the 23rd Indian Division had come in as also the main headquarters of the Royal Air Force, with two squadrons of the RAF Regiment, two RAF Thunderbolt (P-47) squadrons and two Netherlands squadrons of Catalinas (PBY-5). Consequently, in the last week of the month, the British force in the island of Java consisted of one brigade of the 23rd

---

[6] Crockett. *How the Trouble Began—Java* Herpers, March 1946.
[7] Mountbatten's *Report*, p. 271.
[8] Telegram No. SEACOS 523, 17 October 1945, SEAC to Cabinet Offices.

Indian Division at Batavia, another at Bandoeng (with a detachment at Buitenzorg), one battalion at Semarang (together with an improvised brigade under the command of the divisional artillery commander) and a brigade at Sourabaya for the whole eastern half of the island. The last unit was opposed by the Indonesians in the harbour but was permitted to enter after an assurance was given about its real intentions of being messengers of peace and good-will and not the harbingers of Dutch imperialism. As a further proof of British sincerity in this respect, General Christison converted Netherlands Indies Civil Affairs Organisation, which was hated by the Indonesians as an organ of Dutch power, into Allied Military Administration, Civil Affairs Branch, whose task was to engage in welfare services, distribution of supplies and custody and interrogation of prisoners.

But accidents do happen in history and an accident of a miserable nature happened at Sourabaya on 29 October and changed the course of Anglo-Indonesian relations avdersely. As stated earlier, Sourabaya was held by the extremists and the Supreme Allied Commander had no knowledge of it. So when the Royal Air Force dropped leaflets on the city on 27 October, warning its inhabitants to hand over their arms within forty-eight hours or be shot thereafter for default, there was a flare-up in the city. Road-blocks, seizure of motor cars, removal of national flags and confiscation of firearms before the expiry of the forty-eight hours provoked the Sourabayans to fury. They retorted by killing and abducting Dutch women and children and fighting the British force at every point of contact. On 29 October Dr. Soekarno arrived by air, followed by the commander of the 23rd Indian Division from Batavia; and together they succeeded in arranging a truce with the local Indonesian leaders. Later in the day, Brigadier Mallaby, commanding 49 Indian Infantry Brigade at Sourabaya, toured the town with the Indonesian leaders, who explained to the crowds about the agreement made with the commander of the 23rd Indian Division. Some extremists in the crowd shouted down their leaders and shot dead Brigadier Mallaby. Mob rule ensued in the town; British positions and units were attacked everywhere with swords and spears; and a number of Allied prisoners of war were killed. All that the British could do in the circumstances was to retreat and concentrate their brigade in the dockyard area, to rally all available persons among the prisoners of war at Dharmo, which was a mile south of the town, and finally, to warn the city once again, but in more rigorous terms. 'Surrender if you are a criminal and co-operate if an innocent citizen'.

Life elsewhere was no better for the British or the Japanese. At Bandoeng, which is a pleasant hill station seventy miles from Batavia, the Indonesians had very nearly got possession of an internment camp with thousands of Dutch, men, women and children, but the Japanese defended the city succesfully until the arrival of 37 Indian Infantry Brigade. At Buitenzorg two companies of 3/3 Gurkha Rifles rescued quite a large number of captive women and children; at Depok, between Buitenzorg and Batavia, 1,250 Christian women and children were saved and sent to Batavia. At Semarang the Japanese handed over arms and prisoners of war to the Indonesians, while there was fighting at Cheribon, Jogjakarta and other places. In fact as the British penetrated into the interior, to places like Ambarawa, Semarang and Magelang, they saw nothing but fighting, looting, killing, kidnapping and ruthless scramble for weapons of destruction. Everywhere streets were unsafe after dark, canals stank with odour of putrefying flesh, and civilians had to go to internment camps for protection.

By an irony of fate the British and the Japanese came closer together in self-interest, and the British had to use the Japanese to maintain law and order outside their eight bridge-heads. But they prohibited offensive action by their troops and instructed them to fire only when fired upon.

Dr. Van Mook has observed correctly that 'in Sourabaya all the succeeding phases of the French Revolution from the first seizure of power to the Terror seemed to follow each other in a few weeks, ending with a gruesome " people's tribunal " in the principal club, where a number of defenceless Dutch and Eurasians were " tried " and delivered to the mob to be cruelly clubbed and speared to death'[9]. Java was, in other words, in revolt against Holland and had adopted violence and terror to achieve her freedom.

Lord Louis Mountbatten had, in the circumstances, to act warily and thereby bring peace in the land[10]. He outlined his task into two phases, one diplomatic and political and the other military and economic. The first of these belonged really to the Cabinets of the United Kingdom and Holland. Hence he dealt with the representatives of ' Indonesian Free State ' and Holland within Java as two separate parties whose disputes could only be solved by the Government of Holland, but in whose combined or collective welfare the British Government was deeply interested and for whose mutual understanding United Kingdom was ever

[9] *The Stakes of Democracy in South-East Asia.* Op. cit., p. 210.
[10] Telegram No. SEACOS 519, 16 October 1945, SACSEA to Cabinet Offices.

ready to offer any kind of service. It is from this broad and humanitarian point of view that Lord Louis Mountbatten sent his Director of Intelligence to London to explain the true position to the Chiefs of Staff. This officer later went to Holland on the same mission. Unfortunately, the Dutch proved to be obdurate, and the Indonesians adamant, on the question of international status and recognition. There could be no progress in their talks or agreement. On 14 November, Dr. Sjahrir formed a cabinet of moderates and indicated his willingness to co-operate with the foreign powers. Dr. Soekarno, who was the president of the Republic, appealed to President Truman and Premier Attlee for intervention, and to Marshal Stalin for moral support. Other Indonesians expressed the idea of calling upon the Mussalmans of the world to join in their struggle. Lest the political situation should deteriorate for lack of a clear understanding of British intentions in Java, Mr. Noel Baker stated in the House of Commons, on 17 October 1945, that Great Britain recognised only Holland as the ruler of Java. This was further clarified by Mr. Ernest Bevin on 23 November 1945, as follows: ' Our military tasks were, first, to disarm and concentrate the Japanese forces; secondly, to rescue and bring home our prisoners of war; and thirdly, to rescue the thousands of internees in the camps throughout the large island. We had no intention of using any British forces for any other purpose or against the inhabitants. Indeed, our efforts to avoid the shedding of blood have resulted in our being accused of weakness. It is essential for the fulfilment of our military task to secure and maintain law and order, and naturally General Christison has authority to use his forces for that purpose.

' (But) we have no intention of being involved in any constitutional dispute between the Netherlands and the people of the Netherlands East Indies......... We began, however, to advise that negotiations should be opened, and I do not propose to go into any controversy about personalities—of this individual or the other. The Netherlands Government refused to negotiate with Dr. Soekarno. On the other hand, our generals met him and had a talk with him '.

There was one fortunate circumstance within Java, which deserves notice. Whatever the attitude of Admiral Helfrich, commanding the Netherlands forces in the Far East, might be, the co-operation of Dr. Van der Plas and Dr. Van Mook was available. Both had opposed the recognition of Dr. Soekarno in September 1945, but by the end of October 1945, they had agreed to invite him for negotiations. On 1 November, Dr. Van Mook conferred with Dr. Soekarno, on the authority of Dr. Logemann, who was then the minister of Holland for overseas territories. Dr. Van der Plas concurred in the ideas and procedure of his Lieutenant-Governor-General.

EVENTS IN JAVA

November 1945 was more conspicuous for military achievements than political ones. On 22 November, extremist Indonesians, inspired by the example of Sourabaya, killed and dishonoured the dead bodies of twenty Indian enlisted men[11] and four members of an air crew of a C-47 which had crash-landed at Bekasi due to engine trouble. Three days later a force of infantry with a detachment of tanks was sent to wipe out the terrorists and burn the place and raze it to the ground[12]. Lord Louis Mountbatten was naturally shocked at the two massacres but found it late to intervene. So he issued a stern warning: " It was perfectly understandable that soldiers after discovering such an incident should be strongly moved and react as they did but that, whereas reprisals visited deliberately on guilty and innocent alike might be intelligible if taken in the heat of the moment and under intolerable provocation, any form of calculated reprisal whatever or punitive measures of that kind taken in cold blood was absolutely opposed to his policy and would be punished with the greatest vigour ". Elsewhere too the example of Sourabaya was emulated. It had become the symbol of invulnerability, procured by magic amulets and incantations. Unarmed boys tried to rush into advancing tanks and armoured cars in a trance-like mood and mass psychosis. In central and western Java the presence of prisoners of war and the Japanese, with the absence of communications between them and the British made the Indonesians attack almost all places of importance like Ambarawa and Bandoeng.

Two facts however emerged clearly from the fight between the British and the Indonesians. The first was that the British did not swerve from their adopted policy of moderation. None-the-less, they met terror with terror, though only in grave situations like Sourabaya and Bekasi murders. Normally they adopted the principle of discretion as the better part of valour. Major-General E. C. Mansergh's[13] letter to the Indonesian governor of east Java, R. M. D. Soerio, in November 1945, bears testimony to this view, while his letter to General Christison, dated 9 November, assured him that ' I have taken every precaution to delay the use of force,

---

[11] These belonged to 7 Hyderabad.
[12] War Diaries of the 23rd Indian Division and units.
[13] Commanding 5th Indian Division.

to confine the areas to be struck to the most important and then only one at a time. There will be pauses in the operations during which the Indonesians will be able to contact me'[14].

At this time the Supreme Allied Commander was confronted with a difficult problem. At the fourteenth inter-command meeting General Auchinleck had raised the question of employment of Indian troops in Burma and South-East Asia and observed as follows: ' There can be no objection to the employment of Indian troops to deal with any Japanese or disturbances inspired and led by the Japanese in the occupied countries. It is essential, however, that Indian troops are not employed against nationalist movements save in the most exceptional circumstances, as such action would have grave political repercussions in India'. As no solution was found, the question was repeated at the next meeting on 7 November 1945. The Chiefs of Staff informed Lord Louis Mountbatten that the Indian troops ought to be confined to maintenance of simple law and order, that no more Indian troops would be available for reinforcing those in Java and that above all it would be necessary to send them back to India form March 1946. To these they added that the 2nd British Division then in Malaya would not be sent to Java to take the place of Indian troops which would be withdrawn.

All these in effect meant that in December, Lord Louis Mountbatten was to find a political solution for a most critical and difficult military problem. He raised therefore the question of British policy once again. On 3 December, he discussed it with the Chief of Imperial General Staff at Singapore and asked specifically for the approval of reinforcing Batavia with brigades of the 7th Indian Division, evacuating Semarang absolutely and evacuating Sourabaya after political settlement with the Indonesians. The Chiefs of Staff agreed to this as a long-term policy. Ten days later Lord Louis Mountbatten sought instructions for authority to reduce bloodshed by either persuading Dr. Sjahrir's group to cease fire or compelling the extremists and anti-social elements to abide by law. On 21 December he was empowered to adopt the police power to round up and hold in custody the known or suspected extremists, disarm and concentrate the Indonesian elements of police force and take over all transport from the hands of extremists, after duly informing Dr. Sjahrir and publishing it in the newspapers. As a corollary to this, all the Dutch troops were sent out of Batavia, and the Supreme Allied Commander fixed 27th of the month for the commencement of police action against disturbers of peace. The area covered by Batavia, Buitenzorg and Bandoeng was cleared

[14] D.O. No. G/165 dated 9 November 1945, Main HQ 5th Indian Division, SEAC Para 2.

of all snipers, road-blockers etc. by a tactical disposition of troops and undoubted reprisals upon reckless extremists.[15]

The Dutch and the Indonesians protested vehemently against this policy of exclusion. The former complained that they were betrayed. On 30 December 1945, and, as a special concession to Admiral Helfrich, General Christison permitted 800 Netherlands marines to land at Tanjong Priok, but he would allow no more than these. When this order was questioned in the House of Commons on 23 January 1946, Mr. Ernest Bevin said that 'landings of large contingencies of Netherlands troops might have led to a calamity'.[16] Dr. Sjahrir's protest was more reasonable than that of the Dutch. He felt honestly that ' if the British tried to keep law and order by force of arms or by planned military action, the Indonesians would resist to the best of their ability.[17] The Indonesian attitude generally was ' Dutch to clear out or British to be considered as hostile '.[18]

At the same time the Indonesians saw the situation more clearly and realistically than the Dutch. Dr. Sjahrir's visit to important centres in eastern Java had the good effect of subduing the impassioned Soetmo of Sourabaya fame, who agreed to obey Djogjokarta thereafter. The TKR was recognised as the only army of free Indonesia, and, above all, the prisoners of war were well treated. The only confusion yet was the ambiguity of Allied policy in the midst of food scarcity, currency difficulty and anti-Chinese demonstrations. Guerilla warfare could not be avoided or prohibited. Dr. Sjahrir himself spoke of resistance by force when a conference of Allied commanders at Singapore considered force as a means of establishing order in the Netherlands East Indies. In these circumstances, Dr. Van Mook left for Holland on 15 December for consultations, and he was not expected to return before the second week of January 1946. One good result of his visit was that the Dutch Prime Minister, accompanied by the Foreign Minister, his deputy and Dr. Van Mook arrived in Britain on 26 December, and opened discussions with the Government there on the following day.

The Indonesians were more lucky than the Dutch in gaining world estimation. The American press was so outspoken in their favour that the Dutch had to assure America of their honourable intentions. The British newspapers called for the speedy

[15] See Operation Order No. 1 in War Diary of the 23rd Indian Division dated 15 December 1945.
[16] Gerbrandy, P. S.: *Indonesia*, p. 101.
[17] Mountbatten's *Report*, page 275, para 66.
[18] See Major-General Mansergh's D.O. G/165 to ALCNEI dated 18 September 1945, HQ 5th Indian Division South-East Asia Command.

withdrawal of British forces from the Netherlands East Indies while the Soviet press criticised Dutch imperialism and urged the United Nations to intervene. Reports of strikes and demonstrations, sympathising with the Indonesians, continued to arrive from Australian ports.

It appeared that January 1946 would be the beginning of the end of all troubles in the country and that the 'police action'[19] would be attended with conspicuous success. The departure of General Christison on the 28th of that month from his post as the commander indicated that after all the situation in the country had been brought under control. Two days before his journey, Dr. Van Mook had arrived from Holland with Dutch proposals for settlement, and two days later the Allied forces had impressed the troublemakers with the superiority of their strength. The TKR also co-operated most loyally under Dr. Sharifuddin's administration. In fact the last week of January witnessed radical developments in the negotiations between the Indonesians and the Dutch. Criticism of the British policy against the aspirations of the Indonesians led Holland to send a Parliamentary Commission to visit Java and collect full information about the problem there; but it had no control over government policy or over Dr. Van Mook's actions in the country. An explanation of this action of the Dutch Cabinet at this moment may be in fact that both the Dutch and the British had 'reached the joint view that we should indeed acknowledge the right of Indonesia to independence'[20]. Another unexpected event was the deputation of Sir Archibald Clark Kerr as special ambassador of the United Kingdom to Java, but not as an arbitrator. A third important occurrence was the censure of government for using Indian troops in Indonesia and French Indo-China. Simultaneously with this the news arrived in Batavia that Russia had asked the Security Council 'to put an end to the existing situation' in Java and Greece. Nothing could be more auspicious for a people struggling for freedom than this trend of events inside and outside their country.

The narrative of military operations during the month of January is therefore a simple one. In Batavia area, the east was troublesome; Krawang-Tjakampek zone was dangerous and Cheribon was full of extremists. But bullets mixed with bulletins subdued the irresponsibles. Western Batavia too called for action, but it was controlled more easily. The TKR became TKI to symbolise a national army while Semarang developed into a regular theatre of war. These two rather alarmed the British, partly

---

[19] Weekly Intelligence Summary No. 218, para 7, sub para 2.
[20] Gerbrandy, P. S.: *Indonesia*, op. cit. page 137.

because they called for punitive operations. So ALCNEI had to declare that even in the worst situation no punitive action should be undertaken without the prior authority of ALCNEI[21]. He also encouraged the idea of dropping 'peace bulletins' on troubled areas, especially in eastern Java. He transferred Semarang to the 5th Indian Division, approved of extending Sourabaya area of occupation and removed the Japanese from Semarang so as to dissolve the source of irritation to the extremists belonging to that area. A strict but vigilant control was exercised on the press. For example, a newspaper, *Pewarta*, was suppressed for publishing an article inflaming the people on a political issue, with a note that 'such action, whether by word or deed, cannot be allowed. It is to establish and maintain peace, law and order that I and my forces have been ordered here by the United Nations'[22]. ALCNEI also set up courts under Dutch Presidents, one or more members of which were qualified Indonesians to deal with looters, strikers, boycotters and saboteurs. One direct result of this was Soetomo's approach for British recognition[23].

Dr. Soekarno during January 1946 moved to Jogjakarta. On the 5th of the month and with Drs. Hatta and Sharifuddin on his side, he changed his Headquarters from Batavia to Jogjakarta, leaving Dr. Sjahrir and the rest of his cabinet to remain at Batavia. This meant either greater freedom to Dr. Sjahrir, to discuss Dr. Van Mook's proposals (still to come from Holland), or all rights reserved by himself in a far off town of Java. It also gave greater powers to Dr. Sharifuddin as head of the national army.

February 1946 was a period of comparative calmness and therefore it was a most suitable time for constructive statesmanship. All towns except Bandoeng were quiet, but TKI was not above suspicion after its raid on Serpong in the first week of the month. It was hoped that Bandoeng ' could become a Batavia rather than a Sourabaya '[24], and so it turned out to be. On the politico-military side both the Indonesians and the Dutch were preparing themselves for mutual war after the withdrawal of the British, and both of them 'played a waiting game' on the diplomatic table. The Indonesian army was sent to camps for training and ordered to be in readiness for war. Soedirman, Commander-in-Chief of that army, forbade his men from co-operating with the British officers. The idea of a Holy War was abandoned, and the RAPWI were made a bargaining counter for all talks. The Dutch too were

[21] War Diary, 5th Indian Division, January 1946. Log Sheet No. 4 Serial No. 31.
[22] Letter G/820/118 Main HQ 5th Indian Division to AMACAB, Sourabaya.
[23] D.O. G/165 Major-General Mansergh to ALCNEI, 22 February 1946.
[24] War Diary, the 23rd Indian Division, WIS No. 15 dated 27 February 1946.

getting stronger by bringing in more and better trained troops from Holland, whenever an opportunity occurred. But they had to wait until March for doing so more regularly with Supreme Allied Commander's permission and sanction.

On 10 February 1946, Dr. Van Mook submitted the fresh proposals from Holland, to a conference of Dr. Sjahrir, Sir Archibald Clark Kerr and himself. The principle adumbrated in those proposals ran as follows:

" The Netherlands Government............ take the view that the peoples of Indonesia should, after a given preparatory period, be enabled to decide their political destiny.

" Therefore the Netherlands Government .... considered it their duty to do everything in their power in order to create and to fulfil as soon as possible the conditions which will permit such a free decision to be taken and which will assure its international recognition, thereby complying with article 73 of the United Nations Charter.

" The Netherlands Government therefore intend, in consultation with authoritative representatives of the Indonesians, elected from a large variety of groups, to draft a structure for the Kingdom and for Indonesia based on a democratic partnership.

" This new organisation is to be maintained for a limited period, believed to suffice for the fulfilment of the conditions for the free decision referred to above. At the end of this period, the partners shall decide independently about the continuation of their relations on the basis of a then complete and voluntary partnership. Any difference of opinion as to the question whether the period should be extended before a free decision is possible, shall be solved by a procedure of conciliation or, if necessary, by arbitration".

Obviously these terms were unacceptable to the Indonesians who demanded ' 100 per cent independence here and now '. Dr. Soekarno looked upon Netherlands East Indies as one unit and claimed freedom for all its parts.

At this time world opinion was stirring itself on behalf of the Indonesians. In the United Nations Organisation, two resolutions, one by Russia and another by Egypt were moved on 7 February, but both of them failed to secure the necessary support. Moreover, on 12 February 1946, the Legislative Assembly of India passed a resolution, without division, on an adjournment motion, to censure the Government of India on its ' failure to instruct its delegates to the United Nations Organisation to convey the strong views of the elected members of the Assembly on the subject of British-Indian and Dutch operations against the nationalist forces of Indonesia[25]. These moves enthused the Indonesians to greater zeal. At the same time, Holland also came out more enthusiastically with her reform proposals on 12 February 1946. The Chinese Communists of Malaya were allowed to move to Indonesia, with Dr. Sjahrir's permission. The local opinion within Java hardened and Dr. Sjahrir warned that if negotiations with the Dutch failed, foreign 'intervention would be sought'. Bandoeng radio laid emphasis on the example set by Russia in her own revolution as a pattern for Indonesia to follow.

The net result was that Dutch proposals of 10 February 1946 were put into cold-storage. Dr. Soekarno observed, 'This makes no advance'. Contrary to expectations nationalists increased their opposition to the Dutch plan and the extremists revived their terrorist methods against the Dutch and the British. Bandoeng became an active centre of opposition. The Headquarters of the 23rd Indian Division and 49 Indian Infantry Brigade were shifted to that place to save the Japanese who had been sent there for concentration and disarming. Resistance continued to be stiff in Sourabaya area where the British forces were practically encircled.

Sir Archibald Clark Kerr (now Lord Inverchapel) however showed qualities of statesmanship. He became the persona grata of the rival parties within a few weeks of his arrival. He succeeded in convincing them that their mutual interests lay ultimately in a reasonable settlement of their dispute. This enabled him to get the cordial consent of Dr. Sjahrir for Dr. Van Mook's proposition that the Netherlands troops should be introduced into Java early in March and in turn to get the approval of the British Chiefs of Staff for the plan[26].

April 1946 saw a lull in the whole situation. The Indonesians showed evidence of moderation and discipline and forwarded a memorandum on the lines of the Franco-Viet Namese agreement in French Indo-China. This was not acceptable to the Dutch, who resented any mention of the conferment of international status on Indonesia and the transfer of control over Sumatra to them[27]. The negotiations marked no progress and Java again reverted to terror and extremism. However, the Supreme Allied Commander was successful in getting the Indonesian agreement

[25] SAC's real hurdle was his Chiefs of Staff. They would not let SAC either reduce or modify his Indian forces. They said that 'there will be the utmost difficulty in finding British troops to replace them and not only your plans but all plans for the peace-time employment of our forces will need reconsideration'. Telegram No. COSSEA 473, dated 8 February 1946, Cabinet Office to SACSEA.
[26] Telegram No. SEACOS 640 dated 26 February 1946, SACSEA to Cabinet Offices.
[27] Telegram No. SEAC 688, 30 April 1946, SACSEA to Cabinet Offices (not to Dutch).

to the evacuation of Allied prisoners of war and the Japanese by rail from every point in the interior of Java.[28] At this time, Major-General Mansergh took over as the Allied Commander. Lord Mountbatten visited Java and met the Dutch acting Lieutenant-Governor-General, the new Dutch Commander-in-Chief and Dr. Sjahrir. Later he held a meeting of his own officers and the British Consul-General in Batavia, at which Lord Killearn, as controller of foreign affairs in SEAC was also present. Lord Louis Mountbatten decided, as a result of these meetings and further conferences at Singapore, to recommend to the Chiefs of Staff to transfer all but key points in Java to the Dutch from 1 July 1946, for the purposes of law and order and to hand over all Java to them from the end of that month. The Dutch were destined to pay a heavy price for this decision, because west Java was a scene of continued terrorism, Bandoeng was to be defended while Batavia too had its share of nightmares. In Sourabaya there were definite indications of a build-up of an underground organisation. A fast of three days was imposed on TRI and their families to strengthen their spirit for the struggle for freedom and to prepare them for sacrifice for freedom.[29] An attempt was also made to starve the Dutch by a scorched-earth policy.

Consequently clashes between the Dutch and the Indonesians became inevitable in May 1946. The presence of the Supreme Allied Commander until the end of the month averted an immediate war between them. The military situation was largely influenced by the fact that the Government of India and the United Kingdom were asking for the return of their troops, the task of evacuation of Allied prisoners of war was nearing completion, and the political factor of the existence of a conservative government in Holland strengthened the grim determination of the Indonesians to win back their freedom. Java was held by the extremists, and a government loan had been floated there to unite all parties in the cause of independence. However, the Indonesians made a distinction between the Dutch and the British: against the latter they did not wish to fight for they had conceded freedom to India.

Events in the next few months moved with kaleidoscopic rapidity. Terrorism broke out in Java in June, and a state of emergency had to be proclaimed there. The Chinese became the victims of national fury. The Indonesians used mortars and other military stores which the Japanese had left there. The extremist section was in the ascendant; but unmindful of the temper of the people, civil authority over Netherlands East Indies was transferred

[28] WIS No. 20 dated 3 April 1946. 23rd Indian Division.
[29] WIS No. 26 dated 15 May 1946, 23rd Indian Division.

to the Dutch in July 1946. This had the effect of provoking the extremists to further action. Dr. Sjahrir, a moderate in views, was kidnapped by them, but restored a few days later. Dr. Soekarno assumed supreme power and extremists controlled Batavia and other key points.

However, August, the month in which the first anniversary of the Republic of Indonesia was celebrated, brought fresh hopes of peace and compromise, when the Dutch Government appointed a Commission General to decide urgent matters on the spot; and it began negotiations with the Indonesian leaders on 20 September. Lord Killearn acted as an intermediary and ultimately a truce was agreed to on 14 October 1946. These terms were finally incorporated in the Linggajati Agreement on 15 November. Thus ended a difficult political situation and the British-Indian troops were in a position to leave Batavia on 30 November. The occupation was a short one, but it involved fighting leading to 2,300 casualties, in a force of 100,000 men.

SITUATION IN SUMATRA

Next to Java in importance was the occupation of Sumatra, a part of the Netherlands East Indies. This island is situated on the Equator and is about 1,600 miles long and 250 miles wide, thrice as big as Java. The west coast is backed by a mountain range with several peaks over 10,000 feet high. There are clouds and heavy rains on the coast and windward slopes of the mountains; the rain averages more than 100 inches a year, most of it in the two monsoon months of April and October. On the mountain slopes there are often heavy storms. The low marshy plains to the east of the mountain range have less rain than the west coast, and this falls during October to December. The weather is hot and humid in the eastern parts, and even the land and sea breezes are not of much help. The population is over 13 millions, the majority being Muslims.

The main focal points of the island are Medan, which was the capital under the Dutch administration, Padang and Fort de Kock, which were the Headquarters of the Japanese *25th Army*, and Palembang, famous for its neighbouring oilfields. Roads and railways were limited in number, except in the vicinity of large towns, but comparatively good. Rivers which are navigable by shallow draught ships for long distances, form the chief means of communication between inland towns of the alluvial plains of the east. The principal ports of Sumatra are Olehleh, Belawan, Emmahaven, Palembang and Oostahavon, the middle three were mined during the war. Airfields suitable for reoccupation craft were at Medan, Padang, Palembang and Pakan Baroe, while Emmahaven provided an alighting area for flying boats.

Originally it was estimated that there were nearly 77,000[30] Japanese troops in Sumatra. The main concentrations were 28,000 in north Kota Radja and Medan areas, 11,000 in west-centre, Fort de Kock and Padang area, 6,000 in east-centre and 10,000 in south Palembang area. Orders were issued to clear all the Japanese forces from Padang, Medan and Palembang areas. There were also 8 to 9 thousand Japanese air force personnel, chiefly in Palembang area with about 100 aircraft.

The main objects of the reoccupation of Sumatra were:—

"(a) to reoccupy, with sufficient force, key-areas, secure effective control, enforce the surrender and disarm the Japanese forces;

(b) to render assistance to APWI."

Sabang having already been occupied by Royal Navy was a separate responsibility.

There was, apart from guerilla warfare, for which the country was most suited, the problem of internal security, created by a Chinese tribe even before the war. During the Japanese occupation this tribe had armed itself with modern rifles and automatics. They were suspected of being unfriendly to the Allies, thus making movement off the roads and railway dangerous except when it was made in strength.

All matters affecting the civil population were handled through the Netherlands Indies Civil Affairs (NICA) Organisation attached to the Force Commander. But there were also twelve small underground parties in Sumatra, of which eleven were engaged in assisting the prisoners of war, and the remaining one was active in arming the police force of the Medan area in maintaining law and order. All these were in wireless communication with one another.

The force made available for Sumatra consisted of the 26th Indian Division, with a complement of squadrons of air force and a few naval vessels, a Royal Air Force regiment and the existing Netherlands East Indies forces within the island.

It was decided to occupy the following areas which corresponded roughly to the civil divisions:—

(a) Padang   ...   Fort de Kock
(b) Kota Radja   ...   Medan
(c) Palembang   ...   Taloek Beteong

---

[30] Figures given by the Japanese delegates to the Conference at Rangoon on 27 August 1945. The figure mentioned in ALFNEI's Despatch on Sumatra and report of 26th Indian Division, 13 November 1946, is 70,000.

Medan was occupied first of all. Then Padang was taken, but as Japanese offered little opposition to these principal movements, only a small force was sent to the two places. Similar course was adopted in the case of Palembang also.

The general orders were quite clear to the units. Full authority over military personnel and civilians was to be exercised only in key areas, and even there civilians were to be dealt with through NICA. Outside these key areas full responsibility rested with the Dutch authorities who were permitted to ask the Supreme Allied Commander for military assistance through the normal chain of command. The general tasks of the army forces in Sumatra were defined as follows:—

"(a) to secure the Padang area and assume control of Headquarters *25th Japanese Army*,
(b) to secure the Medan area,
(c) subsequently to occupy the Palembang area,
(d) to disarm and concentrate all Japanese forces in Sumatra in accordance with the policy laid down by ALFSEA in August 1945,
(e) to protect and succour all APWI and subsequently to evacuate the deserving among them,
(f) to occupy the key areas until the NEI could take over,
(g) to set up a military administration in the occupied areas,
(h) to set up a message filtering and monitoring service, and
(i) to introduce food and other civil supplies".

The air force was to give tactical support and to fly in priority personnel and stores and to evacuate the prisoners of war and casualties, until a routine traffic was established between Malaya and Sumatra.

The 26th Indian Division began to arrive in Sumatra on 10 October 1945, and by the end of the month it was concentrated in Medan, Padang and Palembang areas with headquarters at Padang. Out of its three brigades (the 4th, 36th and 71st) earmarked for service in Sumatra, the 36th was diverted to Java.

MEDAN AREA

Between 10 October and 5 November 1945 the following units landed in Belawan, the port of Medan:
Headquarters Royal Artillery
6 SWB
Administrative units.

On 10 October 1945, representatives from the 2nd Imperial Japanese Guards met the commander of the Royal Artillery 26th

Indian Division on board HMS *Venus* to sign surrender terms. Headquarters Royal Artillery was established at Medan as Headquarters Medan Area.

The following troops, together with 8/8 Punjab Regiment landed in Belawan during the period 30 October to 5 November 1945:—

    Headquarters 4 Indian Infantry Brigade
    2 Rajput Regiment
    2 Frontier Force Rifles.

On landing, 8/8 Punjab Regiment moved across Sumatra to Pedang to join 71 Indian Infantry Brigade, and 6 SWB came under command of the 4 Indian Infantry Brigade. Headquarters 4 Indian Infantry Brigade and 2 Frontier Force Rifles moved out to the area of Bindjai, about 25 miles west of Medan, on the main road and railway. 6 SWB remained in Medan.

The role of 4 Indian Infantry Brigade was to form a striking force for the defence of Medan, and to be prepared to operate anywhere in northern Sumatra. During November 1945 reconnaissance of the whole area was carried out, including patrols to Fort de Kock in the Padang area, some 200 miles distant, to contact the 71 Indian Infantry Brigade. Elements of 6 SWB moved to Brastagi, about 45 miles south-west of Medan, as advance party for possible moves of 4 Indian Infantry Brigade.

The situation in this area was quiet until 25 November 1945, when a patrol of 6 SWB was fired upon by an organised party of Indonesians in the Brastagi area, with the result that this advance party was withdrawn to Medan.

During November and December 1945, the Indonesians in the town area of Medan were restless but politically unco-ordinated, and patrols and small detachments of the Allied troops were sniped nightly.

By 5 January 1946, the following troops arrived in Medan-Belawan area from India:—

    7 Indian Field Regiment, less one battery
    1 Indian Anti-Tank Regiment
    6 Rajputana Rifles
    Machine-Gun Battalion Frontier Force Rifles
    'A' Squadron 146 Royal Armoured Corps (Armd. cars)
    2 Patiala Infantry.

Up to February 1946, searches and raids for arms and known extremist leaders were constantly made in the town and their immediate vicinity. Opposition consisted mainly of sniping, but road-blocks began to appear outside the towns. The Indonesians had for some time been trying to persuade Indian troops to desert with arms, for which they were prepared to pay large sums of money. And as their good luck would have it, six of them deserted on 8 March with rifles and ammunition, and search parties which were sent after them were waylaid by an ambush, as a result of which the searchers suffered several casualties, including one officer killed and one wounded.

During this month there was also considerable increase in shooting in the town, and raids were therefore carried out day and night on the headquarters of the extremists. On 12 February, the first " battle " occurred, when the 2 Rajput Regiment met many road-blocks and considerable opposition with machine-guns. Consequently, the British artillery was brought into action for the first time.

During April, the Indonesians made frequent night attacks on the Allied Prisoners of War and Internees camps at Helvetia, just north of Medan.

In May, parties of thirty to forty armed Indonesians clashed with the British patrols at various times. On 9 May, a party of the 625th Indian Field Security Section was ambushed; one officer was killed and two British other ranks captured. Brigade operations to trace these captured men were not successful.

In June continuous patrolling was carried out in the town. There were many clashes with the Indonesians and their opposition was sometimes considerable. Frequent brigade operations were carried out and villages in the area were searched for arms and ammunition.

The Indonesians had an excellent warning system in all areas, including the firing of warning-shots by sentries, the use of public and private telephone system, and listening in to radio telephone conversations. Thus the news of the movement of the occupying troops was quickly passed. To defeat this warning system, operations were now mainly carried out at night. Two of these operations, in particular, were successful and resulted in the capture of large quantities of arms and ammunition and the release of 200 Chinese from Indonesian hands.

By the end of August 1946, the Indonesian opposition had become more co-ordinated and more boldly led. In September 1946, all operational troops came under command of 4 Indian Infantry Brigade which assumed responsibility for the whole area. The " set up " in the Medan area on 16 September was:—
    Headquarters 4 Indian Infantry Brigade
    7 Indian Field Regiment, less 5 Indian Field Battery
    ' A ' Squadron 146 Royal Armoured Cars
    6 Rajputana Rifles

2 Rajput
Machine-gun Battalion Frontier Force Rifles
2 Frontier Force Rifles
2 Patiala Infantry.

6 SWB had been disbanded in April 1946, and Headquarters Royal Artillery had moved to Padang in August 1946.

During the period September 1946 to November 1946, the Allied troops met with a determined opposition and encountered many road-blocks and trench system. On 26 and 27 September 4 Indian Infantry Brigade carried out operations with three battalions to clear the area. Determined opposition was effectively dealt with, and the Indonesian casualties were estimated at 43 killed and a further 55 killed or wounded.

By 10 October the whole of Medan area was much quieter. On 26 October 1946, the Netherlands troops started to relieve the SEAC troops; and the machine-gun battalion of the Frontier Force Rifles and the 1st Indian Anti-Tank Regiment embarked for India. That night was the noisiest in Medan.

The arrival of the Netherlands troops was not popular with the Indonesians, and for the first time a convoy on the road Medan-Belawan was attacked. After this, movement on the road was restricted, and all convoys had to be escorted.

By 30 November 1946, the Dutch troops had taken over control in Sumatra, and all foreign troops therefore left.

PADANG AREA

Headquarters 26th Indian Division landed at Emmahaven, the port of Padang, on 10 October 1946, with the following:

Headquarters 71 Indian Infantry Brigade
1 Lincolns
1 Royal Garhwal Rifles.

Headquarters 26th Indian Division was established in Padang and dispositions of major units were as follows:—

1 Lincolns	... south-west of area of town
1 Royal Garhwal Rifles (less one Company)	... north of town
One Company Royal Garhwal Rifles	... Emmahaven, the port of Padang.

On 10 October 1945, 8/8 Punjab Regiment arrived in Fort de Kock, 10 miles north of Padang, from Medan and came under the command of 71 Indian Infantry Brigade. The journey from Medan, about 200 miles to the north, was accomplished without incident.

During October and November 1945, the Allied prisoners of war were concentrated, wired in, and protected by the British troops. These unfortunate souls previously scattered throughout the town, had suffered considerably at the hands of the Indonesians.

On 3 December 1945, the Brigade-Major of the 71 Indian Infantry Brigade and a lady worker were found murdered in Padang. Proclamations were therefore issued imposing a Civilian Curfew and forbidding the carrying of any sort of weapons under penalty of death. Strong action was taken against infringement of these orders. Further, 8/8 Punjab Regiment was moved from Fort de Kock to Padang to strengthen the local force.

In consequence of these measures there were no incidents in Padang from mid-January to mid-March 1946, when Headquarters 71 Indian Infantry Brigade and 1 Lincolns left Padang for Palembang as it was felt desirable to have a formation Headquarters with the senior officers in command, in the Palembang area, where tension was increasing.

During April and May 1946, many raids were made in Padang and local villages, and small quantities of arms and ammunition were recovered. In subsequent months, active operations sometimes became necessary when the Indian troops, particularly of 8/8 Punjab, in the course of their escort duties were ambushed or attacked.

On 5 August, 5 Indian Field Battery (7 Indian Field Regiment) and 2 Kumaon Rifles arrived in Padang from Java, and Headquarters Royal Artillery moved to Padang from Medan. This enabled the whole of Padang town to be brought under effective control.

During September, operations were carried out to clear areas in the vicinity of Padang of hostiles who had been persistently attacking the perimeter.

During October and November 1946, except for minor incidents, Padang was quiet. By 30 November 1946, the Dutch had taken over control in Sumatra and all occupying troops were therefore withdrawn.

PALEMBANG AREA

The 1 Burma Regiment landed at Palembang on 25 October 1945, and was disposed as follows:—

Battalion (less two companies) ...	Palembang Town
One company ...	... RAPWI Block
One company ...	... Airfield

Palembang town was then unquiet, and spasmodic attacks were being made on individuals, specially the Chinese, but no clashes occurred with the Allied troops. In December, however, three naval officers were ambushed, two being killed and one wounded. Tension in the area continued to increase during the early months of 1946. This led to the movement, on 13-15 March 1946, of Headquarters 71 Indian Infantry Brigade and 1 Lincolns into Palembang from Padang. The Indonesians grew suspicious at the arrival of the British troops and showed their resentment by sniping their convoys. On 30 March, a patrol of 1 Lincolns consisting of one officer and fifteen British other ranks was subjected to heavy fire, and was further attacked by two parties of the Indonesians, armed with rifles, spears and swords. The patrol had to be eventually extricated by a company of 1 Lincolns, who suffered some casualties. The Indonesian casualties were estimated at 112 with a minimum of twenty-seven killed. As a result of this action and the fact that the Japanese, who had been guarding the oil refineries in the area, were due to be evacuated, the 3/4 and 3/9 Gurkha Rifles disembarked at Palembang during July 1946.

No further incidents, however, occurred and the handover to Netherland troops, which started in October 1946, proceeded smoothly.

SITUATION IN SMALLER REGIONS OF SOUTH-EAST ASIA

The Bangka Island was reoccupied by Netherlands East Indies forces on 11 February 1946, in the face of minor opposition from the Indonesians. Bali was reoccupied similarly on 2 March 1946, and Lombok on the 27th following, with no opposition, although there were subsequent minor disturbances in the interior of Bali, which were dealt with by the Dutch.

The outer islands (which included Netherlands New Guinea and the whole of the Archipelago except Java and Sumatra) were partially occupied in August 1945 by the Australian forces who could not be relieved of their responsibility until January 1946, when a brigade of the 20th Indian Division was transferred from French Indo-China and a Royal Air Force staging-post was set up at Macassar. A number of Netherlands Internal Security Companies were made available from Australia at about this time, and the Supreme Allied Commander deployed them throughout the islands to eke out his own troops. When he left SEAC on 31 May 1946, there were 36 Native companies and 6 Netherlands companies in the outer islands as well as six battalions formed from the ex-prisoners of war.

The Australian forces reoccupied British Borneo, because they were fighting with the Japanese there and it was to them that the Japanese surrendered in August 1945. In December 1945, Lord Louis Mountbatten visited the Australian forces in British Borneo, Celebes and Dutch Borneo, and on 5 January 1946 he received the control of British Borneo. On the 8th of this month he established a military administration under his own nominees and the Australian forces were thereupon relieved by a brigade of the 20th Indian Division.

On 10 January 1946, the British Cabinet decided to re-establish civil government in British Borneo under the authority of the Colonial Office by 1 March 1946. But apart from Sarawak reverting to the Raja on 15 April nothing could be done to implement the scheme for several months[31].

Thus ended the relief of the Netherlands East Indies from the Japanese occupation which paved the way for the evacuation of the Japanese back to their homes.

[31] Mountbatten's *Report*, page 292.

CHAPTER XVI

The Disarming, Concentration and Repatriation of the Japanese Prisoners of War in South-East Asia

INTRODUCTION

When the Japanese surrendered, their strength in South-East Asia was nearly three-quarters of a million, and they were scattered all over the area. They had in their possession millions of tons of explosives, munitions and weapons, and with these they could be a source of trouble to the Allied forces. Lord Mountbatten was fully conscious of this danger, particularly because he did not have the means to keep them in full control, and took ample precautionary measures to prevent any untoward developments. Instructions were issued to the subordinate commanders that the Allied forces must provide for self-defence, and meet any sudden treacherous attacks. They were asked to arrest at once personnel of the following organisations (subject to confirmation): Kempei Tai, Tokomu Kikan, Hikari Kikan, G. S. Intelligence personnel, War Criminals, and Guards of Allied Prisoners of War. Strict injunctions were issued against fraternisation, as also maltreatment of the Japanese or use of violence against them. Disarmament of the Japanese forces was to be the first task, and in all dealings with them subordinate officers were exhorted to adhere strictly to international conventions.

Lord Mountbatten, at the same time, adopted the policy of dealing with the Japanese through their Supreme Commander. In his report to the Combined Chiefs of Staff he has stated that there was no alternative to this procedure, and added that 'for this purpose I maintained the existing Japanese Chain of Command, through their Supreme Commander, to publish and enforce my orders. I consider that if the Japanese Chain of Command had been disrupted for fear that it might provide the enemy commanders with a means of controlling their forces in resisting us—before we had fully replaced it with our own, it would have been impossible for us to use their forces for our own purposes as effectively as we did'[1]. This policy made it possible to concentrate and rapidly evacuate large numbers of Japanese troops and considerable

---

[1] Mountbatten's *Report*, p. 257, para 4.

EVACUATION OF JAPANESE FROM FRENCH INDO-CHINA

The total strength of the Japanese forces in French Indo-China was estimated originally at 71,000 which was not far wrong. On V. J. Day which was 15 August 1945, the figure stood at 60,360 besides 2,000 civilians. These forces were concentrated mainly in Saigon, Phnom Penh and Tourane areas in the south, in Hanoi and Langson areas in the north, and in detachments of various sizes along the road line of communication and on the Mekong river. In French Indo-China south of 16°N, there were 40,000 Japanese in the 'southern' part. Very little of this number had gone to Siam, when Japan surrendered.

There were three divisional formations in southern French Indo-China, viz. *2nd, 22nd* and *55th*, one Independent Mixed Battalion (IMB) and Headquarters and non-divisional units in Saigon area, totalling 19,000 troops. The strength at Phnom Penh, Tourane and the remaining areas, was 4,600, 3,300 and 13,000 respectively. In Saigon, there were in addition 2,250 personnel of the *Headquarters* of *Southern Army* (part of which was at Dalat) and part of the *Headquarters* of the *38th Army*. The *2nd Division*, which was withdrawn from Burma before it was fully formed, and various non-divisional ancillary units including air (ground and naval) were 9,000 strong. In Phnom Penh, Headquarters of the *55th Division* had been set up with a nucleus of 1,000 divisional troops; elements of the *22nd Division* were also in the vicinity amounting to 2,000; and above all there were a number of small non-divisional units. In the Tourane area the *34th IMB* (with only two battalions) and ancillary troops held 3,300 men. The remainder of 13,000 was mainly made up of:

Army	5,300
Air/Navy	4,700
Unidentified	3,000
	13,000

The remnants of 4 Air Brigade which was now in southern French Indo-China after its fight in Burma, were disposed as follows:—

Saigon	16 Aircraft ...	1,420	personnel
Phnom Penh	19 ,, ...	1,400	,,
Thu Dau Mot	...	150	,, (Navy)

Kompong Chnang	... ...	825	Personnel
Hanoi	... ...	255	,,
Arakor 18 Aircraft	...	750	,,
Phu My (Saigon) 5 ,,	...	550	,,
Bien Hoa Catlai 9 ,, (Navy)	...	300	,, (Navy)
Kompong Trach	... ...	230	,,
Total (Aircraft) 58 Army		5,430	Army
9 Navy		450	Navy

The strength of these Japanese forces in southern French Indo-China, their status and influence, called for the most delicate handling by the Supreme Allied Commander, not only for the reason that anything done in excess of law and morality would lead to serious military and political complications but also because it would bring disgrace to the United Nations.

The Japanese attitude was correct if not cordial. When Major-General Gracey arrived at Saigon on 13 September 1945, he was met by two Japanese Generals and one Vice-Admiral and given charge of airfield straightaway. According to the operation order of 19 September there were 17,700 Japanese who obeyed promptly the strange orders of the British General to disarm the Annamites in the police force, to provide lorries for the British troops, etc. In the following month the British General assigned quite a large number of minor duties to the Japanese, like combing the areas for armed Annamites and hidden arms, guarding bridges, patrolling cross-roads, and garrisoning etc.

In November the personnel of Kempei Tai surrendered and were removed to Surete. All Japanese relieved by the French moved to *Headquarters Southern Army* on the 27th of the month for concentration, while those from Loc Ninh area moved and prepared a block at Chon Thanh in the morning of 9 November. It is stated that by the third week of this month " disarmament and concentration of the 65,000 Japanese services personnel and 6,000 civilians in southern FIC is proceeding well. Nearly half the services total was reported disarmed by 24 November".[2]

Figures given on 17 December 1945 reveal that 42,254 Japanese army and air force personnel had been disarmed and concentrated in south French Indo-China by that date, leaving 15,020 to be dealt with. The latter were chiefly engaged in garrisoning outlying areas. But in view of the considerable progress made so far, it was then expected that all Japanese service personnel

---

[2] Weekly Intelligence Summary, India Command No. 213.

and civilians would have been disarmed and concentrated by the end of the year. The surrender of the last 7,988 naval personnel was accepted at Saigon on behalf of the senior British Naval Officer there on 15 December, and it was hoped that 5,000 of them would be repatriated by the end of the year, if shipping became available. Lest any unforeseen incident should retard progress, Cap St. Jacques was prepared for the concentration of 60,000 persons by middle of January 1946, and Major-General Gracey visited the place on 11 December and approved of the plans[3]. By 15 January 1946, 21,150 disarmed Japanese had been concentrated at Cap St. Jacques[4].

February was the month of the final withdrawal of the British from South French Indo-China. Consequently it was planned to transfer *Headquarters Southern Army* to South Johore in Malaya at the end of the month. The Japanese were still involved against the Annamites, and Baria—Cap St. Jacques were protected by the British and Japanese troops jointly. By 18 February all the 70,000 Japanese, remaining in South French Indo-China, had been concentrated and disarmed except for 3,000 still doing duty in outlying garrisons. 47,000 Japanese were in final concentration areas at Cap St. Jacques, Saigon, Thu Dau Mot, and it was expected that the concentration at Cap St. Jacques would be completed by the end of the month.

EVACUATION OF JAPANESE PRISONERS FROM SIAM

Siam was the easiest country to manage so far as the Japanese were concerned. Information about their strength, distribution and disposition with full co-operation of the Siamese army and citizens in dealing with the Japanese was welcome, and the sacrificing spirit displayed by the Japanese was remarkable.

According to Force Plan No. 2 dated 2 September, the estimated strength of all Japanese forces in Siam was 58,000, disposed as follows:

(a) Bangkok—Kanburi 28,700
(b) Lampang—Ubon 18,700
(c) South Siam (Garrisoned troops) ... 2,300
(d) Unlocated 8,300

There were barely 9 army fighter aircraft, with the Headquarters 4 Brigade still in Bangkok.

In September, the Supreme Allied Commander's forces were still in the process of formation. So the Japanese were left

---
[3] War Diary, 9/12 Frontier Force Regiment, 4 and 11 December 1945.
[4] Weekly Intelligence Summary, India Command No. 221.

free to themselves wherever they were. But they handed four million ticals over to the Allies on 15 September[5], and they held themselves responsible for the safety and well-being of prisoners of war until the Allies could take them over and they promised full information about the strength and disposition of the *18th Area Army*. The RA were appointed to supervise all Japanese camps at Ubon, Nakon Sawon, Lampang and Chiengmai. At the same time instructions were given for the movement of Japanese troops to prescribed areas of concentration:—

No. 1 Area	Chiengmai	...	23,000
No. 2 ,,	Lampang	...	7,000
No. 3 ,,	Nakon Sawon	...	8,000
No. 4 ,,	Pong	...	19,000
No 5 ,,	Nakhon Pathom	...	9,000
No 6 ,,	Lopburi	...	9,000
No. 7 ,,	Saraburi	...	5,000
No. 8 ,,	Nakhon Nayok	...	18,000
No. 9 ,,	Ubon	...	8,000

It was stated that 16,000 Japanese troops would move from Bangkok on 23 September 1945, and the troops outside Bangkok would complete their shift from their respective places to places fixed for them by 27 September 1945[6]. But this was obviously impracticable.

In October the conditions changed most favourably to the Allies. By the end of the month a total concentration of 96,429 Japanese had been achieved; and a considerable number of the remainder, including the Japanese *56th Division*, about 4,000, were moving to the concentration area at Chiengmai. Railway troops on Siam-Burma railway (about 4,500) and railway troops in South Siam remained for essential transport duties and for the move of the Japanese *94th Division* to Malaya. Included in the total were 4,800 troops who remained in Bangkok with *Headquarters 18th Area Army* and for labour duties. The total number of Japanese disarmed by 1 November was 110,131 comprising 1,330 naval, 100,805 army and 7,996 air force personnel. In addition, the 7th Indian Division had a plan under way to concentrate 70,000 Japanese at Nakhon Nayok from several other places[7]. The Japanese *Burma Army* with reinforcements had been caught in Siam in the middle of August 1945 when Japan capitulated to the Allies, and this had to be ordered to move to concentration areas like any other Japanese force. Kempei Tai and such

---

[5] War Diary, 7th Indian Division dated 15 September 1945.
[6] *Ibid.*, G. S. Branch, J. 94.
[7] *Ibid.*, 1 November 1945.

other organisations were wound up and confined to Bangkwang Jail. Civilian Japanese who had surrendered but were not charged with crimes were disarmed and concentrated like military personnel.

By the middle of November, a gradual move of the Japanese forces southwards from Lampang[8] was started at the rate of 2,000 per day. To ensure a constant flow from that place, Japanese were moved from Chiengmai to Lampang and from there to the south. Some of the Japanese in the Chiengmai area were found selling arms in small quantities to the Chinese and Indians. This led logically to the destruction of all dumps without the knowledge of the Japanese. During this month 1,400 tons of arms and stores were dumped in the sea, while 207 Military Mission had handed over all responsibility for the Japanese to 114 Indian Infantry Brigade[9]. At the close of the month the position was as follows: total of all Japanese in concentration area was 83,633; movement of Japanese to final concentration area at Nakhon Nayok and Naung Hoi was in progress, and the Japanese still outside concentration areas and engaged as work parties totalled 7,938. A further 1,553 Japanese KT, HK and personnels wanted for war crimes were detained in Bangkok. Grand total 1,13,005[10].

The attitude of the Japanese towards Allied forces in Thailand was exemplary. They did not show any sign of fraternisation with the Siamese. They said, 'We would have continued to fight willingly were it not for the Imperial Proclamation'[11]. But it was the Allied army which disarmed the Japanese army, because they were now withdrawing from Siam leaving the Japanese to the care of the Siamese.

On 14 January 1946, the Chiefs of Staff authorised Lord Mountbatten to hand over to the Siamese the responsibility for guarding the surrendered Japanese personnel. The figures of disarming and concentrating the Japanese in the beginning of this month were: At Nakhon Nayok 49,590, in Bangkwang Jail and Bangkok camps 1946 war criminals and such like persons in custody; grand total 1,13,238 and disarmed out of these 1,12,630.

The Japanese showed definite signs of deterioration in February 1946, because the date of their repatriation was as far off as ever. On 31 May 1946, therefore, the Supreme Allied Commander stopped all further apprehension of the Japanese and confined the Allied attention to repatriation only[12].

8 Dar Diary, 7th Indian Division, 15 November 1945.
9 War Diary, 114 Indian Infantly Brigade, November 1945.
10 War Diary, 7th Indian Division, 1 December 1945.
11 *Ibid*, Insum 28 November to 4 December 1945.
12 Mountbatten's *Report*, p. 280, para 90.

EVACUATION OF JAPANESE PRISONERS FROM JAVA

The story of disarming and concentrating the Japanese in Java follows a different course from that in French Indo-China and Siam. Here the Indonesians had become an adolescent nation, declared themselves as an independent republic and looked upon the British mission with open suspicion. The Japanese to a very great extent were responsible for this unenviable position of the British, they had not only helped the Indonesians to declare themselves as a republic, but had surrendered their arms and stores to them and themselves had gone into self-exile in the interior of Java.

Lord Louis Mountbatten restricted his task to controlling the key areas and leaving the remainder of the country to the Japanese and the local government. But he soon found himself confronted by a peculiar situation. The Indonesians would not unanimously co-operate, and the Japanese in eastern and western Java were hostile or indifferent. He had therefore to use his influence and strength in getting the maximum help from both with the minimum loss of prestige, and it is on account of this necessity to swim along with the current rather than against it that he changed his policy towards the Indonesians, the Dutch and the Japanese.

He left the Japanese in east Java, more or less to themselves. It was impossible to get at them with the Indonesians having interrupted his communications. He took greater care of central and western Java and presented some strength at Semarang, Ambarawa and Magelang. He built up a really formidable force at Bandoeng with *Headquarters 16th Japanese Army* and 37 Indian Infantry Brigade. Elements of Japanese force were also kept roundabout Batavia.

In November 1945 a terror was created by the extremist Indonesians. Many Japanese joined them, many fought against them and several others stood watching. There was heavy fighting in central Java, roundabout Magdang; and in east Java, the Supreme Allied Commander ordered the *16th Japanese Army* to concentrate all Japanese forces in that area at Sourabaya. ' The Japanese have been ordered ', an order declared ' to bring with them their personal arms and equipment, limited ammunition and all transport, but to destroy all other equipment and warlike stores. They will bring rations for two months '[13]. It is doubtful if this order served any purpose, because nothing remarkable occurred on subsequent dates.

[13] War Diary, 5th Indian Division. Operation Instruction No. 13 dated 30 November 1945.

The strength of the Japanese army in Java in the middle of January 1946 was as follows:

Batavia area	10,469
Buitenzorg area	4,448
Bandoeng area	13,425
Cheribon area	1,074
Total for western Java	29,416
Total for central Java	11,425
Total for eastern Java	Not known

It was realised that the Indonesians were extremely perturbed at the use of Japanese military personnel against them in Java. So the Allied Commander issued a general order that their continued use was politically most undesirable as it was upsetting arrangements with the Indonesians for getting the Allied prisoners of war out of central and eastern Java. The Japanese in these regions were numerically strong and militarily well equipped, and unless a cordial attitude was adopted there could be no chance of concentrating them at all. So far as the Indonesians were concerned they had come to consider the evacuation of Allied prisoners of war and Japanese forces as essential for the success of their struggle with the Dutch for freedom, and so the Indonesian leaders also took a practical view of the duties of the Supreme Allied Commander in Java. An officer of the 7th TRI Division addressed his audience on 31 January 1946, as follows: ' Some may doubt whether co-operation with the British should be permitted. This is a very stupid question. General Christison himself declared once that he was unable to carry out his task without full co-operation from the Indonesians. This task, consisting of maintaining law and order, disarming the Japanese and releasing ex-prisoners of war and internees is imposed upon him by agreement of the United Nations. Hence our help is indispensable and will be beneficial to ourselves '"[14].

But the greater problem of disarming, concentrating and repatriating the Japanese was dealt with in the next month, April 1946. On the 25th of that month 700 Japanese arrived in Batavia from central Java, and the Indonesians started the slogan ' Let us be grateful to Japanese ' with the idea of getting rid of them very early. The rate was fixed at 1,000 per week from central and eastern Java, and it was followed strictly throughout May and June.

The position was very hopeful in June. It is recorded that 42,000 were shipped out of the country by the 5th of that month,

---

[14] *Ibid.* Weekly Intelligence Summary No. 13.

and there were only about 8,000 left in Indonesian controlled areas. By the 18th of the same month, 54,000 were evacuated, and it was then estimated that there could be another 20,000 in the whole of Java, with two to three thousand in Indonesian controlled areas. After this date arrangements were made to lift 2,000 per week by air. Consequently a war diary of 28 June 1946 recorded that the evacuation of the Japanese had been almost completed and it had amounted to 58,000. There were still some 1,500 Japanese south of Buitenzorg to be evacuated. Even these were cleared out on 29 June by pulling pressure on the Indonesian officials concerned.[15]

EVACUATION OF JAPANESE PRISONERS FROM SUMATRA

When the 26th Indian Division arrived at Sumatra, there were about 71,500 Japanese, in the north 33,000, in central Sumatra 12,500 and in the south 26,000. Garrisons had been established in the areas of the larger towns of Medan, Padang and Palembang, but small detachments of troops were scattered throughout the rest of the island. These were mainly at the ports of Koetaradja, Sigli, Belawan, Pakan Baroe, Djambi, Teloek Betoeng, Mana, Piana, Emmahaven and Sibolga. During the early part of Japanese occupation the Japanese were working in the ports and were employed in general administration, but as it became apparent that Allied troops were about to take the offensive on the sea, these troops were employed for the defence of the island's coast. There were also specialists working the oilfields, the silver, tin and gold mines. After the cessation of hostilities the Japanese closed down the mines and the large stocks of raw material which had accumulated at the ports due to shipping shortage over the previous year further increased. Shortly after the arrival of the 26th Indian Division the Japanese were ordered to commence concentrating their personnel for evacuation to Japan. The dispositions of the main Japanese forces were as follows:

North Sumatra
Sabang-Koetaradja	4,000
Medan area	27,630
Sibolga	1,270
Tangjoeng Balai	100
	33,000

[15] War Diary, 23rd Indian Division—Weekly Intelligence Summary for June 1946 and for 10 July 1946.

Central Sumatra
Padang	...	...	...	4,775
Pakan Baroe	...	...	...	2,595
Fort de Kock	...	...	...	5,130
				12,500

South Sumatra
Palembang	...	...	...	12,250
Djambi	...	...	...	5,500
Benkoelen	...	...	...	12,750
Bangka—Billiton	...	...	...	450
				30,950

The planned withdrawal of the Japanese garrison in the Koetaradja area to Medan was hampered by the local Achinese tribesmen. They molested and looted the Japanese attempting to destroy their arms and ammunition before concentration, and during this period managed to obtain a quantity of war equipment from the Japanese. As a result of this and in order to avoid an incident with the locals, it was decided to evacuate that group of 4,022 Japanese directly from Koetaradja and it was the first evacuation to be completed in 1945. Sabang remained under Allied control but the rest of the area was completely overrun by the extremists and the Achinese who now closed down on the Japanese garrisons to the north of Medan for the purpose of capturing or buying arms and equipment. A protective screen of Japanese was laid from Langsa on the coast through Pangkalan Brandan to Bindjai, Arnhemia and Brastagi. The outlying garrisons in the north were withdrawn inside this perimeter and established protective road-blocks and check-posts.

Similar concentration was achieved in central and south Sumatra, but it was not until January/February 1946 that the first batch of approximately 11,259 Japanese was evacuated from Palembang to Rempang Island. These had been withdrawn from Bangka, Billiton, Benkoelen and Teloek Betoeng. As in the north the local extremists looted and bought arms and ammunition from the Japanese and as each area was evacuated the locals assumed immediate control.

At the same time another 5,265 Japanese were concentrated in central Sumatra and evacuated from Pakan Baroe to Batu Pahat in Malaya. These came from the areas of Padang and Fort de Kock and the interior of central Sumatra and were not particularly interfered with by the local inhabitants.

Also during February 1946, 5,706 Japanese had been concentrated in the Medan area and were evacuated from Belawan and Tangjoeng Balai. This evacuation entailed a tightening up of the protective screen around Medan, and, as many Japanese had been withdrawn from the Langsa/Koesla Simpang areas, the northern sector was pulled back into Pangkalan Brandan.

This completed the first phase in which approximately 26,252 Japanese were evacuated. The remaining 45,248 were disposed as follows:—

North Sumatra	23,272
South Sumatra	14,741
Central Sumatra	7,235

The second phase of the evacuation was carried out during March/April 1946. In north Sumatra 11,132 Japanese were evacuated from Belawan and this resulted in drastic changes in the disposition of the remaining Japanese personnel. In order to retain intact the screen around Medan the Japanese were deployed as follows:

Pangkalan Brandan	2,942
Bindajai	1,429
Medan	1,272
Tebingtinggi	2,276
Pematang Siantar	2,039
Taroetoeng	464

Also during March/April, 2,063 Japanese had been evacuated from Pakan Baroe leaving approximately 5,100 in central Sumatra. These were located at Fort de Kock, Pakan Baroe and Pajakoemboe. In phase two 19,200 Japanese were evacuated.

During May/June 1946, the evacuation of Japanese from central Sumatra was completed when over 5,000 left from Pakan Baroe. Padang alone remained under Allied control, the rest of central Sumatra passed completely into the hands of the Indonesians.

In north Sumatra during the same period a further 4,260 Japanese were evacuated from Belawan. No large-scale change in the Japanese defence screen was made. The concentration of all outlying detachments in north Sumatra was completed, and only slight alterations in the locations and strengths of the Japanese check-posts were made.

The situation at the end of June was as follows:

Remaining in north Sumatra	7,455
Remaining in south Sumatra	12,873
War criminals in Sabang	451
Deserters/Missing	518
Dead	485

During July a total of 5,692 Japanese were evacuated from south Sumatra. These were made up of two ship loads to Japan carrying 4,828 personnel, a group of hospital patients numbering 83 and 781 Japanese to Singapore. This left only 7,141 Japanese in south Sumatra who were deployed in the Palembang, Pladjoe, Soengai Gerong and Talang Betoetoe areas.

In north Sumatra 693 Japanese were evacuated to Singapore and 2,592 to Japan during July. The remaining 4,375 were pulled into a tight ring running through Tangjoeng Poer, Bindjai, Berastagi, Tandjoeng Morawa and Tanamara Estate.

There were still 451 war criminals held on Sabang Island and the number of Japanese deserters/missing was 505. The total number of Japanese in the whole of Sumatra at the end of July was 12,472.

In August 2,420 Japanese were evacuated from Palembang direct to Japan leaving 4,721. This figure did not alter until October when a further 1,231 were evacuated. This caused a large-scale thinning out of the personnel in the Pladjoe/Soengai Gerong areas and as a result the Allied troops had to be supplemented and redeployed in areas of the oil refineries.

In October 2,232 Japanese were evacuated from Belawan leaving only 1,839 in north Sumatra. This meant the end of the Japanese screen around Medan and these remaining personnel were concentrated at Belawan. In mid-October two final shiploads of 1,298 Japanese were evacuated leaving 540 in Medan and Belawan.

The final evacuation of the Japanese from south Sumatra was completed during the first week of November 1946 and 2,799 Japanese were shipped out leaving 643 technicians and labourers in the oil refineries at Pladjoe and Soengai Gerong. Included in this evacuation were 150 Japanese war criminals and suspects who were transferred to Sabang Island.

CONCLUSION

On 17 November 1946, the remaining Japanese in Sumatra deployed as follows passed into the hands of the Dutch for evacuation:

North Sumatra
Medan	146
Belawan (Dock labourers)	400
Sabong Island (War Criminals and suspects)	584
	1,130

South Sumatra
Pladjoe/Soengai Gerong (Technicians and labourers)	643
Total remaining in Sumatra	1,773

APPENDICES

APPENDIX A

Memorandum of the General Headquarters Supreme Commander for the Allied Powers

18 December 1945

MEMORANDUM FOR RECORD

Tentative arrangements covering establishment of the British Commonwealth Occupation Force in Japan have been effected between Staff Conferences of the Supreme Commander for the Allied Powers and the British Commonwealth Force as enumerated below. These arrangements have been concluded on a staff level to facilitate establishment of the Force in Japan when directed. It is understood that they are subject to agreement between the Governments concerned and in no way constitute commitments of the parties to specific courses of action. The substance of these arrangements is being communicated by the Supreme Commander for the Allied Powers to the United States Government, and by the GOC, British Commonwealth Force, to the Australian Government, for appropriate action.

1. COMMAND RELATIONSHIPS

(a) Mission:

The British Commonwealth Force will constitute a component of occupation forces in Japan under the supreme command of the Supreme Commander for the Allied Powers. It will be charged with the normal military duties of a force of its size and composition, including military control of Hiroshima Prefecture and such other ground and air areas as may be allocated to it for this purpose, demilitarisation and disposition of Japanese installations and armaments within such ground areas and measures necessary for the security of the Force. These areas do not constitute a national zone. It will accomplish such ground and air patrol and surveillance missions within allocated areas as may be directed. Military Government functions within areas allocated to the British Commonwealth Force will be conducted by U.S. agencies as directed by SCAP. Relationships of the British Commonwealth Force with the Japanese, and routine security functions pertaining primarily to Eighth Army operations as a whole, will be prescribed by the CG, Eighth Army. The British Commonwealth Force will conduct such military operations outside normally allocated areas as may be directed to the CG, Eighth Army for Ground Forces and the CG, Fifth Air Force for Air Forces.

(b) Command Organization:

SCAP will assign ground forces of the British Commonwealth Force to operational control of the CG, Eighth U.S. Army. SCAP will assign operational control of the air component of the British Commonwealth Force to the CG, PACUSA. Such air component will function as a separate air command under the Fifth Air Force. SCAP will assign operational control of Royal Naval Port Party, British Commonwealth Force, to the U.S. Naval Commander exercising jurisdiction over Japanese ports, for operation of the port of Kure. Such assignments to operational control will become effective upon arrival of the forces concerned at Japanese ports of debarkation. Ground Forces of the British Commonwealth Force will function as a corps of two divisions under the command of the GOC, British Commonwealth Forces as Corps Commander. The Corps will be composed of one British-Indian Division of two brigade groups with supporting troops. Logistic organization of the British Commonwealth Force will be as prescribed by the Commander thereof. GOC, British Commonwealth Force will remain responsible for the maintenance and administration of the British Commonwealth Force as a whole.

(c) Command Administrative Channels

(1) GOC, British Commonwealth Force will have the right of direct communication with the British Commonwealth Joint Chiefs of Staff in Australia on administrative matters affecting the Force.

(2) GOC, British Commonwealth Force will have the right of direct access to the Supreme Commander for the Allied Powers for matters of major policy affecting the operational capabilities of the Force.

(3) It is understood that for matters of governmental concern effecting the policy and operations of the British Commonwealth Force, the channel of communication lies from the Australian Government as representative of the British Commonwealth of Nations through the United States Government and the United States Joint Chiefs of Staff to the Supreme Commander for the Allied Forces.

(4) In administrative matters pertaining to relations with United States Forces or with the Japanese, the GOC, British Commonwealth Force will be governed by policies prescribed by Commanders exercising operational control. Such policies will

in general conform to those prescribed for United States Forces. In case of conflict between such administrative instructions received from the CG, Eighth Army and the CG, PACUSA (or his designated representative), the matter will be referred to GHQ, SCAP for decision.

(d) *Liaison*

GOC, British Commonwealth Force is authorised to exchange liaison officers by mutual arrangement with CG's, I Corps and Fifth Air Force. Provisions for liaison between British Commonwealth Force and Japanese Central Liaison Committees in areas occupied, are subject to future arrangements between British Commonwealth Force Headquarters and GHQ, SCAP on Military Government matters will be conducted through the Eighth Army. Liaison between British Commonwealth Force and U.S. Naval authorities will be conducted through Naval Port Director of the port or ports concerned for local matters pertaining thereto. Liaison with U.S. Naval authorities on all other matters will be conducted through GHQ, SCAP.

2. AREAS OF RESPONSIBILITY

(a) The British Commonwealth Force will be allocated Hiroshima Prefecture for exercise of the functions and responsibilities enumerated in sub-paragraph *1a* above.

(b) If proven necessary by reconnaissance, the British Commonwealth Force may be allocated an additional area or areas by SCAP for air base purposes. Within such areas, British Commonwealth Force will exercise the security and surveillance functions and responsibilities prescribed for Hiroshima Prefecture, subject to local modification at the direction of CG, Eighth Army.

3. FORCES

(a) It is understood that the total strength of the British Commonwealth Force will be determined by inter-governmental decision. It is also understood that the British Commonwealth Force plans to maintain its basic organisation as a Corps of two divisions of two brigades each, with suitable air and (air and ground) service supporting elements within the strength eventually determined. Major unit strength will be adjusted to meet the total strength determined by inter-governmental decision. Composition and strength of the air component of the Force is also subject to inter-governmental decision.

(b) It is understood that the British Commonwealth Force may be withdrawn wholly or in part upon agreement between the Governments of the United States and Australia or upon six months notice by either party. It is also understood that reductions will be made in the British Commonwealth Force from time to time in conformity with progressive reductions in United States Occupation Forces in Japan.

(c) GOC British Commonwealth Force will provide SCAP with troops lists including units strengths, upon final determination of the composition of the force.

(d) For planning purposes, the GOC, British Commonwealth Force has submitted tentative designation of units of the Force, current location and availability for arrival in Japan as follows:—

Unit and Location

    Force Headquarters, Australia
    Headquarters Anzac Division, Australia 34th Aust. bde., Morotai
    New Zealand Bde, Italy
    British-Indian Division, Bombay
        (Hq. and 2 Bdes.)
    Force Troops, Australia and SEAC
    RAAF, Labuan (Borneo)
        3 Sqdns. Mustangs
    Hq. Staff Planes (2) and Dte. (Australia)
    RNZAF, New Zealand
        1 Sqdn. (Spitfires)
    RAF
        2 Sqdns. Mosquitos (BR), Madras
        1 Sqdn. Spitfires (Ind.), Madras
        2 Sqdns. Spitfires (BR), Singapore
        1 Sqdn. TC (BR), Rangoon
        Com. Flt. (BR), Madras
    RN Port Party, Singapore
    AF Const. Sqdn., Labuan
    Base and Port troops, various locations.

Target Arrival Dates in Japan

    RN Port Party—28 January
    34th Bde.—1 February
    AF Const. Sqdn.—1 February
    Adv. Ech. Force and Base Troops—1 February
    1st Ser. Air Ground Ech.—1 February
    Hq. Anzac Div.—23 February

Main Body Air Ground Ech.—23 February
Main Body B-1 Div.—15 March.
NZ Bde.—23 March.

(e) (1) It is understood that actual arrival dates of the above units are subject to clearance by SCAP upon evacuation by U.S. forces of areas to be occupied.

(2) Arrangements will be made by PACUSA for staging of air echelons of the Force to Japan via. the Philippines and Okinawa, except for RAF spitfires and airplanes of the New Zealand Squadron, which it is understood will be delivered by water transport.

5. MISCELLANEOUS

(a) *Initial arrangements for establishment of British Commonwealth Force in Japan:*

(1) The Australian Services Mission in Tokyo will be disbanded and its functions taken over by an Advance Echelon, Headquarters, British Commonwealth Force, made up of Australian Services Mission personnel, augmented by three or four additional officers to be designated by GOC, British Commonwealth Force.

(2) Direct communication between the GOC, British Commonwealth Force, or his authorized representatives, and CG, Eighth Army, CG, PACUSA and CG, Fifth Air Force, for matters pertaining to the establishment and operation of the Force, will be authorised by SCAP upon receipt of authority for entry of the Force from the U.S. Joint Chiefs of Staff.

(3) Pending further instructions, travel of staff officers of the Force Headquarters and of preliminary reconnaissance parties and individuals for inspection of areas and other orientation purposes is authorized subject to current clearance procedures by SCAP.

(4) Quartering, subsistence and transportation of advance parties of the British Commonwealth Force will be provided by the Force.

(5) Preliminary movement of casual airplanes of British Commonwealth air forces to and in Japan for staff purposes will be subject to current clearance procedures by SCAP. Temporary use by such air-craft of U.S. facilities in Japan and enroute will be arranged by PACUSA.

(b) *Signal Communications:*

(1) It will not be necessary for the British Commonwealth Force to establish radio communications in Tokyo as SCAP will

be able to handle its required traffic until such time as the Commonwealth Force moves into its proposed area. Matter of co-ordinating the use of codes and ciphers will be worked out by technical representatives of U.S. and British Commonwealth Forces at a later date.

(2) Existing wire facilities used by X Corps will be made available to the British Commonwealth Force.

(3) Courier service in Japan will be continued as presently established by the Eighth Army and Fifth Air Force and will be made available to the British Commonwealth Force.

(c) *Press Releases:*

No press release concerning the British Commonwealth Force will be made pending governmental arrangements for simultaneous announcement in Washington, Tokyo, Canberra, Wellington, New Delhi and London of the formation of the Force. Necessary steps will be taken to insure against premature press reports in this respect.

6. LOGISTICS

(a) The British Commonwealth Force agrees to assume complete logistic responsibility for the support of the Force.

(b) Transportation required for the Force will be furnished from British Commonwealth sources (Rail within Japan excepted).

(c) The British Commonwealth Force will be equipped with tentage.

(d) Considerable housing is known to be available in the area to be occupied. Details as to procurement will be worked out by the British Commonwealth Force and Eighth Army based on schedule of withdrawal of U.S. and arrival of Force units.

(e) Maintenance of the Force will be furnished by the British Commonwealth Force. Plans provide for 90 days supplies to accompany troops, with ammunition to conform to Eighth Army and PACUSA levels.

(f) In as much as strength of British Commonwealth Force is indefinite at this time, tonnages involved in troop and supply movement are undetermined. Preliminary investigation indicates a sufficient port capacity to handle the Force.

(g) Intransit and substantial permanent storage warehousing is available in contemplated areas. The British Commonwealth Force will be prepared to provide such additional storage as may be required.

(h) Air Base facilities in areas allocated to the British Commonwealth Force for such purposes will be made available to the Force, subject to arrangements for continuation of essential United States functions therein. Additional construction and maintenance becomes the responsibility of the British Commonwealth Force.

(i) Upon arrival of its port director personnel the British Commonwealth Force will assume port director functions for the entire port of Kure, under operational control of the U.S. Navy. U.S. personnel will be withdrawn. The Kure Navy Yard will remain under United Sates control.

(j) The control of shipping schedules pertaining to the British Commonwealth Force will be a Force responsibility.

(k) Requirements for a minor increase of the British Commonwealth Force advance Headquarters in the Tokyo Area will be submitted to SCAP.

(l) In area of occupation, requirements for office space, officers' billets, enlisted men's billets, warehouse and ammunition storage areas will be procured through the Eighth Army.

(m) The British Commonwealth Force desired to secure three airdromes. Decisions on this point will be made after physical inspection of existing facilities in Hiroshima Prefecture and, if deemed essential, in adjacent areas. Inspection of Itami airdrome at Kobe as a possible alternate site is authorized.

(n) Bulk petroleum products and packed aviation lubricants will be furnished by the U.S. on a dollar reimbursement basis while all other packed petroleum products will be furnished by the British Commonwealth Force. U.S. Force will deliver bulk products to the water line. The British Commonwealth Force will be responsible for receiving and distributing bulk products. Informal reports indicate that adequate bulk tankage exists in the proposed area of occupation.

(o) Local procurement for the British Commonwealth Force Area will be accomplished in conformance with Eighth Army directives.

(p) Rail transportation will be procured through normal Eighth Army channels.

(q) The British Commonwealth Force agrees to furnish such railway guards as may be required for its own operations.

(r) Yen currency will be supplied through the Eighth Army procedures. Current conversion rate on basis of 15 yen to 1 U.S. dollar will obtain for the British Commonwealth Force.

(s) The British Commonwealth Force will be prepared to furnish pay schedules, both military and civil, to the Eighth Army when requested.

(t) Improvements made to Japanese facilities with U.S. materials will be accepted by the British Commonwealth Force on a dollar reimbursement basis, when such facilities are needed and desired by the British Commonwealth Force.

Lt.-General J. NORTHCOTT, A.I.F.,
Commanding British Com. Force.
Major-General R. J. MARSHALL, G.S.C.,
Chief of Staff, Supreme Commander for the Allied Powers.

APPENDIX B

Occupation Instruction No. 3, General Headquarters Supreme Commander for the Allied Powers

12 February 1946

1. (a) Military control of JAPAN has been established and is being effectively exercised by the Supreme Commander for the Allied Powers. Demobilization of the Japanese military forces within JAPAN has preceded in schedule and is over 98 per cent complete. Approximately 15,000 former Japanese naval personnel are engaged in repatriation duties and 12,000 in mine-sweeping operations.

(b) The Commanding General EIGHTH United States Army is responsible for all land areas (other than that occupied by FIFTH United States Fleet ashore) in JAPAN proper. See General Headquarters United States Army Forces Pacific Operations instructions Number 4 and Number 7 with amendments thereto.

(c) The Commander-in-Chief United States Pacific Fleet, employing the FIFTH United States Fleet and attached Allied Naval Forces, controls the coastal waters of JAPAN and occupied certain Japanese naval facilities in Japan, routes Allied naval shipping and controls Japanese naval and merchant vessels, conducts reconnaissance and essential operations including mine-sweeping and verifies the disarmament and demobilization of Japanese naval forces by inspection and surveillance. See General Headquarters Supreme Commander for the Allied Powers Occupation Instructions Number 1.

(d) The Commanding General Pacific Air Command United States Army, employing the FIFTH United States Air Force, provides the air garrison for JAPAN, aerial reconnaissance and photography, surveillance, air warning, and air support for the Occupation Forces. See General Headquarters United States Army Forces Pacific Operations Instructions Number 4 and 7 with amendments thereto.

2. (a) The British Commonwealth Occupation Force will augment the Occupation Forces in JAPAN and will constitute a component of the Occupation Forces under the supreme command of the Supreme Commander for the Allied Powers.

APPENDIX B

(b) Composition of major units:—
  British Commonwealth Occupation Force—Lieutenant General J. Northcott, CB, MVO, AIF.
  Ground Forces—Lieutenant General J. Northcott, CB, MVO, AIF.
  British-Indian Division—Major General D. T. Cowan, CB, DSO, MC, Indian Army.
  34th Australian Infantry Brigade Group—Brigadier R. H. Nimmo, AIF.
  New Zealand Brigade Group—Brigadier K. L. Stewart, CBE, DSO, NZEF.
  Royal Naval Port Party—Captain J. A. Grindle, RN.
  Air Forces—Air Vice Marshal C. A. Bouchier, CB, CBE, DFC, RAF.
  81st Australian Fighter Wing (3 Mustang Squadrons), RWAF.
  11th Spitfire Squadron RAF.
  17th Spitfire Squadron, RAF.
  96th Transport Squadron, (Medium), RAF.
  4th Spitfire Squadron, RIAF.
  14th Corsair Squadron, RNZAF.

3. (a) General Officer Commanding British Commonwealth Occupation Force will:—
  (i) Progressively establish around, naval and air forces of the British Commonwealth Occupation Force in HIROSHIMA Prefecture, as arranged with the Commander FIFTH United States Fleet (representative of Commander-in-Chief United States Pacific Fleet) and the Commanding General Pacific Air Command United States Army. Dates of arrival of forces in JAPAN will be as approved by this Headquarters.
  (ii) Pass operational control of the British Commonwealth Occupation Force, less Air force units and the Royal Naval Port Party, to the Commanding General EIGHTH United States Army upon arrival of units at ports of debarkation in JAPAN.
  (iii) Pass operational control of air force units of the British Commonwealth Occupation Force to Commanding General Pacific Air Command United States Army upon arrival of units at airfields or ports of debarkation in Japan. Arrange with Commanding General Pacific Air Command United States Army for the staging of air echelons through the PHILIPPINES and OKINAWA to JAPAN as required.

(iv) Pass operational control of the Royal Naval Port Party, British Commonwealth Occupation Force to the Commander FIFTH United States Fleet (representative of Commander-in-Chief United States Pacific Fleet) upon arrival of the Royal Naval Port Party at the port of debarkation in JAPAN.

(v) Subsequent to the establishment of the British Commonwealth Occupation Force in HIROSHIMA Prefecture, progressively established ground and air forces in the areas of SHIKOKU Island and OKAYAMA, TOTTORI, SHIMANE (to include the OKI-RETTO) and YAMAGUCHI Prefectures, as directed by the Commanding Generals Eighth United States Army and Pacific Air Command United States Army.

(b) Commanding General EIGHTH United States Army will:—

(i) Arrange with the General Officer Commanding British Commonwealth Occupation Force for the progressive movement of the British Commonwealth Occupation Force, less Air Force units and the Royal Navy Port Party, to assigned areas in JAPAN. Dates of arrival of forces will be as approved by this headquarters.

(ii) Assume operational control of the British Commonwealth Occupation Force, less air force units and the Royal Naval Port Party, upon arrival of units at ports of debarkation in JAPAN.

(iii) Assign HIROSHIMA Prefecture, and other areas if and when so designated, as the zone of occupation of the ground forces of the British Commonweatlth Occupation Force for the exercise of the functions and responsibilities of Occupation Forces under the Commanding General EIGHTH United States Army.

(iv) Employ the British Commonwealth Occupation Force, less air force units and the Royal Naval Port Party, for such military operations as are required in JAPAN in areas other than the assigned occupation zone of the British Commonwealth Occupation Force.

(v) Subsequent to the establishment of the British Commonwealth Occupation Force in HIROSHIMA Prefecture progressively extend the zone of occupation of the ground forces of the British Commonwealth Occupation Force to include the areas of SHIKOKU Island and

OKAYAMA, TOTTORI, SHIMANE (to include the OKI-RETTO) and YAMAGUCHI Prefectures. See paragraph 3b(iii).

(c) Commander FIFTH United States Fleet (representative of Commander-in-Chief United States Pacific Fleet) will:—
  (i) Assume operational control of Royal Naval Port Party, British Commonwealth Occupation Force upon arrival in the KURE area.
  (ii) Establish the Royal Naval Port Party in the KURE area as arranged with the General Officer Commanding British Commonwealth Occupation Force and the Commanding General EIGHTH United States Army. See Paragraph 4d(iv).

(d) Commanding General Pacific Air Command United States Army will:—
  (i) Arrange with the General Officer Commanding British Commonwealth for the progressive movement and establishment of air forces of the British Commonwealth Occupation Force at designated air-fields in JAPAN. Dates of arrival of units will be as approved by this headquarters. See Paragraph 4e(ii).
  (ii) Assume operational control of air force units of the British Commonwealth Occupation Force upon arrival of units at airfields or ports of debarkation in JAPAN.
  (iii) Assign the air component of the British Commonwealth Occupation Force as a separate air command under the operational control of the FIFTH United States Air Force.
  (iv) Assign to the air forces of the British Commonwealth Occupation Force the primary mission of security and surveillance in the area occupied by the ground forces of the British Commonwealth Occupation Force. Assign other missions as required in support of occupation forces in JAPAN.

(e) (i) General Officer Commanding British Commonwealth Occupation Force will have the right of direct access to the Supreme Commander for the Allied Powers for matters of major policy affecting the operational capabilities of the British Commonwealth Occupation Force.
  (ii) In administrative matters pertaining the relations with United States Forces or with the Japanese, the General Officer Commanding British Commonwealth Occupation

Force will be governed by policies prescribed by commanders exercising operational control. Such policies will in general conform to those prescribed for United States Forces. In cases of conflict between such administrative instructions received from the Commanding General EIGHTH United States Army, the Commander FIFTH United States fleet and the Commanding General Pacific Air Command United States Army (or their designated representatives), the matter will be referred to General Headquarters Supreme Commander for the Allied Powers for decision.

(iii) General Officer Commanding British Commonwealth Occupation Force will retain the right of direct communication with the British Commonwealth Joint Chiefs of Staff in Australia on administrative matters affecting the British Commonwealth Occupation Force.

(iv) Military Government functions within areas assigned to the British Commonwealth Occupation Force will be conducted by United States agencies as directed by the Supreme Commander for the Allied Powers.

(v) (a) Exchange of Liaison officers between the General Officer Commanding British Commonwealth Occupation Force and the Commanding General I United States Corps and FIFTH United States Air Force is authorized.
(b) Provisions for liaison between the General Officer Commanding British Commonwealth Occupation Force and Japanese Central Liaison Committees in areas occupied, will be as arranged between the Commanding General EIGHTH United States Army and General Officer Commanding British Commonwealth Occupation Force.
(c) Liaison between the General Officer Commanding British Commonwealth Occupation Force and General Headquarters Supreme Commander for the Allied Powers on military government matters will be conducted through the Commanding General EIGHTH United States Army.
(d) Liaison between the British Commonwealth Occupation Force and United States naval authorities will be conducted through the Naval Port Director of the Port or Ports concerned for local matters pertaining thereto. Liaison between the British Commonwealth Occupation Force and United States naval authorities on all other matter will be conducted through General Headquarters Supreme Commander for the Allied Powers.

4. Logistics

(*a*) *Responsibility for logistic support:* The General Officer Commanding British Commonwealth Occupation Force will be responsible for logistic support of all British Commonwealth Occupation Forces engaged in the occupation except that certain petroleum products as described below will be furnished from United States sources.

(*b*) *Supply:*
  (i) The British Commonwealth Occupation Force will arrive in the occupation area within 90 days accompanying supplies of all classes. Tentage will be included.
  (ii) After establishment of the British Commonwealth Occupation Force in the occupation area, levels of supply maintained for the force will conform generally to those of the EIGHTH United States Army and Pacific Air Command United States Army.
  (iii) Resupply of the British Commonwealth Occupation Force, except for bulk petroleum products for ground and air forces, will be from British Commonwealth sources.
  (iv) Bulk petroleum products for ground and air forces of the British Commonwealth Occupation Force will be supplied by the United States on a dollar reimbursement basis. The Commanding General EIGHTH United States Army will arrange for delivery of authorized bulk petroleum products to the waterline at which point(s) the General Officer Commanding British Commonwealth Occupation Force will receive and distribute them.

(*c*) *Hospitalization and Evacuation:* The General Officer Commanding British Commonwealth Occupation Force will be responsible for the hospitalization and evacuation of personnel of the British Commonwealth Occupation Force within the occupation area and to overseas destinations.

(*d*) *Transportation:*
  (i) Except for rail transportation, all transportation required by the British Commonwealth Occupation Force for movements to and from the occupation area and within the area will be furnished from British Commonwealth sources.
  (ii) The General Officer Commanding British Commonwealth Occupation Force will procure rail transportation in

JAPAN through procedure as established by the Commanding General EIGHTH United States Army.

(iii) The General Officer Commanding British Commonwealth Occupation Force will furnish such railway guards as may be required for its own operations.

(iv) British Commonwealth Occupation Force Port Director personnel will assume port director functions and responsibilities for the entire port of KURE upon arrival in JAPAN, under operational control of the FIFTH United States Fleet (see paragraph 3a(iv)). KURE Navy Yard remains under control of the Commander FIFTH United States Fleet.

(v) The General Officer Commanding British Commonwealth Occupation Force will be responsible for the control of shipping schedules pertaining to the British Commonwealth Occupation Force.

(e) *Construction and Facilities:*

(i) The Commanding General EIGHTH United States Army will allocate to the General Officer Commanding British Commonwealth Occupation Force such housing as is available in the area to be occupied by that force and as is required by the force. The Commanding General EIGHTH United States Army will allocate in transit and storage warehousing to the General Officer Commanding British Commonwealth Occupation Force as required and available. The General Officer Commanding British Commonwealth Occupation Force will furnish additional storage if required.

(ii) The Commanding General Pacific Air Command United States Army will allocate IWAKUNI airdrome and facilities, and air bases and facilities as required within the area occupied by the British Commonwealth Occupation Force as bases for operations of the air forces of the British Commonwealth Occupation Force. The Commanding General Pacific Air Command United States Army will arrange to continue functions in these bases which are essential to the Pacific Air Command United States Army.

(iii) The General Officer Commanding British Commonwealth Occupation Force will procure in the area of occupation office space, officers billets, enlisted men's billets, warehousing and storage space sufficient for his requirements in accordance with methods and policies

as prescribed by the Commanding General EIGHTH United States Army.
   (iv) The General Officer Commanding British Commonwealth Occupation Force will accept on a dollar reimbursement basis improvements made to Japanese facilities with United States materials, when such facilities are needed and desired by the General Officer Commanding British Commonwealth Occupation Force.
   (v) The Commanding General EIGHTH United States Army and the Commander FIFTH United States Fleet will allocate, as available, berths, piers and unloading areas to the General Officer Commanding British Commonwealth Occupation Force in sufficient quantity to meet British Commonwealth Occupation Force discharge requirements.
   (vi) The Commanding General EIGHTH United States Army will furnish, as available, existing wire communications facilities required by the General Officer Commanding British Commonwealth Occupation Force.

(f) *Miscellaneous:*
   (i) The General Officer Commanding British Commonwealth Occupation Force will be responsible for the completion of demilitarization and disposition of Japanese installations and armament in their assigned areas in accordance with instructions prescribed by the Commanding General EIGHTH United States Army.
   (ii) The British Commonwealth Occupation Force will furnish pay schedules, both military and civil, to the Commanding General EIGHTH United States Army when required.
   (iii) The General Officer Commanding British Commonwealth Occupation Force will require exclusive use of yen currency in the occupation area by the British Commonwealth Occupation Force and will procure required yen currency from the Commanding General EIGHTH United States Army. The current exchange rate on the basis of 15 to 1 United States dollar obtains for the British Commonwealth Occupation Force, conversion from British Commonwealth currency to be at the exchange rate of 3·228 United States dollars to one (i) Australian pound.

5. COMMUNICATIONS

(*a*) *Information concerning Japanese Signal communications facilities:*
  (i) Civil Communications facilities in JAPAN are operated by the Board of communications, and agency of the Japanese Government, in accordance with directives of Supreme Commander for the Allied Powers. The Occupation Forces employ Japanese civil communications facilities to the maximum extent consistent with maintaining essential communications required for the internal Japanese economy.
  (ii) Japanese Military (Army and Navy) communications facilities in JAPAN have been deactivated except where such facilities are required in connection with demobilization and repatriation purposes and for mine-sweeping operations.

(b) For information concerning Allied signal communications see current index to Standing Signal instructions and signal operation Instructions, General Headquarters United States Army Forces Pacific.

(c) Authority has been granted and frequencies allocated for the British Commonwealth Occupation Force to establish a radio circuit between Headquarters British Commonwealth Occupation Force JAPAN and MELBOURNE, AUSTRALIA for transmission of communications authorized under paragraph 3e(iii) above.

(*d*) *Command Posts:*
  (i) Supreme Commander for the Allied Powers—TOKYO.
  (ii) United States Army Forces Pacific—TOKYO.
  (iii) United States Pacific Fleet—PEARL HARBOUR.
  (iv) EIGHTH United States Army—YOKOHAMA.
  (v) British Commonwealth Occupation Force—to be ANNOUNCED.
  (vi) Pacific Air Command United States Army—MANILA Advance Echelon—TOKYO.
  (vii) FIFTH United States Fleet—AFLOAT.
  (viii) Naval Activities Japan—TOKYO.
  (ix) 68th Army Airways Communications System Group—TOKYO.
  (x) FIFTH United States air Force—TOKYO.

(*e*) *Commanding General EIGHTH United States Army will:*
  (i) Provide assistance as may be required by Commanding General Pacific Air Command United States Army in

the integration of the British Commonwealth Occupation Force into the air warning system for the Japanese Islands.
(ii) Make available to the British Commonwealth Force existing safeguard courier service in JAPAN.

(*f*) *Commanding General Pacific Air Command United States Army will:*
(i) Insure that the British Commonwealth Occupation Force is integrated into the air warning system for the Japanese Islands.
(ii) Coordinate with Commanding Officer 68th Army Airways Communications Systems Group United States Army to insure proper integration of the air navigational facilities of the British Commonwealth Occupation Force air units with those of the United States Army Air Force.

(g) Commanding Officer 68th Army Airways Communication System Group United States Army will, in coordination with Commanding General Pacific Air Command United States Army, arrange for the British Commonwealth Occupation Force air force navigation facilities to become an integral part of the navigational facilities of the United States Army Air Forces.

(h) Commander FIFTH United States Fleet will insure establishment of communications by Royal Naval Port Party to adequately control shipping in the KURE Port.

(i) Commanding General EIGHTH United States Army, Commanding General Pacific Air Command United States Army, and Commander FIFTH United States Fleet will:
(i) Allocate radio frequencies and call signs to elements of the British Commonwealth Occupation Force under their operational control.
(ii) Arrange for the transfer of fixed United States communication facilities not required by United States Forces to the elements. British Commonwealth Occupation Force under their operational control in accordance with provisions of 4e(iv) above.
(iii) Arrange for the assignment of Japanese Civil Communications facilities as may be required by elements of the British Commonwealth Occupation Force under their operational control. By command of General MacArthur.

S. J. CHAMBERLAIN,
Major-General, G.S.C.,
Acting Chief of Staff.

APPENDIX C

Directive to the Commander-in-Chief, British Commonwealth Occupation Force in Japan

18 February 1946

APPOINTMENT

1. This directive is issued to you as Commander-in-Chief British Commonwealth Occupation Force (hereinafter referred to as B.C.O.F.) on behalf of and with the approval of His Majesty's Governments in the United Kingdom, Australia, New Zealand and India, hereinafter referred to as the "British Commonwealth Governments concerned".

2. Your command will comprise such formations and units of the naval, army and air forces as may be allotted to it from time to time by the British Commonwealth Governments concerned.

3. Subject to any exceptions expressly mentioned below, you may delegate any or all of the powers conferred on you in this directive to any officer or officers under your command.

OBJECTS AND ROLE

4. The objects of British Commonwealth Occupation Force, from the aspects of the British Commonwealth Governments concerned, are:—
   (a) To represent worthily the British Commonwealth in the occupation of Japan;
   (b) To maintain and enhance British Commonwealth prestige and influence in the eyes of the Japanese and of our Allies; and
   (c) To illustrate to, and impress on, the Japanese people, as far as may be possible, the democratic way and purpose in life.

5. In addition to furthering these objects, you should also bear in mind that the organisation of British Commonwealth Occupation Force and the establishment in connection therewith of the Joint Chiefs of Staff in Australia (hereinafter referred to as J.C.O.S.A.) are regarded by the British Commonwealth Governments concerned as constituting a further development in British

Commonwealth co-operation. You should therefore foster, in your Headquarters and in Force and Base units, the principle of the maximum integration of services and personnel of each country contributing forces to British Commonwealth Occupation Force.

6. You are to take as the military basis on which British Commonwealth Occupation Force participates in the occupation of Japan the Memorandum for Record signed at Tokyo on 18 December 1945, as modified by the provisos set out by the United States Government in its note dated 22 January, 1946 to the Australian Legation at Washington. The Memorandum and provisos have been approved by the United States Government and the British Commonwealth Governments concerned.

7. Broadly, your military role, under the direction of the Supreme Commander for the Allied Powers in Japan (hereinafter referred to as S.C.A.P.) is, within the area allotted to British Commonwealth Occupation Force:—

(a) The safeguarding of all allied installations, and of all Japanese installations awaiting demilitarisation.
(b) The demilitarisation and disposal of Japanese installations and armaments.
(c) Military control. This does not include Military Government.

RELATIONSHIP WITH UNITED STATES SERVICE AUTHORITIES

8. You are placed under the supreme command of Supreme Commander for the Allied Powers to whom you have the right of direct access on matters of major policy afffecting the operational commitments of British Commonwealth Occupation Force. The shore based naval personnel of British Commonwealth Occupation Force come under the operational control of the United States Naval Commander exercising jurisdiction over Japanese ports. The army component comes under the operational control of the Commanding General of the 8th United States Army, and the air force component under that of the Commanding General, Pacific Air Command, United States Army, (P.A.C., U.S.A.) as a separate air command under 5th United States Air Force. Though it is through you that these United States commanders exercise this operational control, you may authorise direct communication between them and your subordinate commanders to the extent you consider necessary.

RELATIONSHIP WITH SUPREME COMMANDER FOR THE ALLIED POWERS FOR ADVICE ON SERVICE MATTERS

9. Should Supreme Commander for the Allied Powers require advice on service matters you are to adopt the following procedure:—

(a) You should deal direct with Supreme Commander for the Allied Powers on all service matters affecting British Commonwealth Occupation Force in respect of the land and/or air services represented in British Commonwealth Occupation Force.

(b) Should Supreme Commander for the Allied Powers raise any question requiring co-ordinated British Commonwealth views on land and/or air service matters outside British Commonwealth Occupation Force's immediate sphere but concerning the British Commonwealth countries represented in British Commonwealth Occupation Force as a whole, you should act as the channel of communication to Supreme Commander for the Allied Powers, obtaining such co-ordinated views as may be necessary through Joint Chiefs of Staff in Australia. If he raises a matter concerning the United Kingdom only, you should refer it to the Prime Minister of the United Kingdom's representative with Supreme Commander for the Allied Powers.

(c) You should deal direct with Supreme Commander for the Allied Powers on naval matters only insofar as they concern the Naval shore Party of British Commonwealth Occupation Force, keeping the Commander-in-Chief, B.P.F., informed.

The Commander-in-Chief, B.P.F., should continue to deal direct with Supreme Commander for the Allied Powers on matters of naval policy keeping you and Joint Chiefs of Staff in Australia informed whenever subjects affecting British Comonwealth Occupation Force are under consideration.

RELATIONSHIP WITH BRITISH COMMONWEALTH AUTHORITIES

10. You are responsible for the command and administration of British Commonwealth Occupation Force as a whole to the British Commonwealth Governments concerned through Joint Chiefs of Staff in Australia, whose instruction to you will be issued through the Australian Chiefs of Staff acting as the agents of Joint Chiefs of Staff in Australia. The normal channel for communications from you on these matters is through the Australian Chiefs of

Staff to Joint Chiefs of Staff in Australia. You are to submit to Joint Chiefs of Staff in Australia monthly reports on the activities and general welfare of your command.

11. On matters of Governmental concern affecting the policy and operations of British Commonwealth Occupation Force as a whole, you are to communicate through Joint Chiefs of Staff in Australia to the Australian Government who act as the representative of the other British Commonwealth Governments concerned.

12. The relations of your subordinate commanders with their Governments and national authorities are governed by directives issued to them by their Governments. You will be given copies of these directives.

13. Subject to any special instructions you may issue, the commander of a Service component of a national contingent may communicate direct with his national Service authorities on matters of domestic administration concerning the personnel of his national Service wherever serving in British Commonwealth Occupation Force. In addition he may make periodical reports on the activities and general welfare of his command direct to his national Service authorities but he is to provide you, and where concerned, the Air Officer Commanding B.C.A.I.R., with two copies of such reports. You are then to pass one copy, with any comments you may wish to make, to the national representative concerned on Joint Chiefs of Staff in Australia.

14. The officer nominated as the representative of a national contingent has the right to communicate with his national authorities, when he considers it necessary in the discharge of his responsibilities, on matters which affect either the general well being of personnel in his contingent or the interests of his Government. In the case of the United Kingdom and India contingents he will communicate through the representative or representatives of his nation on Joint Chiefs of Staff in Australia. Such communication may be made only after prior consultation with you. He is to provide you immediately with two copies. You will at once send to Joint Chiefs of Staff in Australia a copy together with any observations on it which you may wish to make.

CONTROL AND ADMINISTRATION OF BRITISH COMMONWEALTH OCCUPATION FORCE

15. The broad policy for the organisation for the control and administration of British Commonwealth Occupation Force in Japan and for channels of communication in respect of both you and your subordinate commanders in relation thereto is set out

in Appendix 1, " The Organization for the control and administration of British Commonwealth Occupation Force in Japan ".

16. In carrying out the command and administration of British Commonwealth Occupation Force you are to be guided by the principles and policy set forth in the " Plan for a British Commonwealth Force to participate in the Occupation of Japan ". copies of which are being issued to you and to all concerned.

17. Personnel and units from Service components of national contingents forming part of Headquarters British Commonwealth Occupation Force, or B.C.O.F. Force and Base Units are to be regarded as transferred for functional control and general administration. The commanders of Service components of national contingents remain responsible both to you and their national Service authorities for the domestic administration, including disciplinary action and well being of these personnel and units. In the case of the officer nominated as the representative of the Indian Contingent, he, jointly with you, is responsible for ensuring that Indian personnel are not employed on any task or in such manner as to conflict with religious or caste susceptibilities.

MILITARY GOVERNMENT

18. Military Government of the area allotted to British Commonwealth Occupation Force will continue to be conducted by the United States agencies. You have been provided with officers both in your Headquarters and those of subordinate formations for purpose of liaison with the United States military government agencies and, with the sanction of those agencies, for liaison with the Japanese authorities in the British Commonwealth Occupation Force area.

PUBLICITY POLICY AND PUBLIC RELATIONS ORGANISATION

19. You are to be guided in Public Relations matters by the following definitions of the objects of publicity in connection with British Commonwealth Occupation Force and Joint Chiefs of Staff in Australia, which are to be read in conjunction with paragraphs 4 and 5 above: —

(a) *Long Term:*
   To further British Commonwealth co-operation and co-ordination.

(b) *Short Term:*
   (i) To ensure adequate and co-ordinated publicity on a British Commonwealth basis simultaneously in all the British Commonwealth countries concerned.

(ii) To stimulate voluntary recruitment for the Australian and New Zealand contingents of British Commonwealth Occupation Force and to maintain public interest in the Force throughout the British Commonwealth.

20. You are to afford the Press every facility within such limits as are imposed by Supreme Commander for the Allied Powers or as may be necessary to facilitate the policy set out in paragraphs 4 and 5 above.

21. You are to afford the Public Relations detachments with each national contingent full facilities for dealing direct with the Public Relations organisation of their respective countries in accordance with the latter's domestic Public Relations policy. You are to ensure that the activities of these detachments are coordinated in the light of the publicity policy for British Commonwealth Occupation Force set out in paragraph 19 above.

DISCIPLINARY POWERS

22. You are to exercise disciplinary powers in accordance with the warrants that have been issued to you in respect of personnel of each national contingent and Service therein.

FINANCIAL POWERS

23. You are authorised on behalf of the British Commonwealth Governments concerned to exercise financial powers in accordance with the limits and provisions set out in Appendix 2 to this directive. Appendix 2 will be issued later.

PROMOTIONS AND APPOINTMENTS

24. All promotions and appointments and recommendations for promotions and appointments will be made in accordance with existing instructions issued by national authorities. You may, however, direct that certain proposed promotions and appointments, and recommendations for promotions and appointments, be submitted to you for comment before being authorized or forwarded to the national authority concerned.

ALTERATIONS TO ORDER OF BATTLE AND WAR ESTABLISHMENTS

25. You are to refer all proposals for changes in the order of battle or in war establishments (except those of integrated units)

to the appropriate Australian Service Headquarters for clearance in accordance with current instructions.

26. In the case of integrated units and headquarters, in order to facilitate the rotation of staff appointments, you are authorised to vary the nationality of appointments and postings below the rank of colonel or equivalent up to a limit of ten per cent increase or decrease in the numbers of the respective ranks provided initially by each nationality. Where numbers are too small to admit of this percentage being observed, the limit is to be two individuals. Any changes which you make in the terms of this paragraph are to be reported to Joint Chiefs of Staff in Australia without delay. Proposals beyond the above limits are to be referred, in the case of purely air establishments, to R.A.A.F. H.Q., and in all other cases to Army Headquarters Melbourne, for clearance in accordance with current instructions.

27. With the object of conserving British Commonwealth manpower, you should explore the possibility of replacing Service personnel by locally engaged persons to an extent that will not materially impair the fitness of the Force for its tasks. Notwithstanding paragraphs 25 and 26 you may, at your discretion, employ in accordance with this paragraph locally engaged persons to replace Service personnel within your authorised war establishment. Such replacement of Service personnel will be regarded as constituting a reduction in the total strength of Service personnel to be posted against the war establishment which itself remains unaltered.

ALTERATIONS TO WAR EQUIPMENT TABLES

28. Any proposed changes to war equipment tables should be referred to the appropriate Australian Service Headquarters. You are, however, authorised to approve local scales and issues in excess of authorised scales provided these do not result in any substantial increase in provision and do not introduce new types of equipment.

Acting Minister for Defence;
Commonwealth Government of Australia,
For and on behalf of his Majesty's Governments, in the United Kingdom, Australia, New Zealand and India.

APPENDIX D

Directive to the Commander of the Army Component of the Indian Contingent of the British Commonwealth Occupation Forces in Japan

15 October 1946.

APPOINTMENT AND COMMAND

1. This directive is issued to you as the Commander of the Army component of the Indian Contingent of the British Commonwealth Occupation Force in JAPAN (BCOF) on behalf of and with the approval of His Majesty's Government in India hereinafter referred to as "the Government".

2. This directive is to be read in the light of the "Plan for a British Commonwealth Force to participate in the Occupation of JAPAN", and in conjunction with the directive issued to the Nominated Representative of the Indian Contingent and with any directive which the Commander-in-Chief B.C.O.F. may issue to you.

3. You are responsible to the Commander-in-Chief B.C.O.F. for the command, employment, administration and training of the Indian element of the British-Indian Division and such formations and units as may be allotted to it from time to time. You will receive from the Commander-in-Chief B.C.O.F. any directives necessary in respect of this task.

4. You are at all times to ensure that those under your command:—
   (a) represent India worthily in the occupation of Japan;
   (b) maintain and enhance British Commonwealth prestige and influence in the eyes of the Japanese and of our Allies; and
   (c) illustrate to, and impress on, the Japanese people, as far as may be possible, the democratic way and purpose in life.

SPECIAL RESPONSIBILITY FOR DOMESTIC ADMINISTRATION

5. You are responsible to the Commander-in-Chief B.C.O.F. and to G.H.Q. India for matters of domestic administration including disciplinary action in respect of all the personnel of the

Indian Army wherever serving in B.C.O.F., and that arrangements for their welfare are satisfactory.

6. You may communicate direct with G.H.Q. India on such matters, subject to any special instructions which the Commander-in-Chief B.C.O.F. may issue. In addition, you may make periodical reports on the activities and general welfare of your command direct to G.H.Q. India but you are to provide the Commander-in-Chief B.C.O.F. with two copies of such reports.

SPECIAL RESPONSIBILITIES FOR GENERAL WELL BEING OF YOUR COMPONENT AND FOR SAFEGUARDING THE INTERESTS OF THE GOVERNMENT

7. You are to bring to the notice of the officer nominated as the representative of the Indian Contingent any matters which affect either the general well being of the personnel for whom you are responsible under this directive, or any matter affecting the interests of the Government, which you have not been able to resolve through normal channels in B.C.O.F. and which you considered sufficiently important to be brought to the notice of the Government.

DISCIPLINARY POWERS

8. Your disciplinary powers will be in accordance with the warrants or other forms of delegation that may be issued to you and with any other powers that may be authorised.

PUBLIC RELATIONS

9. You are to ensure that those under your command understand the policy governing public relations, which is explained in the " Plan for a British Commonwealth Force to participate in the Occupation of Japan ".

10. You are to ensure that any Public Relations personnel attached to your component conform with the requirements of the Directorate of Public Relations in India with those of the Headquarters B.C.O.F., Public Relations Directorate; also that the Commander-in-Chief B.C.O.F.'s directions for the co-ordination of all public relations activities in B.C.O.F. as a whole are implemented.

FINANCIAL POWERS

11. You are to exercise such financial powers as may be delegated to you by the Commander-in-Chief B.C.O.F., to whom

the British Commonwealth Governments concerned have delegated responsibility for the Administration of B.C.O.F. as a whole, including certain financial powers.

W. J. CAWTHORN,
Major-General,

On behalf of the
Commander-in-Chief in India.

Representative of the C-in-C India, on the Joint Chiefs of Staff in Australia.

APPENDIX E

Directive to the Nominated Representative of the Indian Contingent of the British Commonwealth Occupation Force in Japan

15 October 1946

1. This directive is issued to you as the Nominated Representative of the Indian Contingent of the British Commonwealth Occupation Force in JAPAN (B.C.O.F.) on behalf of and with the approval of His Majesty's Government in India hereinafter referred to as " the Government ".

2. This directive is to be read in the light of the " Plan for a British Commonwealth Force to participate in the Occupation of Japan ", and in conjunction with the relevant paragraphs of the Directive issued to the commanders of the components of the Indian Contingent of B.C.O.F. and with any directive which the Commander-in-Chief B.C.O.F. may issue to you.

3. As the Nominated Representative of the Indian Contingent, you are responsible, in respect of all personnel of all Services in the Indian Contingent, for bringing to the notice of the Government, through the channels prescribed below, any matter which affects either the general well being of personnel in the contingent or the interests of the Government, which you have not been able to resolve in consultation with the Commander-in-Chief B.C.O.F. and which you consider sufficiently important to be brought to the notice of the Government.

4. In particular, you are responsible jointly with the Commander-in-Chief B.C.O.F. for ensuring that Indian personnel are not employed in any task or in such manner as to conflict with religious or cast susceptibilities.

5. Before consulting the Commander-in-Chief B.C.O.F., you are to consult with the senior officer of each of the other Services in the Indian Contingent. Further, in all such cases, you are to communicate to the Government only after full consultation with the Commander-in-Chief B.C.O.F., to whom you are to endorse immediately two copies of your communication.

6. In cases where air questions or matters affecting air force personnel are involved, you are also to consult with the Air Officer

Commanding B.C. AIR and similarly provide him with three copies of your communication.

    7. You are to address communications on matters referred to in paragraph 3 to the Commander-in-Chief in India through his representative on J.C.O.S.A. Should you be addressed direct by the Government on any matter, you are to reply through the channel defined above.

On behalf of the   W. J. CAWTHORN,
Commander-in-Chief in India.   *Major-General,*
                               Representative of the C-in-C India,
                                  on the Joint Chiefs of Staff in
                                             Australia.

APPENDIX F

268 Bde Group Order of Battle and Location Statement as at 2400 hrs. 30 June 1947

Ref. Maps 1/50,000 Sheet: 4549 III 4551 IV 4648 I 4648 II 4649 IV 4653 II 4753 II 4753 III 4847 IV
4849 I 4849 IV 4859 I 4851 II 4850 III 4953 III 4954 IV 5049 III

Serial	Orbat Serial No.	Arm	Unit	Location	Map-Ref.	Remarks
1	734	HQ and HQ Units	HQ 268 Ind Inf Bde Gp	OKAYAMA	892294	
2	735	,,	HQ 268 Bde Def Pl	,,	,,	Dets MATSUE, HAMADA
3	736	,,	HQ 268 Bde Sig Sec	,,	,,	
4	737	,,	Ind LAD Type '1'			
			Ind LAD Type '1' for serial 734			
5	613	Armoured Corps	7 Lt Cav	KURASHIKI	877285	Rear Details only.
6	727	RA	30 Fd Bty RA	OKAYAMA	892294	,, ,, ,,
7	741	,,	16 Ind Fd Bty RIA			,, ,, ,, (at TOKUSHIMA)
8	609	Engineers	350 Fd Pk Sqn RE	FUKUSHIMA	896225	
9	742	,,	429 Ind Fd Coy RIE	OKAYAMA	892294	Dets at MATSUE, KOCHI, TOKU-SHIMA, TOTTORI, YONAGO, ZENTSUJI, HAMADA, (see also note (b)).
10	610	,	907 Ind Wks Sec	,,	,,	att 907 Ind Wks Sec.
11	..	Infantry	Det 7 Mech Equip Pl	TOTTORI	924393	Bn to TOKYO for gd duties.
12	738	,,	5/1 PUNJAB		92493	Bn Band
13	738A	,,	5/1 PUNJAB Band	HAMADA	709324	Det HQ BCOF
14	739	,,	1 MAHRATTAS	OKAYAMA SOUTH	896284	Det UNO
	740		2/5 RGR (FF)			
14A	..	ST	2/5 RGR Band	,,	892294	Bn Band
14B	..	,,	227 Coy RIASC			

APPENDIX F—(Contd.)

Serial	Orbat Serial No.	Arm	Unit	Location	Map-Ref.	Remarks
15	622	ST	8 Coy RASC Civ Tpt, HQ MT, Coy, four Tpt Pls & four RDI's	WADASHI-MIA	963210	Det OKAYAMA. Coy moves to TOKYO later.
15A	622A	,,	8 Coy RASC Tpt Wksp Pl	TOKYO		To TOKYO later.
15B	622B	,,	1753 Comp Pl	TOKYO	670420	
16	624	,,	56 Ind Comp Pl	YONAGO	834385	
17	625	,,	21 Ind Comp Pl	OKAYAMA	892294	
18	626	,,	489 Ind Comp Pl	IWAKUNI	716315	
19	627	,,	591 Ind Sup Pl	OKAYAMA	892294	
20	628	,,	9 Ind Fd Bky Sec	IWAKUNI	716315	
21	629	,,	9 Ind Fd Bkv Sec	OKAYAMA	892294	
22	631	,,	38 Ind RHSD	,,	,,	
23	632	,,	59 Ind Sup Coy HQ	,,	,,	
24	633	,,	756 Ind Sup Sec	,,	,,	
25	634	,,	861 Ind Pet Pl	,,	893296	
26	602A	Med	Band RIASC	KURE	892294	With HQ CRIASC
27	635	,,	92 IGH	OKAYAMA	754243	One Sec OKAYAMA
28	636	,,	80 BGH	,,	892294	(a)
29	637	,,	33 Fd Hyg Sec	,,	,,	With 60 Recep Camp
30	639	,,	48 AMU	,,	,,	,, ,, ,,
31	641	,,	71 Ind Dental Unit	MATSUE	8	
32	642	,,	80 Ind Dental Unit	KURE	754242	With 92 IGH
33	643	,,	20 Ind Dental Mech Unit	,,	,,	,, ,, ,,
34	644	,,	25 Ind Ophthalmic Unit	,,	,,	,, ,, ,,
35	645	,,	5 Subsidiary Spec Centre	,,	,,	,, ,, ,,
36	745	,,	9 Ind Lt Fd Amb	MATSUE	808391	Dets TOTTORI, HAMADA, TOKYO
37	651	Ord	14 Ind MLBU	OKAYAMA	893296	
38	648	,,	Det 221 AOD	KURE	535411	With BOD HIRO
39	649	,,	One Amn Pl 64 OFD	HIRO	761243	
40	650	,,	Half 223 Veh Pk Coy	,,	,,	,, ,, ,,
41	654	,,	208 Ind Ord Fd Pk	OKAYAMA	892294	Det MATSUE
42	655	,,	114 Ind Ord Offrs Shop	,,	,,	

APPENDIX F—(Contd.)

Serial	Orbat Serial No.	Arm	Unit	Location	Map-Ref.	Remarks
43	700	Ord.	9 Kinema Sec	OKAYAMA	892294	Dets KURE, MATSUE, TOKUSHIMA.
44	659	ME	350 Fd Pk LAD	FUKUSHIMA	896285	(b)
45	660	,,	Indep Sec 152 Ind Mob Wksp Coy	MATSUE	808391	
46	662A	,,	1164 Ind Tpt Coy Wksp Sec	OKAYAMA	892294	
47	663	,,	Refrig Repair Component Type 'E'	,,	,,	
48	742	ME	111 Ind Inf Wksp Coy	OKAYAMA	892294	Dets TOKYO, KOBE (2) MITSUI, KURASHIKI.
48A	..	Pro.	204 Brit Pro Coy	,,	,,	
48B	..	,,	47 Ind L of C Pro Unit	,,	,,	Dets KURE, KURASHIKI.
48C	..	,,	268 Ind Inf Bde Unit	,,	,,	Det to TOKYO with Gd Bn. One
49	669	,,	152 SIB Sec	TAKAMATSU	904252	(c)
50	671	Int	29 Brit FS Sec	KURASHIKI	877285	
51	746	,,	904 Brit FS Sec	OKAYAMA	892294	
52	679	,,	551 Ind FSS	,,	,,	
53	684	Canteens	4160 BIS	,,	,,	
54	685	,,	4251 Det Sub HQ	,,	,,	Whit Bde HQ
55	686	,,	4225 Canteen Club	,,	,,	,,
56	689	,,	4226 ,, ,,	,,	,,	,,
57	744	Postal	Bde Postal Unit	YONAGO	834385	Dets KURE, IWAKUNI.
58	..	,,	112 FPO	KURE	754243	Dets HAMADA, TOTTORI.
58A	..	,,	Indian Base Postal accounts Unit	OKAYAMA	892294	With BOD
59	693	Pay	27 Staff Paymaster	(YASUDA BANK)		
59A	..	,,	101 Fd Cash Office	OKAYAMA	,,	With Bde HQ.
60	699A	Welfare	Brit & Ind Div Radio Diffusion Van (IT)	,,	,,	,,
61	699B	,,	Ind Inter Services Broadcasting Unit	OKAYAMA	,,	,,

APPENDIX F—(Concld.)

Serial	Orbat Serial No.	Arm	Unit	Location	Map-Ref.	Remarks
62	704	Welfare	Det SSAHS	Okayama	892294	With Bde HQ.
63	705	,,	50 Amenities Stores (Depots Type 'J')	,,	893296	,,
64	706	,,	Women's Voluntary Services (UK & India)	,,	892294	,,
65	709	,,	50 Unit Institute (BT)	,,	,,	,,
66	710	,,	100 Unit Institute (IT)	,,	,,	,,
67	711	,,	6 Women's leave hostel YWCA	,,	,,	,,
68	712/715	,,	Det FANY	,,	,,	,,
69	716	,,	7 Holiday Home	TAKUMA	863240	
70	716E	,,	KUMAON REGT Band	OKAYAMA	892294	
71	716G	,,	RNF Band	,,	896294	
72	717	PR	PR Det	,,	,,	
73	719B	Camps	60 Ind Recep Camp (2 Brit & 1 Ind Sec)	,,	,,	
74	719C	,,	SSO			
75	..	Edn	Pre-Release & Resettlement Trg Unit	KURASHIKI	877285	Dets 1 MAHRATTAS, 5/1 Punjab, 16 Ind Fd Bty RIA.

NOTE.—(a) Temporarily under command of 268 Bde and awaiting disposal.
(b) Force tps under 268 Bde for local administration.
(c) Force tps under 34 Aust Bde for local administration.

APPENDIX G

268 Ind Inf Bde Gp Occupation Instruction No. 1

Disaster Plan

13 May 1947

HQ 268 Ind. Inf. Bde. GP.

Ref Map: CENTRAL JAPAN 1/50,000 4451-II, 4551-IV, 4753-IV, 4952-III.

GEN

1. The land areas of JAPAN are particularly liable to disasters in the form of earthquake, flood, tidal wave, typhoon, fire or volcanic eruption.

2. Such occurrences present problems which are generally similar to those presented by air raids and in framing plans to meet such emergencies, the principles involved in the now familiar procedure for ARP should be applied.

3. Preparations may be broadly divided into:—
(a) Action to be taken during precautionary period when some warning of an impending disaster is available.
(b) Action to be taken during and after a disaster.

4. It may frequently be impossible to implement previously prepared plans owing to the violence or unexpectedness of the occurrence. Therefore all plans must be highly flexible and considerable improvisation may be required.

SCOPE OF THIS INSTR

5. *The objects of this instr. are:*
(a) To provide plans for the emp. of 268 Ind. Inf. Bde. Gp. in the event of a disaster.
(b) To define principles on which comds of sub areas, units and dets will base their own disaster plans and on which co-ord action will be taken in the event of inability of fully implementing the Bde Disaster plan.

TASKS OF THE OCCUPATION FORCE

6. (a) *Primary task:*
The protection of the lives and property of Allied Nationals.

(b) *Secondary task:*
Emergency relief to Non-Allied Nationals will be given where it is necessary:—
  (i) To alleviate human suffering.
  (ii) To preserve peaceful and orderly conditions.
  (iii) To prevent chaos.

RELIEF MEASURES TO NON-ALLIED NATIONALS

7. (a) Relief will NOT be given to Non-Allied Nationals at the expense of the well being of Allied Nationals or their property.
(b) All relief to Non-Allied Nationals will be effected through US Mil Govt. and JAPANESE Govt. agencies in accordance with Appendix ' A ' attached.

CIV DISASTER PLAN

8. The Prefectural Government of OKAYAMA, SHIMANE and TOTTORI have prepared their own Disaster Plan for the civ population and have now been instr to revise them.

AREAS AND SUB-AREAS

9. (a) Area ... Prefectures of OKAYAMA, SHIMANE AND TOTTORI.
   (b) Sub-Area (i) OKAYAMA   SECTOR ABLE
                               OKAYAMA SOUTH
                               SECTOR BAKER
                               OKAYAMA NORTH
                               SECTOR CHARLIE
                               KURASHIKI
               (ii) SHIMANE
               (iii) TOTTORI

GROUPING OF UNITS

10. See Appendix ' B ' attached.

RESPONSIBILITIES

11. (a) 268 Ind Inf Bde Gp is responsible for initiating, preparations and measures of relief or any general disaster occurring in the prefectures of OKAYAMA, SHIMANE and TOTTORI.

(b) Sub-Areas responsibilities will be limited to area allotted as regards planning, preparation and immediate action. In case of a localized disaster, or one affecting Sub-Areas to a different extent, co-ord of effort will be directed by HQ 268 Ind Inf Bde Gp.

(c) Units are primarily responsible for own camp area and immediate vicinity but may be allotted additional responsibilities.

COMD AND CONTROL

12. (a) In a disaster emergency COMD 268 Ind Inf Bde is assuming op control of all army units located in the AREA and under comd for local adm.

(b) Comd Sub Areas/Sectors will assume op control of all army units located in sub areas/sectors at the time.

(c) Sub-Areas will liaise with their respective Mil Govt team and Air Force fmns.

SUB AREA AND UNIT DISASTER PLAN

13. (a) *Sub-Area Plans*

Comds Sub-Areas will prepare Disaster Plan for precautionary measures and immediate action within sub-Areas. Plans of units under comd will be co-ord by Sub-Area Comd.

(b) *Unit Plans*

Unit plans for precautionary measures and immediate action in event of disaster will be prepared and co-ord with Sub-Area plan.

(c) Sub-Area and unit disaster exercises will be held periodically.

(d) Disaster Plans will be maint up to date and will be handed over to incoming fomns or units on relief.

(e) Three copies of Sub-Area plans of units directly under comd will be submitted to reach this HQ by 1 JUN 47. Units under comd of Sub-Areas will submit three copies of their Disaster Plans to Sub-Areas concerned.

BASIS OF DISASTER PLANS

14. Plans will be based on a system of seven phases as set out in paras 23-29. These states of readiness are based on the degree of WARNING which experience has shown may be expected.

15. The degree of WARNING may vary from several days e.g. in the case of a typhoon to NO warning at all e.g. in the case of an earthquake. Therefore:—
    (a) Any alert may NOT necessarily begin with PHASE 2 and in extreme cases it may be necessary to implement PHASE 6 without previous warning.
    (b) Sub-Areas may frequently be standing to at different states of readiness, since conditions may vary from one locality to another.

EQUIPTS FOR INCL IN DISASTER PLANS

16. *Fire-Fighting*
    (a) Any kind of disaster is almost certain to be accompanied by an outbreak of fire which may assume maj proportions.
    (b) Therefore, normal resources in both equipment and personnel must be augmented as much as possible and extra precautions put into force to check and extinguish outbreaks of fire.

17. *Med*
    (a) Hy calls may be made on med resources, which may themselves be affeced by the disaster. Alternative aid posts will therefore be held available.
    (b) Extra stretchersbearers and vehs for use as amb will be earmarked to stand by when required.

18. *Rescue Squad*
    Rescue squad will be detailed and appropriate tools eqpt and tpt made available for their use.

19. *Sups and Clothing*
    Seven days res ration will be held by units. Stocks of water and clothing will also be held by units ready for use. These will be so located that they have max protection against the effects of any disaster and are readily available when required. Under typhoon conditions dumps should be decentralized into shelter areas (see para 26(b)(iii)).

20. *Mutual Assistance between Sub-Areas and Units*
    (a) In cases where the area affected by a disaster is localized, Sub-Areas/Units will be prepared to render mutual assistance as required.
    (b) Such assistance may incl:—
     (i) The despatch of tps, sups and eqpt.

(ii) The provision of max engr assistance.
(iii) The housing and rehabilitation of personnel evac from the affected area.
(iv) Civ population—See Appendix 'A' attached.
(v) Med.

(c) Tps moving to the disaster area will be armed and will carry two days sup of rations and water.

21. *Looting, Sabotage etc.*

Vigorous action will be necessary to prevent looting, sabotage or other hostile acts both during and after a disaster. They may incl action by subversive elements, under cover of a confused situation, therefore counter measures will be prepared by all units.

EMP OF AC

22. BCAIR is prepared in the event of a disaster to provide AC for the following tasks:—
(i) Recce of affected area
(ii) Dropping of relief sups
(iii) Evac of cas, where feasible
(iv) Courier and intercomn service

STATES OF READINESS

23. *PHASE 1 Normal Conditions*
   Action (i) Prepare and maint up to date Sub-Area/Unit Disaster Plans.
   (ii) Where practicable secure roofs of service type buildings of a temporary nature (e.g. Nis en hut) by means of a steel cable picketed in the ground, as a protection against typhoon.
   (iii) Special Earthquake Precautions—See Appendix 'C' attached.

24. *PHASE 2—Code Word—Pretoria*
   (a) *Situation*
       Warning of a typhoon or tidal wave expected to strike area within 24 hrs. but NOT before 12 hrs. See Appendix 'D' attached para 4(c).
   (b) *Action*
       Issue WARNING ORDER to all tps.

25. *PHASE 3—Code Word—Ottawa*
   (a) *Situation*
       Warning of typhoon or tidal wave expected to strike within 12 hrs but NOT before 6 hrs.
   (b) *Action*
       Issue WARNING ORDER to all tps.

26. *PHASE 4—Code Word—London*
   (a) *Situation*
       Warning of typhoon or tidal wave expected to strike area within 6 hrs but NOT before 3 hrs.
   (b) *Action*
       (i) Issue WARNING ORDER TO all tps.
       (ii) Confine tps to Unit areas, except those on duty.
       (iii) Earmark slit trenches or similar shelters above water level for all personnel as a protection against typhoon and flood.
       (iv) The following will stand to at three hrs notice:
           Firefighting squads
           Med Units
           Rescue Squads.
       (v) In case of a typhoon warning:
           (a) lash down stocks of rations, water, and clothing in vehs,
           (b) lash down dumps of loose timber, corrugated iron or any other material that can be blown away,
           (c) strike tents.

27. *PHASE 5—Code Word—Canberra*
   (a) *Situation*
       (i) Imminent typhoon or tidal wave about to strike the area within 3 hrs (See Appendix 'D' para 5(b).
       (ii) Flood, fire or volcanic eruption NOT as yet constituting a disaster, but capable of developing into one within a short period.
   (b) *Action*
       (i) Implement PHASE 4, if NOT already in force.
       (ii) Place TOPSEC, SECRET or CONFD documents in safes or protected buildings.
       (iii) Extinguish all oil stores, braziers or other naked flames.

(iv) Open wrls comn if NOT already opened.
(v) In case of fire take normal action to control and extinguish.
(vi) In case of flood or volcanic eruption prepare for evac and implement if necessary.
(vii) In case of typhoon, evac to stronger structures all personnel housed in buildings NOT capable of withstanding winds of high velocity. If such stronger buildings do NOT exist move personnel to slit trenches etc. earmarked beforehand.

28. *PHASE 6—Code Word—Napier*

   (a) *Situation*
   (i) Typhoon or tidal wave actually striking the sea.
   (ii) Flood, fire or volcanic eruption of sufficient intensity or size as to constitute a disaster.
   (iii) Earthquake.

   (b) *Action*
   (i) Implement PHASE 5, if NOT already in force as far as conditions permit.
   (ii) In the case of an earth tremor or earthquake take the special precaution detailed in Appendix ' C ' attached.
   (iii) Thereafter as ordered by the local unit or Sub-Area Comd in the lt of the circumstances prevailing.

29. *PHASE 7—After-Math-Code Word—Delhi*

   (a) *Situation*
   Disaster passed (See Appendix ' D ' para 4(d)) or effects under control.

   (b) *Action*
   (i) Report to HQ 268 Ind Inf Bde Gp by the most expeditious means:—
      (a) The location and magnitude of any damage.
      (b) Requirements for assistance.
      (c) Cas.
      (d) Action of tps.
      (e) Any other pertinent infm.
   (ii) Survey comn to determine which rds, rlys and airfds are usable for mov of personnel and sups to and from the affected areas. Report this infm to this HQ.

(iii) Restore, rehabilitate or construct emergency facilities in the following order of priority:
  (a) Water sup.
  (b) Emergency hospital facilities.
  (c) Emergency repair of rds, brs and rlys.
  (d) Provision of emergency lighting and heating facilities.
  (e) Civ population.

TYPHOON WARNING

30. Appx 'C' att gives details of the typhoon warning system op by BCAIR. This system will be regarded as the official authority within BCOF area for issue of warnings regarding states of readiness. Units may however obtain useful corroborative infm from local JAPANESE Weather Bureaux.

31. Warning msgs will be received by this HQ and it will be passed to Sub-Areas/Units concerned by the fastest means.

32. *Visual Sig System*

The following system will be instituted within sub-areas/units wherever practicable in order to provide a visual means of notifying all ranks of the existing state of readiness.
  (a) A flag pole will be erected on the most conspicuous pt within unit areas.
  (b) Flags will be displayed to denote the state of readiness in force as follows:—
    PHASE 2 PRETORIA ... ONE flag
    PHASE 3 OTTAWA ... TWO flags
    PHASE 4 LONDON ... THREE flags
    PHASE 5 CANBERRA ... FOUR flags
  (c) Flags may be of any convenient colour, size or shape.

INTERCOMN

33. *Code Words*
(a) Notification of an impending or actual disaster will be passed by the most expeditious means available using the appropriate code word and detail as follows:—
  (i) Nature of disaster (eg.—typhoon/fire/earthquake).
  (ii) ETA (if applicable) and place.
  (iii) Code Word to implement required state of readiness:—
    PHASE 2 ... PRETORIA
    PHASE 3 ... OTTAWA

PHASE 4	...	LONDON
PHASE 5	...	CANBERRA
PHASE 6	...	NAPIER

(b) *Examples*
" TYPHOON WARNING ETA ... (place) 0223001 LONDON "
" FIRE   ...   ...   (place) CANBERRA ".

34. *Sitreps*

(a) Sitreps from Sub-Areas/units will reach this HQ by 0900 hrs and 1800 hrs during WARNING and Disaster Emergency Period.

(b) This HQ will fwd sitreps to HQ BCOF by 0930 hrs. and 1830 hrs daily.

35. ACK.

R. S. Noronha,
Bde Major,
HQ 268 Ind Inf Bde Gp. Ext 92.

Okayama

Appendix 'A' to HQ 268 Ind. Inf. Bde. Gp. Occupation Instr No. 1 Disaster Plan of 13 May 47.

Assistance to Civil Population

GEN

1. Att at Annx 1 is a brief outline of the arrangements made by the Japanese Prefectural authorities for publishing warnings and for communicating with the Occupation Forces.

2. The Japanese civil authorities are responsible for all measures taken for their own security before, during and after a Disaster. They may, however, receive assistance from the Occupation Forces in the circumstances and under the conditions stated in para 7 of the body of this Instr, subject to the following:

(a) *Relief sups*

Mil sups and eqpt will NOT be made available to the civil population as relief sups, except under the gravest circumstances.

The Japanese maint stocks of relief sups of all natures at UJINA, which are available for despatch to afflicted areas. Mil assistance may however be given to tpt these stores.

(b) *Med*

Japanese civilians will NOT be cared for in Military Hospitals nor will med attention be given them until Allied Nationals have received adequate care.

In circumstances where medical resources of the Occupation Forces are NOT fully emp in caring for Allied Nationals, however, medical personnel may be made available to advise and assist the Japanese as required.

(c) *Other assistance*

Other specialist personnel, such as engrs, sigs, etc. may similarly be made available to assist the Japanese if they are NOT required for the assistance of the Occupation Forces or of Allied Nationals.

RESPONSIBILITIES OF US MIL GOVT

3. US Mil Govt units are responsible for:—
(a) Warning local Japanese authorities of an impending disaster.

(b) Ensuring by supervision and advice that adequate measures are taken by the Japanese local authorities when a disaster occurs.
(c) Requesting military aid from BCOF for the assistance of the Japanese when required, and for the co-ord and allocation of all such assistance given.

RESPONSIBILITIES OF BCOF

4. *General*

Military assistance will only be rendered to the Japanese by BCOF at the request and through the medium of US Mil Govt.

5. *Assistance available*
(a) Provision of engrs with their eqpt if required to assist or supervise Japanese civil engrs in the restoration of rds, ryls, sea walls etc. etc.
(b) Provision of sig personnel and eqpt to assist the Japanese in the restoration of comns, or to est comn with isolated areas.
(c) Provision of med personnel.
(d) Provision of MT to set up an emergency tpt system.
(e) Provision of land, air or sea tpt for the mov of relief sups from Japanese sources. Provision of personnel to supervise the distribution of relief sups.

6. *Procedure*

When a disaster occurs within a sub-area of responsibility Mil assistance so given will be rendered in three stages as follows:—
(a) *Stage 1* (i) Sub-areas will immediately despatch reps by the fastest means to report to the appropriate Mil Govt unit to ascertain their requirements as follows:—
One LO to ascertain requirements of relief sups and tpt, and in the absence of a BCOF Mil Govt LO, to act in his stead.
One Med rep.
One Engr. rep.
One Sig rep.
(ii) HQ BCOF may similarly despatch one Liaison Officer and where possible one Naval Liaison Officer.
(b) *Stage 2* (i) Based on the requests of US Mil Govt and on the advice of the technical reps, the LO will inform the Sub-area concerned what

assistance is required. This will include requests for naval or air assistance.

    (ii) Sub-areas will render the max assistance possible from within their own resources, keeping this HQ infm.

    (iii) Assistance required beyond the resources of Sub-Area, incl requests for naval or air assistance, will be referred to HQ 268 Ind Inf Bde Gp.

(c) *Stage 3*   This HQ will request HQ BCOF to allocate such extra resources as are available.

7. *Allocation of naval or air assistance*

    (a) When naval or air assistance is required in more than one Sub-area of responsibility, its allotment will be co-ordinated by this HQ.

8. *Refugees*

    (a) Should the evac of refugees be necessary, Sub-areas will be prepared, in conjunc with US Mil Govt, to enforce the use of selected routes, in order that the mov of important mil and civ sups and equpt is NOT impeded.

    (b) In exceptional circumstances, Sub-areas will be prepared to est camps for refugees.

Appendix 'B' to Hq. 268 Ind. Inf. Bde. Gp. Occupation Instr. No. 1 of 13 May 47

GROUPING OF UNITS

1. *OKAYAMA SUB-AREA*

   COMD:—C.O. 2/5 RGR (FF)
   (a) *Sector ABLE*
      (i) Tps:—
         2/5 RGR (FF)
         350 Fd Pk Sqn RE
         21 Fd Pk LAD REME
         Water Tpt Pl
         80 BGH
      (ii) Comd: C.O. 2/5 RGR (FF)
   (b) *Sector BAKER*
      (i) Tps:—

268 Ind Inf Bde Sig Sec.	1164 Ind. Tps Wksp sec
30 Fd. Bty RA	111 Ind Wksp Coy
HQ RE	204 Brit Pro Coy
429 Ind Fd Coy RIE	268 Ind Inf Bde Pro Unit
907 Ind Wks Sec.	152 SIB Sec
227 Ind Div Tpt Coy RIASC.	551 Ind FS Sec
59 Ind Sup Coy —38 Ind RHSD	27 Staff Paymaster
21 Ind Comp Pl	Det YWCA
591 Ind Sup Pl	60 Ind Reception Camp
9 Ind Fd Bky Sec	Bde MT Pl
861 Ind Pet Pl	SSO
33 Fd Hyg Sec	MOV AREA OKAYAMA
43 AMU	

         14 Ind MLBU
         114 Ind Ord Offrs Shop
         208 Ind Ord Fd Pk
         9 Kinema Sec.
      (ii) Comd Bde Fire Offr
   (c) *Sector CHARLIE*
      Tps:—
      (i) Pre Release and Resettlement Unit
      (ii) Rear details 7 Lt Cav
      Comd:—O.C. Pre Release and Resettlement Unit

2. *SHIMANE Sub-Area*
    1 MAHRATTA
    Det Sigs (MATSUE)
    9 Lt Fd Amb
    Indep Sec 152 Ind Mob Wksp Coy
    Comd:—C.O. 1 MAHRATTA

3. *TOTTORI Sub-Area*
    5/1 PUNJAB
    56 Ind Comp Pl
    112 Postal Unit
    Comd:—C.O. 5/1 Punjab

APPENDIX 'C' TO HQ 268 IND INF BDE GP OCCUPATION INSTR No. 1 DISASTER PLAN OF 13 MAY, 1947

SPECIAL PRECAUTIONS TO BE TAKEN IN THE EVENT OF EARTHQUAKES

1. *During Normal State (Phase 1)*
   (a) Ensure that all ranks are conversant with the provisions of para 2 below.
   (b) Ensure that orders are issued to, and are understood by all Service or Japanese personnel in charge of Electricity Supply, Gas and Steam Heating installations which sup the Occupation Forces, in accordance with the provisions of para 3 below. Where such installations are Japanese controlled, Sub-areas will request US Military Government to issue the appropriate instrs.

2. *Actions of tps during an earthquake*
   (a) Evac buildings and move rapidly to areas where there is NO danger from falling objects.
   (b) If time allows, extinguish all oilstoves, braziers, electric fires or naked flames.
   (c) When the earthquake is over, inspect buildings for possible damage that might render them unsafe.

3. *Action to be taken by personnel in charge of Power etc. Installations during an earthquake*

   (a) *Electricity Sup*
      (i) All Sub-stas sup electrical energy to Occupation Force Installations will be immediately disconnected from those installations.
      (ii) At local Military Power Stations, switches will be withdrawn to disconnect the Power Stas from their respective loads, and the stas closed down.

   (b) *Gas Sup*
      As in sub para (a)(i) above.

   (c) *Steam Heating*
      (i) Steam will be turned off at the boiler house either by closing the main boiler steam valves or by closing the valves on the stam leader.
      (ii) Where liquid fuel firing is emp, the fuel sup will be turned off.

(iii) Where coal firing is emp dampers will be closed and firing doors opened. It is emphasized that SAFETY VALVES must be maint in first class condition to enable surplus steam to blow off, and for this reason, must be checked periodically.

(d) *Water Sup*

It is essential that water sup remains turned ON to deal with possible fires. In cases where the supply of water is dependent of the sup of electricity, therefore, the sup of electricity to pumping stations must be turned on again as soon as it is safe to do so.

It must be impressed on all ops that the initiative for taking action rests with them, since there will be NO time for the issue of specific orders.

Installations, incl water sup installations, will NOT be put back into op until the local Comd is satisfied that there is no liklihood of danger to life and property by so doing.

APPENDIX H

ENGINEER ORGANIZATION AND WORKS LAYOUT OF BRINDIV ENGINEERS AS ON 31 MAY, 1946

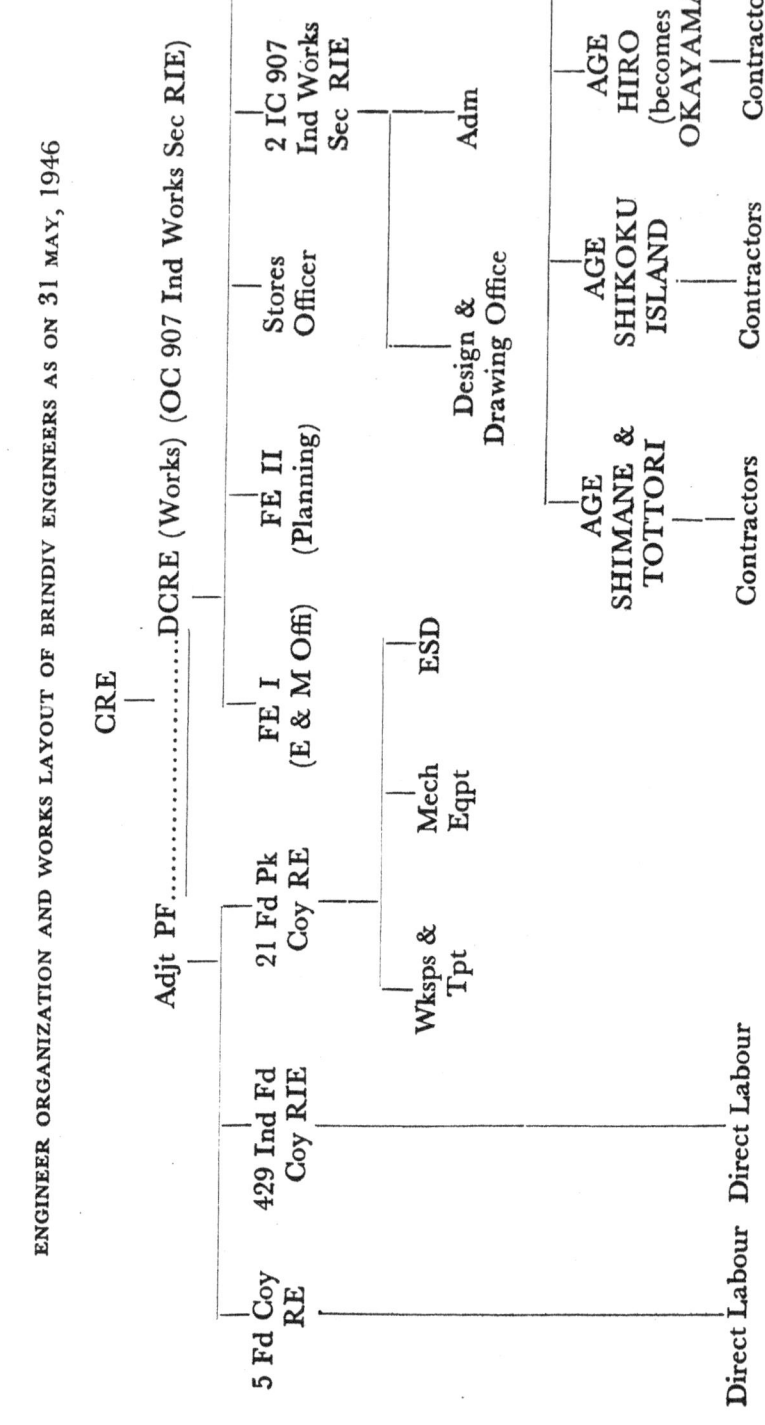

APPENDIX "J"

Split by arms—Indian Army Units/Formations—Japan

	PART "A"—USSR ARMS BASIS														PART "B"—PARENT ARM BASIS												
	FLAT WE				3% RETS				GRAND TOTAL					FLAT WE				3% RETS				GRAND TOTAL				
ARM	Officers	BORs	VCOs	Total	Officers	BORs	VCOs IORs NCsE	Total	Officers	BROs	VCOs IORs NCsE	Total		Officers	BORs	VCOs IORs NCsE	Total	Officers	BORs	VCOs IORs NCsE	Total	Officers	BORs	VCOs IORs NCsE	Total
Staffs	57	51	412	520	2	2	12	16	59	53	424	536*		23	7	281	311	1		8	9	24	7	289	320
IAC	35	3	657	695	1	..	20	21	36	3	677	716		34	1	657	692	1	..	20	21	35	1	677	713
RIA	10	..	206	216	..	..	6	6	10	..	212	222		13	2	206	221	..	..	6	6	13	2	218	227
R Ind Engrs	42	13	1,515	1,575	1	1	45	47	43	19	1,560	1,622		43	21	1,520	1,584	1	1	46	48	44	22	1,566	1,632
Ind Sigs	17	118	323	458	1	4	10	15	18	122	333	473		16	112	323	451	1	3	10	14	17	115	333	455
Ind Inf	50	..	3,061	3,111	1	..	92	93	51	..	3,153	3,204		47	..	3,061	3,108	1	..	92	93	48	..	3,153	3,201
RIASC	21	..	1,104	1,125	1	..	33	34	22	..	1,137	1,159		24	1	1,174	1,198	1	..	35	36	25	1	1,209	1,235
IAMC	48	58	743	849	1	2	22	25	49	60	765	874		56	56	744	856	2	2	22	26	58	58	766	882
IADC	..	..	..	..	..	..	..	..	..	..	..	4		2	2	..	4	..	..	..	..	2	2	..	4
Nurses	36	..	..	42	1	..	..	1	37	..	..	37		36	..	..	36	1	..	..	1	37	..	..	37
IAOC	30	42	796	868	1	1	24	26	31	43	820	894		34	47	812	893	1	2	24	27	35	49	836	920
IEME	15	94	561	610	..	1	17	18	15	35	578	628		14	41	573	628	..	2	17	19	14	43	590	647
Intelligence	2	12	18	32	..	..	1	1	2	12	19	33		3	12	19	34	..	..	1	1	3	12	20	35
Provost	2	55	87	144	..	2	3	5	2	57	90	149		3	55	87	145	..	2	3	5	3	57	90	150
Postal	1	..	52	53	..	..	2	2	1	..	54	55*		2	..	54	56	..	..	2	2	2	..	50	58
Pay	..	..	..	..	..	..	..	..	..	..	..	1		1	..	..	1	..	..	..	..	1	..	..	1
ACC	..	..	..	..	..	..	..	..	..	..	..	6		1	5	..	6	..	..	..	..	1	5	..	0
IGSC	3	10	97	110	..	..	3	3	3	10	100	113		2	10	97	108	1	2	3	3	2	10	100	112
Pioneer & Lab	2	..	408	410	..	..	12	12	2	..	420	422		2	..	408	410	2	..	12	12	2	..	420	422
AEC	..	..	..	..	..	..	..	..	..	..	..	..		5	6	2	13	..	..	..	..	5	6	2	13
IACC	..	..	..	..	..	..	..	..	..	..	..	..		1	23	22	48	1	1	1	2	1	24	23	48
Air Liaison	3	3	3	3	..	..	..	..	3	3	3	9*		3	3	3	9	..	..	..	..	3	3	3	9
Welfare	11	68	78	152	..	2	2	4	11	65	80	156*		13	63	78	154	1	2	2	4	13	65	80	158
Chaplains	..	..	..	..	..	..	..	..	..	..	..	..		6	..	..	6	..	..	..	..	6	..	..	6
Public Relations	6	..	11	17	..	..	..	..	6	..	11	17*		7	..	11	18	..	..	..	..	7	..	11	18
Graves Regn	1	1	..	2	..	..	..	..	1	1	..	2*		1	1	..	2	..	..	..	..	1	1	..	2
Canteens	1	29	60	90	..	1	2	3	1	30	62	93*		1	29	60	90	..	1	2	3	1	30	62	93
Totals	393	497	10,192	11,082	10	16	306	332	403	513	10,498	11,414		393	497	10,192	11,082	10	16	306	332	403	513	10,498	11,398

NOTES

1. The Indian Army Manpower Ceiling comprises the WE and Rfts of all IA Units in British Commonwealth Occupation Force (Including Brindiv).
   (a) Officers (b) BORs of the RE and IACC attached to Indian Units (c) VCOs, IORs and NCsE (d) Members of WVS (I). Replacements will be demanded from General Headquarters (India).
2. BORs other than RE and IACC attached IA Units from part of the British Army Ceiling. Replacements will be demanded from United Kingdom direct.
3. In the case of the commitment for arms marked* in Part B-Parent Arms basis, no parent arms is specified.

INDEX

Agansing Rai, Naik, V. C.: 84
Allied Control Council: 26-7
Anson H. M. S.: 122
Atlantic Charter: 1-2
Auchinleck, General Sir Claude: becomes Commander-inChief, India, 4; visits Brinjap, 83; his views on employing Indian troops in Burma and South-East Asia, 231
Australian Commonwealth Navy Board: 37
Australian Defence Department: 41

Bandoeng: 37th Indian Infantry Brigade in, 228; Headquarters 23rd Indian Division and 49th Indian Infantry Brigade move to, 236
Bangka Island: Netherlands East Indies forces occupy, 245
Bangkok: 218
Barfleur, H. M. S.: 122
Batavia: re-named Djakarta, 222; British forces occupy, 226; 23rd Indian Division in, 227
Bevin, Mr. Earnest: statement in the House of Commons about British intentions in Java, 229
Bladin, Air Commodore F. M.: appointed Chief of Staff to Lieut.-General Northcott, 44; *see also* 118
Brain, Mr. H. N. (Political adviser to Major-General Gracey): 201
Brinjap (Brindiv): principles for the selection of, 77; Major-General D. T. Cowan as Commander of, 78; assembling of, 79; selection of units for, 79-80; Commander-in-Chief, India, visits and his message to, 83-4; Lieut.-General Northcott inspects and his message to, 86; objects of, 86; moves to Japan and debarkation at Kure, 90-1; designation changed to Brindiv, 94; location of Brindiv, 98; move to Okayama, 100; communications and transport for, 107-9; operational duties of, 110; security in the area allotted to, 111; occupational duties of, 114-18; general duties of, 119-21; supervises Japanese general elections, 120-1; liaison with Allied troops, 121-2; liaison with the Japanese, 122; intelligence activities of, 126; training in the units of, 127; manpower problems for, 127-8; armour for, 129-30; Artillery support for, 130; engineers and their task in, 130-3; signal communications in, 134-7; supply and transport for, 137-9; Ordnance stores distribution to, 130-40; Electrical and Mechanical Engineers in, 141-2; education branch in, 142; morale of Indians in, 143; medical facilities for, 144-5; health of the troops in, 145; welfare and other recreational facilities for, 146-50; pay organisation for, 151-2; Public Relations Detachment in, 152-3; British and American correspondents visit, 153; radio programmes and film shows to, 153-5
British Army:
2nd British Division, 230
5th British Brigade, 104, 156
2 Dorset, 153
30th Field Battery, 130
British Borneo: Australian forces re-occupy, 246; Lord Mountbatten visits Australian forces in, 246; Military administration in, 246; 20th Indian Division in, 246
British Commonwealth Occupation Force (BCOF): 16-18; selection of area for, 18-20; strategic, political and economic considerations of the occupation of Japan by, 30-1; objects of occupation of Japan by, 32-4; Joint Chiefs of Staff, Australia vested with the right to control and administer, 35; organisation and arrangements for the control of, 44-7; area allotted to, 45-6; responsibility of, 46; shipping arrangements for, 50; difficulty in getting more Indian officers for, 53; channels of communication for, 55-6; organisation of, 56; Order of Battle of, 57; administration of, 60; dependents' families in, 62-3; amenities and welfare for, 63; maintenance of, 64; supplies and accommodation for, 64-6; movement and transportation for, 66; postal, currency and financial arrangements for, 67-74; lessons from the experience of postal services in, 69; long-term maintenance for, 74; lessons from 75; relationship with National Contingents, 94-5; relief works by, 103-4; re-organisation of, 104-5; recreational facilities for, 147-50; decision to reduce the strength of, 158; plan to withdraw Indian troops from, 158-62; final departure of Indian troops from, 162-4
Budhi Bahadur Thapa, Rifleman: 116

Cawthorn, Major-General: 41, 72; represents Commander-in-Chief, India on Joint Chiefs of Staff, Australia, 86; visits 4 Royal Indian Air Force Squadron in Japan, 126
Cedille, Colonel (French): 201
Chiang Kai-shek: 1, 193
Chifley, Mr. (Australian Prime Minister): 14, 22
Christison Lieut.-General Sir Philip: as Allied Force Commander in Netherlands East Indies, 221; *see also* 223, 225, 227, 232, 254

Clark Kerr, Sir A. (Special Ambassador of the United Kingdom in Java): 233, 236
Clarkol (Special Column): 206
Combined Chiefs of Staff: 4
Combined Chiefs of Staff Committee: 2
Cowan, Major-General, D. T.: as Commander British Indian Division of BCOF, 44; selected as Commander Brinjap, 78; issues message on assuming command, 79; inspects troops at Mashrul Camp and raises ' Force 152 ', 82; leaves Japan and his message to troops, 105; meets Pressmen in the ship *Dunera*, 153; *see also* 85, 95, 116, 150
Cripps, Sir Stafford: 3
Curtin, Mr. John (Australian Prime Minister): 3
d'Argenlieu, Vice-Admiral (French): 205, 208

Derevyanko, General (Russian representative on the Allied Control Council): 27
Devonshire (Ship): 163
Dilwara (Ship): 162
Dunera (Ship): 91-2, 153

Eichelberger, General (U. S. Eighth Army Commander): 9
Etajima: 118
Evatt, Rt. Hon. H. V. (Australian Minister for External Affairs): 15, 156-7; meets General Cawthorn and Indian High Commissioner, 157; writes to Mr. Nehru for retention of Indian troops in Japan, 158

Festing, Major-General Frank: 91
French Indo-China: 192-3; political developments in, 193-4; British forces in, 196; occupation of, 197-8; Lady Mountbatten in, 200; Military position in, 201-2; developments in Saigon, 202; 32 Indian Infantry Brigade in, 202; developments in other parts of, 203-8; the French take over responsibility for, 208-13; withdrawal of Indian troops from, 214-15; Royal Air Force leaves, 215; Franco-Viet Namese agreement in, 236; evacuation of Japanese from, 248-50
Fourteenth Army: 170

Gairdner, General: 28
Gaje Ghale, Jemadar, V. C.: 84, 118
Gascoigne, Mr. (United Kingdom Ambassador to Japan): 28
Germany: 5
Godavari, H. M. I. S.: 124-5
Gracey, Major-General D. D.: 199-200, 201, 212, 249

Hamada: 67
Hatta, Dr.: 220
Hawthorn, Major-General (Commander, 23rd Indian Division): 226
Helfrich, Admiral: 224, 229, 232

Hiro: 138-9, 141
Hirohito, Emperor: 8
Hiroshima: 5, 47-8
Hong Kong: 1, 153
Hugh Hoffman, Brigadier-General: 116

India: proposes integration of Indian Administrative Units for functional control only, 53; agrees to meet the cost of Indian Component in BCOF, 72; share of Pool Account in BCOF, 73
Indian Army:
7 Cavalry: provides the armour for Brindiv, 129; main role during stay in Japan, 129; returns to India for reorganisation, 129
16 Light Cavalry: 213
4th Indian Infantry Brigade: 241-3
20th Indian Infantry Brigade: 199
32nd Indian Infantry Brigade: 210-11
33rd Indian Infantry Brigade: 217
80th Indian Infantry Brigade: 211-13
100th Indian Infantry Brigade: 211, 214
268th Indian Infantry Brigade: 80; Brigadier K. S. Thimayya as Commander of, 81; Brigadier Shrinagesh as Commander of, 105; returns to India as the last undivided contingent of the Indian Army, 144; made responsible for withdrawal of the whole of Indian Contingent from Japan, 158-9; breaks into four echelons, 158; leaves Japan, 165
7th Indian Division: 172, 216-18
17th Indian Division: 79
20th Indian Division: 172, 201, 209, 213, 214
26th Indian Division: 172, 216
429 Field Company Indian Engineers: 116
1 Mahratta: 117
114 Field Regiment: 212
14/13 Frontier Force Rifles: 205, 211, 213-14
1/1 Gurkha Rifles: 198, 205, 212, 214
2/5 Royal Gurkha Rifles: known as the famous " Triple V. C." Battalion, 80; *see also* 115, 117-18, 162
4/2 Gurkha Rifles: 210
4/10 Gurkha Rifles: 205, 212-14
16 Indian Field Battery: 130
26 Indian Field Battery: returns to India: 130
111 Indian Infantry Workshop: 142
23 Mountain Regiment: 212
1 Punjab: 116, 118
9/14 Punjab: 210
Indian Air Force Signals: 134; arrives in Japan, 136; important lessons during the stay in Japan, 137
Indian Contingent: tasks of, 96; means of achieving, 97-8; withdrawal from Japan, 106, 156; negotiations for withdrawal of, 156; warning order and plan of withdrawal, 158-60
Indian Troops: land in Kure, 91-2; take

part in Empire Day celebrations, 102; move to Shikoku Island, 104; liaison with the Japanese, 122-3; morale of, 143; final withdrawal from Japan, 162
Indian Prisoners of War: recovery of, 186-91
Indonesia: declaration of Independence and efforts to defend it, 222-3; mass violence against the British forces in, 226-7; British build up military strength in, 226; negotiations for settlement with the Dutch, 235-6; celebrates first anniversary of the Republic, 238; truce with the Dutch and Linggajati Agreement, 238; clashes with the British patrols, 242
Itagaki, General (Commander, Imperial Japanese 7th Army): 9
Iwakuni: Air port of entry for BCOF: 49; capacity of air port at, 49; air-booking centre at, 66; Indian Air Formation Signals at, 134

Jain, Dr. L. C.: as Economic Adviser to the Commonwealth Representative, 27; promoted as the head of the Indian Liaison Mission in Tokyo, 29
Japan: 1; surrenders and terms of the surrender, 6-8; American troops land in, 9; aims of the Allied occupation of, 10; military objects of the occupation of, 13, 32; Allied troops for, 14; as an American base, 25; Laision Mission in, 28-9; British Commonwealth policy regarding occupation of, 30; strategic, political and economic considerations of BCOF in, 30-1; service families of BCOF move to, 62; concentration and move of Brinjap to, 77-93; severe earthquake in, 103; cyclones in, 110; problem of Koreans in, 111-12; Royal Indian Navy and Air Force in, 124-6; Indian Air Force Signals in, 134-7; Indian families in, 143
Java: Japanese landing in, 2; British and Indian Forces in, 226; revolts against Dutch, 228; British intentions in, 229; events in, 230-8; terror and extremism in, 236-7; evacuation of Japanese prisoners from, 253-5; strength of Japanese Army in, 254
Joint Chiefs of Staff, Australia: 33, 35; vested to control and administer British Commonwealth Occupation Force, 35; composition and responsibility of, 35-6; friction with Australian Defence Department by the overseas members of, 36; Chairman defines the functions of the members of, 38-9; dissolved, 41; functions and achievements of, 41-3; comprised of, 45; directive to C-in-C. BCOF for the mounting of the Force, 51
Jones, Mr. Frederick (New Zealand Defence Minister): 117
Kandy: Siamese delegation at, 217
Katayama Tetsu: becomes Prime Minister of Japan, 121

Killearn, Lord (Controller of Foreign Affairs in SEAC), 237
Kochi: 67
Korea: 112
Kumaon Band: 163
Kure: base port for BCOF, 46; capacity of the port at, 49; reefer storage facilities at, 64; integrated Base Post Office at, 67; advance base facilities at the port of, 85; debarkation of Brinjap at, 91; H. M. S. *Anson* and *Barfluer* visit, 122; Indian Air Formation Signals (IAFS) arrives at, 134; BCOF sports and amusements at, 150

Lawson, Rt. Hon. J. J.: 224
Leclerc, General (French): 200, 201, 212
Linggajati Agreement: 238
Lockhart, Lieut.-General R. M.: 82-3
Longemann, Dr. (Minister of Holland for Overseas Territories): 230

MacArthur, General Douglas: arrives in Australia, 3, 4; enters Tokyo, 9; agreement with Northcott, 15-16; President Truman's directive to, 25; BCOF forms part of occupation Force under, 45; Operation Instruction No. 3 and gives practical shape to MacArthur—Northcott agreement, 51
MacArthur—Northcott Agreement: 15, 16-17, 51, 156
MacMahon Ball: 27
Mallaby, Brigadier (Commander, 49th Indian Infantry Brigade): 227
Mansergh, Major-General E. C.: 230; takes over as Allied Commander in Java, 237
Mashrul Camp: Indian camp at, 81-2; Indian units concentrate at, 82; 'Force 152' raised at, 82
Matsue: 141, 147
Matsuyama: 67
McLachlan, Air Commodore I. D.: 136
Medan: 26th Indian Division concentrates in, 240; Indian troops in, 241-3; Netherlands troops relieves SEAC troops from, 243
Meiji Shrine: 116
Melbourne Army Headquarters: responsibility of: 64-6
Missouri (U.S. Ship): Japanese envoys sign the unconditional surrender on board the, 7
Miyajima Island: 150
Molotov, Mr. (Soviet Foreign Minister): 6
Mountbatten, Admiral Lord Louis (Supreme Allied Commander, SEAC): 4; accepts surrender of all Japanese forces in South-East Asia, 8; accepts personal surrender of Field-Marshal Count Terauchi's family swords, 206; inspects Brinjap, 91; relinquishes responsibility, 215; invites Siamese Military Mission to his headquarters at Kandy, 216; policy in Netherlands

East Indies and Dutch reaction to, 224; sends his Director of Intelligence to London and Holland, 229; raises the question of British policy in Indonesia, 231; visits Java, 237; *see also* 153, 200-1, 209, 211-12, 217, 221, 226, 236, 253

Nagasaki: 6
Namdeo Jadhao, Sepoy, V. C.: 84
Nehru, Pandit Jawaharlal (Prime Minister of India): presses for the withdrawal of Indian troops from Japan, 156-7
Netherlands East Indies: 220; South-East Asia Command takes the responsibilty to maintain peace in, 221; General Christison as Allied Force Commander in, 221; British landings in, 222; situation in, 224; the Dutch take over civil authority in, 237-8; relief of from Japanese occupation, 246
Nimmo, Brigadier (Commander Australian Infantry Brigade Group): 45
Noel Baker, Mr.: 229
Northcott, Lieut.-General J.: 15; agreement with General MacArthur (MacArthur-Northcott Agreement), 15-17; returns to Australia, 21; resumes discussions with MacArthur, 22; as Commander of British Commonwealth Occupation Force, 44-5; visits India, 51; lays down policy regarding fraternisation, 60-1; inspects Brinjap before its departure to Japan, 86; visits General Headquarters, (India), New Delhi and appoints an Indian Officer as his A.D.C., 87; *see also* 102

Okayama: 67, 140-1, 150

Pacific War Council: 3
Padang: Indian troops in, 243-4; disturbances in, 244
Palembang: 1st Burma Regiment in, 244; disturbances in, 245; 71 Indian Infantry and 1 Lincolns in, 245; Netherlands troops take over the control of, 245
Paranjpye, Dr. (Indian High Commissioner in Australia): 157
Patterson, Rear Admiral: 225
Pearl Harbour: 1
Pickard, Lieut.-Col. E. C.: 205

Rajendra Singh, Lieut.-Col.: 165
Ranchi (Ship): 105
RAPWI: 174-5; plans for, 175-6; initial operations to contact, 176-8; care of prior to evacuation, 179; movement of, 181-4; *see also* 221
Red Cross: 185-6
RIASC: Organisation of units in, 139
Richelieu (French Battleship), 207
Robertson, General: 105
Royal Indian Navy: in Japan, 124
Royal Indian Air Force: 4 Squadron arrives in Japan, 93; activities in Japan, 125-6; leaves Saigon, 215
Rydr, Major-General Chase W (U. S. IX Corps Commander): 117

Saigon: military position in, 201; developments in, 202; Vice-Admiral d'Argenlieu arrives in, 205; fighting in, 206-7; French 9th Colonial Infantry Division arrives in, 209; 32nd Indian Infantry Brigade moves from, 211
Sanganaya: 140
Semarang: 233
Seni Pramoj: becomes Prime Minister of Siam, 217
Scott, General: 147
Sharifuddin, Dr. (Head of the Indonesian National Army): 234
Shikoku: 49, 67
Shimane: 49
Shrinagesh, Brigadier S. M.: selected as Commander of 268th Indian Infantry Brigade, 105; message to Major-General Cowan by, 105; ensures no discrimination or communal propaganda in the Units, 144; message from Head of the Allied Government Team at Okayama to, 163; goes to Australia as Indian representative on Japanese Peace Conference, 164
Siam: *see under Thailand*
Singapore: 2
Sjahrir, Dr.: forms his cabinet and expresses willingness to co-operate with foreign powers, 229; visits important centres in East Java, 232
Soekarno, Dr.: organises the country against Colonialism, 221; chooses his cabinet, 223; appeals to President Truman and Premier Attlee for intervention and Marshal Stalin for moral support in the struggle for freedom, 229; Netherlands Government's refusal to negotiate with, 229; moves to Jogjakarta, 234; assumes supreme power among extremists, 238
Soerio, R. M. D. (Indonesian Governor in East Java): 230
Sourabaya: flare up and adverse Anglo-Indonesian relations in, 227; Dr. Soekarno and Commander 23rd Indian Division arrive in, 227; stiff resistance by Indonesians in, 235
South-East Asia Command: 4; issues directions to local Commanders for occupation, 171-3; plans for restoration of law and order in French Indo-China, 195-6; transfers Field-Marshal Terauchi to Singapore, 214; transfers duties to French Military Commander, 215; task of in the occupation of Siam, 217; responsibility of to maintain peace in Netherlands East Indies, 221
Stewart, Brigadier, K. L.: 45
Sumatra: 2; occupation of by BCOF, 180; situation in, 238-9; reoccupation by BCOF and its objects for, 239; 26th Indian Division in, 239; Dutch troops take over control of, 243; evacuation of Japanese prisoners from, 255-8

INDEX

Takamatsu: 67, 139
Takuma: 67
Terauchi, Count (Japanese over-all Commander in South-East Asia): 8, 172-3; surrenders family swords to Lord Mountbatten, 206; transferred to Singapore, 214
Thailand: geographical position of, 215; climate, 216; Allied occupation of, 216; treaty with United Kingdom, Australia and China, 218; elections in, 218; normal conditions re-established in and occupation forces move from, 218; evacuation of Japanese prisoners from, 250-2
Thimayya, Brigadier K. S. (now General): 9; as Commander 268th Indian Infantry Brigade, 81; leaves Japan and his messages to BCOF, 102-3
Tokushima: 67
Tokyo: 19; British Commonwealth sub-area at, 21; Gurkhas in, 115-17; Brindiv guard duties in, 115; 1 Punjab in, 116; Mahrattas in, 117
Tottori: 49, 67, 102

Truman, President: issues directive to MacArthur regarding aims in the occupation of Japan, 10
Twelfth Army: 170

United Kingdom/Indian Element (UKINDEL): functions of, 41
United States Eighth Army: 18, 131; Fifth Air Force, 18
Uno: 67

Van Mook, Dr.: 224; confers with Dr. Soekarno, 229
Van O Yen, General: 225
Venus, H. M. S.: 241
Viwatcha Chaiyant (Siamese Prince): 218

Wadashima: 16; Indian troops at, 130, 139
Wavell, General Sir Archibald P.: 1, 4
Weir, Major-General: 117

Yama, Colonel: arrest of, 124
Yamaguchi: 49
Yoshida, Premier (Japan): 121

Zahir Ahmad, Mr.: 75

www.ingramcontent.com/pod-product-compliance
Lightning Source LLC
Chambersburg PA
CBHW080755300426
44114CB00020B/2732